WOMEN'S HOLOCAUST WRITING

S. LILLIAN KREMER

WOMEN'S HOLOCAUST WRITING

Memory and Imagination

University of Nebraska Press, Lincoln and London

Portions of this work have appeared, in different form, in: "Norma Rosen: An American Literary Response to the Holocaust," in *Daughters of Valor: Contemporary Jewish-American Women Writers*, ed. Ben Siegel and Jay Halio (Newark: University of Delaware Press, 1997), 160–74; "The Holocaust and the Witnessing Imagination," in *Violence, Silence, and Anger: Women's Writing as Transgression*, ed. Deirdre Lashgari (Charlottesville: University Press of Virginia, 1995), 231–46, reprinted with permission of the University Press of Virginia; "Holocaust Writing," in *The Oxford Companion to Women's Writing in the United States*, ed. Cathy N. Davidson and Linda Wagner-Martin (New York: Oxford University Press, 1995), 395–97; "*An Estate of Memory*: Women in the Holocaust," in *Holocaust Studies Annual 1991*, ed. Sanford Pinsker and Jack Fischel (New York: Garland Publishing, 1992), 99–110; "Holocaust-Wrought Women: Portraits by Four American Writers" and "The Holocaust in Our Time: Norman Rosen's *Touching Evil*," *Studies in American Jewish Literature* 11, no. 2 (fall 1992): 150–61 and 3 (1983): 212–22, respectively; "Holocaust Survivors: Psychiatric and Literary Parallels," *Proteus: A Journal of Ideas* (fall 1995): 27–31, Shippensburg PA 17257–2299, © 1995 by Shippensburg University, reprinted with permission; and "Post-Alienation: Recent Directions in Jewish American Literature," *Contemporary Literature* 34, no. 3 (fall 1993): 571–91, reprinted by permission of The University of Wisconsin Press.

Kremer, S. Lillian, 1939–   Women's Holocaust writing : memory and imagination / S. Lillian Kremer.   p.   cm. Includes bibliographical reference and index. ISBN 0-8032-2743-4 (cl : alk. paper) 1. Holocaust, Jewish (1939–1945), in literature. 2. American literature—Jewish authors—History and criticism. 3. American literature—Women authors—History and criticism. 4. Jewish women in the Holocaust. 5. Holocaust, Jewish (1939–1945)—Personal narratives—History and criticism. I. Title. PN56.H55K74 1999   810.9'358—dc21   98-27794   CIP

FOR SARAH LEAH

FOR HER SISTERS WHO PERISHED AND

FOR HER SISTERS WHO LIVED

CONTENTS

PREFACE

Studies of Holocaust literature written before the late 1970s by male critics focused on works by male Europeans and Israelis. Other than a few significant exceptions, prominent critics have given scant attention to the noteworthy body of Holocaust writing by Americans and women. With the intention of extending the canon, this text explores English-language fiction by émigré women living in America whose creative writing is influenced by Holocaust memory and experience, and fiction by American-born women encountering the Holocaust through research and imagination.

Rather than present a definitive survey of women's Holocaust narratives, I offer a close reading of exemplary works and take notice of their relationship to women's testimonies and to the relevant historic context. I have selected texts distinguished by the power of their literary expression and reflective of the diverse Holocaust experience of nationally, culturally, and socially distinct women. These fictions by survivors and their contemporaries who were "not there" offer a widely disparate portrait of female Holocaust experience: women living openly and in hiding in Aryan sectors and women incarcerated in ghettos and camps, passive victims and resistance fighters, the secular and the religious, and eastern and western Europeans of varied political views and social and economic classes. Some of these works have been critically acclaimed and embraced by the reading public; others are neglected works of literary and historic merit. Each makes a significant contribution to shaping our understanding of women's Holocaust experience by graphically and poignantly rendering the trauma of Jewish and half-Jewish women under the yoke of National Socialism. Each provides a glimpse of female-gendered Holocaust experience hitherto unmapped in male-authored texts customarily presented and received as portraits of normative Holocaust experience.

Although this study acknowledges shared themes in male and female Holocaust experience and fictive representation, its principal focus is the distinctive ordeal and response of women as given voice and visibility by women writers born before the end of World War II. The ways gender signification informs fictional Holocaust texts are revealed through representations of maternity, fertility, and sexual assault and depictions of gender- and culturally shaped Holocaust responses. My interest is in the commonalities and distinctions of writing by women who experienced the Shoah directly and by others who learned about it after the fact. Are there significant differences in the Holocaust experiences these writers explore? How does the distanced representation of the concentrationary universe differ from the immediate perspective? How are the philosophical and political implications of the Shoah presented? Are wartime and postwar survival similarly privileged by these writers? To what extent do these discrete cultural voices overlap and diverge?

Mine is not an effort to shift the focus of Holocaust scholarship from Jewish victimization to female victimization. I have no interest in favoring, nor do I consider it morally appropriate to favor, discussion of comparative male/female martyrologies or of competing victimization. That millions of men, women, and children were targeted for annihilation by the Nazis and their collaborators only because they were Jewish or had the requisite number of Jewish grandparents is established historic fact. This text acknowledges that axiom. I argue not that one sex suffered more than the other or that the suffering of one sex was more tragic than the other, only that there are gendered differences in their suffering and response and that women's fictional representations of that experience merit careful study.

Without losing sight of affinities between male and female Holocaust discourse, my analysis underscores their differences, thereby striving to contribute to a more inclusive Holocaust canon. My reading of Jewish women writers is in the tradition of numerous novelists and critics who have broadened the scope of our knowledge of Jewish women's experiential and literary history. I have abjured a reading that places an overriding emphasis on the autonomy of the text and its formal characteristics, preferring instead to read the literature in relation to the historic event it takes as its subject. Textual explication is synthesized with contextual reference, survivor testimony, and historic and psychiatric studies of Shoah-era and postwar survival experience to learn how history is inscribed, translated, and interpreted in literary form. My analysis considers extrinsic contexts of gender and historic imperatives, illustrating how the fictive experience parallels autobiographical, historic, and psychiatric accounts of Holocaust experience and how novelists' characterizations of victims and survivors affirm or contradict the extraliterary findings. The intention is to unite literary explication with sociopolitical constructs that motivated the writing, to perceive how these writers negotiated the complicated interactions among life story, history, and fiction.

Holocaust is the most widely used English term to designate the 1933–45 war against the Jews, a war that began with book burnings and culminated in the burning of human beings in the crematoria and lime pits of Nazi-occupied Europe. Although the word *Holocaust* suggests an apocalyptic destruction, it also has an unfortunate sacrificial connotation related to the biblical burnt offering congruous with a Christian interpretation of Jewish history. The sacrificial connotation of the word renders it morally repugnant. Nevertheless, the word is used throughout this work, for it is the most widely accepted term in popular and scholarly discourse. The Hebrew word *Shoah* is a preferable alternative and is used liberally herein. The biblical word, meaning ruin, calamity, desolation, was reintroduced in modern Hebrew to suggest the cataclysmic destruction of European Jewry that transformed conceptions of God, society, and humanity; yet *Shoah* is free of the affirmative theological overtones of the Greek-derived *Holocaust* and accurately signifies the rupture in the Jewish collective consciousness engendered by the destruction of one-third of the world's Jewish population.

ACKNOWLEDGMENTS

I am grateful to Ilona Karmel, Elżbieta Ettinger, Hana Demetz, Susan Fromberg Schaeffer, Cynthia Ozick, Marge Piercy, and Norma Rosen, who generously agreed to personal interviews for this book and gave their permission to quote from and paraphrase their remarks. Their forthright responses to my questions about their Holocaust writing are vital to my understanding.

The National Endowment for the Humanities has my gratitude for a summer stipend and the award of two grants for Seminars for College Teachers that allowed me to work on this project and share my ideas with colleagues who asked provocative questions. Kansas State University provided time for a sabbatical and numerous travel grants to conduct research.

Portions of this study have appeared in different form in collections of essays: *Daughters of Valor: Contemporary Jewish-American Women Writers*, ed. Ben Siegel and Jay Halio (Newark: University of Delaware Press); *Violence, Silence, and Anger: Women's Writing as Transgression*, ed. Deirdre Lashgari (Charlottesville: University Press of Virginia); *The Oxford Companion to Women's Writing in the United States*, ed. Cathy N. Davidson and Linda Wagner-Martin (New York: Oxford University Press); and *Holocaust Studies Annual*, ed. Sanford Pinsker and Jack Fischel (New York: Garland Publishing); and in refereed journals: *Studies in American Jewish Literature* (ed. Dan Walden and Miriyam Glazer); *Proteus*; and *Contemporary Literature* (ed. Thomas Schaub and Elaine M. Kauvar). I appreciate these editors' permission to publish from my earlier work.

My greatest debt of gratitude is to my husband, Eugene Kremer, who helped me at every stage of the project with wise counsel and loving encouragement.

WOMEN'S HOLOCAUST WRITING

INTRODUCTION

Historic Representation

Holocaust historiography and literary criticism, like virtually every aspect of Western civilization, has typically been male-centered. Because chroniclers of Jewish history, like most historians, privilege male experience as normative, women have routinely been cast at the margins of Jewish history. As Paula Hyman observes, "Most frequently, women were subsumed in a cultural experience whose patterns were defined by the life histories of men. Presuming that the experiences of women and men were essentially identical, historians spoke explicitly of men but implied that women were included in the category of man. By introducing the analytic tool of gender, feminist theory and women's history have challenged the paradigm of ordering human experience according to male norms and then asserting that such a paradigm is universal."[1] Hyman's insight, albeit directly addressing other periods of Jewish history, implicitly encapsulates most noted historians' treatment of women in the Holocaust. Even among the female historians who were some of the first to write about the Holocaust—Lucy Dawidowicz, Nora Levin, and philosopher-historian Hannah Arendt—the feminist perspective is muted.

Throughout the enduring history of antisemitism Jewish women as well as men have directly suffered the aggression of the enemies of the Jews. Women were shackled in bondage in ancient Egypt, massacred by the Crusaders, burned during the Inquisition, slaughtered in the Petlurian and Chmielnicki pogroms and in Stalinist purges. Hitler's genocidal war against Jewry was waged against all Jews. Unlike most wars, in which women's suffering is a by-product of the conflict, Nazi Germany's annihilation program made the destruction of Jewish women a critical strategic objective. As Claudia Koonz observes in *Mothers in the Fatherland*, the Nazi universe was a "society structured around 'natural' biological poles . . . [with] race and sex as the immutable categories of human nature. . . . In place of class, culture, religious divisions, race and sex became the predominant social markers."[2] Jewish women, like all Jews, were first and foremost racial targets, because Nazi racial ideology defined Jewish life as a threat to the "purity" of Aryan blood and culture. Because biology was uppermost in the Nazi genocidal ideology, Germans departed from traditional warfare, which often spared female civilians and children from slaughter. Master bureaucrat Adolf Eichmann "was absolutely convinced that if he could succeed in destroying the biological basis of Jewry in the East by complete extermination, then Jewry as a whole would never recover from the blow."[3] This view of all women as "cell-bearers (child bearers)" doomed Jewish women, for in Hitler's view "one gestating Jewish mother posed a greater threat than any fighting man," and "every child that a woman brings into the world is a battle, a battle waged for the existence of her people."[4]

Though slow in appearing, feminist perspectives have emerged in Holocaust historiography during the last two decades and have become central elements of the Holocaust canon. Germaine Tillion and Konnilyn Feig have written about Ravensbrück, the women's concentration camp. Valuable studies of women in the ghettos, camps, and resistance networks by Joan Ringelheim, Sybil Milton, Marion Kaplan, Vera Laska, Claudia Koonz, Margaret Rossiter, and Esther Katz constitute a significant gendered account of Holocaust history.[5] Marlene Heinemann, Myrna Goldenberg, and Sara Horowitz have isolated gender-based Holocaust experience in women's memoirs.[6] Women's voices are also heard in the work of sociologist Ruth Linden and anthologists Carol Rittner and John Roth.[7] By telling their own stories or writing about women's history, women broaden the critique of Nazism encountered in narratives by men.

Joan Ringelheim is among the pioneers of women's Holocaust history.[8] She argues that when we fail to recognize that men and women suffer oppression differently, we "lose the lives of women for a second time."[9] She is a forceful voice for recognition that "traditional attitudes and responses toward women, as well as gender-defined conditions, made women especially vulnerable to abuse of their sexuality and of their maternal responsibility—to rape, murder of themselves and their children, the necessity of killing their own or other women's babies, forced abortion, and other forms of sexual exploitation—in the ghettos, in resistance groups, in hiding and passing, and in the camps."[10]

Ringelheim's work brings together testimonies of female survivors, addressing gender differences in coping strategies, which focused on transforming starvation into communal sharing, rags into clothes, isolation into relationships or surrogate families, and habits of raising children and nurturing into care of fellow prisoners. Women's testimonies often assert that men were less effective in transforming their familial roles into the protection of others. In her 1991 "reconsideration" of her earlier work based on anecdotal reports of survivors Ringelheim called for scholarly investigation of the claim that women's capacities for enduring the trauma of dislocation, starvation, loss of traditional support structures, and physical and mental abuse were different from men's.[11] A 1993 "postscript" to the "reconsideration" cites Raul Hilberg's recent research in *Victims, Perpetrators, Bystanders* on the number of victims by gender, confirming that gender indeed mattered during the Holocaust, that antisemitism, racism, and sexism were inextricably linked in Nazi theory and practice.[12]

Experience of and response to the genocide was dependent on whether one was religious or secular, separatist or assimilated, and eastern or western European, and even differed among those in the same occupied country—whether one was native-born or immigrant, whether one was incarcerated or in open or concealed hiding, whether one served in the Jewish Councils or fought in partisan and resistance groups, and yes, whether one was male or female. Although the German commitment to the degradation and genocide of European Jewry was firmly rooted in racial antisemitism, Jewish men and women were persecuted in ways unique to their sex. As a consequence of gender and other differences, Holocaust narrators tell distinct stories of enduring and resisting the German genocidal environment. Study of the differences is informative, just as contemplation of commonalities is significant. Attention to gender is a salient component of the larger history and the complete text.

Fictional Representation and Holocaust Literary Criticism

The near absence of representation of women's gender-related Holocaust experience in critically celebrated literature is explained in some measure by the gender of most Holocaust authors and critics. Their work reflects their male experience and perspective. In much male-authored Holocaust writing, however, absence of women and women's voices is explained not solely by male discounting of women's experience but, in some measure, by the historic reality that men and women suffered significant portions of their ordeals in sexually segregated labor and concentration camps. Although most men writing about the concentrationary universe consign women to the margins of their imaginative Holocaust writing, male-authored prewar and postwar fiction features women's stories. From the vantage point of chronological and geographic distance, Aharon Appelfeld and I. B. Singer write prologues and epilogues to the Shoah that amply chart women's Shoah-wrought anguish.[13] Equivalent focus, however, is absent in imaginative writing by men on women's occupation, ghetto, and camp ordeals. Despite their impressive craft and their depictions of the dehumanizing camp experience, the quintessential Holocaust texts by Elie Wiesel and Primo Levi ignore the gender-specific experience of female prisoners. Not until we turn to women's texts do we encounter the depth and breadth of women's Holocaust experience.

Like the historians, literary critics generally privilege men's experience and writing. Treatises by prominent male critics have, more often than not, relegated all but a small segment of women's Holocaust writing to the periphery, when not consigning it to invisibility. Women's experiences are rarely central to the presentation of a "typical" Holocaust story. As Sara Horowitz observes, women's memoirs are less frequently cited in scholarly studies, and significant books by women prematurely fall out of print.[14] With important exceptions, this is also true for women's testimonies and creative writing. Apart from such luminaries as Charlotte Delbo, Nelly Sachs, Ida Fink, and Cynthia Ozick, women's Holocaust writing remains at the edges of Holocaust literary criticism. Elie Wiesel, Primo Levi, Tadeusz Borowski, Jerzy Kosinski, Aharon Appelfeld, Peter Rawicz, Paul Celan, and a score of other men inevitably come to mind when one thinks about critical appraisals of Holocaust writing, whereas only a handful of women are accorded similar recognition.

Modest but increasing attention of prominent male literary critics to women's Holocaust writing may be found in Edward Alexander's commentary on Nelly Sachs, Norma Rosen, and Susan Fromberg Schaeffer; Alvin Rosenfeld's insightful commentary on the work of Sachs and Cynthia Ozick; Lawrence Langer's analyses of poetry and prose by Sachs, Delbo, Ozick, and Ilse Aichinger, and his studies of women's oral Holocaust testimonies; and Alan Berger's perceptive essays on Ozick, Rosen, and Schaeffer.[15] Yet even these male critics, although recognizing important literary contributions by women, neglect gender issues in their Holocaust writing. Among the topics absent in male writing are the ways female sexuality and motherhood added burdens to the normative Holocaust ordeal, the cooperative networks women prisoners developed, and the manner in which female cooperation and interdependence contributed to survival. There may be no conspiracy to silence women's voices. Nevertheless, since their works have received inadequate critical attention, their voices have been effectively suppressed.

Holocaust gender scholarship and literary criticism of women's Holocaust writing have grown impressively during the last dozen years as women assume a more prominent role in Holocaust studies and literary scholarship. An early influential interpretive study of women's Holocaust memoirs, Marlene Heinemann's *Gender and Destiny: Women Writers and the Holocaust*, identifies and analyzes gender-specific themes such as maternity, fertility, sexual assault, amenorrhea, fear of sterilization, and "crimes" of pregnancy and childbirth, and their expression in women's memoirs and in one novel. Other critics focusing on explication and assessment of women's Holocaust fiction are Dorothy Bilik, Sara Horowitz, Sidra Ezrahi, Ellen Fine, and myself.[16] Gender studies and analyses of women's literary interpretations extend the scope of canonical criticism through attention to oft-muted facets of Jewish women's Holocaust victimization and endurance. Just as increased feminist scholarship and the growing influence of women in publishing contribute to the mounting visibility of women's Holocaust writing, men, albeit most often in collaboration with a female editor or scholar, are beginning to incorporate more texts by women in Holocaust anthologies.[17]

Women's Holocaust Experience and Women's Narrative

Women's fiction validates women's history, mourns the dead, empathizes with survivors whose memories are burdened by horrendous trauma, and celebrates regenerative psychological healing and communal restoration. Unlike male narratives, in which women appear as minor figures and often as helpless victims, in women-centered novels female characters are fully defined protagonists, experiencing the Shoah in all its evil manifestations. This writing portrays female communities in ghettos, concentration camps, and resistance units where they are assertive agents, forging communal bonds and struggling for control of their own destinies as they encounter daily rounds of hard labor, beatings, starvation, illness, sexual assault, forced separation from family and friends, and, for some unfortunates, subjection to medical experimentation.[18] Fiction written by women treats women's varied responses to the Nazi universe—accommodation and rebellion, altruism and selfish withdrawal. The texts are densely patterned works locating the individual woman's struggle to survive within the larger configuration of European Jewry's trial.

Émigré writers bring direct experience and witness to their narratives. Ilona Karmel's *Stephania* charts the hospitalization and convalescence of a young survivor, experiences that derived from her own rehabilitation, and incorporates a Cracow Ghetto memoir. *An Estate of Memory*, a tale of women bonding in makeshift camp families to fight for survival, is set in Plaszow and Skarzysko labor camps, where Karmel was imprisoned. Elżbieta Ettinger draws on her own incarceration in the Warsaw Ghetto, her life in hiding, and her resistance work in Aryan Poland. The danger-filled world of the Jewish fugitive is central to Ettinger's *Kindergarten*, a tale of young Jewish girls hiding in Aryan communities, and *Quicksand* follows the life of the survivor in Communist Poland that Ettinger experienced. In a highly autobiographical novel Hana Demetz chronicles the predicament of a child of "mixed race." *The House on Prague Street* recounts the experience of a "half-caste of the first degree," benefiting from one parent's German origins and suffering from the other's Jewish status. In the sequel, *Journey from Prague Street*, the survivor's postwar life in Europe and America is periodically interrupted by Holocaust memory.

Of the writers who were "not there," and therefore work from research and the imagination, two chart the chronology of the Shoah from its prelude in eastern and western European antisemitism, through the development of the Nazi reign of terror, and finally to the aftermath. Susan Fromberg Schaeffer's *Anya*, based on accounts of survivor-interviewees, is a sweeping historical novel beginning with Jewish life in prewar Poland and concluding with the impact of the Holocaust in the lives of survivors. Winner of the Edward Lewis Wallant Award for Jewish American fiction, Schaeffer has impressed readers with the authenticity of her recreation of the Polish Jewish ambiance. Marge Piercy, a widely read poet and novelist, well known for her feminism but less so for her Jewish themes, has turned increasingly to Jewish subjects. Her epic war novel *Gone to Soldiers* includes a thorough rendering of Vichy France, the Jewish resistance, and American Jewish reaction to the Shoah garnered from research, direct contact with French survivors, and observations in her own Detroit neighborhood. Cynthia Ozick, the most celebrated and critically acclaimed of the American-born writers, has incorporated Holocaust themes throughout her literary career. *The Shawl* comprises a brief lyrical account of a mother's witness of her child's electrocution followed by an extended exposition of the atrocity's psychological toll on the mother's postwar life. Norma Rosen, among the most frequently cited novelist-theorists of Holocaust discourse, has portrayed the impact of the Holocaust on nonparticipants and non-Jewish characters. *Touching Evil* and her more recent short fiction reveal the meanings of the Holocaust in the lives of intimates of survivors and nonparticipants engaging the Holocaust as "witnesses-through-the-imagination."[19] Ozick and Rosen draw on the contact survivors have with Americans, meticulously detailing the medical, psychological, and social aspects of survival for the victim and the victim's family. Rosen and Piercy extend canonical themes, by representing American Jews' political and psychological engagement with the tragic fate of their European coreligionists.

Several of the writers treated in this book have long been aware, and appreciative, of at least one other. Cynthia Ozick and Norma Rosen are friends and colleagues. They frequently comment favorably on each other's work and share a predilection for provocative literary and political-social essays as well as fiction. Schaeffer's novel *Anya* was endorsed by Ozick. Whether Ozick's reading of Schaeffer's treatment of the separation and reunion of a mother and daughter influenced her decision to explore a mother's permanent loss in *The Shawl* is open to conjecture. Hana Demetz was moved to write her own story after reading Elie Wiesel's *Night* and Ilona Karmel's *Stephania*.[20] Although the writers' familiarity with one another's work does not signify intraliterary connections among the texts, marked similarities of thematic concern and patterns of development are often evident. All, aside from Rosen, situate their work directly in the Holocaust universe, and all use the rhetorical trope of the eyewitness, either retrieving or constructing testimony as a means for authenticating their novelistic discourse. Some of their works manifest the feminist tradition of privileging the dynamics of mother-daughter Holocaust-ravaged relationships and parent-child role reversal, and others are in the mode of female peer bonding and support. Each eloquently and passionately bears witness to a harrowing chapter of human history from a female protagonist's perspective.

Gendered Perceptions/Gendered Peril

Although they do not write in opposition to patriarchy, the writers I discuss elucidate female gendered experience, thereby beginning to counterbalance the universalization of male experience and interpretation while making significant artistic and conceptual contributions to Holocaust representation. Is women's writing so different from men's that it should be described as evidencing a feminine mind or a feminine style? Yes and no. This book shares Elaine Showalter's view that "women writers should not be studied as a distinct group on the assumption that they write alike, or even display stylistic resemblances distinctively feminine."[21] Rather, women possess a literary history, one deserving explication for its representation of women's lives and history. Cynthia Ozick's argument against the idea and use of gendered language, her desire to make the traditional literary landscape her own, represents the practice of most of the writers studied here. Although, like Ozick, I resist the concept of a separate collective feminine reconstruction of language and culture, I maintain that Holocaust narratives by women writers significantly extend literary representation and interpretation of the Shoah. They do so by introducing female-centered stories underscoring gender-specificity and emphasizing misogyny as complementary to racism.

Comparative study of male and female Holocaust writing evidences both similar and gender-divergent strategies for coping and resistance. Male and female Holocaust texts emphasize the need to combat the dehumanizing Holocaust universe, to depict the radical evil that victims encountered and how they succumbed to or survived the catastrophe, to bear witness for those who died, and to enjoin the world to remember their history. The writers share the recognition that remaining silent or forgetting the victims would further Nazi genocidal goals. Divergent emphases in male- and female-authored texts arise from gender differences and the gendered assault prisoners encountered in the Nazi universe. Nazi subversion of traditional male power, associated with providing for one's family through a career in a profession or business, led to psychological as well as physical hardships. Similarly, Nazi sexism stripped Jewish women of their traditional roles as homemakers and nurturers of children. In male writing the theme of individuality, of one's own resourcefulness, predominates over the theme of communal cooperation. Conversely, the support the women receive from one another sustains them, assures them of their worth, and impels their survival struggle. Male narrators generally dwell on their loss of autonomy and its impact on their failure to provide for and protect their families. The focus of their female counterparts is the loss of family and secondarily the loss of autonomy.

The novelists studied here neither present women as a homogeneous group exhibiting identical beliefs and behaviors nor suggest that gender comprises the totality of women's Holocaust experience. Even so, their writing evidences significant commonalities worthy of critical examination. More often than does male fiction, women's writing delineates the prewar period through graphic description of elegant, abundantly provisioned households. Illustrative are the sense of well-being Demetz evokes in garden, orchard, and home imagery, the table laden with Rosenthal china, the chauffeur-driven cars and servant-run homes emblematic of an Edenic pre-Holocaust life; Schaeffer's representation of peace and prosperity is conveyed in a family's luxurious apartment, her protagonist's exquisite wardrobe, and vacations in spas pampering the body that will be so brutally abused in the coming catastrophe. Employing a polar literary strategy, Ilona Karmel introduces domestic imagery ironically or to highlight disparity in *An Estate of Memory*. She writes of the abundance of grief, "like gifts from home."[22] A woman's incapacity to feed hungry fugitives is likened to the anxiety of a hostess as "more and more were coming, as if to a long-awaited wedding" (76). A camp work site is juxtaposed with normalcy: "As in a home tables for refreshments are set out at the guests' arrival, so here stones, here bricks, and planks were being piled" (195). Karmel's juxtapositions privilege analogy and distinction by drawing attention to parallels but insisting on differences. Her domestic imagery effectively transports the uninitiated reader into the Shoah landscape via familiar idiom and image, simultaneously heightening the reader's perception of the violation of home and hearth at the core of Nazi criminality.

Departing from the conventional approach of male writers, who follow the lead of ghetto chroniclers such as Emmanuel Ringelblum and Chaim Kaplan by focusing directly on the communal life of the ghetto and the organizational structure and dynamics of its administration, women more often treat family dynamics and valiant efforts to sustain familial structures in the hostile ghetto environment. They depict female slave laborers who produce civilian and military goods for transport to Germany yet manage to fulfill their responsibilities as ghetto homemakers, and women who form cooperative networks in the ghettos and camps to feed the starving and nurse the sick. Paralleling distinct patterns in women's Shoah testimony, women's fiction depicting individual and collective oppression differs from male presentations in its characteristic incorporation of uniquely female experiences such as menstruation, pregnancy, and invasive gynecological examinations; its inclusion of strategies women devised in their struggle to endure; and its descriptions of ways women salvaged prewar paradigms of meaning in the face of annihilation.[23] Schaeffer, Karmel, and Ettinger chronicle overcrowding, abysmal housing, starvation rations, lack of sanitation, slave labor policies, early mass killings, and Jewish resistance efforts from the vantage point of the individual rather than by depicting the ghetto hierarchy and organized resistance cells typical in male writing. Some of the writers studied here represent victims' suffering and coping directly through fiction set in ghettos and concentration camps. Others approach these themes indirectly through memory, nightmare, and imagery in post-war settings.

Although men and women suffered many of the same Holocaust hardships, their gender socialization produced divergent responses. Among the most dehumanizing experiences for both sexes was the camp initiation. Prisoners were ordered into shower rooms where they were told to undress, line up to have the hair shaved from their bodies, and be deloused. Men typically write of this experience in terms of loss of autonomy and personal dignity. Stripped of clothing and body hair, the individual was far less visually distinguishable from others and deprived of the outward symbols of communal role as scholar, professional, businessman, community leader; his social status was obliterated. Women, socialized by religious teaching and communal values to be modest, experienced the process, and write of it, as a sexual assault during which they were shamed and terrified by SS men who made lewd remarks and obscene suggestions and poked, pinched, and mauled them in the course of delousing procedures and searches for hidden valuables in oral, rectal, and vaginal cavities. Male writers portray the tattooing process as emblematic of their characters' vulnerability and impotence. Women pay less heed to tattooing and privilege verbal and physical sexual abuse and the humiliation associated with shorn hair and exchange of personal clothing for intentionally ill-fitting, mismatched camp garb. Most prevalent in passages focusing on female anatomy and appearance are references to the deterioration of and assault on women's bodies, loss of menstruation and fear of sterilization, forced abortions, and arid breasts. Because the camp initiation ordeal and much of the continued harassment of female inmates was sexually oriented, compounding the mortal danger they faced as Jews, their writing focuses more intensely than does male writing on sexual intimidation and trauma.[24]

Divergent responses to the excremental camp environments is also gendered. Women accustomed to high standards of feminine hygiene were suddenly virtually without soap, water, toilets, and sanitary napkins and were confronted with dire health problems. Women socialized to invest in their physical appearance—to use makeup, to dress well, to style their hair—were radically defeminized. Charlotte Delbo describes camp women as "lumps of flesh which had lost the pinkness and the life of flesh . . . completing the process of withering and decomposing." She intensifies the deterioration by suggesting that the flesh of the women standing in the roll call "blended in so well with the dusty soil that it required an effort to pick out the women there, to make out empty breasts amid this puckered skin that hung from women's chests."[25] Male writers convey the effect of starvation and primitive sanitary facilities on their protagonists' strength, health, and feelings of powerlessness, but they do not direct attention to the aesthetic and procreational anxieties of their physical deterioration.[26] Vulnerability borne of racism and sexism violently and relentlessly complicated the lives of Jewish women. Rape by the SS was rare because racial laws forbade sexual contact between Germans and Jews and because the SS had an ample supply of their own women and healthier non-Jewish inmates in brothels. Sexual abuse by the SS, however, was common—whether in the form of verbal insults or physical punishment. Jewish women were more often raped by low-level functionaries and encouraged to exchange sexual favors for survival: an extra piece of bread, medicine, a pair of boots, a better job, escape from a selection. Stripping all prisoners for selection inspections and ordering women, in particular, to stand naked in the cold either before or after showers in the presence of leering guards was common.

Pregnancy and motherhood, prevalent in women's Holocaust writing as tropes for female vulnerability or as reminders of the dominance of the life force, are virtually absent from male Holocaust writing and from much critical Holocaust discourse.[27] Nazi sexist and racist policies unavoidably cast mothers of "inferior races" as threats to Aryan purity and therefore destined them for extermination. In contrast, maternity for Aryan women was "idealized and encouraged through extensive legislation to increase the German birth rate."[28] The European model of motherhood was glorified for German women and violently assaulted for Jewish women. Jewish women discovered that bearing children was a crime against the Reich, that their children were to be denied life: condemned, by German decree, to starvation, disease, medical experimentation; doomed to be gassed or tossed alive into crematoria ovens and lime pits. Central to the fictional resistance theme and celebration of women's bonding and mutual support is women's rebellion against the Nazi ban on Jewish pregnancies. Women willingly risk their lives to secure extra food for their pregnant sisters, assist in the clandestine birth, kill the infant to save the mother, and, on very rare occasions, subvert the Nazi genocidal endeavor and support Jewish continuity by smuggling the newborn out of the camp.

Most Holocaust fiction by men and women portrays mothers empathetically and heroically, either as victims or as strong women, often replacing men as protectors of the family and serving as survival guides to their daughters. Departing from much late-twentieth-century feminist writing, which displaces the maternal voice by privileging women as sisters and friends, Holocaust fiction emphasizes both sisterly and maternal bonds. The authority of the maternal voice in Holocaust writing links it to traditional Jewish writing, which routinely rendered maternal figures and influence affirmatively. The absence or presence of diminished fathers and praise for the resourcefulness of mothers are found in the fiction of Ettinger, Demetz, Schaeffer, and Karmel. American-born Jewish women writers fashion Holocaust-era mother-daughter relationships in ways that are consistent with the treatments by their émigré counterparts. Their depictions of troubled survivors is less affirmative, showing these women as obsessive, overly protective of their children, or withdrawn into the worlds of memory and nightmare.[29]

Children: Innocents Betrayed, Innocence Lost

Women's writing focuses far more emphatically than men's writing on the plight of young children, for several reasons: prewar gender-based role distinctions led men to work outside the home and women to labor within, supervising the care and nurture of children; early labor conscriptions and deportations took men and left women and children behind to cope with discriminatory practices at home; and young children were separated from their fathers at the camp entry. Illustrative are Karmel's, Ettinger's, and Schaeffer's treatment of smuggling children into hiding; and Karmel's, Piercy's, and Ozick's delineation of the clandestine birth and murder of a child. Male writing laments the loss of children and addresses fathers' grief but does not center on efforts to save children or on the combined efforts of fathers and young children to survive together; it is more likely to feature older adolescent sons entering the camps with their fathers, as in Wiesel's *Night* or the young boy on the run in Jerzy Kosinski's *Painted Bird*.

Writing by men rarely focuses on intimate Holocaust-wrought father-son relationships in the manner of Wiesel's *Night*. Very young children are more often presented anonymously and en masse as in Wiesel's heartbroken observation of "children in the flames"[30] and Borowski's workers carrying dead infants from transports and tossing a small girl with only one leg onto a truckload of corpses to "burn alive."[31] Women's Holocaust narratives often individualize children, focusing closely on the plight of named and developed young characters rather than on the anonymous mass or a representative child. These children are dispossessed from the security of their prewar position in society and are painfully aware that the adults they had relied on for protection are impotent in the Nazi order. Émigré and native-born American female writers movingly chronicle the shattered lives of children and adolescents as antisemitic legislation designed to enforce social segregation of the Jews produces ever tighter restrictions. Demetz, Ettinger, Piercy, and Schaeffer depict children's indirect encounters with early antisemitic edicts as their parents lose their jobs and property, and their direct experience of exclusion from public venues and deportation to the extermination camps. Demetz and Piercy are particularly effective in portraying the psychic suffering of youngsters separated from gentile friends; banished from schools, libraries, movies, sports events, and public transportation; and stigmatized by the decree requiring them to wear a large yellow star inscribed with the word JEW. Schaeffer and Ettinger dramatize the dire circumstances encountered by children forced from their homes and the radical changes that accompany ghettoization or living in hiding and apart from family. Children's "actions," the rounding up of ghetto children for lethal injection or deportation for "extermination," is reported or finds expression in the fiction of Schaeffer, Piercy, Rosen, and Ozick.

Treatment of the separation of parents from children is markedly different in writing by men and women. The subject receives poignant but brief attention by men. The last view of children as they are marched away with their mothers at the camp railroad ramps is a recurrent scene or memory in male writing. Women develop the ramifications of separation of parent and child at considerable length and in depth, from the occupation period through the final loss and mourning. The dilemma of whether to try to send children to safety among strangers or to remain together as a family is a recurrent theme in Holocaust narrative. Few Jewish families had the option of hiding as a group as did Anne Frank's family. Those who had the opportunity to hide usually separated to reduce the risk of losing everyone or because it was more feasible for children than for adults to be hidden. When the decision was taken to place a child with gentiles, the hidden were living outside the law, moving from place to place, obtaining false papers, "passing" as Christians, learning new names and new family histories. There was constant danger of suspicious neighbors or of the child's inadvertent self-betrayal. Hidden children lived in fear of blurting out their real names, of uttering a Jewish word, of mispronouncing a Christian prayer or forgetting an anticipated religious gesture. Heightening the psychological stress of undeviating vigilance was the pain of feeling abandoned by their parents. Schaeffer and Ettinger show the very young in hiding, children too young to understand their religious identity and consequently untroubled by that dimension of an alien environment. Ettinger also depicts the emotional oppression adolescents experienced in adapting to the customs of people who were often very different culturally and religiously, and Demetz charts the ambivalence and pain of a young girl of mixed race.

Representations of children's ghetto activities vary considerably based on the gender of the author. Male historians and novelists often celebrate the heroism of children as major actors in smuggling operations to supplement the meager supply of food in the ghettos. In ghetto histories by Chaim Kaplan and Emmanuel Ringelblum, or the fiction of Arnost Lustig and Leslie Epstein, children slip through crevices in the ghetto wall, beg or buy food at far lower prices than on the Jewish side, and bring it into the ghetto concealed under their clothing, knowing that if caught, they will pay with their lives.[32] In ghetto representations by women writers the focus is unrelentingly maintained on the children's victimization, starvation, illness, subjection to lethal injection, or deportation to the death camps.

The initial round of concentration camp selections at the train depot was contingent on the deportee's age, health, and gender. Women arriving at the concentration camps with young children were routinely murdered with their children rather than selected for slave labor. Ellen Fine writes, "Being a mother directly affected the chances for survival; being a father did not."[33] The horrors awaiting Jewish women who survived the selection included unique burdens of motherhood: "Coping with pregnancy, childbirth, and infant care made Jewish women particularly vulnerable . . . to physical abuse and mental anguish—whether through abortion by choice, forced abortion, bearing a child, being killed with a child as its actual or supposed mother, bearing a child and not being able to feed it, killing a baby because its cries jeopardized other people or because if the baby were found . . . both Jewish mother and baby would be killed."[34] Pregnant women who eluded the notice of the examining physicians and delivered babies in the camps lost their infants at the hands of Jewish birth assistants striving to save the mother's life or the lives of camp personnel.[35] In the work of an Auschwitz survivor Dr. Mengele is reported to have justified killing women with their children because "when a Jewish child is born, or when a woman comes to the camp with a child already . . . I don't know what to do with the child. I can't set the child free because there are no longer any Jews who live in freedom. I can't let the child stay in the camp because there are no facilities in the camp that would enable the child to develop normally. It would not be humanitarian to send a child to the ovens without permitting the mother to be there to witness the child's death. That is why I send the mother and the child to the gas ovens together."[36]

Shared Atrocities: Gendered Coping and Spiritual Resistance Patterns

Common to the writing of men and women is the focus on prisoners' preoccupation with hunger and the distribution and supplementation of inadequate rations. Women write much more frequently of the ever present paucity of food juxtaposed with prewar plenty. With incarceration, food becomes even more significant. Inmates learn to measure their value to the Germans in terms of the allotment of food they receive. Their conversations and social relationships are food-centered, as are their dreams. Male characters dwell on their hunger or remember enjoying fine meals. Female characters speak of hunger-induced food fantasies, fondly recollect meal preparation, and share remembered recipes. A survivor, Susan Cernyak-Spatz, explains "that these memories mitigated the despair [of] their everyday life."[37] Livia Bitton Jackson, deported from Hungary to Auschwitz at age thirteen, describes how women who worked twelve-hour days on heavy construction sites recounted memories of food they used to prepare at home. She likens them to "shipwrecked musicians thinking musical notes out loud."[38] Male and female responses to hunger differ in other ways. Jewish men do not appear to consider starvation an assault on their masculinity, for they had been reared to shun physical prowess associated with athletic or military accomplishments, valuing instead a life of prayer and scholarship or professional achievement. Women, socialized more often in the universal pattern of trying to maintain good health for procreation and to value physical attractiveness, are characteristically represented as distraught by their diminishing feminine appearance.

Nazi policy required that the Aryan woman be removed from the work force and transferred to the home to function as "guardian of the hearth, bearer of children," producer of and guide to racially and genetically valuable large families. The non-Aryan woman was regarded as fodder for slave-labor Kommandos in the ghettos and concentration camps, where she suffered the humiliation of labor designed to exhaust, to punish, to kill. "Since the work of non-Aryan women was critical to the Reich's labor program," as historian Konnilyn Feig documents, "the Nazis did not hesitate to use women in the most exacting labor. . . . No work was considered too difficult for women. . . . In the rain and the snow the women dug sewers, built barracks, carried rails, and laid railroad tracks."[39] Women were also assigned to the perilous manufacture of armaments, resulting in chemical poisoning. In addition to ghetto and camp jobs, prisoners were leased as laborers in outside Kommandos for German industrialists and businesses that exploited the abundant and ever refurbished slave labor force. When women fell in exhaustion, the SS killed them. For most women, camp labor was debilitating and deadly.

How did women cope in the Nazi universe? Feminine resourcefulness during all phases of the Nazi oppression is a prominent theme in women's testimony and Holocaust literature. Free of the physical marking that circumcision imposed on men, thereby placing them at greater risk of detection, it was easier for women of "Aryan" appearance to conceal their Jewish identity. Aryan-appearing Jewish women feigned Christian identity to escape incarceration, to enhance their mobility for resistance work, and even to gain better food and work details during incarceration. Although biology heightened the vulnerability of identifiable Jewish women, their gender-based domestic training enhanced their survival chances. Once imprisoned, many women exhibited physical and psychological resilience under the stresses of malnutrition and starvation. Female survivors often attribute their perceived lower mortality rate to greater ingenuity than men possessed in applying key domestic skills, such as stretching limited food supplies, mending tattered clothing, and nursing the sick. Their traditional homemaking abilities served them well in nursing one another through typhus and dysentery and tending to one anothers' wounds and proved psychologically therapeutic, helping the victims maintain a vestige of control over their existence. Ghetto historian Leonard Tushnet reported that "clinical research by Jewish physicians in the Warsaw Ghetto confirmed the impressionistic accounts of contemporaries and brought proof to the assertion that women were less vulnerable to the effects of short-term starvation and famine . . . [and that] women also shared and pooled their limited resources . . . better than did men."[40]

The systematic assault on individual autonomy in the concentration camps was occasionally blunted, albeit in small measure, by the victims' resistance, adaptation, and luck, themes treated by both men and women. In contradiction to the unyielding argument Lawrence Langer makes for the absence of death camp heroism and his censure of British historian Sir Martin Gilbert and other scholars who report resistance and heroism in Holocaust testimonies, chronicles, and imaginative writing, it is fair to assert that anything the inmate consciously did to stay alive was an expression of resistance.[41] Numerous survivor testimonies document nonmilitary resistance that was directly responsible for prisoners' survival, material that is iterated in the fiction. Gathering information, helping fellow prisoners, confounding the camp bureaucracy—even the smallest rebellious gesture bolstered inmates' morale. Survival also stemmed from illicit "organization," bartering for goods among prisoners or stealing at the expense of the Germans to obtain food, clothing, medicine, anything needed to prolong life. Organization in the camps included getting work that could facilitate and improve one's physical conditions, but it was mainly confined to trading for or pilfering food and medical supplies. Exchange of goods fostered interdependence among camp inmates. Some of the chief organizers were the workers in the camp warehouses whose job was sorting confiscated prisoner property for transport to Germany. When these "Canada" workers stole warm clothing for their comrades, it was ethical theft, a political act of resistance and social solidarity. Others, who worked in the camp bakery, kitchen, and food warehouses, supplied food for the camp market. "In this way," writes Birkenau internee Olga Lengyel, "theft became ennobled, and even beneficial to the internees. . . . The more one took from the Germans and sent into the barracks of the camp for the use of the internees instead of letting it be dispatched into Germany, the more one helped the cause."[42] When life itself is a crime, acquiring food through barter or theft and maintaining health through illegal purchase of medicine or fraudulent admission to the infirmary are effective forms of resistance. In *The Survivor* Terrence Des Pres cites the mutual assistance men and women displayed as evidence that "the need *to* help is as basic as the need *for* help." He associates the need and response to it with the social nature of life in the camps and the tendency for "gift giving" among inmates, acts that "were enormously valuable both as morale boosters and often as real aids in the struggle for life." The gifts, which were usually food, became a means of sharing vital wealth, "based on the elementary social act of reciprocity or mutual exchange."[43]

Group solidarity worked as an effective mechanism in the concentrationary universe. Individual strength to endure the unbearable arose from the shared need to keep self and group alive. Groups organized according to political, national, and religious affiliation; small biological and surrogate families, even the commonplace two-person friendship, provided inmates with information, advice, and protection. In the group the prisoner was a comrade, not a number, thereby reinforcing each person's sense of individuality and worth in a universe designed to obliterate individual dignity. Most Jewish prisoners, regardless of gender, were conversant with the traditional precepts of Jewish communal responsibility invoked in Torahic and Talmudic teaching to the effect that all Jews are responsible for one another. In addition, gender socialization contributed immensely to the degree and manner of mutual assistance women exercised in the ghettos and camps.[44]

Although there is testimonial evidence and fictional representation of co-operative association among male inmates, the emphasis women survivors and writers place on bonding and reciprocal support is unparalleled in male writing. Women's testimony and creative writing celebrates the formation and effective operation of female sustaining groups. Whether political, religious, or merely circumstantial, whether a network of several or two persons, these women strove to mitigate the physical and emotional subjugation imposed by the Germans. Unlike men, who had typically been socialized to compete against one another and learned nurturing traits under duress, most women were already experienced in the use of such traits. Often cited in testimonies and in the psychological literature as a contributor to women's higher survival rate was their remarkable capacity to create substitute families after the loss of loved ones. Illustrative is Lengyel's observation that women removed one another's lice but men did not and that women tried to keep one another warm during roll call by leaning against one another or putting an arm around another, whereas men stood apart, putting their arms around their own bodies. Lengyel and social scientists who quote her reports generally attribute women's altruistic behavior to their socialization for motherhood and cooperative friendships, and distinguish male camp friendships from those of women by characterizing men as talking with one another, sharing interests and concerns, but stopping short of sacrifice, which was commonplace among women.[45] No doubt there were men who sacrificed themselves for one another, but the preponderance of testimony and creative writing suggests such activity was minimal compared with that reported by women.

In male Holocaust writing interdependence is exceptional rather than commonplace, as in Primo Levi's association with a young man whom he helps feel human by reciting Dante in *Survival in Auschwitz* or the mutual father-son devotion in Elie Wiesel's *Night*. More often, male writing depicts dependence of one victim on another as threatening to the survival of the physically stronger character, as in sons fleeing their debilitated fathers in Wiesel's *Night* and Richard Elman's *28th Day of Elul*. Levi's account of the solitary nature of the male camp inmate is instructive. He writes: "Here the struggle to survive is without respite, because everyone is desperately and ferociously alone. If some[one] . . . vacillates, he will find no one to extend a helping hand; on the contrary, someone will knock him aside, because it is in no one's interest that there will be one more 'musselman' dragging himself to work every day; and if someone, by a miracle of savage patience and cunning, finds a new method of avoiding the hardest work, a new art which yields him an ounce of bread, he will try to keep his method secret, and he will be esteemed and respected for this, and will derive from it an exclusive, personal benefit; he will become stronger and so will be feared, and who is feared is, *ipso facto*, a candidate for survival."[46]

Conversely, female survivor reports and women's Holocaust fiction represent cooperation and bonding for mutual survival as the rule. Representative is Charlotte Delbo's homage to her French companions in Auschwitz who supported her when she felt unable to persist, "as if," writes a skeptical male critic, "one impulse of her story were to reaffirm the strength of human community despite the assault of Auschwitz on its spirit."[47] Germaine Tillion's assessment of women's altruism is typical. The former French political prisoner at Ravensbrück writes, "In the women's camps only the most selfish in character became . . . hardened, while for many the incredible personal suffering only increased their concern for the needs of others."[48] Similarly, many Jewish women attribute their survival to the generosity of friends who shared their bread, helped them withstand a roll call, or nursed them through chronic illnesses. Joan Ringelheim and Sybil Milton, scholars who have diligently studied Jewish female societies in the camps, attest to the importance of women's creation of surrogate families; Milton writes of "small groups of women in the same barracks or work crews . . . bonded together for mutual help. These small families, usually not biologically related, increased protection for individual internees and created networks to 'organize' food, clothing, and beds, and to help cope with the privations and primitive camp conditions."[49] Milton acknowledges that "bonding because of religious or political convictions may not have been specific to women [as it often was to men], but the degree of group cohesion and noncompetitive support available to women seems markedly greater than among men."[50] Similarly, Myrna Goldenberg cites the instances in many female survivor memoirs of "implicitly or explicitly focus[ing] on sisterhood as the sustaining balm of their Holocaust years."[51]

Paralleling the reports in memoir and oral testimony, female bonding and cooperation are crucial to survival in fiction by Piercy, Schaeffer, and Karmel. In their novels, despite every effort by oppressors to dehumanize them and set them against one another, women, suffering gnawing hunger, share food; women, weary from the day's excruciating labor, pick one another's lice and sustain one another through long, painful roll calls; ailing women nurse one another through typhus and other contagious diseases; they share memories, recipes, remembered literary passages, and religious observances to bolster morale and determination in the battle for survival against overwhelming odds. Daughters adopt maternal roles in support of weakened mothers, and women, anguished by the loss of their biological families, create substitute camp families. The novelists echo survivor memoirs in attesting to the social nature of female bonding and in celebrating these unions as essential to women's survival. The critical importance of bonding may be gauged not only from its conceptual and dramatic development in the fiction but from Ilona Karmel's statement of its significance in her own life. She recounts, "One needed to love someone because you couldn't love yourself. If you could love someone, you could come back to yourself. . . . One had to have an image of a person to save oneself from seeing everyone like so much eating, defecating flesh."[52]

The courage and dignity of Jewish women in the face of atrocity were manifested primarily through spiritual and psychological resistance. Women's spiritual fortitude shone brightly in defiance of the ban against religious expression. Despite inherent danger, they observed Jewish ritual and law when possible. Like the men, women prayed, fasted on Yom Kippur, and refused to eat leavened bread during Passover. Unlike men, who had traditionally studied and worshiped communally in study houses and synagogues at prescribed hours, often while clad in prayer shawls, skull caps, and phylacteries, women more often conducted solitary prayer void of ritual garments while lighting candles at home and preparing the household for Sabbath or holidays. Consequently, it may have been easier for women to modify their prewar religious observance and expression for the camp sphere, as suggested by myriad reports of women who smuggled materials from Nazi warehouses and fashioned Sabbath candles, most often by hollowing out a potato and inserting a rag in place of a wick.

Women's prewar memories and visions of a post-Holocaust future function "as a promissory note to redeem the suffering of the present."[53] Historic testimonies often recount scenes of women sharing stories of their family histories and management of households. A young Hungarian inmate of Auschwitz reports that female prisoners recited verses and songs reminding them of home, shared conversations about the past, and discussed books and plays, as a means for temporary spiritual escape from the camp universe.[54] Such testimony, corroborated by many others, confirms that vestiges of humanity persisted in a universe designed to eradicate human dignity and the sense of individual worth. Psychiatrist-survivor Viktor Frankl affirms the beneficial nature of these exchanges, observing that "this intensification of inner life helped the prisoner find a refuge from the emptiness, desolation, and spiritual poverty of . . . existence, by . . . escape into the past."[55] Fellow analyst Joel Dimsdale contends that "time distortion, [whether by focusing] on the peaceful past or a presumably peaceful and happy future," was a way of alleviating the stress.[56] Similarly, Ellen Fine asserts that the reliance on literary memory in women's writing became a means of mobilizing support systems and was part of a joint effort to stay alive.[57] These verbal exchanges recalling prewar experience offered vital, albeit fleeting, distraction from camp brutality, a moment of transcendence from the present, and hope for postwar restoration.

Militant Resistance

One of the popular misconceptions of Holocaust history is that there was no Jewish active resistance, that Jews went to slaughter like sheep. Another fallacy is that resistance movements were exclusively male. Jewish men and women served both in national resistance units and in exclusively Jewish resistance and partisan groups. Women were active in many forms of defiance in Aryan sectors, ghettos, and concentration camps. Opportunities for resistance work depended on many factors, including the Aryan semblance of one's appearance for missions beyond the ghettos and camps and one's job within the Nazi net. Because women were not perceived as traditional agents of political or militant opposition, they often successfully undertook resistance operations men could not. Free women joined male colleagues to collect military and economic information; prepared films, photographs, and microfilms to be sent to the Allies; printed and disseminated information from the BBC and American radio stations; wrote, printed, and distributed news releases, speeches, pamphlets, and jokes about the occupiers and instructions for sabotage of all sorts. The hazardous operations resistants performed required stealing German equipment, sabotaging railways, mining bridges and tunnels, cutting telephone and telegraph wires, and exploding fuel depots, barracks, and vehicles. Resistance continued within ghettos and inside concentration camps as women stole food, clothing, and medicine from the Germans to facilitate survival. Ghetto and camp inmates fabricated radios and disseminated war news through word of mouth to bolster morale.[58] Workers slowed war production and intentionally manufactured defective materials. Prisoners conspired with local partisans, revolted in Sobibor and Treblinka, and destroyed crematory ovens at Auschwitz-Birkenau. As Sybil Milton puts it, "Flight, escape, subversion of the rules, noncompliance, and sabotage on work details were common forms of resistance in every camp and ghetto of occupied Europe."[59]

Benefiting from postwar resistance research and personal memory, several writers discussed here include active resistance themes that debunk the myth that Jews passively acquiesced to Nazism. Piercy treats active and militant resistance substantively; Ettinger employs it in tandem with hiding, and Karmel and Schaeffer introduce active resistance in the ghetto and the camps in the form of work stoppages and escape. Piercy's and Ettinger's women, passing as Christians, work for the resistance in France and in Aryan Poland. The concentration camp inmates of *Gone to Soldiers* and *An Estate of Memory* are saboteurs, learning from old-timers how to debilitate war materials they produce, slack off at production, and keep one another alive with stolen food and medicine. Piercy relied heavily on the voluminous documentation of the French Jewish militant resistance as she wrote the Holocaust portions of *Gone to Soldiers*. Schaeffer's protagonist, based on a survivor with whom the novelist held extensive interviews, is aided by a resistance unit operating in the Vilna Ghetto and a Jew masquerading as a German soldier in Kaiserwald. Drawing on her own experience, Ettinger depicts her heroine's activity aiding the Warsaw Ghetto victims as well as performing numerous acts of resistance in Aryan settings.[60]

Postwar Acclimation

Women's Holocaust coping persisted into the postwar period. At war's end, the surviving remnant of European Jewry often discovered that no other family members were living, that the non-Jews who had benefited from their deportation were unwilling to return their property or help them in any way. Instead, they threatened, and in some instances inflicted, violence on the survivors. Nations of their pre-Shoah residence neither recognized nor wanted to understand the enormity of the Judeocide and therefore ignored the survivors' unique history. Claiming to resist nationalist and racist designations associated with Nazism and fascism, the newly instituted Communist regimes of eastern Europe conspired to dismiss the magnitude of Jewish suffering. All citizens were the same and were to be treated equally, and so the enormity of Jewish losses was, for the most part, disregarded and the survivors' sensibilities dismissed. Economic, social, or psychological assistance was negligible. Unlike gentiles, who returned to their homes and to a communal welcome, Jewish survivors were generally rebuffed, doubly displaced from their homes, left to languish in bleak camps for displaced persons. This abomination is delineated with particular force by Schaeffer and Ettinger, writing about the plight of Polish Jews. In these works, and in those dealing with postwar residence in America by Ozick and Schaeffer, we encounter female survivors applying the lessons of Holocaust survival to their post-Shoah situations.

Émigré and American Cultural Responses to the Holocaust

Not surprisingly, among the fictions by women writers examined here, differences arise that reflect the national or cultural perspectives and experiences of the authors. Although the narratives explore common themes, the émigré and native-born American writers employ distinctive literal and metaphoric Holocaust settings. Each of the foreign-born writers sets her narrative during the period of the Shoah on European soil, focusing on the discriminatory legislation and internment in ghettos and labor and death camps, faithfully presenting the experience of extremity in great detail. American-born writers introduce the ghettos and camps powerfully but sparingly. They focus on the individual's survival struggle rather than the public life or administration of the ghettos and camps and transplant their characters to the American continent, where they are haunted by the past and often struggle with a Holocaust-besmirched present.

Perhaps because the Europeans experienced the moral conflicts of survival, they explore the ambiguities and ethical dilemmas confronted by victims more penetratingly than do Americans. Their characters ask whether survival of the group supersedes responsibility for individual survival, whether to protect themselves during a "selection" knowing that the Nazi quota will be filled by another, whether to allow a needy friend to hide where they had intended to conceal themselves, whether collaboration with the enemy is ever justified, whether resistance is acceptable even if it risks massive retaliation. Spared the moral dilemmas the Europeans faced, the American writers are reluctant to criticize the victims as fellow victims themselves have. The American-born writers are less likely to portray the oppressed as morally flawed or as tormented by the quandary of self-preservation at the expense of another. On the whole, the American writers treat victims while in the grip of the Nazis reverentially, reserving their protagonists' shortcomings for pre- and postwar episodes distanced from the Nazi universe.

Fictional survivors are exemplars of the thesis that no one survives the Holocaust intact and unimpaired. They personify Elie Wiesel's aphorism that for the survivor "the Holocaust continued after the Holocaust."[61] Although native-born American and émigré writers both render postwar survival, the former tend to provide major delineation of survivorship within the Holocaust text, and the émigré writers generally conclude their Shoah narratives with liberation and treat the aftermath of the catastrophe in another work, indicative of the complete rupture engendered by the Holocaust.

Native-born American novelists, fascinated by the individual psyche, privilege survivor trauma. Psychologically troubled survivors dominate the work of Schaeffer, Ozick, and Piercy, characters who bear the wounds Charlotte Delbo had in mind when she wrote,

> I have returned
> from a world beyond knowledge
> and now must unlearn
> for otherwise I clearly see
> I can no longer live.[62]

Like their American male colleagues, their writing centers directly and emphatically on survivors plagued by Holocaust intrusions in their lives, reliving wartime horrors in memory and dream and suffering guilt, disturbance of self-image, professional and educational stagnation, and social alienation.[63] In accord with the findings of psychiatric literature that identify paranoia, emotional isolation, and stress-induced illness as symptomatic of survivor syndrome, the survivor protagonists frequently evidence emotional and intellectual distance from nonsurvivors, unresolved attachment to loved ones lost in environments where normal grief and mourning were forbidden, and disturbing memories, nightmares, and free associations of unrelated postwar images with wartime trauma. Compounding the difficult adjustment to a new culture and continued Holocaust trauma was the survivors' guilt for outliving families and friends. This burden frequently found expression in overprotection of children, failure to pursue prewar ambitions and careers, and living narrowly circumscribed lives, all amply described by the American-born writers. Moreover, these representations echo clinical findings that "the form of the stress response seems to be related [to] . . . the specific content and nature of the trauma experienced." The delusions of Ozick's protagonist conform to the psychiatric theory that "depression is more severe in those who were in concentration camps and lost relatives," whereas the reliance of Schaeffer's and Ettinger's survivors' on wartime strategies to cope with postwar problems reflects anxiety that "is more pronounced in those who were hiding, on the run, and constantly under the threat of being discovered and killed."[64]

Among the most successful conventions novelists introduce to represent survivors' angst are unbidden Holocaust memories, nightmares, and difficulty communicating with nonsurvivors. The fictional nightmares are analogous to survivor nightmares characterized by the dreamer's "over-whelming fear of existential destruction, utter helplessness and complete absence of counteraggression . . . precipitated by auditory or visual percep-tions reminiscent of the concentration camps."[65] Similarly, fictional survivors often exhibit problems that interviewers of Holocaust survivors encounter with subjects "groping to find proper words to express unimaginable and exhausting memories," survivors experiencing "paralyzing, dumbfounding difficulty: the poverty of language to convey emotion and unreal reality."[66] Like their models, the fictional characters contend that no satisfactory anal-ogy exists, that language is inadequate to convey Holocaust reality. They know that even people who invite speech lack the frame of reference to understand it. For the survivors, how and what to tell loom as intractable barriers to communication, yet they are obsessed with the need to share their history.

Several authors present memory either in Proustian terms of "voluntary memory," entailing partial recall and rational ordering, and "involuntary" spontaneous and uncontrolled memory or, in Charlotte Delbo's terms, as "deep memory," memory prodded by sensual stimuli, and "external mem-ory," the memory of thought.[67] The American-born writers explore these significant patterns of memory as they affect characters striving to remain faithful to the past yet straining to escape the most torturous memories. The fiction is strongly influenced but not defined by the psychiatric literature that, by necessity, is devoted to traumatized survivors. The converse to survivor syndrome, survivor mission, is, if not equally engaging, neverthe-less of literary interest to writers who incorporate themes of preservation and transmission of Judaism and advocacy of political Zionism as viable responses to the Shoah. Survivor mission is inscribed in women's narratives on multiple and varied levels. Piercy's protagonist and secondary charac-ters advocate Zionism. Schaeffer's protagonist perpetuates and transmits Judaism's religious and ethical legacy in fierce opposition to intermarriage, and Rosen's survivors' pass on a Judaic legacy to the next generation through observance of religious ritual. Prior to and simultaneous with publication of "Rosa" of *The Shawl*, Ozick's work included numerous characters either moved to initial Judaic study or confirmed in previous commitment in response to Holocaust devastation.[68]

The survivor-writers conflate three characteristically separate roles: the victim who experiences, the eyewitness who reports, and the imaginative narrator who reconstructs or transfigures historic events. When Ettinger writes of the destruction of the Warsaw Ghetto, Karmel of the sadism of the Plaszow commandant, they do so as eyewitnesses, victims who endured the hardships from inside the Nazi universe. Yet each superimposes creative control over the material, coupling the real and invented, experimenting with perception and narrative voice while anchoring and validating the writing in reality. The reader occasionally senses two distinct voices in the works of the survivor writers—the voice of the immediate experience and the reflective voice, the youthful Holocaust-era point of view and the more comprehensive and meditative post-Shoah authorial intelligence. We recognize distinctions between the "I" of the narrative present, in accounts rendered from within the perspective of "planet Auschwitz," and the "I" of the mature writer, who perceives the events of the narrative through a post-Holocaust lens.

From the privileged position of geographical safety and temporal distance, American-born writers produced a diverse body of literature dedicated to memory of an event they did not witness, an event that radically altered the way many people conceive of God, humanity, and civilization. Lacking personal experience, the authority of these novelists arises from the researcher's persistence and the writer's craft. They rely on documentary sources, interviews with survivors, and their imagination. Confronting a cultural code challenging their ethical right to imagine Holocaust suffering, they are often compelled to assert the factual basis of their work. Schaeffer relies heavily on survivor testimony and Piercy on monumental Holocaust research to contextualize their novels. Rosen and Ozick (before "The Shawl") distanced their work from the Holocaust landscape, focusing either on research or on meditation on the philosophical and political implications of the Shoah rather than setting their works in the era of atrocity. Their writing is rooted in psychological realism, anchored in historicity and the effects of the Shoah on postwar lives of victims and empathetic souls who take the history to heart. Émigré and American-born writers alike incorporate eyewitness characters in their narratives and use the eyewitness trope, thereby establishing immediacy and creating the perception of authority. They demonstrate the validity of James Young's insight that "testimony continues to function as the preeminent rhetorical trope underlying the very possibility of a 'documentary narrative.'"[69]

Difficult for any writer, Shoah literature is particularly problematic for Americans, who were spared not only the existential horrors of the catastrophe but, in many cases, lacked substantive knowledge until decades later. Although Ozick, Rosen, Piercy, and Schaeffer were not direct participants in the Jewish experience on the blood-soaked continent, they are profoundly moved by the tragedy, share the burden of Jewish history, and faithfully render and imaginatively reconfigure the catastrophe. The fine writing of talented authors, whether literal witnesses or, to use Rosen's phrase, "witnesses-through-the-imagination," effectively demonstrates that proximity is not the critical measure of authentic literary witness and that it is the artist's power to convey the meaning of the historic which leads to illumination for our time and future generations.

Representation of Holocaust Commemoration

In Alvin Rosenfeld's view, "apart from its genocidal aims, what distinguished the Nazi crime against the Jews was the intent of the criminals to leave behind no witnesses, and hence no record at all. The Holocaust was to be a total, silent deed."[70] Foiling Himmler's objective to relegate Nazism's annihilation of European Jewry to an "unwritten and never-to-be-written page of glory," historians, diarists, and creative writers have recorded the unprecedented criminality of the Third Reich. Akin to the moral commitment of Jewish ghetto chroniclers and diarists to record the contemporary destruction of European Jewry is the determination of physical and psychological survivors to continue the saga into the concentration camp universe, to speak for those who did not survive, and to reflect on the implications of the Shoah. These writers pursue the mandate of the Jewish historian Simon Dubnov, who charged his contemporaries, as the *Einsatzgruppen* were annihilating the Jews of Riga, "Schreib und farschreib!" [Write and record!]. They honor a young Dutch Jewess who chronicled the atrocities perpetrated against Holland's Jews while she labored in Westerbork transit camp before her deportation to Auschwitz. In her posthumously published diary, Etty Hillesum wrote, "I shall wield this slender fountain pen as if it were a hammer and my words will have to be so many hammer-strokes with which to beat out the story of our fate and of a piece of history as it is and never was before."[71] Devoted to the collective memory of an epochal event in Jewish history, writing by the women of this book foils the erasure of history that revisionists and negationists desire, narrates the history as it was, as it never was before and, it is hoped, shall never be again.

Arthur Cohen gives eloquent voice to the religious commitment of witness literature by invoking liturgical injunction to remember Jewish history: "The Passover *Haggadah* commands that every Jew consider himself as though he has gone forth in exodus from Egypt. . . . I was really, even if not literally, present in Egypt and really, if not literally, present at Sinai.

God contemplated my virtual presence then, thirty-odd centuries ago. The fact that history could not prevision and entail my presence is irrelevant. No less is it the case that the death camps account my presence really, even if not literally: hence my obligation to hear the witnesses as though I were a witness."[72] Berel Lang, among others, shares Cohen's view of the Passover liturgical vision of progress beyond collective listening to each Jew's obligation to narrate and regard oneself present at the Exodus and Sinai as the analogue for "the presence of all Jews . . . fixed within the events of the Nazi genocide."[73] George Steiner, whose family had the good fortune to escape Germany, contends "that Jews everywhere have been maimed by the European catastrophe, that the massacre has left all who survived (even if they were nowhere near the actual scene) off balance."[74] The quintessential voice of Holocaust conscience, Elie Wiesel, speaks for most Jews when he concludes, "No Jew can be fully Jewish today without being part of the Holocaust. All Jews are survivors. They have all been inside the whirlwind of the Holocaust, even those born afterwards, even those who heard its echoes in distant lands."[75] And if one takes this awful event into one's consciousness, and happens to be a writer, how is writing about the Shoah to be avoided?

A categorical imperative found in Holocaust narrative is a commitment to Shoah commemoration, a commitment implied by the émigré writers and boldly articulated in the works of the American-born. Commemoration appears as literary theme and narrative form: thematically through survivors' need to communicate history and foil its misappropriation and, in narrative structure, as diary and memoir. Among the literary genres that explicitly invoke historic accuracy, the diary and memoir convey the authority of the witness.[76] Reflective of the significance attached to such historical authenticity is the novelistic appropriation of these testimonial forms. An important literary virtue of diaries, the conjoining of an unmediated direct connection with the recorded events and the expressive point of view of the diarist, is emulated in the fictive mode, and the distanced retrospective stance is achieved by novels constituted as memoirs. Whether immediate or remote, each perspective conveys the aura of authenticity in its references to the historic event. Perhaps because the diarist's vision is limited to the writer's wartime knowledge, often clouded by Nazi deception or by insufficient access to information, most of the writers in this book prefer the survivor perspective, which permits the conjunction of the immediacy of the victim's perspective and the post-Holocaust assessment of Shoah experience, including the impact of the past on the present. These evidentiary genres successfully enhance the impression of authentic historicity, so crucial to Holocaust representation.

In the decades since Theodor Adorno's famous dictum, "No poetry after Auschwitz," literary representation of the Holocaust has been received with near universal acceptance. Critical discourse has shifted to the manner of Holocaust representation in the arts. Adorno's reconsideration and refinement of his position deserves the same recognition his original prohibition was accorded. He has since acknowledged that "the abundance of real suffering tolerates no forgetting . . . this suffering demands the continued existence of art [even as] . . . it prohibits it. It is now virtually in art alone that suffering can still find its own voice, consolation, without immediately being betrayed by it."[77] Confronting moral and ethical questions of what constitutes legitimacy within the contexts of Shoah literature, some assert that eyewitnesses are the only legitimate chroniclers. Such exclusivity is unreasonable. Literary authority and authenticity are neither ensured by personal suffering nor precluded by lack of firsthand experience.[78] Eyewitness accounts may be circumscribed by the experience of the survivors and compromised by Nazi operations purposefully designed to disorient and confuse their victims. The need to imagine the Holocaust is a significant component of the writer's connection to Jewish history and is often perceived as a moral obligation to speak on behalf of the murdered millions denied voice. For some, even those who were "not there," writing is a way of connecting to the collective identity and, for the religiously observant, a means of honoring the biblical commandment to "remember what Amaleq did to you" and to apply the Passover liturgy's injunction to bear witness.[79] Writers who identify with the collective memory of the Jewish people and are willing to merge imaginative transfiguration with evidentiary moorings have legitimate roles in sustaining memory. If legitimacy were to be conferred only on eyewitnesses, silence would ensue with their passing. We would be denied not only the masterful work of nonwitnessing first-generation writers such as Cynthia Ozick but the brilliant work of the second generation and the children and grandchildren of survivors—David Grossman, Thane Rosenbaum, Art Spiegelman, Rebecca Goldstein, Melvin Bukiet, Joseph Skibell, and Aryeh Lev Stollman—whose lives have been directly touched by their parents' tragedies.

Contention now resides in the sphere of Holocaust representation, intensified in studies by theorists of historiography and art who debate the propriety and "limits of representation." Creative writers and theoreticians alike engage the problem of communicating the incommunicable, the predicament of representing experience that has no historic or imagined analogue. Critical discussions of Holocaust representation center on aesthetic boundaries and the legitimacy of artistic expression. Lawrence Langer vehemently objects to a redemptive and heroic vocabulary.[80] Maurice Blanchot calls for a "disaster notation,"[81] and Alvin Rosenfeld warns: "There are no metaphors for Auschwitz. The burnings do not lend themselves to metaphor, simile, or symbol—to likeness or association with anything else. They can only 'be' or 'mean' what they in fact were: the death of the Jews."[82] Saul Friedlander contends that we suffer a traumatic rupture of conventional thought about human nature and civilization as he deliberates about representational adequacy in the writing of history.[83] Berel Lang poses a philosophical argument for privileging historical writing rather than imaginative writing about the Holocaust, asserting "that anything written now about the Nazi genocide against the Jews that is not primarily documentary, that does not uncover new information about the history of that singular event, requires special justification."[84] His objection to literary representation of the genocide is based on the mediation of artifice and its obstruction of the moral obligation to be historically accurate. Lang perceives literature's concern with its own rhetoricity as inevitably undermining accurate presentation of lived experience and historic memory. Geoffrey Hartman's more inclusive approach that "it will require both scholarship and art to defeat an encroaching anti-memory" reflects the current status and probable future of Shoah commemoration.[85] Historic study and creative writing enhance the other's capacity to inform readers. Presumably, history records events objectively and accurately, and literature is given to subjective accounts and creative invention. Yet the historian is also selective, and the creative writer transmits the historian's subject with alacrity precisely because of narrative rhetoricity. The arts will help keep Holocaust memory alive. History clearly has the strength of accurate presentation and analysis of data, but creative literature incorporates historic matter in a search for truth that is more profound than the factual. Using the novelist's skills, the writers studied herein have created a deeply truthful rendition of women's Shoah experience.

Creative writers continue to inscribe their Shoah memories and reflections. In the process of attempting even a partial understanding of the Holocaust catastrophe—whether their subject has been the Holocaust as Jewish history or the impact of the Holocaust on post-Holocaust consciousness—creative writers have fashioned works of singular importance, of moral profundity. Artists and critics alike will continue to grapple with knowing the unknowability of the event and recognizing its resistance to representation. The challenge for the critic lies in bringing a historically informed consciousness to the artist's text. To read these texts fully is to read them historically as well as formally.

ILONA KARMEL

A survivor of the Cracow Ghetto, the Plaszow and Skarzysko labor camps, and Buchenwald concentration camp, Ilona Karmel hails from a large, diverse Jewish family that lived in Cracow since the seventeenth century. Among her kinsmen were ultra-Orthodox Hasidim and Bundists, tradition-alists wearing beards and sidelocks, and modern professionals. Burdened by loss and bolstered by memory, Karmel speaks of her family with great sadness and love, as in her recollection of a revered uncle and great-aunt. The uncle used his store as a front to distribute false identity papers for Jews fleeing the Nazis and distributed his money among relatives who had a chance to survive. He sacrificed his own opportunity for escape in order to remain with his elderly mother. Karmel is in awe of her uncle's filial devotion and his pious old mother's regret that she would end a sinless life in violation of religious law by riding to her death on the Sabbath. In the midst of the abominations the son honored the Sabbath and his mother by preparing a last joyful Sabbath for her: "He covered the table with a white tablecloth, cut the *challah*, said the *kiddush*, and sang Sabbath melodies." Like most of Karmel's family, this uncle and great-aunt perished in the Nazi genocide. It is memories of such people and of her resourceful mother and sister, with whom she was incarcerated, that Karmel uses to produce fiction about "incomprehensible cruelty and . . . a human decency, . . . [unparalleled] in normal times."[1] Karmel and her sister, Henia Karmel Wolfe, began writing poetry in the camps, "a survival instinct," which they brought, "like an offering," to their mother to judge.[2] Since the war, Karmel has written two important novels based on her Holocaust experience and observation. The first, *Stephania*, uniformly praised by critics,[3] was published just four years after her arrival in America and explores ghettoization and survivor memory while eschewing direct presentation of the concentration camp world. *An*

Estate of Memory, the work of a far more mature writer, confronts the camps directly.

Perhaps because she wrote *Stephania* in 1953, so soon after war's end with Holocaust trauma still fresh, or perhaps because she was writing for the first time in an adopted language, for an American audience whom she understood was not yet prepared to accept a detailed realistic account of the concentration camp universe, the Holocaust enters Karmel's first novel only through memory and metaphor. *Stephania* is set almost entirely in a Swedish hospital where a young Holocaust survivor endures surgical and therapeutic treatments of a war-induced back injury, mirroring Karmel's three years of surgical rehabilitation of her legs in Sweden. The protagonist's experience of the Cracow Ghetto emerges organically through the story Stephania relates to her hospital roommates and her recollections. Karmel uses the ghetto love story as an interpretive bridge to help readers approach the unfamiliar world of ghetto starvation, overcrowding, and deportations. Stephania's mental agony is borne of her need to bear witness coupled with her recognition of the impossibility of conveying Holocaust reality to innocent auditors. Her story requires witness but defies conventional communication. No sooner does Stephania begin speaking of the ghetto than she must pause to offer a definition for her Scandinavian listeners and, by implication, for readers: "'It was the place where we had lived the first two years of the war.' Strange, she thought, how you had to explain each word used then, as if a special language had been spoken in those days, a language understood only by those who had lived through them. 'It was— how can I describe it to you?—just a few streets the Germans had cut off from the rest of the city. And walls around them, high walls so that you could not get out when you wanted to. Yes,' she repeated slowly, 'you could not get out when you wanted—that was it—the ghetto.'"[4] Karmel's recognition of the need for a "special language" presented in starkly simple terms is similar to the powerful Holocaust-metamorphosed diction devised by Ida Fink for "A Scrap of Time," in which an adult protagonist recalls her childhood experience of relearning words such as "action" and "conscription for labor" to fit the Nazi genocidal context. These writers' attention to deceptively simple vocabulary shifts is indicative of the affront to ordinary perception, to ordinary comprehension, that accompanied the Nazi assault on language and on speakers of the language.

Karmel's awareness and achievement is on the order of Primo Levi's understanding of the inadequacy of language to make the uniqueness of the Holocaust comprehensible to the innocent. Levi argues: "Just as our hunger is not that feeling of missing a meal, so our way of being cold has need of a new word. We say 'hunger', we say 'tiredness', 'fear', 'pain', we say 'winter' and they are different things."[5] Karmel eases the reader into the virtually unknowable ghetto terrain, employing commonplace images to suggest the oppressive conditions. Her ghetto descriptions range from the documentary to the imagistic. In a realistic rendition of ghetto congestion Stephania explains that fifty thousand people were crowded into a few streets and the number was swelled daily by newcomers from outlying towns and villages. The congestion is even more powerfully evoked symbolically in the young woman's bewilderment at how "it could rain in the ghetto, how the drops could find any space to squeeze themselves in among all those buildings and walls that separated the ghetto from the rest of the city, among all those crowds that filled the narrow streets" (151).

Even the love story is defined and enacted in Holocaust terms. Stephania is attracted to Jan by the dignity he exhibits in the midst of Holocaust humiliation. Distinguished from bent and crouched victims by his erect posture, Jan appears fearless. Replacing traditional romantic rhetoric and tribute, these lovers express their affection through Holocaust-dominated language and gesture. When Stephania discovers that Jan has left the ghetto without his *Ausweis*, the pass permitting him to work outside ghetto confines, she risks her life to deliver the document to him. Similarly, she recognizes Jan's gift of a doughnut as a courageous, loving gesture. Jews were forbidden to enter city shops, but he "just pretended he wasn't Jewish, walked into the store and bought it . . . for me" (320). Uncertain of a secure future, or of any future, these Holocaust-crossed lovers do not utter conventional terms of endearment, do not speak of plans for marriage and family. They express a fervent hope to meet "in freedom," a place they characterize as "streets through which you could walk alone with no guards around you; and [a] home, not crowded with hundreds of people, but real homes where you would have your own room, which you opened with your own key" (322). Just as the Shoah precipitates the lovers' initial meeting, it causes their separation when Jan is deported to a labor camp, and it is the insidious root of their failed postwar reunion, a meeting Stephania resists because she cannot bear to have Jan see her Holocaust-wrought deformity. Karmel skillfully establishes the Holocaust as the agency defining Stephania's postwar persona.

With a few notable exceptions, survivor-writers have focused on the concentrationary period, omitting or giving short shrift to survivor trauma, which has become a major element in American Holocaust fiction. Not only is *Stephania* an early example of a survivor-writer tackling the subject of postwar tension; it is among the first English-language literary creations of a protagonist whose postwar life and thought are significantly plagued by Holocaust memory. Representative are Stephania's thoughts about her parents' deaths and observation to her hospital roommates that gentiles expect to die of natural causes but Jews anticipate an unnatural death. Supporting her contention to the incredulous Swedes, who have lived in a secure, homogeneous society, Stephania forthrightly identifies the anti-semitic source of Jewish vulnerability, but she is too distressed to illustrate her thesis with a recitation of historic evidence. She withdraws instead to private recollection of the unceremonious disposal of a Jewish body by a fellow victim, "dragging it by the legs on the floor, because he was not strong enough to carry it" (260). Too hungry and sick at the time of her mother's death to mourn in the traditional manner, she now grieves at leisure.

Karmel uses Stephania's grief to introduce the complex moral dilemmas of the Holocaust era. At the time of her father's death Stephania considered the dead fortunate to escape the hardships the living endured, and she expressed comfort in the knowledge that his suffering had ended. Guilt for outliving loved ones, among the most poignant aspects of survivor syndrome, is illustrated in Stephania's extended postwar memorial service for her father and in her self-rebuke. Relief has turned to guilt for her impatience and harsh response to her father's wartime impotence. She imagines a tribunal, inviting the judgment of Holocaust colleagues on whether her duty was to save herself and her mother or to compromise their opportunity by remaining with her father, whose Jewish appearance would betray the family. Despite confirmation by her imagined peers that she was duty-bound to act as she did, Stephania adheres to an unrealistic higher ethical standard, one that is removed from Holocaust actuality, and protests that somehow she should have saved all three. Suspicious of her imagined peers' confirmation because "all of them who survived, had done what she did, in a less terrible way perhaps, but still . . . by forgiving her they forgave themselves, too" (263), she seeks the verdict of those untouched by Holocaust experience, naively trusting in their capacity for objectivity. Stephania considers confessing to her roommates but rejects that option, recognizing that they are unqualified to judge because "they had not been there. They would not understand . . . they had lived in a different world" (264). Stephania, like Edward Lewis Wallant's Sol Nazerman and Elie Wiesel's Eliezer, remains her own harsh judge. "It was that I cared about nothing but running away. . . . I left him . . . all alone . . . and just ran away. . . . I could have done something, . . . I could have tried. . . . I could have saved him . . . if I had only wanted to" (265). The victim steadfastly refuses the forgiveness of others, whether survivors or innocents, and, in the end, holds herself morally accountable for abandoning her father.

Stephania is, as most critics perceive, affirmative in spirit. Nonetheless, it does not suggest, as one critic asserts, that when Stephania leaves the hospital ward "she is at last free of the misshapen hump of her past."[6] On the contrary, the Shoah survivor continues to carry the physical and psychological wounds of the Holocaust, which may be dormant or repressed for a time but are likely to reemerge, even decades after liberation. That the Holocaust follows victims is suggested not only in Stephania's psychological and physical pain but in Karmel's use of the Holocaust image of confining ghetto walls to describe the patient's tight, confining body cast. Because the Holocaust emerges only occasionally in Stephania's thoughts and discourse with her hospital roommates, the novel may be read as prologue to *An Estate of Memory*, which elaborates themes introduced in *Stephania* and addresses the more horrendous universe of labor and concentration camps as its primary focus.[7] Whereas *Stephania* explores the relationships and individual development of strangers thrust by happenstance into the prolonged intimacy of a hospital room, *An Estate of Memory* employs a similar structural device in a compelling depiction of women's bonding in the concentration camp world.

Literary critics lavished praise on *Stephania*, hailing Karmel as a "writer with serious things to say and the ability to say them movingly and with forthrightness," an author who has produced "a solid substantial novel" and who "writes with the sure craftsmanship of an experienced writer . . . [and] the balanced maturity of point of view . . . notable in a writer twice her twenty-seven years of age."[8] Although acclaimed at its publication by Archibald MacLeish as "a tremendous achievement," *An Estate of Memory* initially attracted only modest critical attention and limited readership. The difference is reflective not of the author's craft but of readers' limitations and publication during the turbulent Vietnam era. Karmel's tough, unsentimental treatment of victims was at variance with the pathos and redemptive mode many American readers crave in Holocaust writing and film. Audiences accustomed to the sanitized Broadway and Hollywood productions of *The Diary of Anne Frank*, depicting families in hiding and a heroine who naively declares her faith in the basic goodness of humanity, were unprepared for the uncompromising Holocaust realism and moral complexity Karmel offers. Another difficulty is the complex structural form of *An Estate of Memory*, which eschews the linear chronological development or simple flashback of

Stephania. Karmel plunges readers directly into the camp universe in medias res, immersing them in Holocaust chaos, and they, like the characters, must cope with disorientation and navigate a bewildering course without conventional literary connections. Reaching far beyond *Stephania* in its mature style, structural sophistication, psychological depth, and sociological and historic authenticity, *An Estate of Memory* has only recently begun to receive the critical recognition it richly merits, as readers and critics have gained wider familiarity with Holocaust history and writing.

The novel charts the course of four women under duress in the ghettos and camps of Nazi Europe. The sisterhood is composed of Tola Ohrenstein, a nineteen-year-old daughter of a famous mercantile family; Barbara Grünbaum, a young country matron of generous spirit, so Aryan in appearance that she is known as the "big Pole"; Alinka, a fifteen-year-old orphan waif who has worked for the Germans since she was thirteen; and Aurelia Katz, "a professional victim" (138) whose pregnancy provides motivation for the women to band together and nurture life in a universe of death. The women beg and peddle their belongings for one another, feed and warm one another, and tend one another in childbirth and illness—sustaining a supportive alliance in the face of horrendous obstacles to their survival. Their heroic resistance attests to human dignity in the face of utter depravity. Through integration and individuation of the narrative strands that constitute the women's histories, Karmel returns to some ghetto themes introduced in *Stephania* and enlarges the novel's Holocaust landscape by introducing the experiences and relationships of her characters before their incarceration at Plaszow and Skarzysko. *An Estate of Memory* derives its contrapuntal form from its characters' memories and their dramatically articulated wartime suffering.

Forgoing chronological progression from occupation to ghettoization and camp deportation, Karmel invokes pre-camp Holocaust experience by interjecting and juxtaposing spontaneous recollection, conventional flashback, interior monologue, and dialogue within the labor camp time frame. Illustrative is her Proustian presentation of Barbara's pre-incarceration background, an involuntary spontaneous recollection initiated by a seemingly unrelated object. A Plaszow camp fence reminds her of times past and of another fence—behind which her servants concealed her from the Nazis. As memory floods her consciousness, we learn that when she understood that the Germans were "bringing trainloads of Jews to Treblinka and killing them off—with gas" (96), she "burn[ed] with shame" (97) for being free and protected while incarcerated Jews were fighting in the ghettos and partisans were fighting in the woods. That recognition prompted Barbara's departure to join resistance fighters, an action that foreshadows her subsequent abandonment of her comfortable Polish persona for her true Jewish identity and the perils it entails.

Pre-camp experiences are most fully explored in Tola Ohrenstein's flashbacks, which develop several of the novel's secondary Holocaust themes: passing as a Christian, ghetto hardship, and bonding among victims. In a passage characteristic of Karmel's clever, caustic use of imagery drawn from life "in freedom" to chart Holocaust experience, she evokes the Ohrensteins' survival efforts: "The time of their escapes, from a ghetto threatened with deportation to a ghetto safe because the deportation had just ended there; to and fro, to and fro, like traveling salesmen always covering the same territory. . . . As in a spa new arrivals replace guests forced to leave, so here refugees from towns emptied of Jews replaced those deported" (59). Karmel's incongruous pairing of spa guests with ghetto prisoners heightens the impression of the constraint and poverty that constitute ghetto existence. Similarly, Karmel introduces Holocaust reality through shockingly dissimilar figurative language to suggest how commonplace atrocity had become. Arguing against including Tola's father in an escape plan, the Polish facilitator insists, " 'It can't be done, . . . it just cannot,' . . . like a furniture-mover unable to transport too heavy a piece" (61). Tola relies on commercial and domestic imagery to relate her parent's death, "like coins slipped from a torn purse" (64); she remembers children playing "deportation," and the liquidation of the ghetto hospital, where "death was being brought to the sick—like breakfast to bed" (66), juxtaposing domestic kindness with brutality. Tola's impossible choice, whether to flee with her mother or stay with her father, is ironically conveyed in idyllic terms: "Like partners in a dance she kept switching them around" (62). In addition to ironic commentary on the Nazi universe, Karmel's domestic imagery works positively to chart women's nurturing and resistance roles. Barbara Grünbaum's frantic efforts to feed fleeing refugees is represented in terms of a busy hostess preparing for a large social gathering: "Exactly twenty sat down to dinner . . . more and more were coming, as if to a long-awaited wedding" (76). Again, this analogy heightens the discrepancies of ordinary life and the new order, the contrast between a full and empty larder, the extraordinary demands placed on women to provide nourishment from inadequate food supplies. The grotesquerie of the Nazi universe is suggested in the women's preparation for a gas attack: "On this day, just as before a wedding, sewing began; only instead of sewing frill or lace onto the gala dress, everyone was making masks out of gauze, cotton wool, and baking soda" (77). Even the assault of the first bombs is narrated in domestic terms: "From a knife placed carelessly across the bowl a drop of honey hung, elongated like a pendant. . . . And when the drop fell, this was war" (78). Deliberately displacing conventional war imagery routinely employed by male authors with unprecedented use of domestic imagery, Karmel not only heightens the traumatic impact of military aggression on a civilian population but makes war accessible to readers fortunate enough to be free of such experience. Domestic imagery provides a bridge whereby readers cross into the author's concentrationary world, just as Karmel's use of the love story facilitated access to the ghetto experience in *Stephania*.

Karmel evokes domestic recollections in charting distinctive gender accommodation to the Nazi invasion and the subsequent redefinition of Jewish life. Tola's domestic recollections introduce the frustration Jewish men encountered when their status changed from provider and protector to dependent. Dispossessed from business and professions, the men were involuntarily retired. Trapped at home, filling time with prayer and study or manufactured leisure activity while their wives barter for food and keep house, the men are rendered ineffective. Tola's memory of her father's prewar vibrancy is overwhelmed by his submissiveness and resignation, his withdrawal "into the prayer shawl as into a tent" (54). Distinguished from pre-Holocaust war stories depicting women dependent on heroic men for protection and male-authored Holocaust narratives that marginalize women's experience, female-authored Holocaust texts often show women as active family providers and protectors during the occupation and ghetto phases of the Shoah. Because aggression against the Jews was waged not on distant battlegrounds but in the community through isolation in congested ghetto buildings and severe restriction of food rations, women's conventional occupations of food procurement and preparation, nursing, care of children, and domestic sanitation became frontline manifestations of resistance.[9] The fictional examples of inventive maternal resistance and resilience during the early ghetto periods, foreshadowing mutually supportive patterns that become the norm of female society, advance the major theme of women's resourcefulness in feminist Holocaust writing.

In a universe of choiceless choices, victims struggled constantly with untenable alternatives. Parents try to fathom which "resettlement" transport would be best for their family, and their adolescent children try to divine which work detail would be the most secure. In the end, decisions people make are as likely to work to their detriment as to their benefit. At one point Tola must decide whether to heed her mother's advice and escape from the ghetto with a labor group or stay with her parents, hidden in a bunker, in an effort to evade an imminent selection. Another option is for the Aryan-appearing women to escape the ghetto, leaving the Semitic-featured husband behind. Ever vigilant, the hunted pair try to outrun their hunters. Like other interdependent mothers and daughters of Holocaust experience and literature, they find "it was as if they had enough strength between them for only one. When mother led, she just followed like a frightened child. If mother faltered, she took over" (61). Soon it is Tola who "organized their escapes; she who now haughty, now begging, scrounged for the money needed to get out" (60). The managerial skills Tola learns from her mother in the ghetto and during their fugitive period account for the young woman's metamorphosis from dependent child to adult survivor and for her later ability to assess circumstances in the camps and help friends develop and implement survival strategies.

Commonplace in women's Holocaust narrative, and present in each of Karmel's Holocaust novels, is the theme of Jewish women passing as Christians, a practice of desperate Jews who believed their appearance would not betray their identity. Free of the physical marking that circumcision imposed on men, it was easier for women of Aryan appearance to avoid detection. Karmel dramatizes the tension of passing during a train ride Tola and her mother take in the company of outspoken Polish antisemites. The train passes a church, and other travelers lower their heads and cross themselves. Mrs. Ohrenstein, "her arm stiff as after a stroke" (58), follows suit. She peppers their conversation with an invented Christian family and devotional interests, remarking on Aunt Krystyna's book on Saint Theresa, Aunt Krystyna's lovely name days, and another relative, a colonel who went to mass each day.[10] Ensuring the authenticity of her Polish Catholic mask, Mrs. Ohrenstein lards her speech with antisemitic rhetoric: "Yes, they're killing the Jews off . . . yes, serves them right, those leeches . . . yes, perhaps even they are human" (61). The passage reveals Jewish perceptions of well-established Polish antisemitism and is an exemplar of Karmel's astute political observation and sociological verity.

The shame of denied identity, a by-product of Jews passing as Christians, is objectified in Barbara Grünbaum's story. Because her appearance is so Polish, Barbara passes with ease. Eventually, she is arrested, not as a Jew but as a political prisoner. She is incarcerated among Poles who believe she is one of them, even when they are displeased by her articulated concern for the Jewish prisoners. Despite the opportunity to save her life, Barbara is troubled by the bogus persona: "She shammed and lied, while within her, like breath held too long, the truth welled up. She could not bear it any longer, she would speak up. . . . She kept silent; yet the deception pained her, a symptom of ugly craftiness which she knew was ascribed to Jews. . . . Soon it seemed her name had always been Janina Zborovska, her past no more than a picture postcard" (90–91). This short passage testifies not only to the strain engendered by life-preserving duplicity but to the additional tension of the victim's absorbing and internalizing the oppressor's antisemitic enmity.

The primary foci of *An Estate of Memory* are Plaszow, where Tola and Barbara meet, and Skarzysko, where they are transferred and joined by Aurelia and Alinka in a makeshift camp family. The Plaszow camp, located on the outskirts of Cracow, was a primitive place administered by the sadist Amon Goeth. Plaszow was the second largest camp after Auschwitz in the Cracow district and one of the few the Nazis established in the suburbs of a major city. Following liquidation of the Cracow Ghetto and surrounding camps, the number of Jews imprisoned in Plaszow reached twenty-five thousand. The camp was built over two adjacent Jewish cemeteries on a hilly, rocky terrain that stretched beyond to an area of malaria-ridden swamps. Jewish prisoners planed down the hills and drained the swamps. Security was ensured by two rows of high-voltage barbed wire fences and six strategically placed watchtowers, where German guards were ready to fire at any time. Behind the Jewish barracks was a massive grave in which thousands of men, women, and children were buried. Beyond the barbed wire were two more such mass graves. One of them was on a hill known as Chujowa Gorka (Chuy's Hill), which served as the execution site for all the Jews selected as being unfit for hard labor. The camp buildings were constructed of thin boards. Beds were wooden crates, sans mattresses, placed one next to the other. The barracks had no heat, no water, and no latrines. Eventually, latrines were built consisting of holes cut into a board placed over a trough. Here, as in other camps, there was virtually no privacy. The prisoners slept, undressed, ate, washed, and conducted all bodily functions in public.[11] Karmel's powerful descriptions of camp conditions and poignant representation of the impact such circumstances had on inmates are among the best in Holocaust literature.

The main portion of the novel is set in Skarzysko, a forced labor camp for Jews in the Kielce district of Poland, where the foursome live with scores of other women in quarters consisting of mud-splashed, rotten plank floors littered with ash and straw, furnished with slop pails, a double tier of lice-infected bunks, a table, a bench, an iron stove, traces of previous inhabitants, and the smell of "soiled linen and steam; . . . chlorine and urine gone stale" (117).[12] Complicating the health hazards of malnutrition and living in lice-infected filth, Skarzysko's infamous munitions factories, where Jewish women worked, led to either a relatively quick or prolonged and painful death, depending on the chemicals used for production. Of the picric acid unit, she writes: "This was the yellow place. The air declared it— so bitter that each breath hurt, the earth glittering with a phosphorescent sheen, and the trees, a yellow-green lichen eating into their trunks so that they cracked and split in half, the branches denuded but for a scorched fringe trailing through the mud. Behind the trees sprawled puddles the color of phlegm; in the brown canvas spread over squarish piles, holes gaped, their green edges jagged as though gnawed by sharp teeth; . . . 'Picrine' was the name of this place . . . from the picric acid" (115).

Karmel is the peer of the most accomplished Holocaust writers in her capacity to delineate the humiliation, degradation, and brutality of the concentrationary universe. More compelling even than her physical descriptions are her dramatizations of the impact of existing in such conditions, the toll on body and soul of women who had formerly contended with shopping crowds and now swarm between the shelves of their bunks competing for a piece of bread. She recreates an environment where every aspect of normal life is denied, every measure calculated to debase the victims. The fictional world reflects the Nazi pattern of limiting latrine facilities and access in order to foster illness and humiliation among prisoners who are forced to wait, under the pressure of typhus and dysentery, in long lines to use the abominably filthy facilities. Karmel gives human scale to the policy in her passage describing a woman hazarding a beating or death by sneaking into the latrine, "illegal and uncounted" (22), and of a guard deciding which women will have the privilege of relieving themselves during the nights of hard labor. Karmel builds a convincing case for how these policies demoralized and rendered prisoners docile and submissive while so dehumanizing them that Germans could perceive them as a subhuman species fit for "extermination."

Karmel conveys Nazi brutality by emphasizing the slow-paced mass murder of captives through starvation and disease in camps that bred contagion, abstaining from dramatizing the sudden executions that were commonplace in Plaszow.[13] Having been infected with typhus herself, Karmel effectively chronicles the delirium and feverish pain of afflicted inmates: "Intent on the burning within themselves, they panted on their bunks, . . . the inflamed bodies pressed . . . tight . . . the same parched moans, the bedsores, shiny like patches of silk" (292). Beyond the typhus that leaves victims with pale balding heads, shaking on spindly necks, purblind, and half deaf, Skarzysko is distinguished by the doomed picrine people. Unlike the typhus sufferers, for whom there was hope if they could get some decent food, the shriveled, yellow-skinned Picrine people were helpless; "their disease pursued them in the yellow dust, poisoning their breath, poisoning whatever came near them" (120).[14]

Like all the victims in Holocaust literature, Karmel's characters are preoccupied with hunger. Their lives focus on the acquisition, distribution, and supplementation of inadequate rations; their conversations and relationships are food-centered. The women think about food, talk about it, imagine it, dream about it. They rightfully measure their value to the Germans using the calculus of food distribution. The Nazi policy of withholding or disbursing food as punishment and reward permits the prisoners to understand that when they are given food for the journey from Plaszow to Skarzysko, they are meant to survive. Adjustment to the new surroundings is marked by the stages of eating: "First out of hunger; next out of prudence, to store supplies; then out of exuberance, out of sheer luxury" (104).

Response to hunger also reveals the moral code of the prisoner population. To "organize," to steal food from the Nazis, is moral; to steal from a dead inmate before someone else claims the cache is acceptable. To steal from a fellow prisoner, however, is occasion for severe verbal and physical reprimand. A sign of the women's mutual help is their capacity for sharing food and keeping one another from eating the rations too quickly. If one suggests eating early, the other prevents it, since work is impossible on an empty stomach. The prisoners' moral superiority to their oppressors is frequently evidenced in their altruism, in their extraordinary efforts to obtain and share food.

Along with hunger, the agony of roll call is a topic common to all Holocaust writers, as it was to prisoners regardless of their designated categories in the camp universe. The Nazis purposefully transformed a routine bureaucratic attendance check into hours of grotesque and cruel punishment. The entire camp population assembled every morning before work and every evening after work to be counted, sometimes waiting for hours before the counting commenced. Silent and motionless, inmates stood for at least two hours, sometimes all night, clad only in thin rags in pelting rain, penetrating cold, parching heat as "SS officers strolled past the ranks. Any irregularity was punished savagely. . . . Prisoners fainted, collapsed from exhaustion and sickness, simply fell dead on the spot. . . .

To fall and be noticed by an SS man was to be beaten or shot."[15] Olga Lengyel, who worked as a nurse at Auschwitz-Birkenau, contends that the camp administrators subjected prisoners to these brutal roll calls "to break the morale of the deportees [and] . . . to hasten the work of extermination which was the real purpose of the camp."[16]

Abusive as the daily roll calls are, Karmel turns her attention to the terror-filled, often fatal subgenre of the form, the *Strafappell*. The degradation inflicted at these special punishment roll calls, in which women are subjected to cruel individual and collective punishments for offenses ranging from attempted escape to late arrival for roll call, smuggling food, or failing to control one's sphincter muscle while suffering from typhus and dysentery, is the subject of two pivotal scenes in the novel. Among these SS-devised punishments are rigorous calisthenics, beatings, prolonged standing in inclement weather in flimsy clothing, lengthy periods of kneeling on gravel, and death by shooting or hanging in the presence of the entire camp. Karmel's Plaszow roll call scene depicts the shooting of sixty Jews and the flogging of older women, who must endure a minimum of twenty-five lashes administered by strong Ukrainian guards. From the women's discussion of the episode we learn that the sadistic *Lagerkommandant* invented an escape as pretext for this cruelty. The women's sense of their vulnerability is evident in their observation that the German needn't have bothered to fabricate a reason for the punishment.

In a chapter devoted to the Skarzysko *Strafappell* Karmel skillfully alternates realistic description with Barbara's terror-filled stream of consciousness. The women endure several hours of exposure to the cold. They try to warm each other, "first by huddling together, then by kneeling back to back, but it was just pressing cold against cold" (210). Fear spreads as the inmates try to understand the reason for this roll call. They fidget; they whisper; they question whether they are just going to be counted or are summoned for another purpose. The SS man raises his hand, motions with two fingers, and the inmates fall to their knees, like animals obeying a circus master. Pain interrupts Barbara's meditation on her capacity for selfless courage. Cold attacks, and she tries in vain to warm her body against that of another prisoner. Her knees press into flesh-piercing gravel. Temporarily relieved by a makeshift pad fashioned from the hem of her coat and her hands, she is able to sleep in the kneeling position, but pain tearing at her muscles awakens her abruptly. Because Barbara understands no German, psychological angst complicates her physical suffering as she watches the face of an O.D. man (Jewish policeman who worked in the camp) for a clue as to whether she is to be singled out for special punishment for letters she has smuggled out of the camp. Mere chance operates in her favor. By the time the punishment roll call is over, snowdrifts have "buried those kneeling, until they turned to white mounds" (210). Those who can, return to the barracks. The others remain buried in the snow.

The terror of punishment roll calls is matched by the dread of periodic selections. Never immediately evident whether a selection is for a work transport or for death, each such event is cause for alarm. Combining stream of consciousness and third-person description, Karmel faithfully captures the fear that engulfs the women as they learn of an imminent selection. The reader's understanding of the capricious and sudden strategy of selections is heightened by Karmel's decision to juxtapose the selection with a relatively calm interlude in which the women have enjoyed a brief respite from the long night's labor in the absence of the O.D. men. We watch the women scurry, some concealing their money in their clothing, some trying to find hiding places, the older ones rouging their pallid faces with blood, some deluding themselves that only the old, less productive workers will be taken and finally admitting that anyone is subject to selection. This early Plaszow selection scene is fraught with moral dilemmas for the inmates. Tola must decide whether to use her own hiding place or surrender it to another, and if to another, which of several needy candidates is most deserving.

The announced pretext for a later Plaszow selection is an inmate's escape. For this selection, Karmel focuses on Tola's elemental fear engendered by the selection as well as the moral consequences of her defiance as she remains behind hiding in the barracks. Her terror is palpable: "Fear was like an animal; it pounced upon her, clawed, choked her breath, she pounced back, clutched at it, till she forced it under her body and pressed and pressed" (30). Terrified for herself and her co-conspirators, who have first hidden with her in the middle tier of barrack bunks and then deserted their hiding places to attend the roll call, Tola strains to calm herself, to comfort her aching body with promises of future rest, water, food, and fresh air. Her anxiety is heightened when soldiers enter the barracks, throw bedding and pots to the floor, strike rifle butts against the bunks, and drive the women outdoors. Confusion of time and the sequence of her bunkmates' departure, fear of their late arrival at the roll call, coupled with the entry of SS men in the barracks, heighten the rebellious victim's anxiety. As night turns to day and the others have not returned, Tola assumes that they have been transported to another camp, that she is the sole survivor, and that it is just a matter of time until the SS discover her rummaging for a scrap of bread.

Her thoughts alternate from the consummate power of the SS men, who can dissolve ghettos and camps within hours, to the comfort that no camp has yet been liquidated in reprisal for an escape.

Unlike this reported selection, Karmel presents others dramatically, including the selection for transfer to Skarzysko. To the women, it seems a night similar to any other when O.D. men suddenly burst into their work barracks, tear the workers from their seats, kick and push them outside, and drive them to the quarantine barracks, where candidates for execution are temporarily detained. When O.D. men call aside their own relatives, friends, and mistresses, the women believe their doom is imminent. It is during this selection, as the Jewish women are brought out of the quarantine barracks and the Poles are processed for transport to Germany, that Barbara forfeited her relative security among Polish prisoners and joined the Jewish column, self-selecting a more precarious deportation with Jews.

Complementing the realistic portrayals of selections are imagined selections that either evoke or parody the real. During the course of the Skarzysko liquidation Tola's response to a rumor that the women are to be deported to a work camp in Germany registers as a tortured deportation stream of consciousness: "Auschwitz was in Poland, not in Germany; no, Auschwitz was Germany now. Still, just a moment ago he had said something proving it could not be Auschwitz; he had said that only those *arbeitsfahig* would go to Germany. This meant that all not *arbeitsfahig* would be selected. A selection proved it wouldn't be Auschwitz; there was never any selection before Auschwitz" (405–06). This fantasy is juxtaposed with a grotesque parody of a postwar German victory selection of the surviving remnant. The master would present the "indispensables," who were allowed to survive for the entertainment of Germans "so that all could watch the chosen few mate, cheat, denounce, and above all select one another, on and on, till just a handful was left, just two, just one—and he in his last moment still leaping up, his limbs wriggling as though one arm were selecting the other arm, one hand the other hand" (407).

Friendship and bonding, vital means for coping with Holocaust atrocity in the camps, are central concerns in women's Holocaust memoirs and fiction and dominant themes of Karmel's novel. Survivor writing attests to courageous acts of mutual assistance, acts demonstrating the victims' persistent decency, despite their immersion in a hitherto unimagined environment of corruption and radical evil. Group solidarity enhances the individual's chances for survival, providing the victim with someone to nurse her in illness, share food, assist in work, commiserate in hunger and pain, comfort and encourage through depression and fear, and share memories and plans for the future. Often Karmel juxtaposes scenes of gratuitous German violence with vignettes of Jewish women supporting the fallen and beaten in their ranks; offering psychological support to the flogged as they wash bloody, bruised flesh; and sustaining the bereaved who have lost friends and relatives in the punishment roll calls and selections. Like many survivor writers, Karmel incorporates these gestures of mutual assistance to demonstrate that no matter how beleaguered the victims, they struggle to retain the very humanity the Nazis sought to deny.

Like the survivors whose testimonies fill the *Proceedings of the Conference, Women Surviving: The Holocaust*, Karmel's characters form "makeshift camp families" offering loyalty and mutual help. In the Plaszow portion of the novel the women combat hunger, fatigue, and illness and remain conscious during their twelve-hour night-shift labors by singing and joking with one another. The novel's Skarzysko section incorporates a characteristic feature of victim self-help, the vigilant coaching of newcomers by long-term survivors. Old-timers who survived Majdanek advise the recent arrivals to acquire a "cousin," a male who will take care of them and without whom it will be difficult to survive. "Cousins" who worked in other areas were occasionally able to bring an extra piece of bread, medicine, clothing, a work exemption or selection exemption, or an assignment to a better job.

Karmel's scenes of attending and providing for the sick during the Skarzysko typhus epidemic are among the most poignant examples of women's bonding and inmate subversion of camp authority. Starved and sick women, exhausted from slave labor, nurse those who are even closer to death.[17] When Alinka falls ill with typhus, Barbara is at her side, encouraging the half-dead, half-bald child to eat or drink, removing her sweat-drenched clothing, applying compresses, warming her frozen feet, and fanning her burning face. A physician-prisoner contravenes camp policy by registering Alinka as an orderly rather than a patient, a common ruse Jewish doctors and nurses used in their efforts to save patients whose illness would otherwise either go untreated or ensure the patient a place in a death selection.

To help one another through dysentery, typhus, and starvation, the women engage in all manner of commercial ventures to net a piece of bread, a cup of soup, or medicine. Tola haggles with Poles who come to Schmitz, where clothing prices are cheaper. Scurrying from one barracks to another, Tola barters whatever she can—cornmeal, beet marmalade, bread, even clothing from the dead. Initially rejecting an offer to sell her gold tooth because Barbara has insisted that she refrain from such trade, Tola later exchanges the precious commodity to help the typhus-ravaged Aurelia, and Barbara sends instructions out of the camp for the sale of her possessions, hoping to alleviate the suffering of the neediest in her barracks. Devoted to making as many as she can more comfortable, by sharing food, assuming the work of the disabled, and taking on extra work to win an additional potato or cup of soup for a sick comrade, Barbara transforms herself, in the Holocaust crucible, from manor-house lady bountiful to camp savior.

The novel's bonding theme is rendered most thoroughly and complexly in the depiction of the women's shared determination to bring Aurelia's pregnancy to successful term and to smuggle the infant to safety, activities that constitute their primary act of resistance.[18] Long frustrated by her childless marriage, Barbara redirects all her maternal instincts to feeding Aurelia and nurturing the fetus. When she has nothing left to sell, she helps Aurelia by doing laundry and washing floors, managing thereby to buy a few potatoes or a piece of bread. Challenged by Barbara's generosity, Tola vies with her in providing for and protecting Aurelia and her baby. In this place where pregnancy is a crime punishable by death the women rally to the cause of birth and sustenance of new life as an act of faith in the future, despite their understanding that they are heightening the risk of losing their own lives.

Of the three women whose personalities undergo complex Holocaust-induced change, Aurelia's transformation from self-pitying victim to supporter of others in need is most closely associated with the bonding phenomenon. Reversing roles with Barbara, Aurelia comforts the stronger woman when she is close to psychological collapse following a particularly threatening punishment roll call. She encourages Barbara to keep faith in herself by reminding her of past bravery and lauding her influence on the other women; recalling the courage Barbara inspired in others when she responded to Polish antisemitic remarks by declaring she would "rather be a Jew-lover than the Krauts' flunky" (223); and asserting that, during the period Barbara feigned being a Pole, the psychological succor she bestowed on the women was even more gratifying than the bread she shared. The depth of Aurelia's metamorphosis is further revealed as she chides the others for allowing Tola to abandon the group and underscores the crucial importance of group solidarity to their survival mission.

Ruth Angress, a survivor who has much praise for *An Estate of Memory*, describes Karmel's protagonists as people who "cling to relationships that stand out more sharply in a life where selfishness would seem to be identical with self-preservation."[19] The self-absorption that Angress alludes to is a frequent posture of male camp inmates. In *Survival in Auschwitz* Primo Levi writes that men willingly gave a piece of their bread to others only because liberation was at hand: "Only a day before a similar event would have been inconceivable. The law of the lager said: 'eat your own bread, and if you can, that of your neighbor', and left no room for gratitude."[20] Cooperative association among women, which appears to have been the norm, is paramount in Karmel's depiction of human decency unmatched in normal circumstances. When life itself is a crime, the women's cooperative efforts are not only feats of bonding and reminders of human dignity in defiance of the dehumanizing goal of the Nazis but also heroic acts of resistance.

Through careful delineation of resistance efforts, Karmel joins other survivors who explode the myth that Jews went passively to their slaughter. Although camp conditions were designed to make life for Jewish prisoners unbearable, to so weaken them physically and psychologically that they would be incapable of resistance, they resisted physically and spiritually. Lacking weapons or substantive assistance from non-Jewish resistance forces, Jewish opposition to the Germans in the ghettos and camps, of necessity, primarily took nonmilitary forms. The spiritual resistance that served as an index of human dignity under the worst conditions is poignantly illustrated in a clandestine religious observance. An old woman concludes a day of hard labor by voluntarily sweeping the last crumb from the barracks floor before blessing makeshift candles in honor of the commandment to light Sabbath candles. Karmel transforms the mood from Holocaust darkness to Sabbath light as other women appear for Sabbath visits and "the barracks came to resemble a quiet street, where neighbors lean out of their windows to chat with those passing by" (142). Some sing. Some rest. Some delouse and repair their clothes. There are no quarrels, no arguments, no shouting to mar the rare Sabbath tranquility. Karmel's juxtaposition of communal candle lighting, prayer, song, and rest (traditional Sabbath activities) with delousing and repairing clothing (violations of Sabbath sanctity but emblematic of the Nazi universe) maintains the concentrationary reality in the forefront of reader consciousness. Transcendence of the Nazi context was fleeting for the prisoner. So too Karmel's rhetorical juxtaposition allows the reader only a brief respite.

Psychological resistance, far more evident than militant resistance in the camps, was a powerful force for survival and is a critical aspect of Karmel's universe. Private manifestations of such resistance, as in Tola's prepared glances and mental insults countering stares and jeers of the Polish citizenry or Alinka's restorative daydream, and public manifestations, such as collective refusal of food to affirm the imminence of liberation, signify the inmates' retention of their humanity. More often than collective action, individual psychology is the focus. Although the inmate is unable to rebel actively, dream provides the venue for revenge and suggests the prospect of regeneration. In dream, degradation is replaced by superior status. Alinka dreams that a German officer tries to befriend her and that she rejects him in his own language, demonstrating how cultivated she is. Impressed by her rejection of his offers of food, rest, and conversation, the dream-soldier tries to convince his comrades of their misunderstanding of the Jewish people. In contrast to Alinka's dream, motivated by unconscious desires, is Aurelia's consciously conceived daydream of postwar abundance and security, a time of plentiful food, stylish clothing, summer holidays by the sea, and, most significant, reunion with her child and continued friendship with her camp family. Complementing Aurelia's survival reverie is Barbara's, which begins in war imagery and concludes with regenerative images: "The day would come when the boundaries of barbed wire would be razed to the ground. Then all of them would walk out and on, first to a transit place, no longer of war, not yet of peace, a place where no one shouted 'Orderly!', where lights were muted, and food, mild as in childhood, was brought in" (401). Such daydreams of liberation and of regained prosperity shared with fellow victims is a Holocaust coping strategy often noted in survivor testimony and just one indication of Karmel's adroit recreation of Holocaust reality. The dreams of each of the women share visions of comfort, freedom from *Lager* conditions, affirmations of the camp "family" and of reunion with loved ones separated in the war. The survival of relatives is secondary in these dreams, as though that possibility is more uncertain or unreal than the camp group's survival and union. Aurelia's baby, a stranger to her, is more easily imagined in a nearby room than as an immediate presence; Barbara will need time to readjust to the husband she had adored, a man with whom she played a less dominant role than the one she has of necessity learned in her camp leadership position. Barbara's second dream about the postwar period incorporates war and peace imagery, as did the first, but it is more optimistic about the regenerative potential of the victims. Alinka's wedding is to occur on Barbara's estate; the decor will be in the red and white of Poland, white jasmine and red roses, white damask and red wine. They will be surrounded by "relatives returned from the four corners of the earth . . . Aurelia's child, just a bow, white socks and banged-up knees; then she—then Tola, who must, who would be there" (401). Complementing the binary opposites of the candle-lighting scene, Karmel constructs dreams of peace incorporating antithetical images of camp and home. Even Barbara's joyous reunion with her husband is couched in imagery suggestive of Holocaust deprivation, "as if to him, too, she had to grow accustomed, as to richer food" (401), imagery that represents the vision of a starved prisoner, for whom the thought of food is always paramount. Karmel creates a reading experience reflecting the camp experience—the reader's psychological relief generated by the pleasure of hope of a reunion is ephemeral, overwhelmed by the dominant context of camp representation. The dream rhetoric is a brief release from the harsh concentrationary images—never a total escape, only a lull in the avalanche.

Paralleling daydream as psychological resistance is indulgence in prewar memory, as Sidra Ezrahi says, "to relativize the present reality and provide an avenue of mental escape . . . [to] undermine the total sovereignty of the present."[21] Karmel attests to the importance of these exchanges of prewar experience as relief from camp brutality, of briefly and temporarily transcending the present, of maintaining hope for the eventual return to normalcy. Speaking of her own family's coping strategies, Karmel recalls that her mother told the children "the whole family saga, [because] one tried to have one's past with oneself."[22]

Memory works in antithetical ways in Holocaust writing. Memories of family and home, like memories of food, may depress or sustain the prisoner. Zdena Berger chronicles her protagonist's transformation from hope to despair as the past recedes, as memory shifts from the remote past to the immediate Holocaust domain, and as the immediate is projected forward for future memory. Her young woman initially enters the safe world of memory, "close[s] the door on everything outside," and concentrates her gaze on "the house where home was and the door to it a passage to safety." She strains to hear the voices of a future home but discerns only silence. Although the distant past is therapeutic for her, the distant future is unimaginable. Eventually, the Holocaust becomes so pervasive that she contemplates the future in Holocaust iconography "only as another, better camp with more food and two blankets."[23] Moving examples of Karmel's fictional translation of having "one's past with oneself" appear in Tola's memories of her family's economic security and religious piety. Tola recalls her mother's stories of her opulent youth in Warsaw, "where uncles had sped in troikas; Warsaw whence you went to Italy each year" (41); memories of a week-long wedding celebration, of beautiful furniture, fine china, and elegant embroidered silk dresses provide both a dramatic contrast to her present situation and help sustain her pride. Her memories of the family's secure life as partners in a long-established, prosperous business that had been visited by Emperor Joseph are complemented by treasured recollections of Jewish religious life. She remembers her father's return from the synagogue with the "poor man," the obligatory Sabbath guest; his blessing of the wine, "with an intonation that was beautiful" (44), and ushering the Sabbath out with braided candles, wine, and spices. Such memories of the calm beauty and sanctity of traditional Jewish life sustain her in the dark context of the Nazi Reich. These fictive passages are embodiments of psychiatrist-survivor Viktor Frankl's conviction that "intensification of inner life helped the prisoner find a refuge from the emptiness, desolation, and spiritual poverty of his existence, by letting him escape into the past."[24] The novel takes its title from such sustaining memories and from the listener's recognition that most of the people recollected were probably no longer among the living, hence "after the names of husband and child came 'of blessed memory'—the inevitable epithet . . . and memory seemed an estate where those remembered had chosen to dwell" (397).

As the sole woman among the fictional group who has—or at least can believe she has—someone and someplace to return to, Barbara serves as guide to the future. Ezrahi observes that Barbara Grünbaum is "sustained as much by her memory as by her solicitude for her companions—and when she talks about 'after the war,' it is in terms of her life before the war."[25] For Barbara the future is "the past transplanted" (120). Barbara's dream of return to her husband's embrace, to the welcome reception of the household servants, and even to the furnishings in her manor is gradually adopted as a survival dream by the others. In sharp contrast with the disease and death of the camp, Barbara fantasizes her reunion with Stefan and survival of her camp sisters in life-sustaining images of sun and rain; blooming irises, roses, and cornflowers; and abundant crops in the haymaking season.

Psychological resistance also took the form of imagined or planned escape from the *Lager*. The novel's opening scene, distinguishing the red-striped general camp population from women marked with yellow circles denoting them as special risks, women who had been arrested in possession of Aryan papers or had trusted their Aryan looks and lived among the general population until someone denounced them, testifies to the problematics of flight. Tola's escape attempt from a work detail outside the camp is fraught with trepidation. She must worry about not only German police but "a Jewish denouncer, expert at spotting other Jews" (6), and the Polish police, "forever on the hunt for escaped Jews" (7). Despite carefully arranging to change her clothes from prisoner garb to civilian dress and summoning the courage to appear in public, she loses her opportunity when she spies a joint German-Polish police check and aborts her escape.

Although active resistance is limited in the camp sphere, it is not entirely absent. Karmel includes fictive representation of work stoppages and sabotage of products destined for the German war effort that were commonplace in the ghettos and camps. Her secondary characters, minor functionaries and work supervisors, help the prisoners in their resistance efforts. "Standing six," that is, guarding against the arrival of the Germans and their collaborators while others cease working to rest or to warm food, is an important form of active resistance. Organization and cooperation are foremost in standing six. The Jewish supervisor himself gives the order, directing Tola to signal when the camp commander or SS men appear. Foiling selections is another act of resistance, this time enacted by an O.D. man who "spaced the children far apart, and always next to someone short, so that they would appear like adults, only undersized" (71). Karmel casts his effort to save inmates in language that begins with domestic detail familiar to the reader but concludes with the unfamiliar process of sabotaging the Reich's objectives: "Like a hostess before a party camouflaging the worn-out furniture, displaying those still handsome to their advantage, he now sent an old woman to a dark corner, now put a husky girl to the fore" (71). Such imagery, which may seem inappropriate in the camp context, serves to heighten the reader's awareness of the immorality of the Nazi universe and its subversion of ordinary life and makes the unimaginable horrors accessible to those who did not experience the *Lager*.

As Sara Horowitz observes, pregnancy and motherhood tropes are used in diametrically opposed fashion in Holocaust literature — either to represent the ultimate evil of Nazism and women's particular vulnerability or in resistance narratives to represent the Jewish battle against genocide.[26] Aurelia's pregnancy enhances Karmel's bonding theme, and it is also central to her theme of Jewish resistance. In addition to the women's valiant struggle to preserve the expectant mother's well-being, a Jewish O. D. man finds a secluded corner for Aurelia to give birth, and a Jewish doctor assists in the birth. Although the physician uses no medicine to alleviate the pain of delivery or sustain the infant, the women prevail on him to drug the child to ensure its silence during its removal from the camp. Sidra Ezrahi reads the birth of Aurelia's baby as "the most significant event in Karmel's novel, which affirms both the normal life cycle and faith in the future. . . . It is an event which to each of these motherless and childless women symbolizes . . . the regeneration of all her unborn and her dead. Evoking a time when mothers all over Eastern Europe—in bunkers, in attics and sheds, in the forests and most certainly in ghettos and camps—were reduced to suffocating their own babies in a desperate attempt to save their own or their families' lives, the birth and preservation of this baby represents acts of resistance and faith no less miraculous or courageous than the uprisings in ghettos and camps that are celebrated in the novels of heroism."[27] The assertive stance of Karmel's foursome in bringing the child to life and managing its escape from the camp is a validation of life against death, of women's "protective agency" and triumph over their oppressors.[28] Word of the survival of Aurelia's child spreads, and speculation about its escape sustains the spiritual resistance of many women in the camp. If they can believe, as some do, that an underground organization rescued the child or that a partisan fighter actually entered the camp to smuggle the child to freedom, then perhaps they too can be rescued. Just as the act of a young Jewish woman who took an SS man's gun and shot him as she was being led to the gas chamber in Auschwitz became legendary and sustained the spirit of resistance, the fictive act of delivering and smuggling a baby from Skarzysko "was big enough to take upon itself the burden of their longing for proof, for the least sign that out 'in the Freedom' they still mattered" (277).

Another scenario was far more commonplace. Among the painful testimonies of the Holocaust era are those by doctors and nurses who attest to secretly delivering viable babies whom they kill in order to save the mothers' lives.[29] The mothers are told that their babies were stillborn. Although Karmel celebrates her foursome's heroic preservation of a newborn life, she does not allow the reader to forget the more commonplace outcome of camp births, recounting the fate of another baby left to starve in order to preserve the life of its mother.

Thematic development of Jewish-Christian relations, as well as the corollary theme of Nazi antisemitism, is a staple of Holocaust literature. Karmel delineates Polish-Jewish relations in the Polish national context through her characters' memory of prewar and early wartime associations with neighbors, servants, and townspeople; in the camps, where the two groups experience parallel but unequal imprisonment; and in brief encounters between Jewish prisoners and Poles holding camp supervisory positions. Like most Jewish writers, she acknowledges instances of Polish generosity to beleaguered Jews, an authentic, if infrequent, aspect of Holocaust history. During her attempt to escape from a Cracow work site Tola is emboldened by memories of the aid tendered the Ohrensteins by peasants, one of whom warned them of approaching Germans in time to flee, and the help of a trainman who concealed and transported her father to safety despite the published warning of a death sentence for those assisting Jews. Barbara has good memories of harmonious relations with the Poles who worked on her estate and is indebted to her estate manager for repeated acts of extraordinary courage and loyalty: helping her hide for two years, selling her possessions on her behalf after she is incarcerated, and accepting the responsibility for the care of Aurelia's baby while the women are still imprisoned. These singular feats of decency, clearly motivated by compassion for the suffering compatriots, unfortunately pale beside the collective expressions of anti-semitism. The Jewish inmates of Skarzysko know that the Polish prisoners and townsfolk despise them, even in their time of suffering. As the painted Jewish Plaszow inmates are marched through Cracow, they are subjected to the stares and scorn of the free Poles. "Look, . . . ah, look at them! . . . Jews, all painted! . . . Clowns! . . . You wanted the red star and got red stripes instead. . . . Circus! . . . The circus is coming!" (11–12). Thus, in Karmel's fiction the Poles vent their anger not only in customary religiously based antisemitic invective but in political terms, expressing their hostility toward Russia and Jewish communists by condemning all Jews as communists. Polish barrack mates object to Barbara's visits to the Jewish barracks to share her bread. In Skarzysko, where both groups are imprisoned, the Poles abuse and scorn the suffering Jews, whether in a humiliating delousing session or at the hands of a drunken foreman who beats the women and threatens to send them to work at the picrine factory for the least infraction of the rules.

Karmel's recurrent references to Polish collaboration and Jewish percep-tions of Polish betrayal in the Nazi genocide constitute the novel's most serious delineation of the praxis of antisemitism, aside from the Nazi geno-cide itself. Several brief references serve as prologue to a developed scene in which Alinka chides Barbara for thinking that she can gain Polish cooper-ation for smuggling Aurelia's infant out of the camp, when it is Poles who are profiting from Jewish losses. Barbara, who lived among Poles, knows their antisemitism and explains how she will turn it to her advantage by incorporating antisemitic phrases in her speech to authenticate her Catholic persona.[30] Karmel's introduction of a sport trope, "Here it comes, boys, a stag. After him, after the Jew!" (190), is an apt indication of how Jew hunting had passed into the realm of Polish life. Another variant of Barbara's "antisemitic" strategy is to present herself as a peasant woman, en route to her child's baptism, chastising her accusers: "Jesus Maria, you take me for a Jewess, me? Ah, you—you're worse than a Jew, frightening a poor woman out of her wits. A beast would've taken pity on me, but not you; you have no God in your hearts!" (190). Her speech echoes the feigned antisemitism voiced by Tola's mother while passing as a Catholic during ghetto flight and incorporates an ironic closing phrase for good measure. The well-wrought exchange conveys Jewish awareness of and strategy for exploiting Polish animosity and linking the Christian and Nazi variants of antisemitism.

Nazis play only peripheral roles in *An Estate of Memory*, generally appearing as one-dimensional figures portrayed from the perspective of their victims. Typically, Karmel describes the SS metonymically in military metaphors, by their helmets and glistening boots, or as in a punishment scene in which "the arm with the swastika band" (204) designates victims for selection, or as in the Cracow Ghetto liquidation: "the fists, the flailing clubs, and 'Achtung' resounding everywhere" (66). Schneller-Schneller, the Plaszow soldier who escorts the women to work, is known simply by a nickname used by Karmel and others in Plaszow for one of their guards, a name given the fictional guard by the weary prisoners, who hear only his bellowing commands to move faster as he marches them from camp to work.[31] Another briefly sketched German is Skarzysko's Meister Grube, distinguished by the women as kind because he abjures arbitrary beatings and leaves making a picrine selection to his subordinate. Mild as this German may be compared to his colleagues, when Tola contemplates seeking his aid to save Aurelia's baby, she quakes with fear and departs from his presence without asking for his help. Although not overtly cruel, the Meister is a detached agent of the women's agony, one of the cogs in the vast machinery of persecution.

Karmel's most substantial and complex German characterization is the naive young soldier who, moved by Alinka's youth and his own misconceptions about Hitler, shows the girl a measure of kindness. He interrupts Alinka's floor scrubbing to offer her peppermints and expresses surprise that children of her age are incarcerated, going on to insist that Hitler means no harm to children, only to "the capitalists, the big Jews" (182). Evading Alinka's description of herself as representative of ordinary imprisoned Jewish children, the soldier rationalizes, "With you it must have been a mistake. Mistakes are made in a war, in war we all suffer" (182). That a man who is serving in the Wehrmacht remains ignorant of the thoroughness of Hitler's anti-Jewish policies strains reader credulity. Like contemporary postwar Germans who brush aside Nazi crimes, he shifts the discussion from Nazism's victims to the wartime suffering of the German people—the bombing casualties, the hunger, the loss of property in Allied incendiary raids, the vast number of fallen soldiers. Alinka's silence and apparent lack of sympathy for German losses provokes his defense of Hitler: "*Der Führer, Fräulein*, can do no wrong. I know it, I've seen him. But even near him, there are people, who . . . who are not so good" (182). Viewing herself as the spokesperson for Holocaust orphans, Alinka responds to his good wishes about the health of her parents by telling the incredulous soldier that none of the children in the camp have parents anymore, that they have been killed by the SS. The soldier dismisses this report as British "Greuelpropaganda" and warns the girl to resist such rumors. The boy-soldier has convinced himself that parents of children like Alinka are in work camps, and he will not be disabused of that comfort.

Although it is tempting to read the soldier as a representative of German amnesiacs and a forerunner of Holocaust deniers who claimed at war's end that they knew nothing of atrocities, nothing of mass killings, nothing of concentration camps and gas chambers, his self-contradictory role demands another assessment. Camp work soon takes its toll on this serviceman. Instead of offering peppermints, as he did to Alinka, the sentimental devotee of Hitler begins to behave like a hardened Nazi, chasing the picriniacs with a stick and beating other prisoners. Yet despite his apparent fall, Alinka defends him, for in her eyes he remains less brutal than his colleagues: "He beats—not to draw blood like the Picrine *Meister*" (241). That this character is more psychologically and philosophically nuanced than Karmel's other fictive Germans is suggested in Tola's explanation that "he beats because he's crazed by what he sees" (268). It is evident that Karmel intends the reader to accept Tola's interpretation when this soldier responds generously to the women's pleas for help in smuggling Aurelia's baby out of the camp. His mistaken conviction that the Führer means no harm to children is embodied in his response. Holocaust testimonies and memoirs affirm the existence of rare Nazi guards who occasionally helped a Jew in defiance of Nazism, yet this soldier's merciful act is one of dramatic irony, for it is motivated not by his contempt of Hitler but in accord with his understanding of his idol's protection of Jewish children.

The contradictions in the soldier's character reflect Karmel's borrowing from two distinctly different models for his persona. The first, Schneller-Schneller, a strong German peasant who beat the inmates, also treated prisoners kindly. He always ran ahead of prisoners returning to camp from their work sites to see whether a search was in progress at the camp entrance. If that was the case, he warned the inmates so they could discard their contraband along the road and give him any money they had for safekeeping, money he returned in "meticulous little packages."[32] Karmel interprets his brutality as "the frustration of a man who neither could bear his job, nor could handle it. . . . His was the fury of helplessness." The second model, the source for the story about how Hitler meant no harm to the children, was a man for whom Karmel cleaned in the military barracks.[33]

The only historic figure Karmel presents under his actual name is SS Sturmbannführer Amon Goeth, who appears briefly or is the occasional subject of prisoner commentary. Her portrait reflects the grotesque violence routinely found in other memoirists' depictions of the sadistic Plaszow *Lagerkommandant*. In the fiction he strides through the camp accompanied by an attack dog, trained to strike when Goeth utters the word "Jude!" On other occasions he threatens to sever the finger of a woman who has difficulty removing her wedding band, prowls the workshop vicinity, selects old women to be flogged and sixty people to be shot—just to satisfy his savage whim. Beyond the scenes documenting Goeth's sudden capricious atrocities, Karmel renders the villainy of his carefully calculated policy of denying the inmates the meager rations they were allotted by German law. During a camp inspection by an outside German team a Jewish baker is questioned about bread distribution. Before he can truthfully respond "Half a loaf," Goeth "raised his two fingers right above the Commission's heads" (71), and the baker reports that two loaves are distributed weekly per prisoner. Compared with testimonies by Malvina Graf, Bertha Ferderber-Salz, and Henry Orenstein, and his depiction in Steven Spielberg's film *Schindler's List*, Karmel's fictional treatment of Goeth's physical brutality is considerably muted, and the effect of his violence on the victims is privileged.[34]

In contrast to the terror inspired by Plaszow's Goeth, the Skarzysko camp commander is introduced in images that evoke his frailty: "A small parsimonious-looking man, his thinning hair combed carefully over the balding spot, his voice . . . high pitched" (335). It is only the women's fear of his authority over their lives that gives him stature: "It was the petrified silence that made him grow. It seemed that only he knew how to move freely, only he had the gift of speech, while the others—the hundred women bent over their tables—were just parts of a huge machine" (335). Even a weak German holds the power of life and death over a Jew in the world fashioned and controlled by the Nazi Reich. Thus, for Karmel, as for other Jewish writers, the mere presence of the German guard or commander is enough to suggest the terrible power he has over his victims. The environment of carefully constructed fear establishes the oppressor's power. Like other survivor-novelists, Karmel relies on memory of her own limited exposure to the camp commandant and so consequently treats the German leadership in a more circumscribed fashion than do William Styron and Leslie Epstein. Their portraits of ghetto and camp commanders are based on extensive postwar research, apparent fascination with the perpetrator, and representation of radical evil, whereas most Jewish writers identify with and focus on the victims.

Karmel's Germans evidence no moral or ethical dilemmas about their Holocaust behavior. Neither do her Ukrainian guards or Polish foremen. Only Karmel's principal Jewish characters, fighting daily against terrible odds to survive, contend with moral and ethical dilemmas. They apply pre-Holocaust moral standards to the Holocaust universe; they question and decry their own weaknesses; they chastise one another for failing to maintain their own ethical ideals. Even the few who momentarily explain their transgressions by attributing them to the Nazi-imposed universe recant and repent, for they judge themselves and one another by traditional moral codes.

The ethical conduct of the camp inmates must be considered contextually, with an understanding of the concentrationary power structure: an SS aristocracy, a secondary supervisory staff drawn from German allies, and privileged prisoners chosen for their known criminal brutality or their German language skills. German criminals and other nationals were likely to hold privileged positions in camps such as Plaszow and Skarzysko, but Jews served among the lower supervisory ranks, garnering better treatment than ordinary Jewish inmates. The SS policy of using prisoners as block elders, kapos, and work supervisors was effective, for the privileged were obliged to follow German orders. Failure to discipline or make the work crews productive meant death for the supervisors. Success meant extra food, better living conditions, and a temporary stay of execution. Some performed their duties brutally, beating inmates for the slightest infractions of *Lager* rules to impress the SS. Even the kapos and block elders who tried to alleviate the suffering of their charges were part of a system that sanctioned corruption: bribery, arbitrary harassment, and unrelenting physical and mental abuse of inmates. Karmel characterized the supervisory personnel as people to be feared, people from miserable circumstances who grabbed power and generally rationalized their conduct by arguing that if they did not perform their jobs, the SS would do so in a harsher fashion.[35]

Karmel's O.D. men are briefly but judiciously rendered from the perspective of the women they dominate, and not through their own viewpoint. Although there is no doubt they harry and berate the inmates and that some

O.D.'s exploit the women sexually for "gifts" of extra food or deportation exemptions, others endanger their own safety to aid the prisoners and refuse payment of any sort. Karmel modeled one O.D. man on a figure she knew in Plaszow whom she describes as a "big, strapping fellow, feared, dreaded, . . . who was responsible for a large contingent, mostly women, older women, weak-looking women, young kids, being taken to another work camp."[36] The fictional character is represented accurately from the wartime perspective of a female prisoner, but Karmel later revised her opinion of his historic model: "At the time, people felt he was a collaborator." After the war she learned "that he was also a member of the underground, that he played a double role." Karmel conjectures that much of his cruel behavior was a pose to ensure that the Germans perceived him as "trustworthy." Asserting that "classroom morality does not get at those people,"[37] Karmel creates fictional O.D. men in dual or ambiguous roles. They harry the women at work, taunt them, belittle them, but also plot with them to stand six, deprive the Germans of children during a selection, and assist in the birth and secure the escape of a prisoner's child.

Karmel's nuanced prose conveys the range and ethical complexity of the inmates' responses to recurrent threats presented by life in the camps. Less concerned with event than the impact of the event on character, Karmel contemplates the psychological and moral strains borne of years of deprivation and degradation, strains that disrupt group solidarity and cause each woman to withdraw into private grief and agony, private memories of loss and suffering. Although she refers to privileged prisoners in her ethical meditations, the dominant voices in her morality drama are those of ordinary women prisoners, victims whose moral dilemmas arise during the struggle to survive in a universe designed for their destruction. The decisions are agonizing: whether to save oneself or to resist escape knowing collective retaliation will follow; whether to protect oneself during a "selection" or allow another to use one's hiding place; whether and how to control one's tongue rather than lash out against a tormentor, an informer, a denouncer; how much food to eat when everyone is starving; how to decide whose suffering should be alleviated and whose should be ignored; and finally, how to cope with one's own moral transformation.

Extraordinary generosity and meanness of spirit coexist in camp relationships fraught with paradox in women's texts as they do in men's Holocaust writing. The women's moral integrity is manifested in Barbara's plea to the Meister to allow Tola, whom she claims is her sister, to accompany her when, because of her healthy appearance, she is assigned to a relatively good job. Refusing to heighten Barbara's risk by confirming the lie, Tola forgoes the opportunity to improve her own chance for survival at Barbara's expense. When Alinka is assigned a relatively safe job, Aurelia must choose whether to hold her tongue or insist that they be allowed to stay together as "mother and daughter" and thereby risk Alinka's reassignment to hazardous work. Countering Barbara's appraisal that she will jeopardize the child's safety, Aurelia asserts that their mutual support is more vital to the survival of each than is safe work for one. In each instance the women's bond is preserved.[38] The benevolent loyalty evidenced by three of the four women is the standard reported in diaries and testimonies by many camp survivors and is characteristic of behavior Karmel witnessed as women prisoners chose to sacrifice personal safety in favor of remaining with their friends and relatives.

Response to hunger as an index of her characters' moral stamina and ethical standing is a recurrent motif of the novel. As foil characters, Barbara and Tola offer polar responses to Aurelia's needs. On hearing of Aurelia's narrow escape from the Radom Ghetto liquidation, Barbara's reaction, delivered with characteristic hyperbole, is an invitation for Aurelia and Alinka to move to her bunk and a reprimand to Tola for her failure to bring this story to her attention earlier. Tola's reluctance to welcome others into the alliance she has forged with Barbara is premised on a realistic assessment of the additional burden of sharing hard-won but meager "organized" food among four rather than two. Characteristic as this pragmatic assessment is of Tola, so too are her paradoxical herculean efforts to secure extra food for the pregnant Aurelia and to obtain medicine and food for both Aurelia and Alinka during their bouts with typhus. The magnanimity of the starving women is as well dramatized by Karmel as are their lapses. When Aurelia darts from a line of workers passing heavy anti-aircraft shells to retrieve a muddy piece of bread in the road, Tola berates her for endangering the other workers and insists on communal responsibility above individual need. Because starvation is the cause of Aurelia's rash behavior, Barbara excuses but does not justify the conduct.

Tola and Barbara are antagonists created to accommodate Karmel's interest in revealing the variation in and the moral dimensions of victim response to deprivation and brutality. In search of a mission, Barbara begins the concentrationary experience with a vision of her own saintliness and a desire to be heroic. Tola is introduced as a highly self-conscious, defensive, rational loner, yearning to be well regarded. Tola Ohrenstein's story exemplifies gradual accommodation to the concentration camp universe; Barbara Grünbaum's tale is one of constant defiance. The dignity of the victim is preeminent in Barbara's portrait. Her behavior is testimony to the decency of thousands who continually faced ethical dilemmas. Entering Plaszow with the advantage of an assumed Polish identity, she voluntarily abandons the ruse, sacrificing her place in the relatively privileged Polish labor contingent bound for Germany to join her Jewish sisters, whose fate she knows is far worse, conduct Karmel characterizes as acting "from vanity, from a romantic idea of heroism."[39] Despite the danger, Barbara is relieved to return to her Jewish identity, because "she hungered for the sound of her name, longed . . . to speak of herself, . . . and the life that had once been hers . . . she would not spend this war like a parasite, helping no one, thinking of nothing but saving her own skin" (84). Ever vigilant, Barbara guards against succumbing to moral lapses caused by the external and internal evils of the camp: the former are motivated by hunger, typhus, and picrine; the latter, by corruption or selfishness stemming from the desire to improve one's own condition.

Barbara's assertive generosity occasionally provokes the others, who fear that her heroics endanger them even while benefiting them. Tola accuses Barbara of self-aggrandizement, of sacrificing her security in the Polish barracks and joining the Jewish women in order "to be the queen of the ball . . . always the first—first in self-sacrifice, first in grief, first in courage, first in fear" (367). Likewise, Alinka argues that if word reaches the authorities about Barbara's plan to sustain Aurelia's pregnancy and smuggle the child out of the camp, all the women will be in peril. Her aggressive care of the typhus-ridden Alinka foreshadows Barbara's assertive approach to gathering food for the pregnant Aurelia, "pushing and vociferating even against an injustice the size of a missing crumb" (169). Eventually, Barbara's saintly gentleness is compromised under the strain of supervising a hospital barrack and caring for her camp family. So desperate does she become to provide food for Alinka during a typhus bout that she exploits her position as hospital orderly. Observing which patients are dealing with vendors, she begs portions of their food for Alinka and, when necessary, pressures them to share their meager food supply on pain of losing her attention to their medical needs.

Although Barbara's compromised demeanor is far less devastating than Tola's self-interested ethical lapse, she undergoes a significant metamorphosis: from Plaszow saint to Skarzysko benevolent despot. She becomes a fierce disciplinarian of all in her charge, exchanging her sympathetic mode for a command posture. No longer tender and solicitous while nursing sixty patients, she becomes a fiend for cleanliness. Even the sick must air and sweep the barracks and wash when they feel too weak to move. Beating the women without remorse, insulting them without apology, she forces them to battle their illness. The others "had loved . . . her unworldliness, her wild generosity. . . . They grieved to see such unworldliness gone" (169). According to Karmel, Barbara learned that speaking sweetly in conditions of extremity was not always effective.[40] In the concentration camp, discipline had its place, and she had to abandon her saintly image to better serve the needy.

Of the four women, Tola has the most extreme concentrationary metamorphosis. Choosing self-isolation in Plaszow, she is derisively described by others as "the princess," a loner who "would not accept a makeshift family" (7). Later she accommodates to the concentrationary world by bonding with and working on behalf of campmates in Plaszow and Skarzysko, even undergoing voluntary primitive dental surgery to trade her gold tooth for food and bartering scraps of old clothes for the same purpose. Courageous conduct and honesty are paramount in her business operation. Yet despite her achievements and pride in honest trading, she succumbs to years of deprivation. Near war's end Tola abandons her selfless pattern of communal service, turning instead to her own survival and justifying her reversal by asserting that corruption ruled the camp universe and that she would use her opportunity for survival, as had others who bribed an O.D. man or slept with one.

When Tola privatizes her survival strategy, she embarks on a course of conduct that she recognizes will alienate her from the group and perhaps will save her at the expense of others. Sidra Ezrahi observes, "The obliteration of self—and with it, of accountability—appears here as the first sign of compliance of the victim with the system."[41] Tola's deterioration is signaled by the painful rationalization that "anything done for someone else is a sacrifice, a noble deed: but try to do the same thing for yourself and the sacrifice becomes a disgrace. Why? I too am someone: I've no contract for survival. I too am afraid" (342). As Tola succumbs to devastating fear, she transforms herself from civilized aristocrat, to beneficent peddler, to privileged guard.

Karmel prepares readers for Tola's fall from grace by carefully rendering her moral dilemmas early in her bartering career. Troubled by the slightest sign of peer disapproval, Tola questions the appearance of her bartering, wondering how the women are judging her. She knows they trade with her because they believe she's honest. Yet she laments that "a true Ohrenstein would never have sullied himself with such bartering" (293). Later she convinces herself that she has brought dishonor to her respected family name and that the women trade with her only because her prices are the best. She suspects that the women are critical of her: "Could she not have turned into a harpy for her own sake, just to eat well, to get better clothes. . . . Perhaps. If others could do it why not she?" (293). Despite her ambivalence, Tola remains communally engaged; "without knowing why or how, she would find herself up on a bunk washing a sick woman, dressing an infected sore" (294).

Years later, obsessed with self-preservation, Tola applies for a supervisory job that demands that she ensure work quotas and accept responsibility for the production and behavior of her group. Contrary to Barbara's belief that she accepted the job to help the others, Tola confesses that her motive is self-interest: "She wanted safety and the bread that would come later at night" (381). To the charge that she will be a slave driver, that she will be ordered to do something terrible, Tola replies, "Someone else will do it if I don't" (343). Tola's attitude is emblematic of inmates who are willing to do German bidding for self-interest, whereas Barbara and Alinka represent the majority of victims, who recognize the impossibility of serving the Nazis and remaining untainted. Physically satisfied with the extra bread, Tola remains emotionally distraught. During the course of her moral transformation she progresses from determination not to be a mere victim but to be an assertive agent of her own survival, even if at the expense of her prewar principles. She reproaches herself with memories invoking the moral norms and comforts of her former life, memories that might have served as a foothold to the future.

Karmel devotes exquisite nuanced representation to Tola's evolution from hesitant acceptance of her privileged role, to painful accommodation, to hardened acquiescence before her final defiant rebellion. For a time, Tola rationalizes her harsh supervision of underlings and ignores peer disap-proval. She secures her own bread and survival by driving the women in her charge. Spurning Barbara's advice that she motivate the women through self-preservation, to convince them that they must work for themselves, "because if they don't, something terrible might be done to them" (367), Tola asks, "Why should I tell them that they want to live, when it's easier for me to threaten with Rost? Much easier! . . . there's no glory to be got out of me, not a shred. . . . I must be an *Anweiserin* [overseer], in my own way" (367). As work supervisor, Tola leads a double life, constantly plotting how she will manipulate the women to satisfy the Germans and yet find ways to help the women survive. She grows hostile toward her charges, who view her as "the exploiter grown fat on their misery" (378). She is ever fearful that the women are sabotaging her efforts, trying to get away with less labor, standing watch against her barracks arrival as she had earlier done against other supervisors. Before, Tola had been mindful of others' good impression of her; now she has cause to fear their disapproval.

Inmates in positions that require their cooperation with the Germans are considered by the other prisoners part of "them" and no longer part of "we." Yet the inmates depend on the sensibilities of these functionaries for their survival. Although Barbara and Alinka condemn Tola for seeking the overseer position, Karmel helps the reader understand, through Tola's thoughts, how difficult it was to resist the privileged job and how burdensome it was to discharge it ethically. Eventually, the women's resistance overwhelms Tola's intention to perform her duties with humanity and she embraces the perverse brutality of the camp, threatening the women with reports and punishment. Here Karmel explores how the women's relationship has fallen victim to one of the evils of the Nazi system: that of pitting victims against each other by temporarily rewarding a few with life and punishing the masses with persistent hardship and death.

Barbara and Tola, who approach bonding and mutual assistance from different positions, forfeit their lives in pursuit of saving the lives of other inmates. In an open act of resistance, one that is in accord with her benevolent and valorous nature, Barbara defies a German order to include Alinka in a roundup of hospital patients during the Skarzysko liquidation. Barbara commands Alinka to stand fast rather than enter the truck that will deliver patients to their death, and she then pushes the soldier away from the girl. Perhaps to fulfill his quota, perhaps to demonstrate the price of rebellion, the guard sweeps Barbara into the truck. As the truck pulls away and Alinka runs toward it, Barbara at first throws things at her and then exhorts the doctor and O.D. men to hold her, but it is Tola who clasps the child in a protective embrace. The last collaborative effort by Barbara and Tola is saving Alinka.

Tola succumbs to weakness, but she has not been entirely corrupted. Her essential goodwill is evident when she strives to protect the most debilitated women during a selection for extra shell loading by asking the stronger women to volunteer and spare the feeble in their ranks. During the final days of Skarzysko, when she must supervise the women's digging of a mass grave, Tola acknowledges that the price for her survival is too great and determines that she will try to save the women or die with them. She weeps purgative tears "for what has been done to her and for what she has done to those . . . with whom she would soon be together" (433). Like one of

Nomberg-Przytyk's characters who resigns her privileged job in the camp warehouse, Tola forsakes physical safety for spiritual survival. In the epilogue we learn that during a death march Tola approaches a girl to warn her that a guard is taking aim at her, and the bullet intended for the girl fells Tola. In risking her life to save another, Tola is redeemed.

Whereas Primo Levi invites the reader "to contemplate the possible meaning in the *Lager* of the words 'good' and 'evil,' 'just' and 'unjust'; . . . to judge . . . how much our ordinary moral world could survive on this side of the barbed wire," Karmel poses the same questions indirectly. She too ponders the elastic moral boundaries of the *Lager* universe, the erasure of moral absolutes, the moral ambiguities born of necessity that distinguish the thievery by Amon Goeth from that of his victims, who "organize" food and medicine or make deals for special privilege to forestall death. Levi wrote that the Nazi plan was designed "to annihilate us first as men in order to kill us more slowly afterwards."[42] Like Levi, Karmel demonstrates the tragic implications of the plan in her fiction.

Ilona Karmel's women, like Levi's men, unlearn and relearn human possibilities. Karmel describes her writing as an effort "to understand human beings in those events and find something redeeming in a single individual."[43] That objective is masterfully realized in Alinka's maturation from adolescent faultfinder to compassionate friend, in Aurelia's surcease of selfish demands and maturing contribution to community, in Barbara's reformed charity, and in Tola's spiritual redemption. Although only Aurelia's baby and Alinka survive, the spirit of all the women—their sacrifices, their relentless struggles, their nurturing kindness in a setting designed to strip them of any semblance of humanity—lives on in the estate of reader memory. Karmel has imagined these women and recreated her own camp universe with historic truthfulness, psychological complexity, moral integrity, and literary artistry.

ELŻBIETA ETTINGER

Elżbieta Ettinger, like Ilona Karmel, has fictionalized her Polish wartime experiences. Aside from a four-month period in Majdanek, Ettinger was in and out of the Warsaw Ghetto, spent time hiding in Aryan settings, and served as a partisan engaging in sabotage.[1] Her contribution to Holocaust testimony began with the reports she filed while imprisoned in the Warsaw Ghetto. A student in underground classes, she was among the legion of contributors to Emmanuel Ringelblum's compilation of clandestine writing on daily life in the ghetto.[2] Ettinger conveyed her information to her teacher, who was one of Ringelblum's close collaborators. She supplied details concerning "teachers, subjects, the conditions under which [youngsters] studied, the drop-out rate, . . . the progress . . . made." She also reported on beggars, street singers, thieves, and roundups as well as "the number of corpses of starved children and adults strewn in the streets every morning."[3] On the Aryan side, Ettinger fought in a resistance unit that "blew up bridges and killed a number of German officials."[4] At war's end, unlike most surviving Jews, who were disheartened by wartime and postwar Polish antisemitism and emigrated to Israel and America, she remained in Poland, obtaining two advanced degrees, one in political science and one in English and American literature. She was employed by the government in foreign trade and later as a translator. Escalating antisemitism made her foreign trade position untenable, and she turned to translating and writing literary criticism.[5] Ettinger's hope that a nonpolitical field such as literature would make her life as a Polish Jew bearable proved false, and she accepted a fellowship at Radcliffe Institute in Cambridge with a Harvard University appointment. While at Radcliffe, under the auspices of a Bunting Fellowship to write on the law in American fiction, she began her Shoah novel, working on it only at night in the mistaken belief that she had to dedicate her daytime hours to the declared Bunting project.[6] Her decision to write *Kindergarten* stemmed from her wish to counter prevalent American misperceptions of the genocide, Polish antisemitism, and Jewish passivity.[7]

Within the settings of the Warsaw Ghetto and Aryan Poland the major characters of *Kindergarten* experience Shoah-wrought transformations: from housewife to resistance fighter, from innocent schoolgirls to experienced fugitives, from antisemite to Jewish benefactor, and from self-confident partisan to suicidal paranoid. Although the major characters are women, male characters are more visible in *Kindergarten* than in much Holocaust fiction written by women because the novel's ghetto and Aryan settings were free of the sexual segregation common to the concentration camps. *Quicksand*, the sequel to *Kindergarten*, charts the life of the Shoah survivor living in Communist Poland in an environment openly hostile to Jews.

Kindergarten is a third-person narrative presented from the point of view of Elli Rostow, who comes of age during the Shoah under an assumed Christian identity. The brief prologue, dated 1962, introduces Elli as a Shoah-haunted survivor brushing imagined gas away from her child's crib. Memories of her dead relatives and fragments of key events that are developed in the central recollected narrative flood her consciousness, and she complains, "They never let me alone, the same pantomime over and over, . . . I try to forget, I try so hard, not to see their eyes anymore, not to hear their voices, not to smell their sweat, not to feel their anguish."[8] Sensitive to the survivor obligation to bear witness, she believes, "They wait, they do not want to be forgotten, they know I promised, they will never let me forget, never" (2). Ettinger's secular protagonist does not embrace the liturgical tone of Rachel Auerbach, who wrote, "And if, for even one of the days of my life, I should forget how I saw you then, my people, desperate and confused, delivered over to extinction, may all knowledge of me be forgotten and my name be cursed."[9] Yet she is compelled by history and a promise given to her grandfather to remember and bear witness.[10] Like most writers who restrict development of the postwar period in their fiction, Ettinger accentuates the battle for survival in wartime, focusing on the victims' responses to Nazi oppression and Polish complicity.

Ettinger's achievement, like Ilona Karmel's, stems from her recognition that it is impossible to reconstruct the Shoah in its destructive totality and her decision to adopt a discourse of discontinuity to convey the disruption in the lives of European Jewry. Fittingly, her compositional method interrupts narrative flow to evoke Holocaust rupture. Rather than use lineal, chronological progression, she presents the story in a complex series of juxtaposed dramatic scenes, flashbacks and flashforwards, meditations, and diary entries.[11] The text loops back and forth on itself, juxtaposing dramatic presentation and diary meditation to illuminate political and psychological themes. The novel's intricate structure counterpoints ghetto incarceration with dramatic action and Elli's diary accounts with fugitive experiences. In place of the original plan to use the diary as a self-contained section, Ettinger wisely shifted to intermittent and nonchronological presentation of diary entries, which further complicates and clarifies the text. Like Marge Piercy, Ettinger is politically astute and uses the diary form to chronicle public events as well as private responses. The diary entries record official administrative edicts, the incremental stages of occupation and ghettoization, and the impact of these public decisions on private lives. The diary also provides a record of the sisters' lives as they were before catastrophe struck, thereby suggesting the magnitude of their transformations. Entrée to Elli's thoughts and emotions, to her metamorphosis from free citizen to ghettoized pariah, from innocent girl to instant adult, is realized in the diary's discourse. It has been noted that Ida Fink's style conveys her view that "what happened to the Jews disrupted the very foundation of the genre of narrative—the underlying continuity of time."[12] Ettinger's style suggests that she shares that view. Like the writers of the *Oneg Shabbes* archives to which she contributed, her fictional scribe is aware that the Jews of Warsaw are living history and that it needs to be recorded. Rather than use the diary primarily as a historical chronicle of the Warsaw Ghetto, however, Ettinger introduces diary entries intermittently, either as expository referent or as contrast to the "free" fugitive status of the protagonist, retaining the beleaguered voice of the victim throughout.

Like Karmel and *Oneg Shabbes* ghetto historians, diarists, and journalists who plunge the reader into the midst of daily life and death, Ettinger begins her novel in medias res, a narrative style imitative of Shoah displacement and disorientation. She abandoned her early plan to begin *Kindergarten* chronologically, depicting the family in transit from Lodz to Warsaw, and instead thrusts the reader into a violent deportation action, perhaps because she considers the Great Deportation of the summer of 1942 the decisive turning point in the fate of Polish Jewry.[13] Not until a later diary entry, quoting and dating the deportation edict, do readers understand that the novel's setting is the Warsaw Ghetto and learn that "Jews must report . . . at the assembly point. . . . Those employed in the *Judenrat*, in the Jewish police, and in the workshops were exempt. Below, in smaller print, the people were ordered to bring a change of clothing for the trip to labor camps in the East. Scribbled in ink was the amount of bread and marmalade waiting at the *Umschlagplatz* for those who would report without delay" (67). Iteration of the edict conditions allows readers to see it through dual perspectives of ghetto residents, who were ignorant of its true import, and their own post-Holocaust frame of reference, confirming the Nazi ruse that would end in murder. In contrast to the highly charged language of the dramatic scene presented from the victims' point of view, the edict's diction reflects the Nazis' methods for organizing orderly deportations from the ghettos to the concentration and death camps: exemption of the ghetto's prominent members, whose survival depended on carrying out German orders against the Jewish population; the ruse of promising survival through labor; and the inducement of food to entice the suspicious but starving ghetto populace to volunteer for the transports. Choral voices in the dramatic scene speak of forced labor battalions, temporary reprieves through essential labor passes, and roundups. References abound to Jewish efforts to survive through work, bribery, or hiding and to the German counterplan for population control and depletion through the use of Jewish police, starvation, disease, and deportation to the extermination camps. The urgency of the situation is conveyed by shouting voices; by residents scurrying to remove the boards of their "tombs," their hiding places; and by the notice that "the daily quota for the deliveries to the trains waiting in the *Umschlagplatz* . . . had recently been increased" (5). Disappearance of "people who had exchanged fortunes for working passes . . . [signifies] the German workshops had lost their status as sanctuaries" (5) and objectifies a ghetto in its final period of existence. The deportation scene privileges the variety of victim responses. Even as they are being transported to the trains, the captured try to negotiate survival. One has a friend working in a service battalion, another has a friend who knows which Germans to bribe, yet another thinks she will be released when she makes clear that she has a grandson in the German army. The victims are herded to "the vast yard [which] had of late become a sort of stock exchange [where] some transactions even led to liberty" (6).

The arbitrary nature of the deportations is conveyed by reference to the elderly and young, able-bodied and infirm, men and women being driven into the trains together. Chance rules in the chaotic atmosphere. As the seventeen-year-old protagonist is about to enter the train, a stranger takes her arm, signals the guard, and walks her to the ghetto gate, where he signals another guard, slips a piece of paper into Elli's hand, and watches her pass safely. Resistance organization and luck spare the protagonist while two of her elderly aunts and a young cousin are taken in the deportation. To the supervising Nazis, the deportees are no more than inventory, pieces of merchandise to ship from one venue to another. Business imagery invoked to describe the *Umschlagplatz* juxtaposed with description of the victims as "a herd of animals in a trap" (6) invokes the Nazi view of Jews as subhuman and heralds their doom. Ettinger's scene has immense dramatic force, thematic suggestiveness, and psychological impact. Beyond its power as a poignant introduction to the novel's primary resistance motif, its events are the substance of the protagonist's crucial prologue memory. Drawing on Charlotte Delbo's classification of Holocaust memory, Lawrence Langer has distinguished this form of temporal recollection as "durational" rather than chronological; it retains its constant presence and has greater traumatic effect than chronological recall in the survivor's memory.[14]

Elli's rescue from the deportation offers the first sign that she is linked to the ghetto resistance group. Before chapter's end we discover her living in a ghetto basement with two resistance fighters who snatched her from starvation and nursed her back to life. Elli is advised that her mother's order to smuggle her out of the ghetto will be honored. The mechanics of escape are difficult but straightforward: for a hefty price, a Polish woman working in a ghetto factory agrees to let Elli use her entry permit; her uncle, working with the resistance on the Aryan side, will direct her escape. The next day she departs from the control point with a group of Polish workers, and her career as a fugitive begins.

After initiating readers into the most deadly of ghetto experiences in the dramatic opening scene, Ettinger backtracks through flashback and diary entries to trace the prewar and early occupation conditions leading to the deportations. Shifting from the site of the family's current Warsaw tribulations to their Lodz origin, she summarizes their humiliation and harassment under early Nazi occupation, mirroring that of the city's large Jewish population. Elli's diary entries chronicle the response of family members to a host of anti-Jewish decrees within the first few months of civil rule in transmogrified Lodz, now incorporated into greater Germany. The Germans order Jews to wear yellow, six-pointed stars on the chest and back, restrict their movements, confiscate their property, and snatch them for conscription into forced labor brigades. Elli's father is exiled from his office; an aunt has her bank vault plundered by the Germans; a cousin is badly beaten; uncles and aunts are deported or killed; Elli is physically assaulted; and she, her mother, and sister are caught in roundups and forced to wash latrines, scrub public streets for hours, and shovel snow. By 1939

Grandfather Weil is convinced by reading the German press that "the end of this war will see the end of European Jewry." Although he cannot predict the means of destruction, he is certain that "their range and quality will match German efficiency, order, and cruelty" (27). His pre–ghetto era expectations are confirmed in a later statement based on direct observation: "They proclaimed a total solution to the Jewish problem. Maintaining ghettos is only a partial solution. Liquidating them is the answer" (70). Advised by an ethnic German friend of encroaching danger, the paterfamilias persuades the men to flee to Russia and he and the women depart for Warsaw, as yet unincorporated into the Reich.

In Warsaw the family encounters new but equally repugnant regulations. Instead of yellow stars, they must wear white armbands with a blue Star of David. Housing is scarce but available at inflated rates in a dilapidated "quarter which has been overcrowded as long as it has existed" (88). By forcing Poles to leave the district and Jews to move in, the Germans have begun geographically isolating Warsaw Jews as prelude to removing them from Poland's economy and culture.[15] Ettinger conveys the swift progression from hope for a peaceful ghetto existence to the harsh reality in a series of diary entries. In her 4 November 1940 entry Elli reports her teacher's encouragement that the children continue to study languages over "there." By her 15 November entry the violence and repression that will characterize ghetto life have multiplied: her cousin sustains a serious head wound; the ghetto is being sealed: "Heavy guards—German, Polish, Jewish policemen—are watching the ghetto outlets. Along the walls—on both sides—patrols. Day and night" (103).

The reader of Anne Frank's diary can be charmed by her brightness, humor, and curiosity and beguiled by her unquenchable hopefulness, because it is the writing of a person removed from the atrocities and hoping to survive. One experiences no such delusion in Elli's Rostow's diary. The reader of Frank is spared the life outside the attic and the life awaiting her after capture. *Kindergarten*'s readers encounter Shoah reality from the vantage point of a girl enduring its many vicissitudes. The Rostow diary passages echo themes of historic testimonies: early trust resulting from isolation among fellow Jews; ensuing starvation, disease, and deportations; criticism of the ghetto leadership; and the rise of Jewish resistance. Elli refuses to eat, wash, or talk. She lies in bed "struggling against . . . waves of consciousness" (66). Her sister, Lili, tries in vain to rouse, dress, and feed her. Malnutrition takes its toll as Elli develops ulcers and Lili stops menstruating. Ettinger decries not only the German rationing system, calculated to deplete the population through malnutrition, but the inequity of the food distribution.[16] That food was available but withheld from the starving population demonstrates the Germans' intention to operate the ghetto as a preindustrial death camp. Evoking the plight of forty-three thousand who perished from starvation during the first year of the ghetto's operation, Elli's April 1941 account describes the decline of former classmates: the transformation of a healthy young boy to hunger- and typhus-altered bald beggar; the best in physics working in a soup kitchen to support her family; the class beauty living on the Aryan side with a German officer; and the brightest having contracted tuberculosis. Each is a tale of promise aborted. Shoah-wrought metamorphosis is evident even in mother-child relationships; a former indulgent, overprotective mother is now seemingly impervious when her son suffers broken ribs and facial wounds. Having previously cried at the slightest provocation, she sheds not a tear, "her face . . . a stony mask" (106).

Ettinger focuses primarily on ghetto hardships, yet she conveys the heroic efforts of the beleaguered population to maintain its culture, echoing Ringelblum's *Oneg Shabbes*. Classes were held for children. Yiddish and Hebrew writers were studied in reading circles. Lectures and literary programs were organized. An underground press operated. Theater groups and musicians performed. The clandestine operation of these activities following the daily struggle for subsistence attests to dogged Jewish resistance to the Nazi degradation campaign.[17]

Representative of the effective prose charting ghetto existence is chilling theater imagery evoking an illegal venture beyond the ghetto walls, as the youngster concludes: "I felt so strange walking through these 'Aryan' streets as if I were on a stage, a resentful audience staring at me, waiting for me to trip. I do not belong there anymore. I felt out of place among these people, moving freely, walking at ease, brightly dressed, laughing, talking. . . . It all made me sick. . . . The food choked me. . . . The people frightened me. I felt something mounting in me I couldn't even name. When we again passed the gate at Chlodona Street and I put on my armband, I felt relieved" (93). Captivity is reality; liberty is unreal. Liberty is now a theatrical performance, an essentially unconvincing one. Psychologically, Elli has internalized her role as pariah and finds no satisfaction in deluding the enemy. Instead, she fears being recognized as a Jew. Her waking nightmare follows her into a disturbed sleep as she dreams that she and her mother and sister are in a restaurant, each with a large yellow star plastered on her forehead.

The diary is also an effective vehicle for Ettinger's exploration of Jewish identity and antisemitism. Two diary entries dated a year apart take up the subject of assimilation. At the end of 1940 Elli recounts an exchange between her grandfather and an uncle who announces that "if he could only help it, he wouldn't bring up his child as a Jew" (109). The Old Man recognizes the tendency of parents, motivated by the desire to spare their children the discrimination Jews have consistently endured in Christian Europe, to make this decision. Nonetheless, he rejects the practice, for it means "living in deceit" and raising an emotional cripple who will pass on the illness to future generations. A year later Elli, an assimilated Jew, like Ozick's Rosa Lublin, writes of her estrangement from the ghetto's ritually dressed Hasidim, whose language she does not understand and whose manner of expression she disdains. She belongs to a Polish culture, tradition, and future. The grandfather, who often speaks as the novel's moral register, observes that Elli's comfort with Polish identity is based on her expectation of belonging to the nation. Her parents' failure to educate her Jewishly before the external imposition of her Jewish identity causes her alienation. Reflecting Ettinger's training as a political scientist, the old man's discourse persuasively shows that Jews have been lulled by the illusion of assimilation to think they will be absorbed by the host culture, only to discover that they will be rejected. His is the voice of Jewish advocacy arguing the virtue of proudly maintaining cultural and religious identity: "We should seek for a status of equality among people we are living with, without ever forgetting who we are, without denying ourselves. Man must know who he is and where he comes from before he decides what he's going to do with his life—if he wants to live what I call a life" (273).

Returning to dramatic presentation of ghetto life, Ettinger depicts the challenges Jewish Councils faced in their conflicting roles as agents of the Germans and advocates of the Jews. The Warsaw Council office becomes a Wailing Wall, "always ringing with lamentation, curses, threats. . . . Men and women, pulling hair from their heads, . . . seized by fits of rage, hysteria, despair" (75). When Elli pleads with a Judenrat official for work permits for elderly relatives, the clerk ridicules her for underestimating the enemy, for thinking they can be fooled. Her effort to obtain work cards for the elderly is a reasoned response to Nazi practices that designated categories of valued workers to be saved. Victims were encouraged "to believe that the lot of individuals would be diversified, and in each case dependent on individual merit. The victims had to think . . . that their conduct did matter; and that their plight could be at least in part influenced by what they were about to do."[18] Although the reality of arbitrary Nazi rule emerges in the deportation of two young family members in possession of valid work papers and the sparing of the undocumented old grandfather, the victims' desperate belief that individual merit signified security explains Elli's efforts to persuade the authorities to spare her relatives as essential workers.

Ettinger invokes one of her favored rhetorical strategies, the political debate, to render judgment of the *Judenrat*. In a disputation with Elli, her cousin Daniel refuses to justify the actions of the Jewish Council on the basis of " 'the abnormal situation,' the 'instinct for self-preservation,' 'the pressures of danger,' and all that crap" (56). He claims the moral high ground, reminding her that all ghetto Jews live in the same abnormal situation, which does not excuse the *Judenrat*'s benefiting from the hardship of fellow victims. Daniel's position accords with Hannah Arendt's thesis on the tragic complicity of the councils in the misery of their people,[19] and his tone evokes the prophetic rebuke found in Chaim A. Kaplan's 2 December 1941 entry in *The Scroll of Agony*.[20] Daniel offers a devastating critique of council members' profiting from the misfortunes of the masses: "Jews making fortunes in the ghetto, Jews doing business with Germans, trading Jewish slaves, enjoying themselves in restaurants and clubs, serving in the police force side-by-side with Germans and Poles, working in the *Judenrat*, created to show that Jews themselves destroy Jews" (56).

A more sinister collaborative effort to achieve a *Judenrein* Europe is found in the cooperation of Polish citizens. Despite Ettinger's disapproval of Americans, whom she believes focus on Polish antisemitism while failing to acknowledge Poles who assisted their Jewish compatriots, her own writing bears out the overwhelming proportion of Polish betrayal of Jewry and "the Jews' collaboration with the Germans."[21] The novel's most convincing portrait of Polish assistance is found in four women who are bound together as war widows, women with whom Elli's mother, Maria, had cultivated a relationship for a year before sharing the secret of her true relationship to her daughters. Passing as a war widow herself, she developed a close friendship with the four, who operate a restaurant in the city where her daughters are hidden. Maria and these women are united as women, as military wives, and as members of the underground. Beyond reference to these loyal and generous women and the network of Poles on which Maria relies to shelter people, albeit for a lucrative fee, Elli's uncle explains Polish failure to hide Jews in their homes as arising from fear for their own safety rather than from animosity.[22]

The novel's most powerful discourse on the subject of Polish-Jewish relations occurs during a debate between Elli and Daniel, who is experienced in dealing with Poles who protect fugitives. Elli's position, that Daniel is unfairly judging an entire nation "for the prejudices of a handful of blockheads" (55), pales as he observes that "before the Germans started 'Mein-Juden-Kampf' they knew they'd get assistance here without asking for it" (54). Daniel argues: "The problem is not with those who will not help us. The problem is with those who help the Germans. . . . If the rest would just stay indifferent, . . . You probably realize the Germans can't very well tell a Jew from a Pole, unless it's a Jew in Hasidic robes. But the Poles can, even if the Jew makes every effort to obliterate the damnable stigma, to create a more welcome Slavic image of himself" (54). Daniel understands why Poles won't risk their lives to help Jews but not why they risk their lives for money. He fears leaving the house, not because of Germans but because of Jew-hunting Poles. He reminds Elli that their family chased after Polish documents for her because as a Jew she would be sheltered only for an exorbitant fee. Similarly, when the old man argues that the younger family members must escape the Warsaw Ghetto while he and the other elders stay on, he fears putting the refugees in harm's way at the hands of Polish Jew hunters. Profiting from Jewish misery is again rendered dramatically in the response of Poles to news of the ghetto liquidation and their arrival "to buy what the residents had to sell" (82). The grandfather tries to make a deal with a Polish ghetto worker willing to sell the use of his pass. He asks for cash or gold each time a family member uses the pass. As the grandfather tenders what he owns—a house, two factories, and land—the Pole insists on a further document ensuring that no survivor may contest the grandfather's will.

Complementing political debates are midnarrative history lessons. Grandfather Weil recounts historic antisemitism as he struggles to persuade his granddaughter to leave the ghetto, noting Poland's continued medieval anti-Jewish mentality: "Here Jews continue to be destroyed with the zeal and fanaticism of the Crusaders. . . . There are brief periods of peace, then they hear The Voice and the old Lied starts again. This wall has shut us out from the life of our fellow Poles; but it has also protected us from them" (80).

Shifting from staged lecture and debate to dramatic representation of Jews coping with antisemitism, Ettinger presents hidden Jews privy to expressions of Polish antisemitism.[23] Elli and her sister, Lili, living under false identities in the Aryan territory of Chelm, learn from a new landlady that their room had been occupied by a Jewish woman thought to be a Catholic. Incensed at the woman's audacity, the landlady remarks: "The more I think about it the more angry I am at her. Mind you, to expose me to such a danger! To lie so impudently, so shamelessly! . . . A cheater, arrogant, selfish, ruthless, like all Jews! They'd do anything, insult God and man to have their own way" (149). A neighbor tells of encountering a Jew hiding in a church: "The impertinence of the Yids has no limits! There is nothing sacred to them" (107). Another tells of having met Jews who had escaped from an east-bound transport, seeking to join the partisans: "Ha, ha, ha, just imagine, these little Yids fighting side by side with our brave boys!" (107). The fugitives are constantly in danger of denunciation by Poles who resent Jews who have escaped Nazi control, and Elli routinely hears expressions of antisemitism from Poles unaware of her Jewish identity.

Ettinger's fictional rendering accords with survivor-sociologist Nechama Tec's moving account of silence-induced angst in the face of flagrant anti-semitism she experienced as a child in hiding: "We had to be silent about our past, present, and future. Often we had to listen to anti-Semitic remarks. No matter how much this might hurt us, we could not object. Breaking the silence could mean death. Silence became deeply ingrained in all hidden children."[24]

Shifting from the sphere of private insult to its logical public demonstra-tion, Ettinger turns her attention to the most serious fictional and historic judgment of Polish antisemitism—refusal to arm Jewish fighters during the Warsaw Ghetto uprising. Ettinger reminds us that Poland's behavior was congruent with other nations' abandonment of the Jews, in the voice of a choral character whose rebuke is inclusive: "We declared war bare-handed, equipped with bricks and stones. Let those answer who are responsible for that. We were annihilated not by Germans only but by all people, here and everywhere, who let us down, who were silent" (189).[25] Similarly, Daniel asks, why condemn Germany for the genocide, for the "whole world did not believe they would do what they said they would. . . . It's not their fault they found willing collaborators in this country. It is ours. I do not know of any other statesman who informed the world ahead of time in detail, in writing, and in deed, what he was going to do" (56). The grandfather echoes Daniel's judgment in his own anticipation of postwar assessments. In an ironically prophetic deliberation the old man foresees postwar attribution of guilt, "the measuring and weighing of the dimensions of complicity, tons of paper being printed, millions of words being said, only to conclude that the really guilty ones are the victims; for without them the problem of guilt would never arise" (73). The preponderance of the novel's thematic and dramatic evidence confirms the prevalence of vibrant Shoah-era Polish antisemitism. Despite Ettinger's defense of her countrymen, articulated in Elli's contention that one has no right to judge people by human standards in an inhuman time, the forceful and thoroughly developed moral arguments of Daniel and Grandfather Weil confirm Poland's ethical bankruptcy.

Not only is there scant evidence in *Kindergarten* of Polish magnanimity toward Jews; even those who hide fugitives are, in the main, unaware that their "guests" are Jewish. As Nechama Tec reminds us, a "condition affecting the ability to withstand the persecution and death was the level of anti-Semitism within a given country." In accord with Poland's long-standing antisemitic tradition, denunciation of Jews was pervasive. Even if more Poles were inclined to help Jews, the sociologist notes, "in a society hostile to Jews, Jewish rescue by Christians was likely to invite disapproval, if not outright censure, from local countrymen."[26] Despite her protestations and several scenes showing Poles assisting fugitives, Ettinger's hoped-for correction of American "misperception" of Polish anti-Jewish collaboration is not realized. Her own treatment in *Kindergarten* vigorously supports the opposing conclusion.

More successful is the author's effort to dispel the myth of Jewish passivity in the face of Nazi aggression. A resister herself, Ettinger repudiates the conventional underrepresentation of Jewish organized resistance and offers one of literature's most comprehensive treatments of resistance. Through primary and secondary characters she dramatizes resistance inside and outside the ghetto among men, women, and children of all circumstances, linking the themes of resistance and Holocaust-wrought character transformation. Abel, a resistance leader to whom Elli reports as the Warsaw Ghetto Uprising is in its last phase, cites the ghetto fighters' declaration of war and Jewish resistance in temporarily thwarting the annihilation machine.

The authenticity of Ettinger's representation of ghetto resistance is reinforced by her attention to the crucial role of young smugglers, children who could squeeze through the openings in the ghetto walls or crawl through sewers to bring in food. They dug holes under walls or hid near the ghetto gates, sneaking by when bribed or inattentive guards looked the other way. Historian Nora Levin explains, "So desperate was the need for food that not even the death penalty for smuggling (decreed in October 1941) could stop it, for strict obedience meant a lingering death by starvation."[27] Children were often the only buffers between their families and starvation. Ettinger honors the child smugglers through the activities of Elli's cousins. Danny works with his older cousin in the Warsaw Ghetto, "passing through that damned wall twice a day, . . . smuggling food" (52). This young boy—like those of Elie Wiesel, Arnost Lustig, Ida Fink, and countless other Holocaust chroniclers—has matured quickly under duress, learning how to negotiate with his elders and willing to take risks on his own.

The novel's active resistance theme is centered in Maria's character. Elli's mother is a member of a partisan group operating from the Aryan side. Discussing the background and transformation of Maria, whom she identifies as the real heroine of her book, Ettinger explained that Maria (Ruth) "is the offspring of a wealthy Jewish family, who had a loving husband, who never was tested in her life and she stands the biggest test of all." With the advent of the Shoah, Maria, until then a bourgeois housewife, "had to become a stranger in many respects to her own daughters, . . . to tell them, from now on you are such and such, you are not my children."[28] Not only does Maria hold the family together; she engineers an escape for several members, providing their false papers, finding them sanctuaries and places of employment, paying their hosts, and serving the larger resistance movement in several capacities. She is representative of the women Emmanuel Ringelblum celebrates as "the heroic girls, . . . [who] boldly travel back and forth through the cities and towns of Poland. They carry Aryan papers identifying them as Poles or Ukrainians. . . . They are in mortal danger every day. They rely entirely on their 'Aryan' faces and on the peasant kerchiefs that cover their heads. Without a murmur, without a second's hesitation, they accept and carry out the most dangerous missions."[29] Like Vladka Meed of the Jewish underground, who smuggled weapons into the ghetto for the Warsaw Uprising, helped fellow Jews escape, and provided those in hiding with false documents and other assistance, the fictional Maria travels from ghetto to ghetto, resistance job to resistance job, delivering information, maintaining links between dispersed Jewish populations, and smuggling arms. That the children know something of Maria's role is evident in Elli's diary reference to her mother and to Uncle Michael, who works in the Lublin district: "None of us is allowed to talk to friends about their trips, documents, business" (99). Just before the Warsaw Ghetto is sealed, Maria arrives with food and money, and once it is sealed, she manages to have her daughters smuggled out.

In the main, Maria is presented through Elli's perspective. Because the young woman's knowledge of resistance operations is limited, readers gain little knowledge of Maria's work, but they learn much about Elli's perceptions of changes in her mother's demeanor. Uneasy about her own Jewish appearance, Elli is critical of Maria's apparent Aryan adaptation: "Mama says she's not good at playing two parts; once it was decided she was *rein arisch* she sticks to it" (122). Resentful of her mother's perfected Aryan pose, Elli is unable at this stage to understand the necessity of total adoption of the Aryan persona and misinterprets it as a form of distancing. A prisoner of the ghetto, Elli recoils from her mother's apparent detachment from ghetto reality and wonders whether she should confess "that I've got so used to starved corpses lying in the streets that I don't see them anymore? That I conceal the food I carry so as not to be robbed by somebody who is hungrier than we? Or perhaps that I'm sometimes so dizzy from hunger that I don't understand what I read?" (262). She is hurt by Maria's mournful tone when she speaks of the family, one that contrasts sharply with the fervent tone reserved for her resistance colleagues. Maria's confession that resisters on the Aryan side don't really understand the suffering of those in the ghetto confirms Elli's perception of her mother's transformation from Ruth Weil to Maria Chmielewska: "She justifies them, because she lives in their world, not in ours. The change in her is not only an outward one. . . . It's just that she isn't the same anymore" (261–62). In contrast to the naive protagonist's point of view, the authorial voice celebrates Maria's Polish appearance and manners, "the way she talked and laughed and drank vodka and held her glass, fitted her new identity perfectly. Her voice became more harsh, her language less refined, her gestures brisk and sure. She could drink heavily with the millers, laugh and joke with them, . . . when she seemed a little drunk, it was because she wanted to seem so. She was perfectly balanced. There was neither exaggeration nor slackness in her manner. She clearly did not underestimate the foe, real or potential" (47–48).

Unlike their mother's role, the daughters' resistance is initially limited to surviving as Aryans in plain view of people who could denounce them. For "Aryan Jews," the task is surviving outside the law, moving from place to place, obtaining false papers, passing as Christians. According to a woman who lived the experience Ettinger fictionalizes, "the common denominator of Jewish life on the 'Aryan side' was fear! Fear of the Germans, fear of the Poles, fear of the blackmailers, fear of losing one's hideout, fear of being left penniless. . . . The so-called 'Aryans' had to blend with their surroundings, adopt Polish customs, habits, and mannerisms, celebrate Christian religious holidays, and, of course, go to church. They had to watch their every movement, lest it betray nervousness or unfamiliarity with the routine, and weigh their every word, lest it betray a Jewish accent."[30]

Although Ettinger dramatizes the remarkable courage needed to operate clandestinely under Nazi occupation, her portraits of young girls in hiding focuses on the pain to the individual psyche generated by the sustained risk of discovery and denunciation. Elli is transformed from assured young woman facing dangerous ghetto situations with ingenuity to fear-obsessed victim, and Lili plummets from high-spirited optimism into madness. Drawing on her own experience, Ettinger represents the stress associated with adapting to the customs of people who were often very different culturally and religiously and the burden of creating new identities for self and fictitious relatives. For those whose appearance is Aryan and who have good forged papers, it is not their physical existence that must be concealed but their Jewish identity, the possibility of blurting out a Jewish word or getting a Catholic prayer or tradition wrong.[31] The pressure of eluding blackmailers, the constant need to alter identity and relocate, the incessant fear of discovery, and the need to be faithful to the assumed character caused severe psychological stress and made the life of the Jew on the Aryan side a harrowing experience.

The ghetto adolescent who feels a measure of betrayal by her mother's meticulous adoption of the Aryan persona must also become proficient in feigning her assumed identity. Her uncle warns: "You are not you; you are somebody else" (15). She must remove all traces of Jewishness from her appearance and language, trust no one, and appear confident. By this stage of the war being a blue-eyed blond is no longer enough; now Jews are recognized by emaciated faces, melancholy eyes, uncertain gestures. She will have to act and react automatically, because "everybody is your enemy; everybody wants to report on you. . . . You must get rid of this air of a frightened animal. Your 'good looks' [Polish appearance] are good for nothing with that terrified expression. . . . Many people get caught because their fear is conspicuous. . . . They betray themselves. Or they trust; and others betray them" (16). Elli's uncle begins her education in passing as a Christian by hanging a silver cross on her neck and giving her a Catholic prayer book. She must quickly memorize "Our Father," the "Hail Mary," the "Apostles' Creed," and the "Rosary of the Blessed Virgin Mary" and later add to her repertoire. She must be careful to avoid Yiddish words or telltale intonations in her speech patterns. She must even stay clear of partisans, for "there is one point about which some partisans agree with the Germans—that is the Jews" (19). Although she is to think of everyone as her enemy and assume everyone wants to report her, she must look as though she trusts everyone.[32]

Hoping to convince another family of her Polish Catholic identity, Elli regales the housewife with tales about her invented Catholic family. Just as Ilona Karmel's Orenstein matriarch flaunted her religious relatives, so Elli fabricates a Catholic girlhood from her reading and speaks of "the

long white dress she had worn at her first Holy Communion, [of] her late
aunt's [church] wedding . . . at which she was a bridesmaid, of the annual
family Christmas tree, . . . and the sumptuous Easter breakfasts which lasted
until night" (85). Elli shares much in common with Ida Fink's Catholic
impostor, who must step outside the anxiety-ridden self to concentrate on
the contrived role and "put on her armor."[33] The first time Elli went to Mass
"she was acutely aware of the danger of being a newcomer. . . . All nerves,
she was watching the people in front of her. She knelt when they knelt, rose
when they rose, crossed herself, beat her breast, and repeated, 'Mea culpa,
mea culpa, mea maxima culpa'" (86).

Scrupulous attention to maintaining the false persona is evident in the
impostor's every thought and gesture.[34] Elli must convince people that she
has met her own mother only once before, that she has never been in her
home. A domestic, a neighbor, or a stranger met by chance in the house or
village might denounce her. She analyzes the words of her host, reconstructs
overheard conversations between maids and farmhands, and reviews her
own statements for content that might betray her true identity. Beyond
the terror based on her imagined failures, real danger lurks everywhere,
for the house where she lives is likely to be raided by Germans searching
for partisans or ghetto escapees. Moreover, a neighbor wants to know why
she is not registered with the local police, and another is worried about
"all those kikes roaming around, sneaking into the most incredible places"
(106). The need for swift and frequent relocation is evident when Elli flees
her sanctuary because her forged papers, when they finally arrive, show her
name as Warska rather than Barska, the name she had been using.

The authenticity and thoroughness of Ettinger's representation of the
fugitive status is commendable. Beyond the risks of discovery she charts the
loneliness of the fugitive by juxtaposing the psychological terror of living in
hiding with the psychological security of living among one's own people in
oppressive times, albeit even in captivity: "Hiding in holes, eluding daylight,
coming out in darkness, trembling at every knock at the door, knowing that
constant fear, that endless waiting till they get you." Despite starvation and
disease in the ghetto, "the danger was not immediate, not present every
second, in every cell of your flesh" (54). Daniel distinguishes between the
Germans, humiliating themselves by ghettoizing Jews, and Jews, being
humiliated while in hiding, living as hunted prey. The psychological security
of being among one's own people as respite from the stress of conducting
resistance operations on the Aryan side is movingly expressed by a resistance
fighter who worked in a position similar to Maria's. She notes: "The somber,

stilled ghetto streets were dearer to me than the cheerful bustle of the streets on the 'Aryan side.' The ghetto was a dreary place, but it was my own, real world where I could be myself. Here I had no need to maintain the forced smile I wore before my Polish neighbors. Here I did not have to listen to snide remarks from the Poles that the Jews had it coming to them and that Hitler was purging Poland of the 'Jewish plague.' Here I did not have to live in constant fear of being unmasked as a Jewess. I was among my own."[35]

Again and again, Ettinger's girls are compelled to change identity and residence, either because a neighbor is suspicious or because the Germans are searching the area for ghetto escapees and partisans. So bizarre is their situation that when Maria transfers the girls to a partisan area in Janów, where they are they reunited, Lili greets Elli as a stranger, even though they are alone in the room. New forged documents identify them as sisters, and Maria advises them to construct a biography that will allow them to play the parts so well that they believe their forged personas to be their true identities.

Ettinger's description of the girls studying the identities of their fabricated families reveals the enormous tension such dissembling occasions. The study session highlights the grotesqueness of learning a false biography. They memorize their "parents'" first names, the dates and places of birth, their "mother's" maiden name, the names of their maternal and paternal "grandparents." Like students, they reiterate their lessons and quiz each other until they are secure in their new biographies. Ettinger heightens the poignancy of these family inventions by juxtaposing the dramatic study session with a diary entry of remembered authentic family affections and loyalty, a harmonious vision of everyone in the extended family at home together "talking long into the night" (98), remembering "old family stories, long-dead aunts, uncles, cousins, . . . dozens of names, maiden names, wedding dates. . . . They can trace off-spring in all parts of the world along with their children and grandchildren who seem to multiply without end" (99). Elli's memory of prewar visits to her grandfather's home with many cousins in attendance conveys the joy of a large Jewish family, like so many that Hitler's war destroyed. The ghetto context for this reverie and the imagined families are trenchant departures from and reminders of vibrant prewar Jewish family life.

Followed closely, Maria's advice could lead to the schizophrenic circumstances noted by prominent scholars Nechama Tec and Saul Friedlander. Addressing the psychological toll of those in hiding, Tec observes: "Sometimes we were so caught up in the new part that we actually forgot who we really were. Though helpful, this temporary forgetfulness was emotionally costly. For many of us, giving up our true identity created an emotional void and made us feel anxious, worried that we would never recapture our past. We also felt ashamed for giving up what had been cherished by our parents, by those we loved."[36] Friedlander writes of so complete an adoption of the feigned role that his Jewish identity was temporarily lost: "I had passed over to Catholicism, body and soul. . . . Thus, in my own way, I had become a renegade: though conscious of my origins, I nevertheless felt at ease within a community of those who had nothing but scorn for Jews. . . . Different name, different religion, different self. Simulation, dissimulation: How does one know who one is?"[37]

Paradoxically, the most dangerous yet safe situations for Jewish Aryan impostors are within German territory. In their last incarnation the girls are employed in Chelm, Lili in the flour mills belonging to an ethnic German loyal to Poland and Elli in Die Treuhandstelle für verlassenen Judenbesitz (Trust Office for Abandoned Jewish Estates), a bureau actually handling confiscated Jewish property.[38] Identification as an indispensable Polish worker ensures Elli security from the draft for forced labor in Germany. Although it is unlikely that Jew hunters would expect their prey to be in German institutions, the situation is fraught with psychological pressure. Every day Elli faces an exhibit entitled *DIE JUDEN SIND DAS UNGLÜCK DER WELT!* (the Jews are the world's misfortune). Her boss greets latecomers with an ominous threat: "*Arbeit macht das Leben süss* [work makes life sweet]. That's what you would learn in a labor camp if you can't learn it here" (117). Fear of detection is pervasive. A summons to the employer's office is alarming. A directive that she accompany her boss on a mission outside the office leads Elli to believe he is delivering her to the Gestapo. On this occasion, which her apprehension has led her to misjudge, Elli doubts her capacity to withstand torture and is consumed with guilt that she will have foiled her mother's heroic rescue efforts. Promotion to secretarial assistant puts Elli in an awkward and more dangerous position, for now she has contact with commanders of the local SA, SS, and Gestapo, and her duties require her to accompany her boss to arrest hidden Jews. Compounding the terror of discovery and the emotional stress of working with German officials is her complicitous guilt: "Here I am, a companion to the murderers of my people, feeling relief it's not me, it's not my mother, not my sister. Why don't I tell him, go ahead, shoot me, I belong to them?" (166–67).

Spared the direct violence captive Jews experience in the grip of the Nazi universe, the fugitives cannot escape indirect contact with such brutality. As they walk to work in Chelm, they witness emaciated Jewish slave laborers being herded to their work sites. Not far from the camp's watchtowers, Elli stumbles over "something." "Something," she discovers, is a Hasid, his face covered with dried blood and dirt. "A single earlock was glued to his cheek; a bloody flap of skin was hanging where the other was torn off" (125). Further examination of the face reveals a boy of fifteen or sixteen: "One of his eyes hung out; the other, wide open, was glazed with horror. The Hasidic robe was torn on his chest, near the bare feet lay a skullcap" (125).

The second half of the novel shifts the resistance theme from reports of Maria's activities to dramatic presentation of active resistance by Elli and her associates. In the privileged position of German office worker, Elli garners information useful to the resistance forces and keeps abreast of developments in the ghettos. She learns of the liquidation of the "Jewish Quarter" of Chelm and the murder of those who tried to evade deportation, much as Ettinger herself did when she worked in a German office.[39] She learns of the Warsaw Ghetto Uprising while overhearing a German officer objecting to the official designation of Jews as "the enemy," for it elevates the subhuman to the status of battlefield opponent. Overcoming her concern that because she is unable to fire a gun or dress a wound she would be useless, Elli leaves her job without permission and returns to the ghetto.

Her protagonist joins Jews in the ghetto uprising, yet Ettinger is unaccountably parsimonious in her account of the insurrection. A single oblique reference to Elli's having lost her glasses, "which had gotten smashed in battle two days before" (173), attests to her role in ghetto combat. Ettinger opts for a summary report of mortar shells exploding, detonations, fire, and the sight of streets that are "a jungle of stones and bricks, . . . monstrous piles of charred bricks, melted iron, broken pipes, smoldering wood" (174), and many corpses, rather than dramatic representation of the heroic uprising. The battle is briefly presented through Elli's report of ghetto losses to an underground leader and her expression of regret that the insurrection had not begun a year earlier. Her communication is characterized as "dry and terse with no adjectives and no comments. So many killed, so many wounded, no arms, no medicines, no food, no water" (182). Ettinger suggests the strength of the ghetto fighters in a single brief reference to the changed function of the ghetto wall. Not only is it a symbol of Jewish imprisonment; it now "kept off the Germans who wouldn't enter the ghetto except through cleared paths and in close order; and it became instead a bulwark and passage for the insurgents" (171). Thus Ettinger intimates the historic circumstances of the makeshift ghetto army's holding off Hitler's forces and causing them to retreat, regroup, and enter the ghetto with trepidation previously unheard of, forgoing anticipated dramatic representation of the insurgency. More successful than her treatment of the insurrection is her manner of conveying the desperation of the ghetto inhabitants who have escaped to the sewers. They wade through "waves of thick quaggy drainage" (170) and struggle to breathe for sixteen hours underground. Those lucky enough to reach an exit encounter a trap, manned by Germans and their willing accomplices, who extend "a helping hand to the emerging person, pull him out, and at the moment he grasped the situation, push him back and snap the iron lid down" (171), a game the tormentors called "push-pull."

Judgment of the victims and their non-German enemies concludes the Warsaw uprising segment. Typical of her political discourse is a polemic delivered by Abel, the rebel leader, repudiating the charge of Jewish passivity, the conventional ploy of blaming the victim "for lack of courage, dignity, physical fitness, for submissiveness, passivity, resignation. It's all fake; it's a dirty lie. Any group of people, systematically humiliated, cruelly treated, deprived of dignity, mentally and physically tormented, hungry, sick, cold, can be reduced to submission" (189). Abel follows his defense of nonmilitary resistance, the daily battle of staying alive behind the wall, which he lauds as "a higher degree of resistance than the use of weapons" (189), with notice that the failure of the insurrection is, in some measure, due to the Polish refusal to arm Jews. Even if some assistance materializes, it will be insufficient. Hope for success is superseded by realistic expectation of arms denied. Escapees despair that facts and figures will not move the world to support endangered Jews. The only response Jewish people can expect is Polish complicity and worldwide acquiescence to the annihilation of European Jewry.

Ettinger shares the focus other women writers give women's experience, although her fiction does not enter the gender-segregated world of the camps. Her women are, nevertheless, additionally vulnerable, and occasionally empowered, by virtue of their gender. Sexual assault is present from the early occupation period, as Maria discovers when she is caught in a roundup for humiliating manual labor and then suffers harassment by a Nazi officer who finds her "so jung . . . so schön" and expresses his admiration in a manner that implies rape. When she returns home, Maria sits, "staring blankly ahead" (34), and talks of an acquaintance who committed suicide with her two daughters. Lili tends her wounded mother, convincing her that they can stand a lot as long as they are together. Similarly, a Polish extortionist hiding a group of fugitives insists on payment in cash and sexual favors, forcing himself on the women. Conversely, because Ettinger's women are relatively free, opportunity presents itself for women to use men's sexual appetites to their own advantage. When the refugees determine to kill the extortionist who has promised to betray them, they not only ply him with liquor but distract him by playing to his lust.

More often than victims of sexual assault, Ettinger's women are presented as maternally vulnerable. The desperate efforts of Jewish women to save their children are suggested by the attempt of Elli's fellow worker to ignore her child and depart alone with an arresting officer. She fails. Affronted, the officer slaps her and demands the child. In another instance a woman who escaped the ghetto with her infant after her husband was killed changes hiding places nine times in two months because of the Semitic features of her daughter. Finally, compelled to abandon the child for fear of endangering all the other refugees, she lapses from grief and despair into madness.

The fate of children in the Shoah, a common theme among women writers, finds thorough explication in Ettinger's universe, in the ghetto realm as well as on the Aryan side. Ettinger is particularly adept at delineating the special precariousness and precociousness of children whose parents have had to leave them, children who learn adult behavior and assume adult responsibilities early. Such a child is Elli's young cousin Emmi, whom Maria delivers, wrapped and tied up as a bundle, to live with her daughters. After the child's mother finds a hiding place for herself, she trusts that the family will care for her child. The four-year-old, who "is always ready for the road" (129), knows how to refrain from asking embarrassing questions, knows how to promise that she will be good so her cousins will want to keep her. When Elli and Lili are at work, the child is left alone for twelve hours in an unheated room. If she goes outdoors, she risks getting lost, or worse, being questioned by strangers. They leave her sleeping in the mornings with breakfast and lunch prepared, meals she eats in reverse order. For a few weeks Emmi greets her cousins with good cheer on their evening return home. Then the precocious child becomes "more and more restless in her solitary confinement. . . . Though she never complained, often when the girls came home they'd find the food untouched and the child squeezed in a corner. From the moment they entered the room she [manifested the signs of psychic stress by] . . . desperately cling[ing] to them, till she was in bed" (137). In a decision that verges on the incredible, the girls accept an offer from the nearby camp guards to care for Emmi while they are at work. The young soldiers enjoy romping with the child, and she thrives under their guardianship.

Emmi's Shoah-induced maturity is evident not only in her ability to sustain her false persona with the soldiers but in later efforts to nurse the despondent Lili. "She would walk around as if on the tips of her fingers; she knew a patient needed silence. The four-year-old would change the compresses on her head," serve meals, and keep vigil at the bedside. Early maturity became a matter of life and death for Jewish children, and evidence of their bravery and sound judgment, tempered by fear and luck, engages several chroniclers.[40]

Emmi's story is that of a child saved, an uncommon experience of Jewish children caught in the Nazi net. Though the plotline of *Kindergarten* precludes addressing the fate of deported children, Ettinger evokes the more routine Shoah experience of Jewish children. She presents a distanced projection by contriving a situation that enables her protagonist to glimpse a transport of Dutch children bound for an extermination camp: "They were nicely dressed, . . . holding each other's hands. . . . The children looked healthy, well nourished but there was something dreadful in their silence. . . . When [a railroad worker] approached the car in which the children were solemnly standing, the biggest girl said, '*Wasser bitte*.' . . . The worker looked up at her, . . . and after a while was back with a bottle of water. The first shot hit him precisely in the small of his back. The second shot smashed the bottle which the girl was holding in her hand" (286–87). So astonished is Elli by this sight that at first she assumes she is losing her mind. Hours later she is still sitting transfixed in the station until she is helped away by two other resistance workers, one of whom derisively responds to her shock, "She must live in a cozy place with Mummy, Daddy, and a host of aunts. Not used to such shows" (287).

Madness and suicide loom throughout the novel. Ettinger charts the disrupted lives of major and minor characters, either by introducing characters when they have already lost reason or life and then describing the route that led to the catastrophe or by delineating the progressive transformation from clarity to derangement, the movement from fighting for survival to rejecting existence that is externally controlled and persistently degraded. Madness is Ettinger's central metaphor and objective correlative for the Nazi world. She injects cameo portraits that brilliantly and rapidly foreshadow or echo the principal characters' loss of sanity. Illustrative is the demented young mother Elli encounters while sequestered with a group of fugitives following the Warsaw Ghetto Uprising. The woman approaches Elli, a stranger, with a series of anguished questions about her lost child: "Was she all right? She slept when I left her. I tucked her in the blanket to keep her warm till somebody finds her. She is a sweet girl, isn't she? . . . Is she missing me? Tell me, does she speak about me? Have you your own children? Does she play with them?" (192). After her monologue we learn the cause of her madness: she was forced to abandon her child to save the lives of eleven others in hiding.

The novel's metamorphosis theme takes a tragic turn as Lili's transformation lurches from her self-designed Aryan persona to torture-induced madwoman. Falsely denounced as the lover of a partisan by a rejected suitor, Lili is tortured by the Gestapo, a scene the reader is spared. The severity of her experience, however, is conveyed in her prolonged lapse from consciousness and brutalized appearance. Her long hair is clotted with dry blood, her lip deeply cut, her dress torn to pieces, her underwear stuck to bloody skin. Hours after her release Lili mumbles a disclaimer about her origins and family: "I don't know . . . I can't tell . . . I don't know" (144). Her denial of having been in a ghetto and insistence that her mother is dead reveals either that she was suspected of being Jewish and interrogated accordingly or that her fear of being detected as a Jew during questioning was uppermost in her thoughts. The psychological consequence of the Gestapo assault is immediately evident. When she regains consciousness the following day, "she lay silent, her blank eyes fixed on some distant point" (146).

Ettinger renders Lili's descent into madness through oscillations between periods of withdrawal and aggression. Unlike Maria, whose reaction to rape transported her from numbness to active participation in the resistance movement, Lili remains detached. She walks stooped as though trying not to be noticed, confines her conversation to Emmi, and is either openly hostile to or oblivious of Elli. Her moods are erratic, and her responses and demeanor are marked departures from her previous behavior. Claiming to have seen a man take their documents, presumably for delivery to the Gestapo, she causes Elli five days of intense fear of imminent arrest before admitting she fabricated the story for fun. She now hates the sister for whom she endured torture, and her behavior is that of a deranged victim.

Jean Améry, who sustained Gestapo punishment, makes clear in "Torture," one of five essays in his powerful book of testimony, *At the Mind's Limits*, that the ordeal does not end with liberation. Such is Lili's fate. Her experience at the hands of the Gestapo has eradicated her spirit of rebellion. She announces and carries out a plan to confess to and seek the assistance of her Gestapo interrogator. Transformed by a beating that was accompanied by the interrogator's promise to save her and her family in exchange for a confession, the emotionally and physically battered girl repeatedly writes long confessions volunteering the information she withheld under duress: the family members' real names, prewar address, and present domicile. Lili's collapse is further evidenced in her delusion that Elli is an instrument of the

Germans, trying to save her own life in exchange for betraying Lili. As her paranoia develops, she moves out of the shared apartment, insisting that Elli tried to murder her. During the sisters' last exchange, when Lili is en route to an asylum where Maria has placed her for her own safety and that of the others, Lili begs Elli to deliver a letter to her German interrogator.

The impact of the extended dramatic presentation of Lili's mental anguish is heightened by juxtaposition with several short diary entries characterizing the formerly vibrant young woman who planned to attend medical school in France. Uncowed then by German edicts and restrictions, she had refused to wear her armband and frequented forbidden restaurants. The wraith of Chelm once had the strength to nurse Elli during a period of despondency and console Maria by insisting that they could stand whatever came their way, "as long as we are together" (35). As long as there was life, she had maintained, there was hope.

Elli's madness, unlike Lili's, is triggered not by one experience but by witnessing ever-increasing violence, beginning with participation in the gruesome assassination of a self-declared informer, a Pole who is bleeding the ghetto escapees for all the money he can while threatening them with denunciation. Fear of return to Nazi captivity and certain execution emboldens otherwise innocent victims, who kill him and dismember his body for disposal. Elli's reluctance to kill is diminished after this encounter. Threatened by a Nazi when she is captured in a resistance mission, she kills him with impunity rather than allow him to deliver her to the Gestapo. Later, from the vantage point of safety, she is traumatized by the realization that she can kill with greater ease the second time.

In one sense it appears unseemly that Ettinger would foreground the assassination of the Polish betrayer as the most ghoulish scene of the novel, the most prolonged violent scene of the text. Distasteful as such emphasis is, its purpose may be defended in its depiction of the lengths innocent people were driven to in the Nazi realm. The pure are unable to remain pure in the Nazi universe. Although the scene may be based on a historic resistance mission, it has a feel of the fantastic. If it is a fantastic invention, it provides the figurative means for making the transition from the rationally constructed categories of the real world to the horrendous inversions of the Nazi universe.

Representative of the suicidal approach to despair is the early introduction to Grandfather Weil through Elli's discovery of his body, hanging in their ghetto lodging. The suicide of this heroic, fully developed figure is a shock for the adolescent protagonist. Ettinger expands the suicide motif in brief references to minor characters such as Emmi's father, who stands over the child's crib, knife in hand, proclaiming the ghetto is no place for children, and shortly thereafter kills himself. A terse diary entry records the death of Uncle Abram, who "hanged himself this afternoon while Aunt Wilhelmina and Rita were out for tea with some friends" (240). The first suicide is rendered as a shock for Elli; the second testifies to the absurdity of the Nazi world.

The last third of the narrative charts Elli's turbulent relationship with a lover whose loyalty she doubts and from whom she keeps her Jewish identity secret. Like the episodic structure of the picaresque novel, allowing the picaro to encounter a vast array of characters and experience, the novel of open hiding, by virtue of the fugitive's need for frequent relocation, introduces a large cast of characters. Elli discovers on return to Chelm from the Warsaw uprising that, in retaliation for absence without leave, she has been transferred to another office. This job shift is Ettinger's vehicle for introducing new characters and experiences. Here Elli develops a relationship with a partisan who eventually becomes her lover. Adam is the son of a Dachau prisoner, a German who remained in Poland after the First World War as a university dean and refused to resume his German citizenship. Refusing also to become *Reichsdeutsch*, Adam, a reformed antisemite, lives under the name and documents of a Polish schoolmate killed at the beginning of the war. Ignorant of Elli's true identity, he confesses his prior history of anti-Jewish violence. In Adam's story Ettinger offers the inverse tale of a guilt-ridden German risking his life to help a Jewish family he had earlier harmed. He has been haunted by the staring eyes of the proprietor of the last store at which he broke windows. Chance brings the assailant and victim together again, and the repentant Nazi saves the family of his former victim. Adam confesses this history to Elli, whom he believes is a Pole, for he wants her to help the family should he be arrested for his partisan activities.

Fear of detection is so prevalent in the fugitive's thinking that she hides her Jewish identity even from the man she loves: "If only she could have told him everything, if she could give him a day-to-day account of her misery and fear" (250). Such honesty is an unaffordable luxury. She wants the emotional relief of sharing her history with Adam, of talking about her family, of explaining why she returned to the ghetto and what happened there, of unburdening herself about killing the Polish extortionist who threatened to betray the ghetto escapees, of sharing her daily fear and loneliness. Ever suspicious that she could be confessing to an informer, however, she reveals nothing. Elli has much in common with Ida Fink's protagonist of "A Night of Surrender," who remains in adopted character for a short time after liberation, justifying herself to her lover and herself by acknowledging: "My knowledge of the world and of life was one-sided: I knew death, terror, cunning, how to lie and trick. . . . I rewarded him with the life story I had patched together over the last three years; it moved him as it was meant to. I was sorry that I was still lying, but consoled myself with the fact that the true story would have been a hundred times more horrifying."[41]

Elli's transition from common-sense vigilance to paranoia results from the accumulated stress of witnessing the arrest of other Jews passing as Christians, participating in the assassination of the Pole, killing the Nazi officer in self-defense, family reversals, and Adam's insistence on bringing her into contact with his resistance associates. Further complicating Elli's situation is a warning from Maria that Elli has been denounced and that Maria too expects imminent arrest, for she can no longer pay for the silence of Poles who know her Jewish identity.

Most novelists take their survivor protagonists to liberation. Ettinger concludes *Kindergarten* with the victim's surrender to madness, triggered by her belief that Adam has betrayed her because of her decision to leave him. Having witnessed the dire consequences of Lili's denunciation by a rejected suitor, Elli is convinced that the German soldiers in Adam's company have entered their apartment to arrest her. The novel ends abruptly, with blood dripping from Elli's slashed wrist. She declares her readiness to be taken away and begs the soldier to let her take Emmi. "Why? This is not a Kindergarten" (310) is the German's response. So convincingly does Ettinger render Elli's terror that the reader forgets for a moment that the uniformed German is a deserter intending her no harm. It is a melodramatic ending, but one in keeping with the theme of Shoah anxiety that results in madness. That innocence can never replace Holocaust knowledge is evident from Elli's final mad scene and from the prologue's reference to her fearful brushing away of imagined gas from her child's crib. The reader has been prepared for Elli's descent into madness and attempted suicide by parallel plots involving secondary characters and Elli's assessment of her own overwrought state: "She had failed the dead, betrayed the living. She was tormenting the man who loved her because she wanted to save her dignity. . . . She was capable neither of living or dying, of giving love or accepting it. She felt she had passed the limits of damnation" (251).

The novel's prologue, introducing Elli in 1962 as a nervous mother, is powerful in its own right. Revisiting the prologue after completing the novel helps the reader understand the fragments, the broken shards of lives that dominate the survivor's thinking. The prologue, we now realize, is the novel in miniature: "Lili, Emmi, David, the Old Man . . . Lili handing her the envelope, . . . Maria's stony eyes . . . the departing train . . . Emmi spasmodically clinging to her hand, . . . Aunt Paula mounting the truck . . . Danny's black eyes burning with rage . . . the young girl with long plaits cutting off the cord . . . Lili frantically writing . . . Adam . . . you'll stay with me or I'll make you stay . . . the young girl rehearsing prayers . . . look everybody straight in the eye . . . don't turn back . . . never turn back . . . never . . . never . . . you are what is written in these documents, that is the only truth, no other truth ever existed . . . you will never forget . . . I will not, Grandfather, I promise . . ." (1–2). This passage introduces the reader not only to memories the novel will unearth but to the fragmentariness and abrupt shifts in Ettinger's prose that suggest the difficulty of writing about the Shoah in a conventional mode of narrative representation. Holocaust rupture is mirrored in textual rifts and discontinuities.

Immediately after the Warsaw Ghetto insurrection in *Kindergarten*, Elli addresses the subject of maintaining historic memory, anticipating a time in the future when those who abandoned the Jews of the ghetto will come by the hundreds of thousands to bury the dead and care for the living: "I believe they will never forget what happened to us. They will tell it to their children and impose on them a burden never to forget" (190). At the time, it is unclear whether the mourners she has in mind are Poles or Jews. *Quicksand*, a more bitter novel than *Kindergarten*, resolves the question.[42] The new Poland chooses not to remember its lost Jews; it temporarily accepts its invisible Jews to rebuild the nation and then returns to outright persecution.

By virtue of the novel's postwar Polish setting, Ettinger's treatment of survivorship is markedly different from that of novelists who set their fictions in America and Israel. Elli Rostow is the virtual antithesis of the survivors who populate American Holocaust writing. Rather, she shares the characteristics of those Jews remaining in Poland after the war who were dedicated to Polishness and rebuilding their war-ravaged country, as expressed by Iwona Irwin-Zarecka:

> For them, the present and the future had priority, not the past. They were eager to and they did participate in the often exhilarating work of creating a new society. . . . They not only accepted, but frequently propagated the model of "silent Jewishness," keen on rendering the whole issue irrelevant, both in public and in private. . . . In a way

those Jews were migrating symbolically into the world of Polish priorities, Polish concerns, Polish values. . . . The lessons drawn from the Holocaust . . . were detrimental to any maintenance of Jewish identity; complete assimilation was the ideal to the near exclusion of all other options. The very distinction between Jews and non-Jews was to disappear together with the "Jewish question," securing and secured by the Jew's "invisibility." Jewish martyrology was thus all that was to remain of the Jewish presence, a constant warning of the dangers of chauvinism and prejudice.[43]

Persecuted as a Jew in the Shoah, the post-Holocaust protagonist would like to believe that she is a Pole among like-minded Polish citizens, that her Jewish identity is inconsequential in the new Poland. She retains her wartime pseudonym, Warska, deluding herself that she does so "not to deceive but because she believes that in a socialist country no one cared whether she was Jewish or not" (30). She is sincere, if mistaken, in her conviction that under socialism, nationalism will disappear, that something better will be created. Her misconception is objectified through a series of characters, including a figure Elli knew in the ghetto who is more insightful and realistic about the enduring nature of Polish antisemitism. This diplomat changed his name after the war from the Jewish Alex Berg to the Polish Aleksander Gorski, claiming, "It is better for our cause when Poland is represented abroad by ethnic Poles. . . . Otherwise foreigners will think that no one but Jews supports our government" (62). Later we learn that he was directed to adopt a Polish-sounding name. Ettinger caustically notes the commonality of the pattern: Berg, Herzberg, and Goldberg become Gorski, Borowski, Szeryn. Characteristic of early postliberation Jewish invisibility, Elli and the cousin with whom she shared many harrowing ghetto experiences are cautious about anything that might invoke the past. They dare not share their Holocaust thoughts. In a nation of survivors there is tacit understanding that there is no need to discuss the subject of survivorship. Jews in Poland maintain a silent vigil.

Elli's use of a false name is a consistent part of a larger pattern of subterfuge pervading her relationship with her Communist bosses and bureaucrats, behavior based on wartime survival strategies: "For years she had lived a masquerade. She lied and she lied until her life had become one huge lie. . . . In the process of saving her life she had bartered away some part of herself" (30–31). She, like other fictional survivors, including Susan Fromberg Schaeffer's Anya and I. B. Singer's Broder, reverts to wartime strategies to deal with postwar difficulties: "Scraps of her wartime coaching in survival—in lies, camouflage, and alertness—came back" (221).

As she brings the reader up-to-date on Elli's biography in *Quicksand*, Ettinger redirects her focus from *Kindergarten*'s emphasis on the trials of fugitives to Elli's resistance work. In the first volume Elli leaves the ghetto before its liquidation, and attention is focused on her life in hiding. *Quicksand* suggests that Elli escaped only during the liquidation of the Warsaw Ghetto and that "she had been left on the 'Aryan side' with a set of amateurishly forged papers which transformed her from Elli Rostow to Elli Warska, Roman Catholic, clean" (8). We learn from an expository passage that she married Adam, now identified as her commanding officer in the underground army. "So, she had Adam and, more important, she had a gun. The danger of getting caught as a Jew and exterminated like vermin was over. The nightmares—strangulation by gas, elaborate tortures, parading naked in front of elegant, jocular German officers—ceased to haunt her. Her gun put her life in her own hands" (8).

In addition to third-person exposition, Elli's past is conveyed in clips of dialogue with her cousin about "the guerrilla unit she had joined, the subversive operations they carried out, the derailed ammunition trains, blown-up buildings, killed Germans" (56). *Quicksand* thus fills in the gaps of Elli's resistance career, accounts for her survival, and carefully explains: "She had joined the [Polish] resistance against the Nazis because she could not make it alone. The resistance had guns and ammunition. She had listened to their patriotic speeches knowing that their Poland, 'the bulwark of Christianity,' was not what she was fighting for. She did not fight for the London-based government-in-exile or against the Moscow-based Polish 'communists and traitors.' She fought for her life" (6).

Lengthy political debates by ideological proponents ensure that political themes are at the heart of *Quicksand*. Ettinger also represents psychological tension in the postwar life of the Shoah victim. Spared severe impairment, Elli nonetheless experiences a malaise and expresses views that are commonplace in literary representation of survivors. Elli exhibits the impatience of survivors, like Ozick's Rosa Lublin, who fret over the innocence and ignorance of people spared direct Shoah knowledge, of people who have not availed themselves of postwar studies. Working as a translator, as did Ettinger, Elli derisively anticipates the naive questions of an Englishman to whom she has been assigned as interpreter: "He'll ask me questions, all the stupid questions foreigners always ask. Where did she survive the war? Oh, in Warsaw! How horrible! Is it really true that the Germans shot small children? How dreadful! Did they really set fire to every house in this poor, wrecked city? Incredible!" (18). Like Saul Bellow's Shula in *Mr. Sammler's Planet*, she appears to be a religious schizophrenic, continuing to kneel and recite Catholic prayers at bedtime, "a wartime precaution which had grown into a habit" (48). She mistakenly attributes the disinterest of her absentee second husband to her wartime history: "Why would an elegant Englishman want her, 'You're a survivor,' vermin that escaped extermination . . . hands dirty up to the elbows, bad dreams, ugly nightmares" (105). Later she assesses her life in terms of Shoah angst and postwar hardship: "Thirteen years on the run. Behind the ghetto wall, in bunkers, cellars, trenches. The end of the war meant only a more perfect solitude. With time to count the dead" (114).

As for most survivors, unrelated contemporary anxieties provoke wartime memory. She associates her English husband's request that she remove her glasses with the wartime imperative for a non-Jewish appearance: "The familiar tune started in her head. Rouge lipstick no good your eyes everyone can see you're afraid the hair is alright now that its blond but the eyes sunken fearful you must look like a healthy self-confident Polish girl these damn glasses your eyes are still more exposed can't you do without glasses for a while at least" (100–01). This stream-of-consciousness recall cast in the form of a run-on, unpunctuated sentence suggests the ever present urgency of the past, the harried fugitive in breathless flight from her oppressors. As is the case for survivors described in the psychiatric literature, Elli's wartime trauma surfaces at unexpected times, triggered by contemporary situations. She resents having to travel to a publisher's conference in Germany and experiences great anxiety throughout her stay. Despite her fluency in German, she is unable to speak a coherent sentence for several days. Encountering uniformed German customs officers, she reaches for a gun she no longer has. Approached by a passerby for directions, she hands over her passport, imagining that he had barked, "Your identification, Fraulein." During negotiations "she looked at the Germans sitting opposite her without seeing them" (130). Like survivors who manage to function satisfactorily by repressing memory for a time, only to discover that they are affected by deep, enduring (if latent) memories, Elli realizes, as she translates for the Polish delegation investigating charges and countercharges by the North and South Vietnamese, that the past retains its hold on her. Contemporary Asian violence jars the survivor's memory of Nazi brutality. Decapitated and desecrated bodies of Vietnamese in the Asian killing field inspire a nightmare of the Warsaw Ghetto in flames, "an angry crowd . . . milling outside the wall screaming for the Jews to come out. The boy's curly hair was caked with dry blood as was the yellow star on his chest. . . . The woman holding the boy's hand was wrapped in a white prayer shawl. The leather straps of the phylacteries kept the two split parts of her head together. 'Don't be afraid,' she comforted the boy gently. 'We'll be dead by tomorrow'" (225–26). The boy in her dream runs toward her, begging her to wait. His dark curly locks are "now covered with light blond baby fuzz" (226), signifying the guilt Elli feels for surviving because of her Christian appearance while more obviously Jewish victims perished, including a million and a half children.

The unstable emotional relationships charted in the psychiatric literature on survivor syndrome find expression in the fictional postwar life Ettinger portrays. Like I. B. Singer's Herman Broder, Elli Rostow leads a volatile and troubled emotional life. She has divorced her first husband. She seeks love and protection from the men she encounters and enters a series of intimate relationships, living with one man for the comfort of his well-provisioned apartment, with another for consolation from a unfortunate second marriage to a man she loves but who ignores her after their marriage, which he entered only to deceive another lover. Obsessed with her absentee second husband, Elli even becomes depressed about the "charmed life" she lives at the expense of a cousin, and she occasionally returns to her own meager existence. This behavior exemplifies the findings of a leading expert of the Nazi Holocaust, Judith Kestenberg, who has observed that among these children, depression in middle age is a sign of incomplete mourning and unacknowledged anger: "Despite the resilience of hidden children, the years of being hidden or hiding oneself have their residual effects."[44]

Ettinger enhances her treatment of survivorship by counterpointing the emotional and political insecurity of the Polish Jew with that of the Polish émigré to Israel. Elli's cousin Daniel Weil, another transplant from *Kindergarten*, is her political foil. In contrast to her unquestioning faith in Communist Poland's acceptance of its Jewish survivors at this stage is Daniel's observation that there is no significant difference between German and Soviet camps—each smells of corpses. Unlike Elli, who is eager to overlook Polish collaboration in the slaughter of European Jewry, her cousin Danny reminds her of Polish complicity, of "the ovens [to which] our fellow-countrymen so eagerly helped . . . [commit the Jews]" (126). An apologist for her fellow Poles, Elli seeks to mitigate her compatriots' collaboration, as she had in *Kindergarten*, by universalizing culpability, citing American and British refusal to bomb the rail tracks leading to the camps, the unholy behavior of the Holy Father, or the Jews in Palestine who worked on behalf of building the state rather than rescuing European Jewry. Among the figures from Elli's past who reappear in the sequel is Abel, the Jewish resistance leader, now in Poland as a member of an Israeli diplomatic delegation.

While Elli leads a disjointed life, still a stranger in the land of her birth, Abel is at home in his adopted land, a full citizen of a Jewish nation. Unlike Elli, who has floated from one insubstantial relationship to another, the healthy Israeli immigrant is married to a sabra, has two children, and is engaged in nation building. He feels useful and expresses joy that his children "will grow up free from this hideous bargaining for equal rights. They don't have to prove they're loyal. It's taken for granted" (304). Through the juxtaposition of a debilitated, demoralized postwar Polish Jew with a vibrant Israeli, Ettinger introduces the concept prevalent in Israeli writing, that of rehabilitation through nation building and the ascendancy of the Israeli over the Diasporan Jew.

Elli's political transformation from patriotic Pole to disillusioned would-be émigré coincides with the return of bureaucratic institutional anti-semitism, recast as anti-Zionism. The safety and well-being of Poland's Jews are systematically curtailed in compliance with Soviet anti-Zionism, and Elli's distress mounts. Her Shoah past emerges as imperfect analogue to the despotism of Communist society. Contemporary angst arising from the convergence of Nazi and Soviet oppression in her life is objectified in a dream sequence. She wanders through the ruins of the Warsaw Ghetto, climbs the wall covered in pieces of broken glass and barbed wire, and repeatedly fires a gun. Dreams springing from fear of Soviet anti-Jewish measures coalesce in her unconscious with German anti-Jewish measures as she dreams that she is put into "a cage filled with gas because she refused to confess that [her cousin] Boris collaborated with the Nazis" (250).

The tension between her loyalty to the dead and to the new socialist state is manifested in recurrent nightmare and flashback. She and her two cousins are walking in the mountains and singing: Daniel intones the Kaddish, and Boris sings the "Internationale," while Elli tries to satisfy both, alternately singing a line from each. Figuratively torn by each culture, she is literally torn by each of the cousins, one pulling her down toward an empty pit and all her dead relatives, the other holding her up. Flashbacks such as the one of her German sojourn dramatically reinforce the connection between Soviet and Nazi oppression. Another link is Elli's adaptation of her wartime survival strategy to the Soviet situation, a trait she shares with hidden children who translate their wartime skills to postwar life, their ability "to put on 'a good act,' determination to succeed at all costs, taking care of others, and learning to be cared for."[45]

For the most part, *Quicksand* is composed in a straightforward realistic mode. Flashbacks are easily recognized and share none of the looping quality of those in *Kindergarten*. Shoah matter enters the postwar fiction subjectively and subconsciously through dream or directly in survivors' dialogue. Of greater interest to Ettinger than the emotional security Boris provides Elli in his role as party functionary is what he offers in his role as confidant. Elli is able to speak honestly with him not only of her disillusionment with Communist Poland but of the extermination of Jewish intellectuals in the Soviet Union. Only rarely does Ettinger resort in this novel to a stylistic construct resembling the confusion, the rupture the survivor feels as contemporary reality yields to psychological terror. Beyond the disturbing scenes set in Germany, Elli sustains a fall while tripping over a remnant of a red brick wall wrapped in barbed wire: "She fled, wet and breathless, her hands and knees bleeding. The way home became a nightmare. If she were not extremely careful she would end up in the ghetto, behind the wall, and would have to climb it again, and this time they would get her" (137).

Representation of survivor angst through dream and nightmare are conventions Ettinger shares with native-born American novelists. Elli's beloved Lili and Maria emerge in dreams and memories confirming the pain of her solitary survival. She dreams of begging Lili to run to the ghetto shelter as bombers approach. By the time Lili complies, it is too late. In another instance, motivated by her own deterioration wrought by contemporary political anxiety, Elli sees Maria in a surrealistic vision emerging from a wall that opens to facilitate her arrival and then changes to a barbed wire fence. The survivor's response is schizophrenic: "She did not know whether it was safe to call her 'mother' or use her wartime pseudonym" (307–08).

The protagonist's experience with Polish antisemitism links *Kindergarten* and *Quicksand*. Ettinger contrasts Elli's childhood exposure to romantic tales of Polish heroism and sacrifice with her adult knowledge that the glorious visions of a free Poland were not intended for the Jews. She learned of the quotas for Jews in the Polish universities, quotas designed to exclude intellectually gifted Jewish students. She discovered that Jewish students were allotted separate seats in the lecture halls, that they were stabbed on university premises by their Polish fellows. In the present period of the novel Poles detest the "kikes [who they believe] sold us out to the Reds" (34). Poles speak of "them" to signify the Reds and their Jewish partisans and speak of "we" to signify the Catholic Poles at the other end of the political spectrum. Even under Communism, which was to end sectarian hatreds, antisemitism flourishes. Policies permitting Jews to hold prominent party and government posts are revoked because the Polish masses have become intolerant of "the excessive participation of Jews" (271) in powerful positions. The Soviet masters of Poland, already engaged in their own major antisemitic program, oblige their puppet state enthusiastically, using the acceptable political rubric of anti-Zionism in place of socially gauche anti-Jewish slogans. Elli's metamorphosis is accelerated as her Jewish associates lose their jobs, verbal attacks on Israel become commonplace, and trumped-up charges of being Israeli agents are lodged against Polish Jews.[46] In *Kindergarten* quicksand operates as a substantive image of impending doom. The image is used to herald the protagonist's realization that the ghetto has been transformed from secure haven to assembly point for deportations: "Because they still lived, on the surface of the quicksand indeed but not sucked in, her faith in God grew. Now, she saw He had just lulled her. He had cheated her. Heavy hands were dragging her deeper and deeper" (68). In the sequel quicksand is the controlling metaphor for the Polish Jew's recognition that once again life is precarious and she will be submerged if she does not escape.

Political reassessment is at the heart of *Quicksand*. Beyond the rhetorical convention of integrating political debate into the dramatic context, the underlying theme is the correlation of Soviet and Nazi totalitarian regimes and the central role antisemitism plays in each. Blatant postwar Polish antisemitism persuades Elli to declare herself a Jew, for she will no longer maintain her silence when the old hatred pollutes the body politic. The novel concludes with images of bright flowers that lose their luster, shrivel, and die when they are brought home, as has the brief season of Jewish acceptance in postwar eastern Europe. Poland is again mired in the quicksand of antisemitism. Elli Warska willingly returns to her Jewish identity by reassuming her rightful name, Elli Rostow, symbolically separating herself from the land of her birth and the center established by the Nazis for the genocide of European Jewry.

Ettinger has made indispensable contributions to the literature of the Shoah. Her fictional rendition of the dynamics of fugitive status shares much with the social and psychological insights of respected social scientists. Like Ilona Karmel, Elżbieta Ettinger writes autobiographically and authoritatively, crafting a profoundly disturbing book engaging readers in the horrors of hiding in Nazi Europe. By virtue of her experience, her treatment of women in the resistance is more comprehensive than that of most writers. Further, her politically astute exploration of the life of a survivor in Soviet-dominated Poland illuminates important dimensions of survivor syndrome and postwar Polish-Jewish relations.

HANA DEMETZ

Born in northern Bohemia (Sudetenland) in 1928, the child of a Czech-Jewish mother and a German-Catholic father, Hana Demetz lived through World War II in Czechoslovakia but was spared the fate of full Jews in Nazi-occupied Europe. She lived openly in Czech society and never experienced the ghetto or concentration camp, as did Polish Jews Elżbieta Ettinger and Ilona Karmel. Although Demetz suffered relatively minor indignities because of her "mixed race," as a member of an extended Jewish family she witnessed the harsh effects of anti-Jewish legislation. Relatives were deprived of their rights and property or "transferred" to Theresienstadt, a camp described in promotional propaganda as "a model ghetto" and "a Jewish reservation" but in reality a grim fortress town whose exit was Auschwitz and other extermination centers.[1] Demetz credits Elie Wiesel's "shattering" words and Ilona Karmel's *Stephania* for her decision to write her family story.[2] Departing from her plan to produce a three-volume tome on the order of *The Forsythe Saga*, Demetz composed a powerful, highly compressed single volume celebrating her family and recording the tragedy suffered during the Nazi occupation of Czechoslovakia. *The House on Prague Street* is a beautifully crafted, lyrical understatement whose setting, albeit at a discreet distance from ghetto and concentration camp, succeeds nonetheless in conveying the character of life under a hostile occupation. Demetz does not share the political discourse of the Austrian exile writer Elisabeth Freundlich, whose literary mission has been the delineation of Nazi crimes, but is resolved to overturn a climate of indifference toward teaching the Holocaust.[3] Written in German to counter the failure of German schools to teach the history of World War II, *The House on Prague Street*, published in 1970, enjoyed critical acclaim and was serialized in the press.[4] The English edition, translated by Demetz herself, appeared ten years later.

Raised a Catholic and designated a *Mischlinge*, or half-Jew, by the Nazis, Hana Demetz brings a Holocaust perspective to her work that is substantively different from that of Jewish survivors. Unlike Karmel and Ettinger, who suffered virulent antisemitism, Demetz and her autobiographical protagonist were comfortably assimilated into Czech society and adopt an elegiac, melancholy tone toward their European domicile. *The House on Prague Street* is structured as the recollection of Helene Richter, a young girl living in a privileged position among people who suffer Nazi-imposed anti-Jewish legislation but do not understand the full implications of events befalling them. Unlike narratives that chronicle Holocaust experiences of Jewish women separated from their families, living under false identities or interned, and enduring sexual assault, disease, beatings, starvation, and slave labor, Helene's tale, set entirely within a family context, alternates between reports of hardships borne by her Jewish relatives and her comparative ease as a half-caste. Like Czech Jews deceived by the Germans to think the ghetto would be an autonomous Jewish region and Demetz's own Aunt Ella, who took a cocktail dress with her to Theresienstadt in anticipation of afternoon tea, Demetz's characters harbor unrealistic expectations. The protagonist, akin to the author, has her first inkling of the degree of torment people experienced when she sees "the transports of prisoners . . . in the railroad stations . . . the third or fourth of May, 1945."[5]

Continually shifting from first- to third-person perception, from youthful perspective to superimposed adult retrospective, Demetz balances a young girl's Holocaust-era ambivalence with the mature author's psychological and moral reflection. The progressive stages in Helene's understanding of the Nazi violation of her family and neighbors, their transformation from valued citizens to disenfranchised pariahs, parallels her metamorphosis from assimilated Czech to despised half-caste. Demetz calibrates and recalibrates Helene's relationship to her world, chronicling her change from adoring daughter and granddaughter to detached observer as her maternal relatives and parents move from the elite to the socially rejected and economically dispossessed. Ordinary generational conflict, romantic fantasies, and teenage identity crises coexist in Helene's world with expropriations, deportations, and killings. Helene's thoughts and concerns are those of adolescence—friends, boys, school, movie stars, parental shortcomings—heightened by the tumult of war. The authorial voice and skillful juxtapositions convey the ethical complexity of the divided self confronted with an uncommon history.

Demetz conveys the chaotic nature of life under German rule by careful juxtaposition of prelapsarian Europe with Nazi-occupied Europe. She treats four generations of family history, evoking life as it was for assimilated European Jewry from the mid–nineteenth century through the Holocaust. Shifting locales from the family's ancestral house on Prague Street in Bohemia to the Richter dwellings in Moravia and Prague, the novel traces the helpless torment of the German loyal to his Jewish relatives and the disintegration of assimilated European Jewry from its prewar integration to postinvasion disruption of social and political normalcy.

The prewar peace and prosperity enjoyed by the assimilated middle-class Jewish population before the advent of Nazism is evident in the spacious house on Prague Street with its ample domesticity and generous hospitality. In the manner of family sagas of the sort Demetz originally intended to write, the early section of the novel establishes the Löwy family history, beginning with the narrator's great-great-grandfather, who "had come to the small town from Prague shortly after the Austrian Emperor signed the law permitting Jews to move out of the ghettos."[6] A grandson of the famous Rabbi Löw, he remains faithful to Jewish law and maintains a distinctive Jewish appearance among his gentile neighbors. With his good name and a small handcart he builds a modest transport business. Later his son, Helene's great-grandfather, expands the business to employ several drivers. He builds the house on Prague Street, intending it to shelter future generations of the family. Departing from his father's traditional observance, he takes the road of assimilation and is rewarded with commercial success. The family's social acceptance is evidenced when the mayor, doctor, and town councillor serve as pallbearers at his funeral. Helene's grandfather, Max, inherits and enlarges the business and gains the respect and affection of his community by building the town's first hotel, landscaping a public park, and forming a choral society. Grandfather Löwy's brothers add "international luster to the good family name: their textile mills hummed not only in Warnsdorf but also in faraway Bucharest" (20). Another brother is a banker in Prague, and the fourth lives a "wild life" in Berlin and writes poetry.

Because Helene's Jewish awareness is formed through her Löwy family experience, the author's delineation of Max Löwy's attitudes is central to his character development and, even more significant, to the portrayal of Helene's values and behavior during the German occupation. Although a descendant of "one of the most illustrious Jewish families in central Europe" (3), Max considers himself first and foremost a Czech nationalist and consequently directs that he and his family be "taken off the roster of the Israelite congregation" (5). As a man who wonders audibly what good it can do him to be a Jew in Europe, he is representative of many who sought, early in the twentieth century, to live as completely assimilated Europeans.[7] A totally assimilated Jew who considers himself a citizen of the country in which he lives, Max Löwy holds no special loyalty or allegiance to religiously affiliated Jews. His pre-Holocaust isolation from the Jewish community dramatically foreshadows Helene's peacetime tolerance of her German grandparents' disapproval of her parents' marriage and her arrogant pique at Jewish displeasure with the union. The rise of Nazism institutes a shift in her attitude marked by an ironic comment on her paternal grandparents' sudden recognition of her parents' marriage: "They had already sided with the mighty" (9) and urged their son to divorce his Jewish wife.

Through her use of an assimilated Jewish Czech–Catholic German family, Demetz highlights the distinctively modernist approach to antisemitism. As Zygmunt Bauman demonstrates in *Modernity and the Holocaust*, "Modern anti-Semitism was born not from the great difference between groups [that characterized Christian antisemitism of earlier periods] but rather from the threat of absence of differences, the homogenization of Western society and the abolition of the ancient social and legal barriers between Jews and Christians." Since assimilated Jews of Max Löwy's ilk and Jewish converts to Christianity eliminated their distinctions from their non-Jewish neighbors, *"the distinctiveness of the Jews had to be re-articulated and laid out on new foundations."*[8] Religious antisemitism would be replaced by racial antisemitism, on the level of natural law from which there could be no escape, excluding Jews first from positions of power and influence and finally from life. Such is the course followed in *The House on Prague Street*.

In contrast to the dominant tropes of lost professions and Aryanized businesses signifying Jewish displacement in male writing, women writers frequently introduce tropes of confiscated homes and or decaying gardens to denote diminished Jewish status and early stages of Nazi oppression.[9] It is instructive to compare the use of garden imagery in the Holocaust work of Polish-born Israeli Ida Fink and Czech-born Hana Demetz, as each uses the garden to suggest the vanishing place of Jews in the lands of their birth. In "The Garden That Floated Away" Fink uses a surrealistic approach to convey the incomprehensibility of early Aryanization and discriminatory legislation to a child awaiting her father's negotiation for false identity papers. Fink underscores the contrast between the familiar and its perverse dislocation under Nazi rule through a child's observation of a neighbor's garden adjoining their own: "The garden of our childhood friend suddenly shuddered, swayed, began to pitch and roll, and slowly, slowly it began to float away, like a huge green ocean liner. It sailed away slowly but steadily; the distance between us grew quickly, the garden got smaller and disappeared. It had floated away to an inaccessible distance, far beyond our reach."[10] The scene of the disappearing neighboring garden heralds the German-imposed separation of Poles and Jews as the initial step toward deportation and annihilation of Polish Jewry. The garden itself disappears, marking the insubstantiality of Poland's effort to rescue its Jews. Demetz focuses solely on affluent Jews' diminishing prospects in a series of ritualistic birthday celebrations marking the family patriarch's transformation from citizen to pariah. The first party, set in the prewar era, is a tableau of serenity. Abundant flowers and fruit from the family garden and orchard symbolize the Edenic quality of pre-Holocaust life, a scene exuding high spirit and good fortune emblematic of the good relations between Czechoslovakian Jews and gentiles.

The Löwy family's metamorphosis is realistically unfolded to juxtapose pre-Holocaust freedom and prosperity with Nazi slavery and destruction. In the first birthday scene Max Löwy, surrounded by a large, exuberant, and prosperous family, plays the role of charming host and paterfamilias, accepting the warm greetings of the town dignitaries. The quality of life just before the advent of Nazism is suggested not only in Grandfather Löwy's prominent place in his community but also by the opulence the second generation enjoys, as evidenced in their chauffeur-driven Hombers, elegant fashionable clothing, Rosenthal china, and servant-run homes. Through her skillful depiction of this affluence, Demetz effectively dramatizes the austere reversals that will befall these innocents under Nazi rule.

Whereas the first birthday party scene establishes the family's good fortunes, its conclusion and subsequent celebrations convey the declining status and security of Czech Jews. Portending the end of the paradisiacal peace is the after-dinner discussion by the men as they linger over coffee and cigars. The conversation is dominated by the specter of German anti-Jewish demonstrations. Yet despite this anxious undercurrent, these Jews insist that Czechoslovakia will not tolerate German-style antisemitic injustices, a credible view in light of the nation's peaceable integration of Jews and non-Jews.[11] The menacing note sounded in this scene regarding German anti-Jewish policies is forcefully heightened in the next scene, staged early in the occupation. Supplementing the reports of suffering German Jews are signs that danger is close at hand for Czech Jews. The talk centers on the Löwy uncles' diminishing prosperity. By this meeting, the banker has sold all his stock, the manufacturer is reconciled to the loss of his factories, and Max has lost the warehouse and yards. Max Löwy's decision to sell his car lest this possession offend powerful antagonists and his judgment that the women of the family must refrain from wearing elegant clothing echoes the survival strategies taken by many assimilated German Jews. Economic losses are soon matched by civil restrictions. Nevertheless, when some of the uncles speak of emigrating to western Europe or America, Max denounces them. He argues for steadfast devotion to the homeland and believes Czech Jews will escape the fate of German Jews. The Löwy patriarch is an authentic example of the undivided loyalty European Jews felt for their countries and their misplaced faith that their contributions would provide them safe haven against the Nazi menace.

By the time of the third birthday gathering, Czechoslovakia is a police state. The celebration reflects the guarded behavior and peril of Czech citizens under Nazi occupation. Gentile neighbors, who had candidly honored Max on each birthday, now appear surreptitiously and risk grave consequences for their loyalty to the Jew. Max sends these men away, fearful that they will be denounced for consorting with him. The man who thought he could make himself a Czech among Czechs by the eradication of his name from a Jewish congregational register has, under the Nazi regime, become a ghetto Jew once again. Unlike the religious Jews of I. B. Singer's and Elie Wiesel's fiction, characters whose identities are grounded in Jewishness and who are therefore able to retain their self-worth despite Nazi oppression, Max Löwy, whose self-esteem is dependent on non-Jewish affirmation, has nothing. Löwy's demoralizing transformation from respected businessman and community leader to scapegoat is meticulously depicted as each outward measure of his status is stripped. The active, engaged patriarch and citizen becomes a withdrawn, embittered, passive victim whose progressive disengagement from society culminates in voluntary silence. Unlike the muteness of Jerzy Kosinski's boy in *The Painted Bird*, which emanates from the terror of experienced atrocity, Max Löwy's silence figuratively and realistically conveys his sense of Holocaust rupture, but it is also a mark of moral defiance. Max chooses not to commune with the forces that have trampled on civility to further the cause of a political movement whose essence is radical evil. Silence is the only option of the impotent man of honor.

The disposition of the house on Prague Street and the fate of its displaced residents help readers understand the effects of sharp curtailment and eradication of every facet of hard-won European Jewish emancipation. Generously provisioned to accommodate twenty-four houseguests in the first birthday scene, the family home is requisitioned for German use and later confiscated. Under the Aryanization program characterizing

Nazi hegemony, Jews were deprived of their property and denied entry to public facilities.[12] Illustrative are decrees that barred Jews from public institutions, libraries, and schools; forbade them to appear on the streets after eight in the evening or before six in the morning; and banned them from intercity travel, taxicabs, automobiles, and bicycles and from the first carriage of streetcars. Demetz highlights the irony of denying the Löwy family access to the town park and the hotel the patriarch gave his Bohemian city. Revocation of Jewish property and civil rights was soon followed by the denial of human rights. Max Löwy's refraining from walking beside his granddaughter or speaking to his son-in-law reflects laws that prohibited Jews from associating with their gentile neighbors and even from consorting with their German relatives in public. Helene's growing comprehension of the strain of occupation is expressed on her return to Prague from a visit with her grandparents. Her choice of detail and diction conveys the family's decline, ranging from the public humiliation of eradicating the Löwy name from the hotel to expropriation of the family home and demotion of the grandmother from lady of the house to housekeeper.

Novelists of the Holocaust often choose to convey Jewish displacement by dramatizing the entrance of strangers in their homes, strangers who have come to take inventory or outright possession of their property. Demetz and fellow Czech novelist Jiri Weil approach this phenomenon differently yet manage to achieve similar impressions. Consider Weil's protagonist as he witnesses usurpers inspecting his apartment:

> Pavel entered the room, followed by a man and a woman. They didn't say a word. They didn't look at us; they pretended not to see us at all. I remained sitting at the table, and in my embarrassment I began to stir the tea I had drunk long before. They only looked at the objects in the room. They caressed the furniture, took the pewter mugs in their hands, felt the upholstery of the sofas. They calculated loudly between them the quality and sturdiness of various objects; they discussed how they would move the furniture around. We were already dead. They had come to claim their inheritance. Pavel accompanied them silently into the other rooms and into the kitchen. We could hear their happy voices. They returned to the living room again and went by us. They looked about once more, as if counting all the objects in the room so that not a single one could escape them. We kept sitting with our empty cups. Only when they left did they look at us, but I noticed that they were actually looking at the teacups, spoons, and sugar bowl. Pavel

showed them back to the hall. He was there for quite some time. They were probably inspecting the carpet and the armchairs. Then we heard the loud slamming of the door.[13]

In Weil's passage the Jews are already invisible to their avaricious beneficiaries. Only the property their departure will make available is of importance. Despite the objective description and tone, the victims' seething embarrassment and anger emerges brilliantly. Demetz treats the same subject with characteristic avoidance of confrontation and embellishment. She offers instead a spare report by a hearsay witness of the outcome of Nazi appropriation of Jewish property:

> The following summer I could not go visit my grandparents because an order had come to vacate the old house on Prague Street within a week; a room had been assigned to them in town. My father . . . went to help them move. When he came back, he brought my mother a box filled with yellowed family photographs. She sat over it for a long time, crying. It was all that remained of the attic in the old house. (71)

Demetz refrains from enumerating the confiscated property. But she has earlier described the house in great detail so her readers are aware of the magnitude of the theft. Observing that "an order had come to vacate the old house . . . a room had been assigned," her passage not only conveys the dispossession and sadness that Weil's writing imparts but censures the corrupt powers that legitimate this theft and the bureaucracy that implements governmental decrees in the modern state. The victims of the bureaucratic action are personalized through their emotions, whereas their tormentors are rhetorically depersonalized through their distanced and unfeeling manipulation of edicts. A more dramatic confiscation scene emerges when an aunt responds by killing the Nazi officer who attempts to requisition her home. In turn, she is killed and her family deported. Among the new tenants are three boys: "Swastikas were sown on the sleeves of their brown shirts, and swastikas decorated the medals on their chests" (90).

As Helene struggles to live normally, the intensification of Nazi oppression exacts its price on her parents and their relatives. Once exuberant and filled with the joy of life, Frau Richter is transformed from a spirited rebel to a waif who saves a portion of her meager food rations to send to her family in Theresienstadt. Because all her energy goes to help the transported and incarcerated, she endangers her own health and fails to give Helene the attention she wants. For Helene, the more troubling parental metamorphosis is her father's transformation from Germanic hero to bullied coward. Broken by a series of harsh reversals, he has become a man in whom his daughter recognizes fear and passivity.

Paralleling historic accounts of Nazi escalation of anti-Jewish legislation in occupied Europe, Demetz uses the contours of history to reveal how even the privileged Jewish spouses of Aryans were deprived of civil rights and isolated from the general population and how their Aryan mates were humiliated and intimidated. Powerless to act on their own behalf, the Richters await each new restrictive ordinance, each new decree that deepens their degradation. Through Herr Richter's plight we learn of the disgrace suffered by a German loyal to Jewish relatives. He loses his job for refusing to divorce his Jewish wife in defiance of the prohibition of marriage between Jews and Aryans. Depressed by his situation, he withdraws and forfeits his paternal rights and inclinations to protect his daughter from Nazi hooligans. It is through Marie Richter's character that the debasement of the semiprivileged Jew is most fully articulated. Marie complies with the decree that Jews must register and carry identity papers marked *Jude*. She must add a name to her own when "the Germans had ordered that every Jewish woman call herself Sara" (76). In accord with the order that all Jews over six years of age wear an identifying badge consisting of "a six pointed star, as large as the palm of a hand, on a yellow background bound in black and containing the word *Jude* in black letters," she dons the infamous star whenever she leaves home. Through reference to the provisions allowed Helene and her parents, Demetz describes the discriminatory food rationing that allots the least food to full-blooded Jews, slightly more to half-Jews, and still more to non-Jews. Denial of access to transportation, public buildings, and entertainment is similarly illustrated in the family travails.[14] Because of a loophole in the Nuremberg Laws exempting Jewish spouses of non-Jews, Marie Richter eludes deportation. Yet she dies by Nazi decree when she is deprived of medical care because of legislation that denied Jews treatment by gentile doctors and outlawed patient visits by Jewish doctors after curfew.

As a *Mischlinge*, located hierarchically between the disfranchised "full Jew" and the valued German *Volk*, Helene is exempt from full discrimination. Although she is affected by the shrinking sphere of Jewish options, as the child of a German she remains relatively safe and is spared the injustices her mother and other family members endure. A fully assimilated Czech whose Jewish identity is more a function of ancestral history and Nazi decree than self-image or personal commitment, Helene has the perspective of the aggrieved individual whose most elemental notion of self-definition has been violated. Her humiliation at school is the counterpart of the adults' oppression in professional and civic realms. As a half-Jew, she is the target of a vicious pro-Nazi instructor who discards the restraint he had exercised under the Czechoslovakian administration to give full vent to his antisemitism. She must listen to the German professor rail against "the cowardly dog, the Jew-Bolshevik" (79) who killed Reichprotector Heydrich. This teacher compounds Helene's discomfort through a series of escalating harassments: first by looking at her angrily, then by ignoring her despite her obvious talent in his subject, ridiculing her in class, pulling her hair, and finally, sexually molesting her. Like Jewish women in ghettos and camps, Helene suffers her teacher's molestation, powerless to escape his cruelty. Even more painful is her discovery that her parents cannot protect her from this outrage. When she complains about the teacher, Frau Richter advises her to stay out of his reach, and Herr Richter explains that a Jew cannot seek redress for wrongs inflicted by a Nazi. Finally, she endures the embarrassment of expulsion when the principal instructs her to gather up her belongings in conformity with orders he has received "by which all Jewish mongrels must leave school immediately" (96).

Although the novel is based almost entirely on events and people the author witnessed in her own immediate circle of family and acquaintances, Demetz supplements the family chronicle with inclusion of public events as reported to the populace and heard in radio broadcasts. A lamppost loudspeaker blares news that "a heroic U-boat had sunk thirteen thousand tons in the Atlantic during the night . . . [followed by] drums and fifes [playing] 'We shall bring England to her knees'" (67). From the same source Helene learns of the destruction of Pearl Harbor and the German declaration of war against the United States. Radio broadcasts also chart the progress of the war: "Once a halting voice listed names of border towns that had been given up to Hitler without a single shot" (48). Although it is illegal, even for Aryans, to listen to foreign broadcasts, the Richters tune to a Swiss station that reports the battle of Stalingrad and the bombing of Dresden. Helene's impression of Hitler is of "a voice that threatened and chided and yelped . . . until it turned hoarse and was finally drowned by martial music and wild cries" (31).

Forgoing fictional delineation of the ghettos and camps by virtue of her protagonist's half-caste status, Demetz hints at Nazi physical brutality in a brief vignette of the gratuitous violence and degradation Jews suffered under occupation. Helene witnesses the streetcar entry of four soldiers to examine identity papers: "The soldiers, who were holding guns in their hands, omitted no one. A man wearing a star stood on the outside platform—the only place where Jews were allowed to ride. He was eager to show his papers, but the soldiers slapped and hit him and took him away. He looked back once, very calmly, as if expecting that someone would come to his defense. But all the people in the streetcar looked straight ahead, each one for himself, as if nothing had happened" (78–79). The scene represents both the commonplace anti-Jewish violence of the Nazi regime and the silent acquiescence of European bystanders. A scene focusing on witnesses' reactions to the victim's condition rather than the actual infliction of punishment is illustrative of the novelist's tendency to evoke brutal events rather than dramatize them.

Typical of Nazi mass reprisals for individuals' resistance acts is the detention and torture of Helene's uncle following the murder of Reichprotector Heydrich. As mother and daughter wait in a corridor of Gestapo headquarters, where they have brought a change of clothing for the uncle, "the second skull came out, and the thin old man in striped pajamas followed him. He was clutching the package now, and he looked at me as he limped past" (94–95). The man has been so tortured that Marie is visibly shaken and Helene fails to recognize him. Marie expresses her horror by driving her nails into the palm of her daughter's hand. After her mother informs her that the passerby was her uncle, Helene feels her head spinning as she asks: "How could Uncle Rudolf look like that? Was it really he?" (95).

The rapidly escalating plight of the Löwys is conveyed through Helene's point of view and is therefore merely intimated rather than fully explored. We learn that an uncle is unceremoniously discharged from his own export business when it is expropriated for a German; that a stranger is billeted in the family home on Prague Street, where the elder Löwys are temporarily tolerated and eventually evicted; that an assimilated aunt and uncle jump to their deaths, sharing the fate of many upper-class assimilated Jews who elected suicide rather than accommodate to pariah status. Helene registers these calamities virtually without commentary, rarely articulating sympathy for the dispossessed and occasionally exhibiting disinterest or impatience with their concerns. In contrast to the brief notations of these dire events, she gives more thorough attention to relatively minor concerns. When the edict is issued ordering Jews to wear yellow Stars of David with the word *Jude* emblazoned on the fabric, Helene characterizes people by their distinctive proud or humiliated responses: "Some had sewn theirs carefully and neatly onto their coats, using many tiny stitches, as if the stars were to remain fixed on the coats for years and years. . . . Others . . . attached them sloppily, with safety pins" (71). Frau Richter "had sewn her star slightly lower, below her chest" (71), the better to conceal it with a deftly placed handbag when she had occasion to be in public with her Aryan family, much as Jiri Weil's protagonist wanders the city hiding the unnamed word on his chest with his briefcase. In contrast to his wife's cautious Jewish defiance of Nazi rule, Herr Richter bitterly proposes that he and his wife walk openly together, she displaying her yellow star and he, his Iron Cross. In contrast to Jiri Weil's fugitive Jew, for whom the star is seen as an erasure of humanity, a vehicle to expose him and to view himself as his enemies do, Marie Richter refuses to succumb.

The most poignant means Demetz uses to chart the progress of the Holocaust are the departures and disappearances of family members through emigration and deportation. They begin in 1938 with the voluntary emigration of a Viennese part of the family to Australia at a time when Max Löwy confidently assured them: "Nothing will happen to us here, don't you worry. We belong here" (36). By 1942, when Helene is fourteen, her Uncle Fritz's family is sent to an undeclared destination in one of the first transports. The members of this transport have numbers sewn above their stars, an ominous sign that they are bound for a concentration camp. The dramatic power of this scene emerges from the juxtaposition of Helene's innocence regarding the transport's destination and the reader's postwar knowledge. The next deportation is much more emphatically developed. The Löwy grandparents are part of a transport whose destination we later learn is Theresienstadt. And finally, we discover from a summary statement that by 1944 all the family members "were gone now with the transports" (107). From Theresienstadt the grandparents, aunts, and uncles are sent to Birkenau. In the next paragraph Helene notes that only the youngest aunt continued to send the official postcards once a month announcing her good health. Helene's innocence is poignantly revealed in her wonderment about the old people who are no longer permitted to write.

The novelist's decision to select a protagonist of mixed heritage allows her to investigate experiences outside the realm of full Jews. As a pupil in a school designated for *Mischlinges*, Helene Richter associates with others who have German ties. Through an inadvertent bureaucratic failure, Helene's school friend, Susi Renner, remains a member of the Nazi Girls Union and attends its meetings. Dressed in a swastika-marked uniform, she joins other girls to sew and knit for the military effort and to visit hospitals to sing for wounded soldiers. Following her initial dismay at Susi's association with Nazi youth, the impressionable fifteen-year-old Helene attends a meeting with her and finds the atmosphere congenial. It is not long before Helene is lured into Susi's world and confronts moral dilemmas arising from fraternization with German cadets. Illustrative of Helene's divided loyalty between her Jewish mother and racially mixed friends and her German associates are juxtaposed scenes of her accommodation to both groups. First, we encounter her surreptitiously garbed in a borrowed dirndl dress and white kneesocks, looking "very Aryan" (100) and feeling very self-satisfied while singing sentimental songs about the homeland for the hospitalized soldiers. The inappropriateness of Helene's association with German soldiers is suggested in the next scene, depicting Frau Richter waiting all day in the cold at the Prague fairgrounds for a final glimpse of her parents, who are part of a Theresienstadt transport. Similarly, when Helene is sexually harassed by a cadet, she expresses her revulsion in terms of Jewish loyalty: "Suddenly I thought of my mother again: for heaven's sake, what was I doing at Milowitz? . . . My mother was right. They were trash" (115). Yet after singing at a military hospital, she weeps both for the wounded Germans and because she knew she had "betrayed" her mother by feeling compassion for Nazis. Helene's sympathy for German cadets seems implausible to the post-Holocaust consciousness, but Demetz asserts that adolescent girls do not consider the politics of war; they respond to boys as in peacetime—they seek a handsome face, someone amusing.[15] Another factor for inclusion of this perspective may be that the book was originally intended for a German audience, which would have embraced such a scene more readily than others might.

Helene Richter, like the author at her age, has no sense of belonging to the Jewish people, no commitment to their civilization, and insufficient knowledge of the magnitude of the tragedy befalling her Jewish relatives.[16] Unlike the Jewish women in the works of Karmel, Ettinger, Piercy, Ozick, and Schaeffer, who have no option but total Jewish affiliation, Helene is plagued by ambivalence, torn between the wish to enjoy security as a German and occasional pangs of guilt for the suffering of her Jewish relatives. She quickly discovers that a Jewish family is a liability, a hindrance to life's pleasures and good fortune. As a young teenager, she shares with some other Holocaust chroniclers, such as the unincarcerated Anne Frank, an overwhelming desire to lead a normal life despite the dire times. In contrast to her childhood identification with her aggrieved grandfather, revealed in her refusal to enter the city park because he is forbidden entrance, and in her declaration that expropriation of her uncle's business is unfair, Helene's adolescent response to increasingly severe Jewish deprivations leads to her resolve to resist entrapment in the dreariness of her Jewish connections and instead to participate in the German world. In the face of mounting public restrictions and dangers, Helene, like Anne Frank, occasionally withdraws into daydreams of movie stars and boys. Unlike the attic-sequestered Jewish Anne, however, Helene also escapes existentially by virtue of her half-German identity. In the company of her German father and aunt she enjoys privileges her mother is denied. She rides on public transportation, eats in restaurants, and attends public entertainments. She cultivates the friendship of her German maiden aunt, the one paternal relative who acknowledges her, and she falls in love with a sensitive German soldier. Although Demetz asserts her limited purpose of delineating Helene as an innocent seeking adolescent pleasures, the mature authorial voice repeatedly reminds the reader that the special privileges and contradictions inherent in *Mischlinge* status divided the Jewish community, for they heightened the realization that solidarity with other Jews meant suffering whereas distance offered survival.

The protagonist's coming of age is marked most notably in her experience of love. A chance meeting with a German lieutenant who retrieves her windblown hat turns into a classic story of forbidden love that flourishes despite the war. During the early period of infatuation, when Gerd pays Helene a visit, she has a moment of panic wondering how he would feel if he knew she is "a filthy half-Jew" (131). Holocaust reality invades even this idyllic romance. During their dinner dates Gerd orders ample food and multiple desserts, a sharp silent reminder to Helene of the meager food rations her family shares. Gerd must return to his unit, and when Helene sees him again in uniform, she realizes she "had forgotten about all that, the uniform and the Hitler Youth emblem with the swastikas" (137). Despite the racial laws and her mother's displeasure, Helene is hopelessly in love with this boy, who is equally enchanted. Feeling compelled to tell him she has a Jewish mother, Helene is prepared to accept rejection, but Gerd confirms his love and promises to honor the woman who raised Helene. His declaration says much for his character, for he is subject to harsh discipline under the race-mixing laws. The lover who remains faithful to the half-caste, the husband who refuses to divorce his Jewish wife, and the German aunt who shares her rations with Jewish relatives all reflect the author's commitment to include decent Germans in the novel.

Hard times intensify as the German net ensnares baptized Jews and finally the privileged children of mixed heritage. Helene, though better off than the other Jews of the family, is drawn more deeply into the war near its end; like Demetz, she is conscripted into a labor unit to manufacture hand grenades.[17] The closest she comes to the brutality Jews in the camps suffered is being slapped by an SS man because she could not get out of his path quickly enough while carrying a heavy load. She experiences something of the tension and fear of victims working in close proximity to Nazi masters free to exact any punishment or perpetrate any crime they wish against non-Aryans.

The novel's resistance theme is focused both internally, within the family structure, and externally, in defiance of German decrees. Like a majority of men in Holocaust works written by women, most of the men in this novel are so devastated by the many forms of oppression that they withdraw from their former dominant family roles. Again like those in much Holocaust writing by women, Demetz's women, long socialized to nurture and cope, adapt to imposed limitations and injustices more imaginatively and stoically than men. The women often become more assertive or retain active nurturing roles. Illustrative of this dichotomy are the positions taken by Max Löwy and Herr Richter in opposition to those of Aunt Klara and Marie Richter. After playing a dominant role in business and family, Max suffers each diminishment of autonomy with dignity until all rights are stripped from him and he capitulates in Theresienstadt by withdrawing into a self-imposed silence. Similarly, Herr Richter's early active resistance, marked by refusal to divorce his Jewish wife, dissolves when his daughter is molested by a teacher and his wife is denied medical attention. Aunt Klara, however, who had earlier demonstrated her independent spirit aesthetically, resists the intrusion of Nazis who have come to confiscate her home by shooting one of them. Marie Richter regularly defies Nazi decrees in large and small ways. Practicing the sort of generosity and initiative that was common to Karmel's Barbara and Tola, Marie saves a part of her meager rations to provide more food for Helene or to send some to the family in Theresienstadt. Marie does what she can to spare her daughter the pains of Nazism, finding a private school for her when she is dismissed from public school, encouraging her to attend the opera with her father and go out with friends, and consoling her when she is disappointed by her father's inability to protect her. Her more public acts of resistance include concealing her star, removing the star from her coat in a successful effort to secure services for her daughter without prejudice, removing valuables from her sister's confiscated apartment despite danger of discovery by Germans, and bartering on the black market for food to send to her relatives in Theresienstadt, despite her knowledge that the entire family will be locked up if she is discovered.

In contrast to the other writers considered here, whose German characters are all associated with official Nazi policy, Demetz includes decent German civilians who are portrayed sympathetically. For their loyalty to Jews during the Holocaust, they suffer at the direction of the Nazis, and for being German nationals, they suffer Czech vengeance at war's end. In scenes dwelling on the utter madness of revenge Demetz refers to radio broadcasts exhorting the Czech people to kill Germans wherever they could be found, "kill them all, every man, woman, and child" (174). At the liberation of Prague, the Richters' German friends and family are evicted from their homes and brutalized by Czech mobs. In very powerful scenes, oddly among the few dramatizations of violence in the novel, we see Czech Revolutionary Guards confiscating Aunt Annel's apartment and shooting her and Richter, whose heroic efforts to pacify the mob fail.[18] Germans now suffer some of the same injustices the Nazis perpetrated. Czechs issue Germans ration cards to limit their food supply. As a German, Herr Richter is denied treatment in Czech hospitals and dies of his wounds. Richter had violated the law of the Reich by having his wife cremated so as not to bury her in a Jewish cemetery. A year after liberation Helene discovers that the plaque showing her mother's married Germanic name offends crematorium administrators, who intend to remove it but relent when Helene proves that her mother was Jewish.

Demetz, who wrote her book to remember her family members and to counter the failure of German schools to teach Holocaust history adequately, is among the ranks of those who contend that forgetting the Holocaust would compound the tragedy. She addresses the theme of Holocaust memory explicitly in Marie Richter's dialogue and implicitly in Helene's character. In her effort to ensure that future generations know what the Nazis did to their victims and that the atrocities be seen from the victims' point of view, Marie insists that Helene accompany her to witness the results of German crimes and implores her to bear witness at war's end. Responding to an aunt's wish to spare Helene the sight of her grandparents' decline from proud householders to boarders in a single room of another's house, Marie Richter argues: "Let her see it all. . . . Just let her see everything. Someone will have to know about it later on" (91). Similarly, after Marie has Helene accompany her to Gestapo headquarters, where she sees her tortured uncle, Marie urges her daughter, "Remember that well" (95).

After years of alternating between Holocaust evasion and confrontation, Helene encounters Holocaust reality, the quintessential Shoah image—a cattle car filled with Jewish concentration camp survivors who no longer bear resemblance to the living. At a railroad crossing Helene unexpectedly sees the results of Nazi violence: "A train of cattle cars . . . standing in the station, SS men with pointed machine guns before it. . . . We all stared mesmerized, because the cattle cars were full of people. . . . But they were not really people, they were skeletons in striped suits, with numbers on their chests" (171). Demetz is concerned here not only with the implications of the Nazi crimes against Jewry but with the response of the onlookers. One bystander judges the criminals and laments the condition of the victims: "That's how they're sending them back, the sons of bitches." Another confesses that he "didn't believe it when the BBC announced it" (171). Silence ensues because there is nothing more to say. Although she refrains from commentary, it is clear that Helene is at the threshold of comprehension of the catastrophe, at the threshold of understanding that those who perished and those who survived deserve witness and commemoration of their humanity. When she realizes that she is the family's sole survivor, that no one will return, her innocence is shattered.

The house on Prague street is the metaphor that serves as the novel's structural and symbolic foundation. Between the opening and closing frame Demetz charts the life of the family members of the house, sharply juxtaposing the civilized decorum and decency of the prewar period with the destruction, decay, and death of the Nazi era. The novel concludes with Helene's bittersweet perspective. She still dreams of the old house, its colors and textures, its plants, its attic filled with memorabilia of family history—dreams in which she is happy. But when she returns, she finds new tenants. Emptied of its rightful family dwellers and its Aryan usurpers, the house on Prague Street is finally inhabited by concentration camp survivors. The interior is devoid of grace and warmth; its entry hall is covered in ashes and charred logs, evocative of the physically burned-out lives of its former owners and of the emotionally seared lives of its current tenants. The grounds reflect the transformation of the family fortunes from prewar to Holocaust times. In the early years of the novel orchards and gardens flourish, yielding abundant fruit and flowers symbolic of the Edenic lifestyle of assimilated European Jewry. The concluding scene of withered orchard and weed-besotted garden symbolically attests to the demise of European Jewry, as successfully as the brilliant cinematography of *The Garden of the Finzi-Continis* conveys the altered state of Italian Jewry.

Unlike the Jewish protagonists of other novelists, who return to the family dwelling to be spurned by the gentile householders who have usurped their place, Helene finds an ironic reversal. The ancestral home is inhabited by emaciated, black-garbed concentration camp survivors who had suffered as Jews and who now live in the house built by Helene's observant great-grandfather to house many generations of Jews. The survivors have the moral imperative and assert their need to be left in peace. "They were all so quiet . . . all of them pulled up their coat sleeves, all of them showed me their bone arms. . . . All wore numbers on their arms, and all were so quiet as they looked at me. Then the oldest spoke. He said, 'Go away, child, and don't come back. Don't disturb us. You don't know, you haven't seen. You haven't suffered. You haven't endured. We are the last. Don't disturb us'" (186). Although this conclusion is inconsistent with the historic pattern and does not meet with Helene's approval, it is aesthetically pleasing to find the house on Prague Street again inhabited by Jews. The newly initiated protagonist will presumably learn more of the victims' tragedy and perhaps become the witness her mother envisioned. For Helene, this traumatic scene reveals the irreversibility of what had transpired. Like her Jewish family members, she has lost everyone and everything she held dear. This is an apt symbolic ending for a novel that has conveyed the unprecedented evil of Nazi Germany without explicit reference to mass murder but through the experiences of ordinary people and the shattered innocence of a young girl.

The Journey from Prague Street chronicles Helene's postwar odyssey from Communist Czechoslovakia to Germany and eventually to freedom and prosperity in America.[19] Uncharacteristic of novels exploring the lives of survivors, this work does not present a Shoah-obsessed character. References to and memories of the war years are circumscribed and play a subordinate role in this domestic novel, which records Helene's unhappy marriage to a brilliant and egocentric academic, her second marriage to an American Jew whose family hailed from the same area as the Löwys, and her burgeoning perception of her own worth.

Like its predecessor, the novel is highly autobiographical. Demetz now takes a postmodernist self-reflexive turn, however. She attributes much of her earlier writing to Helene, including "a memoir of growing up in Central Europe before and during the war, about her family which no longer existed" (92). Duly incorporated into the narrative is an account of the favorable critical reception for The House on Prague Street and a notation that Helene met her second husband as a result of his admiration for the book.[20]

The novel is structured as a series of short, juxtaposed entries contrasting Helene's reflections on her marriages, occasional reminiscences of Shoah losses, and incidental citations to her writing. Written in the first and third person, as Helene is approaching sixty and taking stock, she claims to "have had too many lives" (3) with a past that occasionally overwhelms and disorients her: "Events overlap, reference points disappear, people who belong to one life suddenly appear out of context, in another" (3). The German/Jewish ambivalence that marked the younger character persists in the postwar reflections, generated by her discovery that Gerd is alive. Although Helene is pleased to know that he survived the war, her first reaction is inability to forgive him for "being part of it," a mark of her postwar consciousness. Yet this reservation does not preclude a brief adulterous reunion with him while her philandering husband is otherwise occupied.

Although the Holocaust past will not fade away, it is less pervasive in her life than in the lives of Jewish survivors in fiction by Ozick and Schaeffer. Of interest to readers of Holocaust literature is the sequel's relation to *The House on Prague Street*, its recall of family members and their flourishing lives in prewar Czech society and Helene's initial reaction to news of Gerd's survival. Her response suggests, albeit temporarily, a more earnest connection to her Jewish family's Holocaust history, culminating in her reflections on the girl that was, the family that was no more, "the family [that] had been lost in many transports, had been gassed, had died of broken hearts, of crushed hopes" (11). More sustained Shoah thought enters Helene's life with her marriage to the American, with whom she returns to Europe to visit his family's ancestral village. Helen's most thoughtful lament for her family appears on this site, where the synagogue and Jewish cemetery remain intact. This visit leads to her elegiac contemplation of the divergent roads the great-great-grandfathers had traveled and the consequences for their progeny, one who had the good fortune to emigrate to America in the nineteenth century and the other who remained in Europe, resulting 140 years later in his family's demise.

SUSAN FROMBERG SCHAEFFER

Susan Fromberg Schaeffer's critically acclaimed Holocaust novel, *Anya*, reads as though it were issued from the pen of a survivor. Yet Schaeffer is a native-born American. Commitment to Shoah remembrance is the vital connective tissue linking Schaeffer with survivors who write from direct experience. Holocaust diarist Etty Hillesum, who had enjoyed a privileged life in Amsterdam, vowed to be "the eyes and the ears of a piece of Jewish history." In the Westerbork transit camp, in the company of Jews from all over the Netherlands, she resolved she would be "the thinking heart of the barracks."[1] Schaeffer's fiction attains immediacy and authority by its "imitation of a memoir through the first-person narrator, who relates her memories of the collision of her life with the Holocaust."[2] *Anya* was conceived as a work that would perpetuate memory of the Shoah and those directly affected by it.[3] The survivor-protagonist, whose life has been irrevocably and radically altered by the Holocaust, shares Hillesum's purpose, advising readers, "I want you to [have] . . . my memory . . . memory is a form of reality."[4] By her rhetorical adoption of the survivor's voice, Schaeffer establishes an aura of legitimacy and honors the survivors who shared their stories with her. The protagonist addresses readers directly regarding the detail and accuracy of her chronicle: "I am going to take you into the apartment of my parents, the apartment where I was born, and where I lived until I was married. . . . I want to be sure that you can see this apartment, that you can picture it so clearly you feel you are walking through it. . . . It is so easy to think that you know what something looks like, what something was like, and really have no idea at all. . . . I want you to go through this apartment so you have a memory of it: my memory. . . . Undoubtedly I have done some retouching, have repainted some of the walls and plastered some of the cracks, but memory is a form of reality after all" (9). If one substitutes the word

Holocaust for *apartment*, the passage stands as confirmation of Schaeffer's rhetorical stance, which allows her to fuse meticulous representation of historic detail with novelistic artifice. Although she invents characters or aspects of their lives, Schaeffer remains steadfast in her assertion that her fictional rendition of the Holocaust is grounded in truth.[5]

Schaeffer acknowledges that before writing the novel she had no interest in World War II or the Nazis, for as she understands, she was a member of the generation that had a "phobic reaction to the Holocaust era."[6] The genesis of the novel lies in the author's adult discovery that an acquaintance of hers, an antique dealer whom she thought she knew, was a Holocaust survivor. In quest of what the Holocaust "really meant instead of what it was supposed to mean," she undertook ten months of protracted discussion with the antique dealer and wide-ranging interviews with others in her primary informant's survivor network. Although survivor-interviewees and the novelist shared the goal of preserving Shoah history, their interests diverged. Schaeffer "wanted to write a book which began with a normal life . . . [that would be] interrupted . . . when history collided with it" and sought information about life before the war. The survivors needed "to talk about their experiences when they really became dreadful, beginning with the ghetto." Searching to extract meaning from their hardships, most of the survivors told Schaeffer how they were rounded up, treated in the ghetto, and transported to and persecuted in the concentration camps.[7]

Anya's European ambiance is an amalgam of information gleaned from survivors, the author's grandparents, and regional picturebooks. Schaeffer credits her informant for providing her "the bones of the dinosaur" but explains that her impressions of European Jewish family life originated from many conversations with her grandparents. Contributing to her skillful recreation of prewar Vilna is Schaeffer's study of photographs of Vilna's streets as they appeared before and after a bombing raid and following rehabilitation.[8] Her descriptive passages of the Savikin home fuse reports from Europeans with decor appropriated from her own home.[9]

Anya conforms to and departs from dominant American literary representation of the Holocaust. Like most American writers, Schaeffer introduces a survivor-protagonist battling Holocaust trauma. She departs from the principal American mode, whose focus is survivor trauma, however, by employing the survivor experience as a frame for extended flashback and development of the prewar, wartime, and postwar European drama. The elegiac prologue and epilogue, set in the America of 1973, frame the central Holocaust chronicle and attest to the permanent physical and psychological impact of the Holocaust on the lives of survivors. The fifty-two-year-old protagonist conveys the continuing enormity of Holocaust disruption in her life and that of her husband by contrasting her early expectations for postwar regeneration with the brutal realization of Holocaust-wrought limitations. An impressive nightmare sequence of German anti-Jewish violence simultaneously registers the survivor's elemental loss, terror, and displacement and functions as a Shakespearean dumb show, introducing both the novel's Holocaust universe and the theme of survivor guilt: "People . . . preparing themselves for war . . . another big group of men going into the room in German uniforms, and they begin fighting with the others. Then they are all screaming and yelling terribly. During the fight, music was playing, German songs, very loud, and suddenly, . . . people were naked and streaked and smeared with blood. . . . I came out . . . from where I was hidden, and start to help with the dead, putting them on the rough shelves like merchandise. . . . At first, I cannot tell who the bodies are. Then I recognize many of them: One was my dead brother, but then it wasn't my dead brother, but sister, and the music was so loud" (5).

In addition to intimating the survivor's troubled psychological condition, manifesting a life that has been disrupted by war, the fragmented sequence forecasts the novel's chronological development in the episodes that follow, recording the Nazi occupation of Poland, ghettoization, deportation, and state-sponsored genocide. Juxtaposition of this dream with Anya's lighting of Yom Kippur memorial candles clearly establishes the author's elegiac tone, her lament for the loss of European Jewry, and her commitment to Holocaust remembrance.

"In History," the section following the prologue, is a vibrant social-cultural tapestry of pre-Holocaust Vilna that helps readers comprehend the impact of Shoah transformation. Readers trace an idealized family of devoted, amiable parents and four intelligent adolescent and young adult children, representatives of prelapsarian upper-middle-class assimilated Jews, living in a city that is home to a large multiethnic population of Poles, Lithuanians, Russians, and Jews. The American novelist's capacity for authenticating the cultural ambiance of Jewish Vilna is evident in the family's Russian and Polish fluency and in its assimilationist values and cultural preferences. In accord with the survivor's recollection of an idyllic youth, this portion of the text charts her lustrous youth and education. As the prewar section culminates, readers have learned of the Savikin family's privileged lives, the protagonist's promising medical career, her courtship and marriage to an adoring young engineer whose Hasidic family welcomes her, the birth of their first child, and the couple's exhilarating cosmopolitan Warsaw life.

Beyond capturing the ambiance of prewar assimilated east European Jewish life, "In History" provides an index by which to measure that life's decline and obliteration. Schaeffer's densely textured portrait of the Savikin world sharpens the subsequent Holocaust metamorphosis. The family lives in a spacious, tastefully furnished apartment, meticulously managed to reflect Mrs. Savikin's devotion to her family's contentment and well-being. The expansive home is the model against which to read ghetto overcrowding in cramped quarters. The lengthy passages on prewar food preparation heighten the impact of later citations on starvation. Whereas male Holocaust writers masterfully recount the pervasive hunger that characterized the Jewish ordeal in the ghettos and camps by addressing the current tribulations, women writers concretize the perception even further by contrasting present hunger with past abundance, allocating considerable space to detailed description of prisoners' memories of prewar food preparation, as in Karmel's work, or to extensive depiction of prewar profusion of food, as in Demetz's birthday scenes. Schaeffer contributes to the convention by describing how summer's produce was prepared for winter and for sumptuous holiday preparations:

> A hundred and fifty pounds of potatoes . . . small watermelons were pickling, small pears and plums and apples packed . . . wonderful preserves from rose leaves and apples, . . . two hundred pounds of flour, two kinds, one flour for white bread, and one for dark bread; one hundred pounds of sugar; all kinds of cereals, kasha. . . . The house was full of everything. Then, before the big holidays, before Passover, . . . and Chanukah, something else started. The geese who were in cages in the woodshed were taken in and slaughtered and stuffed . . . fattened up for the holidays. . . . honey wine was made . . . and the cherry liquor made from enormous black cherries. And right before the holidays would come *matzohs*, in a very big box, almost as tall as Vera, sixty pounds of them. (42–43)

Periodic intrusions into the idyllic atmosphere, as in Mrs. Savikin's recollections of the Russian pogroms of her youth, reports of a contemporary attack on female Jewish university students, and a brief reference to Hitler's *Mein Kampf*, convey the historic pattern of violent antisemitic outbursts and foreshadow the approaching European storm. Full-fledged anti-Jewish violence emerges in the novel's third section, titled "Biblical Times," an allusion to a Savikin ancestor's characterization of an onerous period as "living through biblical times, [when] the living will come to envy the dead" (149). The family ordeal parallels collective Jewish experience: exclusion from hitherto public places, curfews, confiscation of personal property, dismissal from employment, mandatory wearing of yellow stars, subjection to state-choreographed anti-Jewish street violence, forced separation from the non-Jewish population in sealed ghettos, followed by death or deportation to the camps.

The political sophistication of Schaeffer's treatment is evident in her juxtaposition of the fall of two Polish cities: Warsaw's rapid collapse in the face of Hitler's blitzkrieg and the relatively slow capitulation of Vilna. Anya's Warsaw Holocaust experience begins abruptly with her young family's flight across the beleaguered city, dodging falling bombs and tumbling buildings to reach the home of her in-laws, where they spend the first days of the war among praying Hasidim. By virtue of her Aryan appearance, Anya safely ventures outdoors, where she witnesses the campaign of isolating Jews for degradation and humiliation: dark-haired Jewish women are hauled off to the forest to be raped and murdered; young Jewish males are abducted from homes and public thoroughfares, conscripted for hard labor from which they will never return; and old Orthodox men are beaten and humiliated by soldiers hacking their beards and earlocks, defiling their religious garments, and burning their holy books.

The pact between Hitler and Stalin ceded control of Vilna to the Russians, whose mission was to obstruct rehabilitation of the Polish army and implement the region's transfer to Lithuania, newly incorporated in the USSR.[10] Vilna remained a relatively safe domain, for the Russians refrained from Nazi-style brutality, limiting their abuse to pilfering Jewish households. Like Polish Jews who hoped to survive Nazi militarism under Soviet dominion, the Savikins soon discovered that life was fraught with gratuitous economic and social corruption that could work to their detriment or benefit. Soldiers strip their household of its furniture, but a colonel seeking to advance his favor with Anya arranges employment for her father, husband, and her. With the dissolution of the Hitler-Stalin agreement, the Germans occupy Vilna and anti-Jewish violence accelerates, culminating in mass killings and ghettoization. The arrest and fatal beating of Anya's father portends the Jewish future in Nazi Europe. Deposit of Savikin's unrecognizable body with hundreds of others in public gardens ringed with barbed wire is a visual foreshadowing of the approaching genocide and an allusive evocation of the brutal July 1941 assault on the Jews of Vilna. Despite the witnessing narrator's limited perspective, post-Holocaust readers can interpret the scene as synecdoche for the Ponar Wehrmacht and Einsatzgruppen massacres of almost 50,000 people.[11]

Among the most memorable contributions Schaeffer makes to American Holocaust literature are her renditions of ghetto and labor camp. Although she does not identify the fictional ghetto as one of two in Vilna, her scenes evoke authentic conditions and experiences in the larger of the two.[12] Notwithstanding her disinclination to read the voluminous histories of the period, Schaeffer's extensive interviews with survivors enabled her to depict ghetto conditions and specific administrative conduct that parallel the accounts of historians, particularly Leonard Tushnet's *Pavement of Hell* and Yitzhak Arad's *Ghetto in Flames*.[13]

Constituted as physical and psychological antechamber to the concentration and death camps, the larger Vilna Ghetto was located near the medieval town ghetto, the worst section of the city, its buildings rotting and its plumbing primitive.[14] Anya and her family are assigned to the space of people who had just been sent to death, their bread left half-eaten, their linens still warm. This is the likely genesis of Anya's revulsion decades later at "the sight of . . . dishes with eaten food, leftover food, that frightens [her] to death" (487). The room, suffocating in summer and freezing in winter, is shared by Anya's family and forty others who have the use of but one toilet and one hotplate. The day after the Savikins arrive, thousands of newcomers are herded into the ghetto, prompting Anya's mother to warn that the Germans will kill "extra" people and that their family is vulnerable, since laborers are more valuable to the Germans than are intellectuals.

Though Schaeffer's reliance on survivor memory enables her to achieve a credible fictive voice and convincing evocation of ghetto experience on the individual family level, her resistance to historic research contributes to indeterminate portraits of the ghetto elder, the Jewish Council, and the organized resistance forces. Eschewing Leslie Epstein's technique, in *King of the Jews*, of extensively rendering public figures and a large cast of ghetto residents, Schaeffer employs an intimate cast that more fully engages readers' sympathy. Instead of dramatic encounters with the Jewish leadership or German overseers in the manner of Epstein, Schaeffer's characters merely refer to administrators and their policies. In place of Epstein's sustained development of the Lodz elder, Chaim Rumkowski, via documentary and invented pastiche, Schaeffer alludes to the Jewish leader of the Vilna Ghetto, Jacob Gens, by the name Ganz, intimating that he is capable of granting special privileges to his inner circle.[15] This description accords with historic accounts that "Gens built around himself a strong apparatus, well fed and well housed."[16] The practice conformed to the German policy of rewarding privileged prisoners with better food and housing. The factual account also suggests the paradoxical role of ghetto elders, seen in the contradictions inherent in their positions. Ganz capitulates to and subverts German instructions. He supervises ghetto deportation assemblies and cooperates with ghetto resistance forces. By making Ganz the agent of Anya's child's escape, Schaeffer acknowledges the historic figure's cooperation with the United Partisan Organization, activity that led to his execution nine days before the entire ghetto was liquidated.[17]

As in all the ghettos, sustaining life on starvation rations in Vilna depended on one's capacity to supplement allotted rations through smuggling, purchasing food clandestinely, or obtaining a privileged job that was rewarded with extra food or offered opportunity for theft.[18] The porous wooden fence surrounding the Vilna Ghetto allowed Poles to barter precious food for cash and valuables that Jews had brought with them or had hidden on the Aryan side.[19] In addition to provisions delivered by their loyal family servant in the early days of ghettoization, the family is entitled to better rations because one son-in-law works with ghetto police and the other with the Jewish Council. Illegal ventures complement these advantages. Anya uses the opportunity created by her work for Gestapo wives to smuggle in small amounts of food on her nightly return to the ghetto. Later, as a member of a work group at a local mill, she steals flour in small sacks fitted under her armpits. Despite all these machinations, the food supply is woefully insufficient.

Schaeffer's portrayal of ghetto life mirrors the view of chroniclers who explain the pivotal role luck plays in survival as opposed to the exercise of individual will. The impossibility of relying purely on good decisions and survival strategies when dealing with a deceptive power whose purpose is to confuse, degrade, and eventually annihilate its victims is suggested by an early scene based on the historic model of a call that urged ghetto residents to register with the *Judenrat* for work. Eager to improve the family's living conditions, Anya's husband, Stajoe, wants to volunteer. Heeding his mother-in-law's plea for caution, he escapes the mass murder that awaited the five thousand who registered.[20] Chance is also at the heart of the grandmother's escape during an "action" that cleared the ghetto of the elderly. Anya's young daughter, Ninka, is terrified by the arrest of another old woman who shares their room and screams "Momma!"—her name for her grandmother. Only because the soldiers assume Ninka is calling her own mother does the grandmother avoid detection.

Again and again, Mrs. Savikin argues that her children should not take jobs that will bring them in direct contact with the Germans. She warns, "It's better sometimes to stay away and do without the extra potato" (179). Despite the matriarch's admonitions, her daughter and sons-in-law work with the Jewish Council and in the Gestapo ghetto office, thereby gaining the family a private room and better food. Soon the Gestapo retaliates against all the privileged workers and their families for an alleged infraction of the racial laws prohibiting sexual liaisons between Aryans and non-Aryans. The Savikins lose six family members in the assault, and shortly thereafter Stajoe is tortured and executed on a trumped-up charge. Privileged jobs not only failed to protect; they often put Jews in harm's way. The matriarch's prophecy of biblical times has materialized: the family of eleven that entered the ghetto has been violently reduced to three. Anya, like most protagonists of women's Holocaust narratives, must now rely on her own resources to sustain her seriously debilitated mother and helpless child. To make matters worse, the threats presented by hunger, disease, overcrowding, and primitive sanitation are joined by ever more frequent death selections of children, the aged, and the infirm.

Among the most heartrending aspects of women's Holocaust narrative is the Nazi assault on Jewish children and the valiant but futile efforts of their parents to save them. Some found refuge for their progeny in Catholic orphanages; others paid large sums of money to gentile families to shelter the children in their homes. A fortunate few among Jewish mothers were able to accompany their children to isolated farms and rural towns where, with the aid of false identity papers, they passed as Christians. As chronicled in Ettinger's autobiographical novel, parents with resistance connections occasionally managed to send their children into hiding with known benefactors. Others, like Schaeffer's young parents, who had economic means but no political connections, faced the dilemma of whether to relinquish a child to strangers who might abandon or exploit it or have the child share the fate of the family. The prevalent disinclination of Poles to save Jewish lives coupled with a decree condemning gentiles to death for sheltering Jews effectively circumscribed opportunities for sanctuary. Most Jewish children, like those in the writing of Ida Fink and Susan Fromberg Schaeffer, accompanied their parents to the ghettos and either preceded or joined them in mass graves and crematorium ovens.

One of the finest writers of the European catastrophe is Ida Fink, who lived as a child in a Polish ghetto through 1942 and then in hiding until the end of the war. She writes with power and restraint of the tragic fate of parents and children in *A Scrap of Time*, a haunting, delicately crafted collection of stories about the lives of ordinary people confronting the extraordinary circumstances of the Nazi universe. Representative of her exquisite tales is "A Spring Morning," relating a couple's excruciating decision concerning what to do with their five-year-old daughter when the Gestapo arrive to evacuate the Jews from their town. "If we had known," the woman said softly, "we wouldn't have had her. But how could we have known? Smarter people didn't know. She'll forgive us, . . . won't she?" The child understands that the approaching trucks signal their doom: "The child knew! Five years old! The age for teddy bears and blocks. Why did we have her? She'll never go to school, she'll never love."[21] Schaeffer, too devotes considerable attention to Anya and Stajoe's grappling, prior to ghettoization, about the best course for themselves and their infant. Anya's rejection of her husband's early plea that they flee with the two visas in their possession and leave Ninka in the protective custody of strangers seals the fate of the entire family.

Anya's struggle to preserve the life of her child is underscored by frantic attempts to secure food, illegal drugs, and hospitalization when Ninka contracts diphtheria, an illness that will condemn the child to lethal injection if the Germans discover her condition. Ninka's diphtheria is treated only because the ghetto doctor risks his life to care for the child of his former medical student. The absurdity of struggling to get Ninka well so that the Germans can later kill her is the catalyst for Anya's decision to smuggle her daughter out of the ghetto.

Complementing the emphasis in women's Holocaust writing on separation of mothers and children, and the heightened danger to mothers of young children, is the physical and psychological suffering of children. During the early ghetto period Ninka is fortunate to be surrounded by an extended family, for in their cooperative efforts the women are able to take time to play with her or tell her a story. Anya's sister, Vera, gives her a doll that the child names Vera Mouse, a doll that will later link her to the family she has forgotten. Schaeffer reveals much about Ninka's capacity to cope with the hardships of daily existence through play and story.[22] Vera tries to tell the child a winsome story about a golden egg, a story that would have charmed her in peacetime, but the hungry child rejects the fantasy, craving only a real egg. And when she is given an egg and asked whether she wants to feed her doll, the answer is a resounding "No!" Ninka will play with her doll, tell her stories, and put her to sleep. She will not squander precious food on her. The child's stories and language reflect Holocaust reality in the manner of Ida Fink's five-year-old in "A Spring Morning," who understood that the trucks were coming for her family. Similarly, Stajoe worries about how to tell Ninka that her storytelling Aunt Vera has been killed, but Anya insists that she knows. Fink's focus in *A Scrap of Time* is on the agony of anticipation or the pain of recollection rather than moments of extreme suffering in the ghettos and camps. Schaeffer concentrates on the endurance at the core of the Holocaust landscape.

Representation of the Holocaust understanding of these fictional children comports well with the assessment of Aaron Peretz, a Kovno Ghetto survivor who explains that children would "play grave-digging: they would dig a pit and would put a child inside and call him Hitler. And they would play at being gatekeepers of the ghetto. Some of the children played the parts of Germans, some of Jews, and the Germans were angry and would beat the other children who were Jews. And they used to play funerals. . . . The Jewish child was prematurely grown up. We were amazed to observe how children three or four years old understood the tragedy of the situation, how they clammed up when it was necessary, how they knew when to hide."[23]

In the relationship of Anya and Ninka, Schaeffer fuses two major themes of Holocaust literature: resistance and parental separation from or loss of children. She presents the ghetto separation of mother and child objectively in language devoid of emotional intensity. Mrs. Savikin and Anya prepare the child for transfer to a gentile family. They wash, dress, and preen Ninka and carefully instruct her to go with a Jewish ghetto policeman, who will deposit her at a church outside the ghetto gate; from there she is to depart with a stranger who will offer her something to eat. Thus, in the bizarre Nazi-controlled universe a mother counsels a child, in an ironic reversal of normal parental instruction, to accept gifts from and invitations to accompany strangers. Although Anya does not explicitly tell Ninka that they are parting, she warns the child, who seems to understand instinctively, that she must look cheerful and conceal the truth about her ghetto incarceration. Only after Ninka is beyond the ghetto walls does Anya articulate her despair, screaming and collapsing. Unlike most parents, who have no recourse to assistance, Anya is able to save her child through the intervention of organized ghetto resistance forces and the implied cooperation of Jacob Ganz. Through the same resistance organization she learns that Ninka is living with a judge and his wife who have secured false Lithuanian papers for her.

During the ghetto liquidation scene we discover what Ninka's fate would have been had Anya failed to smuggle her to safety. Snatched from ghetto rooms and hiding places, their parents impotent to protect them, children are given death injections. Babies, pulled from mothers' arms, are smashed against walls, their brains splattering. Mothers who resist are attacked by guard dogs, and their children suffer a similar fate. Anya watches as mothers, like a woman in Tadeusz Borowski's "This Way to the Gas, Ladies and Gentlemen," deny or surrender their children on command, because childless women are employable and therefore worthy of life. Although Borowski and Schaeffer present a similar situation, their tone and perspective vary markedly, due to differences between the observers' gender and prisoner status. Borowski's narrator is a male Polish kapo at Auschwitz who unloads arriving prisoners from the transports and dispatches their belongings to the camp warehouse. His lot is better than that of Jewish prisoners, for he reaps scraps from the Nazi plunder of foodstuffs, clothing, and valuables confiscated from the new arrivals. In Borowski's world, where the differentiation between tormentor and victim is blurred, the prisoner kapo claims to feel no pity for the Jewish women and children bound for the gas chamber, only fury with the victims, whose presence requires his own at the ramp. Yet he is sick to his stomach watching another privileged prisoner attack a "young, healthy, good-looking" woman who tries to save herself by deserting her small child. Outraged by such apparent lack of maternal loyalty, the Russian knocks the woman down, berates her as "a bloody Jewess . . . a whore . . . bitch," and tosses her, with her child, onto the truck bound for the gas chamber.[24] Borowski's hardened male prisoner engineers the death of mother and child, and the narrator is distressed at his companion's brutality but uninterested in the mother's plight. Schaeffer focuses not on the perpetrator's but on the woman's emotional reactions. Her young mother finds maternal surrender of children incomprehensible yet bears no animosity toward her ghetto sister. In contrast to the male-authored scene, which is dramatized in all its fury, Schaeffer presents hers indirectly as a postwar recollection, an example of the frightful aspects of the Nazi universe that account for the survivor's long-term trauma, a mother's lament for a woman whose child was murdered.

Unlike Borowski, Ida Fink, and Cynthia Ozick, who dramatize parents' witness to the slaughter of their children, Schaeffer consistently adopts an indirect method. This aspect of parental agony is mediated by Anya's impressions and response rather than in the voices of the victimized women. Fink's direct approach in "A Spring Morning" is far more compelling in its focus on the parents' witness. As Fink's family is being marched to the deportation trains, the father desperately attempts to save his daughter by instructing her to run into the crowd in front of the church to seek help.

The child obeys; the parents march forward and hear a furious shriek: "Ein judisches Kind!" followed by a shot. Rather than shoot the grieving father, the German officer punishes the parent further by forcing him to march forward carrying his dead child.

Role reversal between parents and mature children, commonplace in ghetto and concentration camp and a recurrent theme in women's Holocaust writing, is another means Schaeffer uses to suggest the debilitating effects of the ghetto. Anya's and Mrs. Savikin's capacities to slip into each other's roles shows a fluidity of boundaries between the women that includes intergenerational psychological interaction and union. As we have seen, in the early stages of ghetto imprisonment Mrs. Savikin is strong, wary, and knowledgeable in dealing with the enemy, representative of a paradigm of able mothers visible in the Holocaust fiction of most women writers. She insists that Anya maintain a good physical appearance to convince the Nazis that she is fit to work and is therefore fit to live. Through a growing pattern of role reversal paralleling Mrs. Savikin's deterioration, Anya becomes the maternal protector, securing food for her mother and hiding her during "actions." During the ghetto liquidation, their final scene together, Anya daubs her mother's lips and cheeks with rouge as the elderly parent "stood still, like a good child" (211), and bribes a guard to allow the aged woman to march with those younger and healthier toward the waiting transport. As they try to pass another checkpoint, the women are forcibly separated, Mrs. Savikin sent to the extermination line and Anya pushed onto the train bound for the Kaiserwald labor camp. The novel's last ghetto scene rings true to the historic account of the 1943 Vilna Ghetto liquidation. The older population was dispatched to Ponary to be shot, five thousand others were sent to Majdanek death camp, and the able-bodied were consigned to serve in the vast slave labor empire that included Kaiserwald.[25]

In a study of women's Holocaust testimony Sara Horowitz isolates a final conversation with the mother who perished as a critical factor in the surviving daughter's struggle to live. Of the psychological and moral benefit of the mother's parting words, Horowitz writes: "They give the daughter permission to survive and to rebuild her life. . . . The mother's words contain a moral imperative, both collective and personal. On a personal level, the message urges the daughter neither to imitate the Nazis nor to absorb the image they project of her, but to retain a sense of self predicated on the mother's values. On a collective level, the words make of the daughter a witness, enjoining her to remember the victims, to tell the story of those who perished and cannot speak for themselves."[26]

Mrs. Savikin's last service to her daughter is to arm Anya with hope by prophesying that she will survive. The mother's parting words: "You will live! You have someone for whom to live!" (212) become Anya's mantra.

Transition from the ghetto is achieved in a brutal cattle-car transport to Kaiserwald. As Cynthia Haft observes of French concentrationary writing, the trip may be viewed metonymically.[27] Overcrowding, hunger, thirst, and lack of sanitary facilities are meant by the Nazis to reduce the victims to subhuman status and to presage camp conditions. One hundred and fifty people are packed into the boxcar, crammed so tightly that they cannot fall down. Anya leans against two other women who are pressing against her and sleeps while standing. For the most part, the physical hardships of the journey dominate Schaeffer's writing: "The wheels of the train turned, the wheels of the body turned, the wheels of hunger spun, the mind jammed and played the same scenes over and over" (216). The train stops briefly to clear out the dead and take on a kettle of water, and Anya gazes longingly at the forest, imagining the Polish peasants enjoying their normal lives, and she briefly considers jumping from the train. Anya's liberation fantasy is juxtaposed with a real escape by a woman who summons the strength to pull two boards loose and jump free. Within moments a shot is heard. During the forty-eight-hour train ordeal Anya wavers between capitulation and willful assertion, occasionally withdrawing behind her eyelids, sometimes gaining solace from memories of her parents, other times fearful that she has crossed the border to insanity. In the end, instead of a precipitous escape effort, Anya's will to survive is manifested in heeding her mother's admonition to look her best to impress the Nazis that she is strong enough to be of value in the slave labor force.

"The Lion's Jaws" chronicles Anya's ordeal in Riga's infamous work camp, where half the inmates were women working for the Wehrmacht and Luftwaffe.[28] Gertrude Schneider, survivor of Kaiserwald and author and editor of three books on the Latvian Holocaust experience, writes of the traumatic Kaiserwald reception created by "professional criminals," gentiles serving prison terms at the camp, who shouted obscenities, beat, and kicked the defenseless Jews on arrival until they were inside the camp gate. Schneider's description of the induction process confirms the novelist's rendering. Schneider writes:

> After all remaining possessions were taken away, . . . the prisoners were taken to the showers, a procedure which turned out to be both painful and complicated. First, everyone had to strip. Then, the SS men, with

much relish, would examine the hair of each person for lice. At that point, there were no lice, but still, whenever they felt like it, the Nazis would order long hair on a woman cut very short, or a man's head shaved. Body hair, too, was removed, and a vile-smelling solution was smeared over armpits and pubic area. Finally came the shower, either ice-cold or scalding hot. Then, dripping wet, they would receive "new" clothes. These were all rags and invariably, the taller inmates got very short garments, while the short and skinny people almost fell out of theirs.[29]

Unlike the survivor's sparse journalistic report, which attributes "relish" to the SS men, the novelist's dramatic rendition incorporates self-damning dialogue and graphic juxtaposition of the women's pain with the soldiers' pornographic sadism:

"This is a segregation point; some of you go on from here to other camps, the rest stay here. First is a physical examination. So, . . . you take off all your clothes and leave them on the side of the barracks and then come outside." . . . So we stood there in the winter sunlight. . . . "So," one said approaching me, "lice, eh?" He pinched my nipples. "And how is this, after the trip, all dirty, eh?" He pulled my pubic hair. . . . My stomach was heaving and heaving. . . . "Gasoline for you," he said, "for the lice," and then the next man came along and it began again. My breasts were so sore I could feel the pain in my toes. . . . "So . . . we will take your clothes; they're filthy—I'm surprised at you girls, your age, too— . . . we take care of your hair. And stoop over when the men get to you; they have to check your rectums for ringworms and bleeding; it's for your own good, only for your own good." . . . We saw the hair falling from the heads of the women, . . . My blond hair! Look how they're taking it off in chunks. . . . He was finished with me. I put my hand up to my head. It was rough and prickly, . . . Then a man began coming down the rows with a canister of gasoline and another clipper; he clipped the hair under our arms, then our pubic hair. "Why should it hurt so much?" I wondered, and then came the gasoline from the can, poured all over my hair, from head to toe. "Bend over," he ordered, pouring it down my back, then spreading my behind, pouring it in. It burned; . . . I was drenched in it. . . . I was biting my lip from the burning. (221–23)

Racism and sexism characterize the guards' strategy for forcing their victims to realize their utter loss of autonomy in the camp universe. The novelist's selection and arrangement of detail and her focus on assaulted female anatomy impart an even more effective understanding of the humiliation and degradation imposed on the women than does the survivor's powerful but objective, less lurid account. Whereas the survivor-historian's description focuses on the commonality of experience men and women endure, the novelist's prose specifically genders the humiliation with emphasis on women's vulnerability implicit in shorn hair, mauled breasts, probed rectums, and chemically burned vaginas—offenses transparently mischaracterized as medical procedures "for their own good" that simultaneously sexually assault the victims and strip them of feminine attributes.

The dramatic contrast with a camp induction scene written by Primo Levi suggests that although men experienced the procedure as humiliation, their psychological and physical discomfort was not gender-based. Levi writes brilliantly of the dehumanization prisoners endured in Auschwitz, describing it as a loss of individuality and autonomy.

> When we finish, everyone remains in his own corner and we do not dare lift our eyes to look at one another. There is nowhere to look in a mirror, but our appearance stands in front of us, reflected in a hundred livid faces, in a hundred miserable and sordid puppets. We are transformed into the phantoms glimpsed yesterday evening. . . . In a moment, with almost prophetic intuition, the reality was revealed to us: we had reached the bottom. It is not possible to sink lower than this. . . . Nothing belongs to us anymore; they have taken away our clothes, our shoes, even our hair; if we speak, they will not listen to us, and if they listen, they will not understand. They will even take away our name: and if we want to keep it, we will have to find ourselves the strength to do so, to manage somehow so that behind the name something of us, of us as we were, still remains.[30]

There is not a word in the male writer's devastating description suggesting sexual assault or concern about diminished sexual attractiveness or procreative capacity. The reductive experience denies men the trappings of social status and assaults their personhood rather than their sex and gender.

Gendered also are Schaeffer's clothing tropes to represent the pre-Shoah and Shoah-era status of Jewish women. As a matter of policy, ill-fitting clothing is distributed to the women as one element of their humiliation, a short dress to a very tall woman and a huge dress to petite Anya. This scene is an inverse echo of a prewar fitting in which Anya and Vera engage the services of a sought-after designer who will create two stylish outfits for each sister. When the "prickly head" camp inmate shivers in a cold shower or observes women drying themselves with an old sweater, the reader remembers the luxury of Anya's pre-Shoah life: two women washed her hair: "one half of the head at a time, . . . after the third rinsing, . . . [they] would take the half of the hair that was washed and comb it and braid it [and as she held a towel over the braid,] they would start on the other side" (227–28). These images of love, cleanliness, order, and comfort underscore the brutal conditions at the camp. Schaeffer can refrain from explicit juxtaposition of these parallel scenes, for her early descriptions of the opulent life of the protagonist are so detailed that the reader contrasts the prewar passages with their ghetto and camp counterparts.

In addition to gendering the brutality of the induction scene, Schaeffer fuses bonding and resistance themes in this and subsequent scenes of the Kaiserwald initiation. Anya's capacity to withstand the soldiers' brutalities during the camp induction without comment and to keep her wits about her is essential to her own survival and to that of a young girl so paralyzed by fear that she is unable to follow orders. Sonya, whom Anya met in the transport, is representative of those overwhelmed by terror, those whose spirits are broken by the indignities they are forced to bear. Anya's virtual adoption of Sonya ensures the waif's inclusion in her own survival plans. Like many women who cite the model of their mothers' competence and ingenuity as essential to their own survival and the help they extend to friends, Anya follows her mother's model in her protective embrace of the pathetic, forlorn girl. The women are assigned to barracks, and Anya selects a bunk for them far from the door, the better to escape random selections, a bunk on the top tier in the center of the barrack to be out of range of discarded lice. Without explanation, Anya simply commands Sonya to follow her lead, for the girl is unable to think in concentrationary terms and is still guided by prewar judgment. Innocent of the hygienic virtues of the fourth-level bunk Anya has selected, Sonya complains of the inconvenience of climbing to such heights without benefit of a ladder. Like the supportive inmates of Ilona Karmel's *Estate of Memory*, Anya repeatedly tries to buoy Sonya's spirits, counseling her to think of life after the camp rather than succumbing to the indignities of the present. Anya is the source of the discipline, advice, and love that Sonya must have to resist the forces dedicated to her destruction.

Representative of Schaeffer's able delineation of Kaiserwald adversity is her depiction of the starved and ill-clad women engaged in backbreaking labor despite inclement weather. Pieces of Anya's skin freeze on the pump she uses in her construction job. Her hands are so cold she is unable to grip her bowl and loses part of her maggoty soup, scorching rather than nourishing herself with the meager rations. The first time the ninety-pound prisoner tries to hoist a heavy canister of gasoline she feels as though she "would crack in half at the waist" (229). Eventually, she lifts and fills canisters, moving like a robot, working faster and faster until another prisoner cautions her to slow down lest she become exhausted and weakened, a likely candidate for a death selection.

Eschewing Karmel's focus on the dynamics of the camp community, Schaeffer centers her attention on an individual and treats the group primarily in connection to the protagonist. She introduces the tension of communal interaction under the pressure of extreme deprivation by briefly shifting attention from her idealized protagonist to group dynamics. Like Karmel, she incorporates evidence of jealousy and selfishness among the camp inmates, thereby heightening the text's reliability as authentic representation of women under duress, demonstrating how chronic hunger and severe physical deprivation reveal the worst and best in victims. Anya recognizes that her barrack mates will be jealous because she works in the commandant's warm house rather than in construction during the bitter winter, that they will envy the shoes she is given to prevent her from tracking blood on the commandant's polished floors. Envy and resentment lead to violence when possession of a crust of bread is a paramount concern. A thief is accorded swift judgment by starving peers: she is beaten to death. Antithetically, and more characteristically, hunger leads the women to endanger their lives for one another. Like Karmel's Barbara and Tola, Anya risks punishment to smuggle food for hospitalized inmates. On one occasion she is flogged for stealing two eggs for her sick friend. The beating leaves her barely able to stand and walk. Like survivors who describe inmates using their privileged jobs to help barrack mates and friends, Anya takes advantage of her cleaning job in the commandant's household to systematically pilfer food for hospital patients. Responding to a guard's protective admonition that she stop this reckless behavior, Anya justifies providing the women with food, for "they're sure they'll be cured if they can have these special things" (248), and because she hopes their blessings will keep her distant from the death selections.

Schaeffer's Kaiserwald scenes characteristically forego the horrors of Auschwitz, its medical experimentation and torture blocks, its Zyklon B shower rooms and crematoria. On occasion, however, Schaeffer elevates the dramatic presentation of routine labor camp hardship by symbolic evocation of death camp atrocities. She invokes the crematoria metaphorically in a scene of the women locked in their barrack, helplessly watching as flames engulf an adjacent building. The women can do nothing but await their turn to burn. Schaeffer's description of the women, like "ants in a jar," at once suggests their helplessness in the face of German power and evokes Nazi-Deutsche diction likening Jews to vermin. In this section Schaeffer's prose captures the impotence and terror of the inmates in a manner that is reminiscent of the description by Auschwitz and Belsen survivor Zdena Berger of women's vulnerability as they are stored in overcrowded barracks with boarded windows, "women in boxes."[31] Knees pulled up to her chin, Berger's protagonist feels another's knees in her back. Someone in front of her sits on her feet. Her elbows poke other elbows, and she cannot straighten her arms. The women remain caged in these wooden containers, silently watching the darkness, anticipating death, expecting to fill the chimney, much as Anya's barrack mates expect to go up in flames.

Far different from the futility established in the barrack fire scene is Schaeffer's treatment of resistance from within and beyond the walls of ghetto and labor camp, through individual and collective agency at every stage of the Holocaust. During the ghetto phases Stajoe uses his position as building commander, a post that made him privy to advance notice of house searches, deportations, and death selections, to inform the family, enabling them to cheat the executioner. Mrs. Savikin's repeated concealment in a large Russian stove evokes the historic expertise of Vilna Jews at creating "malinas" — cellars, bunkers, attic closets, secret rooms, all sorts of hiding places where the endangered waited out the raids.[32] Schaeffer's Vilna ghetto residents, like their historical models, are more aware of German intentions than were the Warsaw Jews, who believed the Germans were merely trying to extract as much money from their hostages as possible, or the Lodz Jews, who believed they could save their lives by being a productive and indispensable slave labor force.

Although Schaeffer's decision to work only from the testimony of personal acquaintances and their circle has the virtue of dramatic immediacy and authenticity, the novel is circumscribed by the small sampling of witness experience and knowledge, by what those interviewees wanted to communicate or believed the interviewer wanted to hear.[33] We learn of the wider role of resistance in *Anya* only through occasional reference to beleaguered Jews and isolated Christians risking their lives to smuggle medicine and food into the ghetto and to convey children out and conceal fugitives. They accomplish these feats with the assistance of the Jewish police, inmates who have permits to work outside the ghetto, and the rare sympathetic Pole or Lithuanian. There are brief references to and a single appearance of "the electrician," a member of a resistance network, who confirmed plans for an adoptive family and logistics for smuggling Ninka out of the ghetto and brought news of Stajoe's torture and murder.

In the sexually segregated barracks of the camp universe, relationships developed between the women and privileged male prisoners, known as "cousins." These benefactors, working as camp doctors, kapos, block leaders, and labor supervisors, would, for political or personal motives, provide their favorites extra food, better jobs, and advance warning of "actions." Crucial to Anya's survival and eventual escape from Kaiserwald is her association with a protective male. Unlike women who were protected openly by Jewish fellow prisoners in Karmel's world, however, Anya's unlikely patron, Erdmann, is a Jew masquerading as a German soldier. The convention of Jews passing as Christians to flee the concentrationary world takes the bizarre form here of a metamorphosed Jew using his feigned persona to remain at the core of the Nazi orb, like the impostors of Jakov Lind's *Counting My Steps* and Solomon Perel in Agneiska Holland's film *Europa, Europa*. In contrast to those venues, which realistically tie Nazi pretense to public Jew-baiting, Erdmann neither harms Jews nor speaks ill of them in the company of fellow officers. He works within the German military to evade detection, as he pursues a dual mission of personal survival and assistance to Jewish prisoners. For Aryan-featured Anya, he secures a position as a cleaning woman in the camp commander's quarters. In this context he provides her with extra food, surreptitiously assists her with the heavier cleaning chores and encourages the *Hauptmann* to order warm clothing for her winter marches from the barracks to his home. With Erdmann's recommendation, Anya makes herself indispensable to the commandant as a Russian translator, assisting with interrogation of prisoners of war. Her new work is less physically demanding but more psychologically stressful. Guarded less closely, Anya begins to consider escape and reunion with Ninka, especially after Erdmann implores her to flee before a scheduled tattooing.

Although Erdmann's story has precedent in Holocaust history, it is fictional invention, the most far-fetched of the novel, and is reflective of the American tendency to privilege individual heroism.[34] Erdmann exploits his German disguise to alleviate prisoner misery by allowing a slave laborer a short rest during work, by providing additional food and securing a better job for an inmate, and most valiantly, by orchestrating Anya's escape and reunion with Ninka. Schaeffer renders the fantastic somewhat more credible by framing it in realistic detail. Relying on knowledge of SS corruption, Erdmann passes off his accomplice in Anya's escape as a black marketeer doing business in Kaiserwald. Another realistic element is Anya's deferral of the escape plan because Erdmann's risk is too great. When his conspiratorial role is less detectable, Anya flees. Erdmann's explanation that by appropriating a German identity he facilitates aiding fellow Jews reflects the resistance work of Jews in "special circumstances" on behalf of their beleaguered brethren. Anya and Erdmann exemplify a theory of psychiatrist and Auschwitz survivor Victor Frankl, who argues that "the sort of person the prisoner became was the result of an inner decision, and not the result of camp influences alone; that the inmate had a measure of choice regarding response to atrocity; that apathy could be overcome, irritability suppressed; that . . . [one] can preserve a vestige of spiritual freedom, of independence of mind, even in such terrible conditions of psychic and physical stress."[35] Like the survivors Frankl commends, Erdmann and Anya maintain their dignity as they act generously to protect others. The novelist's treatment of Anya's resolve to survive is congruent with Frankl's view that a prisoner's will to live was dependent on having a future.

Schaeffer renders Anya's fugitive period dramatically and metaphorically, in days marked by an alternating pattern of triumph and defeat. On a metaphoric level, gender-specificity surfaces in Schaeffer's incorporation of two commonly treated aspects of women's writing on the subject of menstruation—the awkwardness and danger of bleeding, which would bring unwanted attention, and the diametrically opposed signification of regeneration through return of normal menstruation. Anya's unchecked menstrual flow is perilous to her moving about Riga undetected. She is terrified of her "blood, . . . all over Riga, a trail, like in Hansel and Gretel" (269). Yet her period is also a symbol of restoration, of improved health related to her privileged work status in Kaiserwald that facilitates her escape and approaching reunion with her daughter. On a dramatic level, danger of detection is not limited to gender-specific conditions. Threatened by a Gestapo search party while visiting Ninka at the Rutkauskus home, she hides in her daughter's bed, under the weight of two heavy mattresses, a poignant echo of her husband's concealment in his parent's Warsaw home during the early roundups. This internment imagery in conjunction with her concealment in an oven suggests the persistent likelihood of her arrest and return to captivity. The brush with death and deliverance occurs on her birthday, which falls in April, the celebratory season of Jewish delivery from Egyptian bondage.

Separation and reunion of mother and daughter, absent in male Holocaust writing, is thoroughly developed in women's writing, and Schaeffer explores it with great sensitivity and psychological complexity. Throughout the novel

Schaeffer maintains the theme of sundered families, especially the separation of mother and child, as a subtext of every plot complication. The majority of works by women feature an adolescent daughter or young adult who tells her mother's story. Schaeffer extends the pattern by presenting three generations and adds complexity by departing from the mutually supportive mother-daughter association of mature women to address the peril-fraught and ambiguous relationship of mother and helpless, dependent child, whose separation leads to temporary estrangement. Unlike the mother-daughter relationship of Mrs. Savikin and Anya, which was developed in prewar normalcy, Anya's relationship with her daughter is configured primarily by Holocaust suffering and separation. The relationship undergoes severe emotional shifts alternating from hate to love, suspicion to trust, resentment to attachment. Fiercely protective of her child's welfare, Anya willingly risks the dangers of her escape from Kaiserwald and her search for Ninka. Grateful for Ninka's safety, she nonetheless resents not only her benefactor's usurpation of the maternal role but her daughter's transference of filial affection to the Lithuanian woman whom she now calls "Mommiti." This rancor may be understood and judged psychologically credible in light of Susan Suleiman's analysis of women's indignation in the face of "maternal-splitting." Suleiman contends that mothers are often anxious about transference of children's affections to surrogate mother figures who care for them.[36] Anya's jealousy is motivated by fear of displacement in her child's affections by an "other" mother who has accepted responsibility for the child's safety.

If, as Suleiman and other feminists argue, anxiety is provoked in peacetime by "maternal-splitting," how much more intense must the phenomenon have been in the Holocaust context, despite the biological mother's intellectual awareness that surrendering the child to another meant saving its life. How bitter it is to know that the survival of one's child depends on a stranger's protective custody and that only in time will the child understand that circumstance. Anya expresses her anger in interior discourse as she is concealed in an oven during a Gestapo raid: "If it wasn't for that miserable child who called Onucia Mommiti, and me, beggar, I could have spent the rest of the war . . . in complete safety. I sat there hating her. . . . I wished I were back in the camp" (300). This inner maternal discourse may be shocking, yet on reflection it is credible. Had war not interrupted her life, she might have continued to resist the "masochistic-feminine willingness to sacrifice" that traditional psychoanalytical theory attributes to good mothers.[37] Shoah transformation engenders behavior that situates her directly in this psychoanalytic sacrificial paradigm: on several occasions Anya willingly endangers her life on Ninka's behalf. Her inner thoughts, however, reveal her anger with the reality that maternity is an obstacle to her survival. Although her behavior is a response to a more fundamental code, the honesty of her thought attests to the tension between maternal love and self-preservation.

Ambiguity governs Anya's feelings toward Onucia Rutkauskus. Acknowledging her jealousy of the woman who has usurped her maternal role and her child's affection, Anya also feels deep shame for harboring such feelings toward the woman who has done her a great service. Because she takes comfort from the security and love Onucia has provided Ninka despite the dire consequences for harboring Jews, Anya's enmity dissolves. Each woman is acutely sensitive to the jealous love the other has for Ninka, and they bond in that love. Paralleling the maternal figures' competition for the child's loyalty is the child's need to conceal her affection for Anya from Onucia. Despite her youth, "she felt the terrible undertow of jealousy between all of us" (291).

Schaeffer is one of the few novelists to chart the toll of separation on mother and child with thorough development of both maternal trauma and the child's psychic wounds. When Anya finally locates her daughter at war's end, in a Catholic orphanage where she was placed after her surrogate parents' arrest, mother and child are strangers once more. Their reunion is fraught with reverberations and inversions of the clandestine farm meeting. Ninka remains emotionally divided by her Holocaust experience, continuing to claim her Lithuanian identity, insisting that her mother is Onucia, and prating Catholic prayers while vehemently spurning her true identity. To make matters worse, Anya is unable to recognize the starved, lice-infested creature as her child. At this stage the child views adults as temporary protectors and asks Anya how long she will keep her. Only when Anya identifies the Vera Mouse doll is Ninka convinced of their relationship and ready to relinquish her assumed Lithuanian identity. Healing begins, and within a short time the pattern of parent-child role reversals emerges as Ninka nurses Anya through an illness.

The Savikin family saga gains its credibility from Schaeffer's dramatic parallel to the collective history. Her overt linkage of Nazi racism and traditional Christian antisemitism provides a broader contextual base for the family narrative. Aside from the courageous efforts of a few righteous gentiles, antisemitic Christians menace Jews at every stage of the narrative's chronology. "In History" situates Nazi antisemitism in the continuum of European history. Its connection to antecedent Christian antisemitism is depicted in Mrs. Savikin's recollection of discriminatory Russian Czarist-era law, which prescribed a Pale of Settlement that segregated Jews to certain geographic areas where they could live and work. She also recounts the peril she and her sisters experienced during a 1914 pogrom when they slept in coffins to elude rampaging peasants intent on rape, pillage, and murder of local Jews. Another mass murder claimed her brother's life. Prewar Polish economic and cultural antisemitism is revealed when, despite stellar qualifications, Anya must beg the university head to admit her to medical school because she is a Jewess. The violent face of Polish antisemitism emerges in a misogynist assault with iron nails on Jewish university women by their classmates, whose goal was to "go after the faces of the beautiful girls, and demolish them" (59). Polish collaboration in the Nazi genocide is evident when a boy betrays Anya's father to unsuspecting German soldiers and when a German believes Anya is a Pole because she spews antisemitic rhetoric as a way to gain access to the site where her father's body has been dumped among "hundreds and hundreds of bodies" (162). The novel's antisemitic violence is neither the exclusive province of hooligans encouraged by civil and church authorities nor attributable to mob hysteria. Furthermore, it is not limited to the Holocaust era but is shown as pervasive in prewar Poland, as well as at the height of the Nazi terror, when the family attorney refuses legal assistance to Stajoe, who is under a Gestapo death threat, and in the postwar period, when a bank colleague of Anya's father dupes Anya into delivering black market goods. These fictional examples of the Polish educated elite's embrace of anti-semitism intimates the genocidal accountability of the German intelligentsia and professional class, the engineers who designed the gas chambers, the physicians who engaged in human medical experimentation, and the judges who upheld racist legislation. Members of the Polish lower classes are gleeful beneficiaries of Jewish suffering. Peasants descend on the Savikin household like "a swarm of black bees filling the house" (167). Later Anya compares them to vultures: "They were robbing our house as if they were plundering our graves, [she charges]. . . . It made no difference to them. According to the peasants, we were already dead" (170). Schaeffer's representation of the Poles' theft of Jewish property shares the bitter tone of survivor Berta Ferderber-Salz, whose memoir, *And the Sun Kept Shining* . . . , attests to the plunder. She writes: "Poles hastened to the Jewish houses from all parts of the city and took what they could. Property that had been acquired through the hard work of generations was lost forever. The Jews who entered the ghetto had no property; they were paupers."[38]

More sinister than the pillage of Jewish possessions is Polish betrayal of Jewish compatriots to the Nazis in full knowledge that the innocents will be killed. Schaeffer's moral outrage is conveyed in a scene mediated by the well-meaning, loyal Christian servant who reports: "They're collecting Jews. . . . The little children will point out who are the Jews on the street, and they will grab them" (160). Astonished, Anya inquires whether they will be jailed, and Anzia replies, "No, not at all, . . . the little boy said they wanted to kill. The soldier said he would teach him to shoot squirrels so later he could shoot Jews" (160). Three years later, when the Lithuanian population is well acquainted with the fate of Jews under Nazi dominion, Anya finds that such acquiescent attitudes about surrendering Jewish victims to their killers have not abated. In the guise of a gentile co-worker, Anya is privy to the sentiments of ordinary laundry women who relate the tale of a woman who unknowingly harbored a Jewish child: "Imagine it, taking it in, you think it's normal . . . and it turns out to be a Jew" (311). Female protective and nurturing attitudes toward helpless children are grotesquely inverted to illustrate antisemitism's insidious character.

Schaeffer's treatment of the postwar Polish refusal to return the bounty of Holocaust-era thievery and the sporadic murder of Jewish survivors is reflective of American-born writers' tendency to devote considerably more attention to pre- and postwar Holocaust history than do European émigrés. Anya experiences such hostile response from Poles who had no intention of losing the benefits they accrued from Jewish losses in exchange for delivering the owners to the Nazis.[39] Neighbors who looted the Savikin household would rather see Anya and Ninka perish than return even a small portion of their ill-gotten gains. Their greed demoralizes Anya, making her feel she is a burglar in her parents' home, and triggers her first postwar nightmares. Equally greedy are peasants who would rather see survivors starve than sell them food at fair rates. The price Anya must pay for two eggs is her mother's recently retrieved diamond ring.

Dramatic presentation of Anya's changing response to antisemitism signifies the positive evolution of her Jewish identity. Prewar passivity gives way to wartime and postwar militancy. Gone is the girlish need to engage in self-mutilation out of guilt for having escaped unscathed while her classmates were disfigured. Gone are the timidity and terror that gripped her while her home was looted by Polish peasants. After being schooled in ghetto and labor camp, Anya risks denunciation during her fugitive period by rebuking a woman for giving Ninka antisemitic drawings and instructing the child to avoid Jews or risk being devoured. Similarly, when former neighbors reject her plea for return of a portion of her family's property, she brings Soviet soldiers to their home to press her case.

The realistic mode and historic breadth of the novel are advanced in Schaeffer's meticulous economic and political contextualization of postwar Poland. Rather than conclude the novel with liberation or a perfunctory summation of postwar European corruption before whisking her protagonist off to America, Schaeffer adheres to her pattern of scrupulous attention to detail, resulting in a richly textured tapestry of postwar political intrigue, individual and state antisemitism, and black market corruption. Typical of victims who continue the practices they employed to survive the camps, Anya forges alliances of mutual support, finds help for Ninka's medical problems from her former medical school professor, and accepts aid from a resourceful street urchin who not only facilitates her reconciliation with Ninka but helps her outwit the criminals who have implicated her in black market activities. In addition to the physical and psychological toll of her ordeal, Anya is entangled in the bureaucratic and political machinations of Communist Poland and denied permission to emigrate to Israel. Central to her postwar rejuvenation is a Jewish-American philanthropist working for the United Nations Relief and Rehabilitation Administration through whom food, medicine, and passage to America for mother and child are secured.

To illuminate what the Holocaust meant to her heroine, Schaeffer believes she had to reveal not only what Anya lost but what she became. Anya exemplifies Elie Wiesel's aphorism that for the survivor, "the Holocaust continued after the Holocaust."[40] Survival does not presage a return to prewar normalcy. She feels the sharp contrast between returning home and returning to life. Anya remains forever wounded, forever disillusioned, and nothing will reconstitute the wholeness of her being. "And Then There Were None" continues her story twenty-five years into the postwar period, establishing the searing, long-term influence of the Holocaust on the survivor's life. In contrast to the prologue's brief, dramatic, and metaphoric introduction to survivor hardships, the epilogue develops the topic reflectively. As for many survivors, the Holocaust dictates everything about Anya's postwar life. Her decision to remarry is founded on her pride in her second husband's successful delivery of his father's murderer to trial. She and Max live and work in a run-down neighborhood in order to be among fellow survivors, the only people they trust and the only people who "can understand what it was like" (475). They abort a pregnancy and forgo having children to avoid afflicting a child with the psychological freight of their own Holocaust trauma. Anya's postwar parenting of Ninka is dominated by their Holocaust history, revealing "many of the clinical characteristics observed in

survivor patients: overprotectiveness, overidentification with children, . . .
and obsession with health in the form of insuring proper nutrition."[41] It is
in her fiercely protective relationship with Ninka, who is both a link to the
past and hope for the future, and in her concern for the welfare of Ninka's
children that Anya's postwar commitments to the continuity of Judaism and
the Jewish people manifest themselves.

Schaeffer endows Anya with characteristic symptoms of survivor syndrome. The survivor still perceives herself as psychically attached to Kaiserwald by "an invisible umbilical cord, infinitely elastic and infinitely strong,
one that could never be cut" (362). Powerfully associated with life and
nurturing, the umbilical image is ironically inverted in the Holocaust female
consciousness as a restraint, a chain depriving the victim of a normal life, and
so functions as a symbol of Holocaust despair and the trauma of survivor
syndrome. Body images prevail in the memory of a humiliating beating
while she was "bent over a bench, naked from the waist; . . . the guard
dipping his leather tongs in water before beating [her] across the bottom"
(362). Even in America feelings of insecurity and fear of renewed persecution
recur. She proclaims: "I am used to danger. I can't understand a life without
it. . . . If suffering isn't there, I have to find it" (475). She experiences chronic
depressive states, a guilt complex, nightmares, psychosomatic complaints,
and deadened feelings, describing herself as "one of the walking dead" (474).
Guilt vexes her conscious hours and her dreams as Anya blames herself for
failing to save her family. She is tormented by the discrepancy of the death
of her loved ones and her own survival. Again and again she dreams that her
dead parents are inquiring about her welfare and urging her to join them.
Underscoring the trauma is her dream of a family reunion in a mansion
filled with the objects that adorned the Savikin home, material things that
objectified the loving, respectful family relationship. Similarly, because she
feels responsible for Stajoe's death, having refused to escape Poland with
him, she dreams of his jealousy of her life with Max and of his insistence
that she join him.

Although her postwar life is governed by the Shoah, Anya meditates
on its impact and her Holocaust metamorphosis infrequently and unsys-
tematically, a pattern established before liberation. In a rare introspective
sequence, set in a barnyard stove where she is hiding from the Gestapo,
Anya correlates the rhythms of the stove to the rhythms of the Kaiserwald-
bound train, rhythms that unleash a flood of memories kindling an epiphanal
insight: "My life was not continuous; it would never be continuous again.
Something, the world, or history, had intervened like a terrible editor of

a movie, snatching out handfuls of characters, changing the sets wildly" (301). From this point Schaeffer abruptly shifts from film to train imagery and back to film editing, suggestive of Holocaust disruption and survivor splicing: "Life is a train constantly crossing the border from the past to the present. . . . The war had transported the whole train into the future which looked the same as the past, where all the rooms were the same, and none of the people were the same and none of the people spoke the same language. And now my mind was doing it, too, cutting pieces of the film randomly with clumsy scissors, without anesthetic, and the victim never knowing anything had been taken" (301). The fragmented prose and shifts from tropes of film editing to train movement attest to her wartime emotional anxiety and project a future defiled and impaired by Holocaust memories. The film imagery in her reverie anticipates the brief postwar meditation on chronic Holocaust intrusion in the aftermath of the war. While rationalizing the increasing frequency of dreams in which she converses with her parents many years after their deaths, Anya observes, "The film which has recorded the story of my life was spliced one third through to an irrelevant reel by a maniac, . . . what began in the past will never continue in the future" (469–70). This passage figuratively and grammatically yokes the individual's destiny to the collective fate of the Jewish people.

A critical manifestation of Anya's trauma is her incapacity to pursue her prewar career ambitions. After a quarter of a century of life in America Anya juxtaposes her pre-Holocaust ambitions, when she thought she could accomplish anything, to her Holocaust-infected perspective of limited expectations and narrow options. Attempts to recoup her medical career, even in the amended role of nurse, fail. In sharp divergence from her prewar and wartime capacity to work with severely ill patients, even to perform a primitive operation on a friend, she is unable to assist during an operation in a well-equipped American hospital or tolerate the sight of a terminally ill child. Career interests and professionalism have lost their significance for this shattered woman, as they have for Saul Bellow's Arthur Sammler, Edward Lewis Wallant's Sol Nazerman, and Cynthia Ozick's Rosa Lublin. Instead of pursuing her medical career, Anya retreats to an antique shop, reminiscent of the one in which Schaeffer discovered her primary survivor-informant, a confined space Anya symbolically characterizes as "so tiny sometimes I feel as if we are living in a coffin" (471). Like Sol Nazerman's cage in *The Pawnbroker* and Rosa Lublin's cramped antique shop and seedy hotel room in *The Shawl*, the claustrophobic environment serves as literary trope for camp incarceration.

Like most survivors, Anya experiences voluntary and involuntary Holo-caust memories. Representative of the latter and suggestive of the horrors she tries to repress is a memory of a Gestapo officer dashing a little boy into a tree, the child's "skull shatter[ing] like an egg" (473). Troubled by such persistent memories, Anya seeks a psychiatrist to help her repress the past and achieve a healthier present, "to make me forget the whole war; that terrible thing that killed everyone, that changed me so terribly. . . . I would have him make me forget everything up to the minute I came to this country" (485).[42] Because the psychiatrist is a survivor himself and recognizes that memory of a people's past history is essential to its continuation, he refuses the patient's request and advises her to make better use of her memories. Eventually, Anya herself realizes both the futility of forgetful oblivion and the concomitant moral imperative of sustaining Holocaust memory and commemorating the martyred millions. Newly inspired, she cultivates memory, for in dream and memory her family lives. The idea that memory not be restricted to the private realm but be transcribed for future generations is implied in the protagonist's closing affirmation: "I am putting my feelings on paper. Paper has patience" (489). Anya thus joins divers fictive Holocaust witness scribes, including I. B. Singer's authors and journalists, Arthur Cohen's scribe, Ozick's letter writer, and the diarists of Ettinger, Piercy, and Rosen.

Although Anya experiences the trauma described under the psychiatric rubric of "survivor syndrome," she also exhibits the antithetical manifes-tation, a dedication to Judaism and the Jewish people some observers have dubbed "survivor mission." Her aim of preservation and regeneration is not enacted in the communal realm, as with Chaim Potok's survivor rabbis, yeshiva teachers, and Judaic scholars, or in the political sphere of Zionist nation building, as with Marge Piercy's survivors. Anya's resolution is manifested in her writing and in the private domain of facilitating Jewish continuity by thwarting her daughter's romance with a gentile. This mission, albeit played on a small domestic stage, suggests the larger restorative cohesion and perpetuity of the Jewish people. That Anya resorts to one of her wartime survival strategies, posing as a Christian, to sever the relationship indicates how seriously she relates this mission to Jewish survival. Appearing before the boy's priest wearing a cross, Anya offers to save his parishioner for Christianity by financing his trip to Greece. Succeeding in this objective, she then pawns her mother's jewelry to send Ninka to Israel. This scheme, too, is successful. Ninka marries an Israeli Jew who emigrates to America, where they have a family that Anya prizes. Anya's assertive dedication to the preservation of the Jewish family is consistent with the pattern of Savikin family devotion amply recorded throughout the novel and reflective of her Holocaust-shaped communal and religious conviction.

Among the most significant themes of Holocaust literature is the impact of the Shoah on the religious identity of characters. Anya's Shoah-configured religious evolution is less sharply defined than that in the characters of Wiesel, Singer, Potok, and Ozick, whose discourse is derived from traditional Judaic protest and affirmative codes. Her thought appears as a byproduct of folk belief rather than familiarity with formal philosophic or religious systems. The product of a nonorthodox family that honored Jewish values primarily in terms of ethical comportment and holiday commemoration, Anya is religiously naive compared with men educated in Judaic law. Her belief in an intervening deity remains unwavering, despite Holocaust history, which taxed the convictions of the Judaically educated in the worlds of Wiesel and Singer. Throughout the novel she attributes her good fortune to God's protection: initially, when she is spared disfigurement by the nail-wielding university fraternity men; later, when she follows the advice of a mystic regarding Ninka's fate; still later, when she is spared in a selection; and finally, when she reflects on her Holocaust history. Schaeffer explains this conviction in psychological terms, for by believing that rescuers were available when needed, Anya evades responsibility for being saved while others perished. Believing in God when traditional believers faltered or rebelled is a "guilt- reversing mechanism, because if God wants you to be alive, you don't have to feel so guilty about being alive."[43] Unlike the protesting Orthodox survivors in the fiction of Singer and Wiesel or the secular skeptic in Richard Elman's *28th Day of Elul*, Anya never denounces God's Holocaust silence, never judges God guilty of Holocaust injustice, never puts the crucial questions of how and why the power she believes to be benevolent failed to intercede on behalf of the innocent. She places blame squarely on humanity: "I do not believe that anyone is as happy about the human animal as they were before" (473). If she could articulate a philosophic position, it would most likely conform to Emil Fackenheim's insistence on reaffirming God and Judaism, arguing that to do otherwise would give Hitler a posthumous victory. She would probably agree with Fackenheim, who does not seek to explain the Holocaust, because its enormity transcends all traditional explanations of suffering and evil, yet affirms the orthodox position on the centrality of God in human history and the covenantal bond between God and Israel.[44] Anya is silent on theodicy. Schaeffer, however, symbolically confirms the survivor's spiritual longings when the old loyal servant returns a silver Noah's Ark basket to be presented to Ninka at her wedding. Schaeffer's selection of this artifact evokes God's covenant with Noah to refrain from destroying the world and symbolically confirms that humanity, not God, bears responsibility for the Shoah. In Anya's insistence that Ninka marry a Jew and in her retrieval of the Noah's Ark basket she clings, as Alan Berger astutely argues, "to hope for post-Holocaust redemption in the form of Jewish continuity."[45]

Schaeffer's meticulous recreation of prewar European middle-class Jewish life and the enormous breadth of her Holocaust canvas, covering ghetto, labor camp, and postwar displacement, has earned accolades from readers and critics. Recipient of the Friends of Literature Award and the Edward Lewis Wallant Award, *Anya* is frequently cited for its comprehensive and authentic representation. Typical of the critical acclaim is Edward Alexander's 1979 assessment of *Anya* as an "extraordinary achievement . . . probably the best American literary work on the Holocaust."[46] In 1974, at the time of its publication, no other American-born writer had so realistically, systematically, and comprehensively delineated ghetto and labor camp and charted the transformation from emancipated, assimilated European Jew to hounded pariah of the Nazi universe. Yet despite the novel's primary realistic mode and panoramic vision, Schaeffer conveys the impression of the essential incomprehensibility and mystery of the Shoah in her reiteration of Anya's prewar assessment of *Mein Kampf* as a fairy tale and in Ninka's postwar characterization of the workings of the crematoria as "a fairy tale about cooking people in ovens" (449). In these repeated references to fairy tales the contemporary American realist acknowledges that the Holocaust universe resists comprehension and "far exceeds the limits of the imagined world."[47]

CYNTHIA OZICK

Paradoxically, although she is one of America's most accomplished novelists of the Holocaust, Cynthia Ozick insists that Holocaust narratives are unnecessary. She is "not in favor of making fiction of the data, or of mythologizing or poeticizing it."[1] Asserting that "the subject is corrupted by fiction and that fiction in general corrupts history," Ozick explains that the Holocaust enters her work "unbidden, unsummoned."[2] She prefers not "to tamper or invent, or imagine, [the Holocaust] yet . . . [she has] done it. . . . It comes; it invades."[3] Finally, Ozick confesses, she "cannot *not* write about it. It rises up and claims [her] furies . . . [because her] brother's blood cries out from the ground."[4] Unlike Susan Schaeffer and Norma Rosen, who were unburdened by Holocaust awareness in youth, Cynthia Ozick, a child of Russian-Jewish immigrants, understood European anti-Jewish violence, experienced antisemitism herself, and learned about Nazi crimes against Jewry. She vividly recalls Father Coughlin, "the 'radio priest' who preached anti-Semitism" during the Depression, and being tormented as a "Christ-killer" for refusing to sing Christmas carols in school assemblies. A classmate, whose parents were German immigrants, informed her that Hitler "had to put the Jews in concentration camps, because they are political prisoners." In response to the antisemitic German legislation of the 1930s her parents participated in the widespread Jewish economic boycott of Germany by refusing to sell Bayer aspirin in their pharmacy at a time when *Bayer* was synonymous with *aspirin*. The Ozicks forfeited precious income during the depths of the Depression to fulfill what they recognized as a moral responsibility to their European brethren. The example of her parents' protest reverberates in Ozick's refusal to purchase German products and her rejection of public speaking invitations in Germany—not because her protest will hinder the German economy but as a memorial to the Jews slaughtered in the Shoah.[5] Her memorial is most fully realized through her artistic genius, which has given life to a superb body of commemorative literature. From her first published novel, *Trust*, which attributes an American's political and religious transformation to Holocaust witness, to survivors' recollections in *The Cannibal Galaxy* and imagined evocations in *The Messiah of Stockholm*, to numerous engagements with Holocaust and post-Holocaust themes in short fiction and confrontation with Holocaust denial in a play, the Ozick canon evidences ever more complex religious, political, and psychological meditations on the Shoah.[6] Inspired by a single line in William Shirer's *The Rise and Fall of the Third Reich*, "about babies being thrown against the electrified fences," "The Shawl" marks the sole instance in which Ozick locates her fiction within the lice-infested, disease-ridden, death-dominated concentration camp universe and focuses exclusively on the gender-based Holocaust suffering of women and the murder of their innocent children.[7] Reminiscent of Ilona Karmel's startling introductory paragraph in *An Estate of Memory*, Ozick begins "The Shawl" in medias res. Rosa Lublin, a young mother, her concealed infant, and Rosa's niece, Stella, struggle to survive a death march from one concentration camp to another. Rosa confronts the choice that plagued many Jewish mothers, whether to entrust her child to a stranger's goodwill or to conspire to preserve its life in the mother's own vulnerable setting. She considers passing her baby to a woman along the road, a choice fraught with danger for mother and child, since the penalty for stepping out of the line of march is death. Should Rosa successfully approach a stranger, other perils would arise. The unexpected transfer might so startle the stranger that she would drop the bundle and inadvertently injure the child. If, on the other hand, the stranger were to realize the Jewish mother's intent, she might reject the child and denounce the mother. Unlike Schaeffer's ghetto mother, who had the cooperation of the Vilna Ghetto leader and the resistance fighters in securing the help of a known Jewish sympathizer, Rosa's only options are to give her infant to a stranger or keep the child in her own life-threatening sphere.

Throughout this magnificently compressed seven-page story, Ozick refrains from the conventions of Holocaust literature that meticulously detail camp physical conditions. Instead, she deftly introduces images conveying the horror of "a place without pity," a place characterized by "bad wind with pieces of black in it," an "ash-stippled wind"; a place of "stink mixed with a bitter fatty floating smoke that greased Rosa's skin."[8] The collection's central symbol, the shawl, assumes magical survival properties in the short story, serving as Magda's daily source of shelter, nourishment, and concealment.

Selecting metaphors aptly juxtaposing nature with the perilous manmade Nazi universe, Ozick describes the shawl-swaddled infant as "a squirrel in a nest" (4), the shawl forming her "little house" (4). Absent are dramatization of food "organization" and the psychological effects of hunger manifested in dialogue and dream. Ozick renders starvation in concise metaphors and similes. Stella's "knees were tumors on sticks, her elbows chicken bones" (3). "A walking cradle" (3), Rosa is so frail and thin that she successfully conceals Magda between her breasts under a shawl that covers them both. Unable to nurse, Rosa gives her baby almost all her food and the corner of a shawl to suck, for "Magda relinquished Rosa's teats, . . . both were cracked, not a sniff of milk. The duct-crevice extinct, a dead volcano, blind eye, chill hole" (4). That the tragic circumstances of the infant's conception and murder are causally linked to Nazi genocide is figuratively established by Magda's Aryan appearance and her Jewish vulnerability. In contrast to the mother's dark coloring, the infant has ideal Teutonic features: blue eyes and blond hair. Although the hair color associates her with the patrilineal line, Ozick alerts readers to the child's perilous destiny, noting that her blondness is "nearly as yellow as the Star sewn into Rosa's coat" (4). Similarly, though the child's Aryan features lead to Stella's declaration that Magda is "one of *their* babies" (4), her belly fat with air, legs pencil thin, voice mute, and head and body lice-infested reveal her Jewish identity and vulnerability to Aryan persecution.

By counterpointing nature imagery on the other side of the steel fence, "butterflies in summer; . . . green meadows speckled with dandelions and deep-colored violets; . . . innocent tiger lilies" (8), with camp excrement, "thick turd-braids, . . . that slunk down from the upper bunks" (8–9), Ozick suggests the unnaturalness of the Nazi mission and the transitory character of Jewish life in the camps. Butterflies yield to crematoria flames as the Jewish reverence for life succumbs to the technologically charged carnage of the Nazis. Confirming the perverse morbidity of the Nazi system is the humming of the electric fence: "sounds in the wire: grainy sad voices" (9). Ozick's passage is reminiscent of Charlotte Delbo's juxtaposition of the world inside the electric fence with that outside, the contrast of an Auschwitz spring with a Parisian spring: "The smell was so strong and so fetid that we thought that we were breathing not air but some thicker and more viscous fluid that enveloped and shut off this part of the world with an additional atmosphere in which only specially adapted creatures could move. Us. A stench of diarrhea and of carrion. Above this stench the sky was blue. And in my memory spring was singing."[9] Delbo's passage, based on the prisoner's memory of spring, suggests burgeoning life, a momentary respite from Auschwitz. Ozick allows no respite. She contrasts the camp sphere with the landscape just outside the fence, highlighting external nature's renewal despite the Nazi perversion of human nature. Ozick symbolizes the indifference of the outside world to life in the camps, suggesting that this human cataclysm merits a complementary breach in nature.

In the camp sphere, normally joyous childhood milestones only fore-shadow danger and death. Magda's first tooth is described as "an elfin tombstone of white marble" (4), and her first steps are but a new source of terror for Rosa, who fears that the mobile but uncomprehending child will stray into the sight of a German guard and death. When she misses the wrap that Stella has usurped to warm her own frozen body, Magda toddles into the roll-call square crying, uttering her first sounds since Rosa's breasts dried, and Rosa feels "a tide of commands [hammering in her] nipples" (8). Uncertain whether to run for the shawl or retrieve Magda without it and chance her continued screaming, Rosa opts for the shawl. She returns too late. In the climactic scene Magda reaches toward mother and shawl as a German guard sweeps the infant up and tosses her onto the electrified fence. Whereas the fantastical mode of Ozick's first reference to children in the camps, in "The Pagan Rabbi," incorporated rescue of an infant similarly tossed against the electrified fence but saved as "the current vanished from the terrible wires," the realistic mode of "The Shawl" demands Magda's death.[10] Dramatic presentation of Rosa's witness to the electrocution of her child evokes the ghastly experience of hundreds of thousands of Jewish women who witnessed the murder of their children, a central theme in women's Holocaust writing.

Ozick heightens German/Jewish dichotomies in the electrocution scene through use of contrasting imagery and linguistic patterns, images that accent the discrepancy between the natural order and German perversion of the life force. When the guard hurls the child at the electrified fence, Magda "swimming through the air . . . looked like a butterfly touching a silver vine" (9). Rosa must resist the instinctive maternal response, "the wolf's screech" (10) ascending through her body. She must deny her body in order to save it; she must still her despairing voice and mute her grief, stop her legs from running to the electrocuted child, and suppress her maternal impulse to honor the survival instinct, for to retrieve her baby's charred corpse will invite the guard's bullet for herself. Even her scream will be a prologue to death. Rosa muffles her cries in the shawl, now her life preserver. Ozick metonymically signifies the humanity of the Jewish mother and child by employing human parts—arms, legs, head, belly—and rhetorically diminishes the murderous Germans by interjecting inanimate metonymic tropes such as "helmet" and "boots" to signify Aryan disregard for Jewish life. Similarly, her focus on breast imagery underscores the maternal character of Rosa's suffering. Her anxiety for her child's survival as well as the life force and its antithesis are repeatedly conveyed through breast imagery. Complementing the characterization of failure to nourish the child by describing the breast as a "chill hole" is "the tide of commands that hammered in Rosa's nipples" (8) as Magda takes her fatal walk in the *Appelplatz*.

Although critics uniformly praise "The Shawl" as a brilliant Holocaust evocation, one must wonder whether the phrases at which we marvel breach Ozick's prohibition against poeticizing the Shoah, whether they violate Theodor Adorno's injunction opposing linguistically beautiful Holocaust constructs, lest the beauty of the language detract from the horror of its subject. Amy Gottfried interprets Ozick's artistry as fashioning "a startlingly graceful scene of liberation. . . . In choosing to beautify a child's electro-cution, Ozick risks glossing over the horror of the Holocaust in favor of aesthetics."[11] Later Gottfried qualifies her assessment, acknowledging that Ozick does not deny the brutality of the Holocaust. Rather, she denies the Nazis' intention to wipe out Jewish resiliency by creating a graceful death scene that provides a moment of transcendence.[12] Although the imagery of the butterfly and silver vine is undeniably aesthetic, it succeeds in focusing on the atrocity rather than calling attention to itself. The forcefulness of the image intensifies our horror and speaks to the perversions of the Nazi universe. Beyond emphasizing the outrage of such a death, lyrical delin-eation of Rosa's perception of her infant's landing on the electrified fence foreshadows the mother's pattern of denial in the novella. She disavows the child's German paternity in "The Shawl," and in the sequel she denies her daughter's death in postwar fantasies of the child's maturation.

Gottfried's transcendent interpretation complements Alan Berger's com-pellingly persuasive reading of Ozick's reiterations of the shawl's magical attributes and life-sustaining quality as evoking the traditional tallit, the prayer shawl worn by observant Jews.[13] In Berger's view the coalescence of shawl and its fragrance, characterized as aromatic spices that are customarily associated with the Havdalah service, supports a redemptive interpretation positing the preservation of Judaism even in the realm of absolute evil. Although the shawl imagery, juxtaposed with the spice imagery, suggests the plausibility of such an interpretation, it is out of character for the dejudaized

Rosa we come to know in the sequel, and Ozick unequivocally denies that she intended the shawl to represent the prayer shawl.[14]

Despite the story's exquisite imagery, redemption is not operative in the electrocution scene. Following a public reading of "The Shawl," Ozick flatly denied Holocaust redemption, arguing that "in thinking about the Holocaust, we have to take into ourselves a different possibility, an alien thesis: one that we have never been taught, one that goes against our moral grain, that seems . . . repugnant. It is that *this* time there was no redemption, the Red Sea did not open, nobody walked through the parting of the waters, the waters remained high and cold and deadly and closed. Nor did the tomb of salvation open to release the spirit of redemption; the tomb of salvation remained shut and sealed. . . . This time, those very powerful models that are the controlling metaphors of our civilization will not be made to work."[15]

Perhaps Ozick's use of the shawl is derivative, an intertextual tribute to Schaeffer's *Anya*, which Ozick praised.[16] Anya believes that her "magical scarf" (271), bearing the embroidered image of a church, has saved her life by helping her identify the actual church being used as a sanctuary for war refugees. Similarly, Rosa is convinced that the shawl has protected Magda by nourishing and concealing her. Another resonance of Schaeffer's text—Anya's examining a sick child and characterizing its single tooth as staring up at her "like a tombstone" (387)—appears in Ozick's reference to Magda's first tooth. It seems plausible that Ozick's decision to write about a mother's loss of a child was prompted in some measure by her interest in exploring a situation antithetical to the one Schaeffer treated. Anya's child survives. Rosa's is murdered. Each mother's postwar character is dominated by her Holocaust trauma: Anya's parenting is obsessive and overprotective; Rosa is in perpetual mourning for her child. Other parallels between the texts abound: the protagonists are ambivalent about communicating their Holocaust stories; they abandon their prewar career interests in the sciences; they own and operate antique shops; and they have difficulty with or disinterest in English despite their prewar linguistic proficiency in several European languages. Ozick's introduction of "the magical shawl" may thus be a visible homage to Schaeffer. In any event, like other superb writers who borrow, she makes the image her own. Schaeffer had used her magical scarf as a plot device. Swerving from that influence, Ozick integrates the shawl completely and profoundly in her short story and novella. Supporting the argument for such correlation, whether conscious or unconscious on Ozick's part, is her acknowledged literary borrowing from Malamud's "The Silver Crown" in "Usurpation," a story about literary influence, and her affirmation that the Holocaust childhood biography of her protagonist in "A Mercenary" resembles that of the boy in Jerzy Kosinski's *Painted Bird*.[17]

The power of "The Shawl" derives from metaphor, dramatic and poetic concentration. Its sequel, "Rosa," is discursive, encompassing a wider historic scope. The reader is directed to Rosa's pre-Holocaust history and to the psychological burden of post-Holocaust survival. Beyond introducing verbal echoes to confirm character constructs of "The Shawl" in "Rosa," Ozick reverberates key images and tropes—shawl, fence, and electricity—to link the two narratives, thereby suggesting the Holocaust's pervasive intrusion in the survivor's psyche. In an astute midrashic interpretation Joseph Lowin contends that Ozick "means for the two stories to stand not in a diachronous relationship one to the other, a relationship in which one story would follow the other chronologically. Rather, Ozick means for the two stories to stand next to each other in a synchronous relationship, in which one story 'always' contains the other and comments on it."[18]

Continuity between the narratives and linkage between the historical past and the present is suggested by the novella's imagery and metaphor. Anticipating the infant's electrocution in "The Shawl," Rosa perceives that "sometimes the electricity inside the fence would seem to hum" (9); and at the precise moment Magda's fragile body "splashed against the fence, the steel voices went mad" (10). In the second narrative images of electricity and shawl revive memories of the child and its brutal murder: "The holy . . . babe . . . thrown against the fence, barbed, thorned, electrified; grid and griddle; a furnace; the child on fire!" (31). The electrified fence surges through the survivor's mind "inside a blazing flying current, a terrible beak of light bleeding out a kind of cuneiform on the underside of her brain" (69). The shawl, which Stella accuses Rosa of treating as a religious relic, is the story's most powerful objective correlative for maternal loss. Frenzied by the expectation of receiving Magda's shawl, Rosa remembers the child in a series of fused shawl, fence, and electricity images, images that evoke the concentration camp and solidify the connection between Rosa's postwar trauma and its Holocaust inception. Electricity and shawl images merge to signal the rare failure on the occasion of the shawl's arrival in Miami to "instantly restore Magda, as usually happened [with] *a vivid thwack of restoration like an electric jolt*" (62; italics added). Finally, the electricity image reintroduces the theme of Magda's German patrimony as Ozick fuses electricity and hair imagery. In "The Shawl" Magda's blond hair signifies a German father. In "Rosa" reference to electric static in Magda's hair, "as if the peril hummed out from the filaments of Magda's hair, those narrow bright wires" (66), conveys the mother's pain generated by Stella's innuendos about Magda's Aryan paternity. Holocaustal imagery pursues Rosa in Miami, whose "streets were a furnace, the sun an executioner" (14), its barbed wire–fenced beach "littered with bodies" (47). Rosa "felt she was in hell" (14). Recurrent shawl, fence, and electricity images effectively unite short story and novella, establishing the Holocaust as the genesis of Rosa's troubled postwar life.

Despite her physical absence, verbal echoes from the initial text reinforce Stella's hovering presence and influence in the second narrative. "The Shawl" opens with delineation of "Stella, cold, cold, the coldness of hell" (3); ravenous; and jealous of Magda's maternal care. Certain "that Stella was waiting for Magda to die so that she could put her teeth into the little thighs" (5), Rosa repeatedly accuses the teenager of regarding Magda "like a young cannibal" (5). Although Rosa's concern for Magda is characteristically expressed in terms of cannibalism in "The Shawl," it is Stella's effort to warm herself that leads to Magda's death. Consequently, in the sequel Rosa contemplates Stella's guilt primarily through references to cold: "She was always cold. The cold went into her heart" (6–7). The coalescence of *cold* and *heart* reverberates from the short story to the novella, as does the cannibal reference. In contrast to the adulatory salutations in Rosa's letters to Stella, "Dear One, Lovely, Beautiful, . . . Angel" (15), the grieving mother harbors contempt for her niece and repeatedly refers to her as a cold and heartless "Angel of Death" (15). Ozick shifts the "cannibal" designation for Stella from the subjective case in "The Shawl" to the objective case in "Rosa." Indulging her hatred in "cannibal dreams about Stella, [Rosa] was boiling her tongue, her ears, her right hand, such a fat hand with plump fingers" (15). The dream reflects Rosa's judgment of Stella as accomplice to Magda's murder. Confirming Rosa's subconscious assessment is her verdict in a letter to Magda, charging that Stella "was always jealous of you. She has no heart" (44), implying, in the shift from past to present tense, a causal link between Stella's tragic Holocaust transgression and her postwar moral failures.

"Rosa" portrays the title character at fifty-eight, nearly four decades after the events recounted in "The Shawl," and explores the protagonist's prewar life as well as her wounded postwar psyche. Here Ozick delineates the transformation from promising young woman to aging victim who suffers the long-term effects of concentration camp deprivation and the loss of a child and maintains an ongoing relationship with Stella, whom she still blames for Magda's death. Measuring time and life by the Holocaust, the survivor classifies three ages of human experience: "The life before, the life during, the life after. . . . The life after is now. The life before is our *real* life, at home, where we was born" (58). "During" is, of course, the Hitler epoch. For Rosa, "before is a dream. After is a joke. Only during stays. And to call it a life is a lie" (58). Increasingly tormented by the loss of her child and public indifference to her Holocaust witness, rather than healing with the passage of time and distance from the site of her trauma, Rosa destroys her New York shop and withdraws into the hell of Holocaust memory. Her only brief solace is lamentation and reveries of imagined lives for her deceased daughter. The lingering impact of the Holocaust in Rosa's life reflects the situation of many survivors, such as Fania Fenelon, a member of the only female orchestra of the concentrationary universe. Thirty years later, Fenelon writes in *Playing for Time*, "I've never left the camp; I'm still there, I've spent every night of my life there, for thirty years. . . . Death, life, tears, laughter, everything was multiplied, disproportionate, beyond the limits of the credible."[19]

Ozick dramatizes the severity of Rosa's lasting torment by placing her in sharp juxtaposition to Stella, who appears to enjoy life despite her past. She has no dramatic role in the narrative, yet Stella functions as Rosa's psychological foil. Readers cannot know whether Stella is free of Holocaust trauma, for she is kept offstage and we do not enter her thoughts and dreams. Her post-Holocaust adjustment is made manifest through letters to Rosa and Rosa's commentary. In contrast to Rosa's perpetual mourning, Stella apparently tries to suppress the tragedy and actively pursues a return to normalcy. Stella is attentive to renewal, to her healthy appearance, to her job, and to taking psychology courses. Mired in the past, Rosa subsists on a starvation diet and maintains a slovenly appearance, her hair disheveled, her clothing in ill repair, her room in disarray and virtually bare. Emblematic of their polar attitudes is Stella's embrace of English and Rosa's stubborn attachment to Polish. Rosa's English is faulty. Her syntactical misstructuring and fragmentation evoke the Holocaust-wrought ruptures she endured. Stella's gift to Rosa of a striped dress leads Rosa to conclude that Stella is acting "as if innocent, as if ignorant, as if *not there*" (33). For Stella, the dress is, presumably, a simple aesthetic selection. For Rosa, it is a direct link to the camps. Resisting what she perceives as Stella's Holocaust repression, Rosa writes, "A devil climbs into you and ties up your soul and you don't even know it" (15). Stella is determined to pursue a life that will diminish the lasting destructive impact of the Holocaust on her postwar life. Rosa, "a madwoman and a scavenger" (13), remains strongly fixated on the past.

Antithetical survivors, Rosa and Stella each perceive the other as mentally ill. For Rosa, the shawl is a holy emblem of her child which she approaches "on her knees" (44), as if kneeling in prayer. For Stella, it is Rosa's "trauma," "fetish," "idol," "relic," and she likens Rosa's adoration of the shawl to that of a benighted medieval worshiper of a false relic. Rosa feigns acceptance of Magda's death to appease Stella's dementia and to convince Stella of her own sanity, but her letter-writing is founded on the pretense that Magda lives. Perhaps because she was only fourteen and did not lose a child, Stella appears unsympathetic to Rosa's trauma and urges her to emerge from her self-imposed Holocaust prison. A letter chastising Rosa for worshiping the shawl warns, "One more public outburst puts you in the bughouse" (32–33). Stella's diction and tone confirm Rosa's charge that Stella is heartless. The threat is modulated only in Stella's last sentence, urging Rosa to live her life. Stella fails to understand Rosa's prolonged mourning, mourning formed of memory, which Lawrence Langer describes as possessing "a durational integrity that exists outside the flow of normal time."[20] Unlike those who lose their children to natural causes or accident and are able to grieve and recover, parents who lost children in the Holocaust are intensely injured by postponed grieving, by the state-sponsored murder of their children, and by the world's acquiescence to their murder. So dreadful is Rosa's memory of Magda's murder that she cannot repress or dismiss it and "get on with life" as others urge.

From Rosa's perspective Stella has freed herself of Holocaust memories and anxieties by consciously repressing them. As Rosa sees it, Stella mistakenly believes in a new world: "Every vestige of former existence is an insult to her" (41). A perpetual victim, Rosa mocks Stella's concern for "after" and attributes the younger woman's failure to realize her goal of marrying an American to repressed fear of the past that sullies the future. She repudiates Stella's attitudes in letters to Magda and in conversation with an acquaintance, charging that "Stella is self-indulgent. She wants to wipe out memory" (58). Rosa is like Wiesel's Eliezer of *Day*, who realizes, "I think if I were able to forget I would hate myself. Our stay there planted time bombs within us. From time to time one of them explodes. . . . It's inevitable. Anyone who has been there has brought back some of humanity's madness."[21]

Stella's characterization implicitly questions whether post-Holocaust normalization is possible or whether it is, as in Rosa's view, evidence of dysfunction. Writing of transgenerational aftereffects of the Holocaust, Dan Bar-On, a professor of behavioral sciences, argues that the Holocaust survivor's wish for normalization could be both functional and dysfunctional, that the return to "normal life" could become dysfunctional if "the survivors avoided a psychological mourning process, thereby becoming inwardly committed to the past they did not work through."[22]

In contrast to Stella, Rosa is representative of survivors who admit to regular, daily associations and memories of the Holocaust in their waking hours and Holocaust nightmares in their sleep. Rosa's survival is bitter—the hell of lost family, lost aspirations, lost language, lost life, the hell of failed communication with those who evade her Holocaust testimony and those who would exploit her history. Separated from the family she loved, the culture she loved, the language she loved, Rosa views life as a chain of dismal encounters differing only in degree. She explains, "Once I thought the worst was the worst, after that nothing could be the worst. But now I see, even after the worst there's still more" (14). Ozick's sensitivity to the long-term trauma endured by Holocaust survivors is analogous to the poet Nelly Sachs's hauntingly resonant fragile voice in "Chorus of the Rescued," pleading:

> We, the rescued,
> The worms of fear still feed on us.
> Our constellation is buried in dust.
> We, the rescued,
> Beg you:
> Show us your sun, but gradually.
> Lead us from star to star, step by step.
> Be gentle when you teach us to live again.
> Lest the song of a bird,
> Or a pail being filled at the well,
> Let our badly sealed pain burst forth again
> and carry us away—[23]

In contrast to the Freudian view of trauma as temporary, resulting in the patient's recovery and return to equilibrium with the passage of time, post-Holocaust psychiatric theory posits lasting trauma borne of a situation in which the individual not only "daily confronted death and degradation" but is in a context of "a new reality totally at variance with the framework of social and moral reality that one had once taken for granted."[24] Trauma experienced in this manner becomes the defining element in a person's life and the reference point for the future. Within this model even adults fully formed psychically at the onset of the trauma may be severely affected. Ozick's Rosa is thus shattered and transformed.

Rosa's room is an objective correlative, reflecting her unhealed postwar existence, and her physical appearance signifies her diminished interest in life. She lives in a "a dark hole" (13), a hotel room containing a bed, an ancient dresser-top refrigerator, and a one-burner stove. Clutter and filth sully the room, which is described as "a shipwreck." A disconnected telephone attests to the lodger's alienation from others. Hair askew, button missing from her dress, she is "the reflection of a ragged old bird with worn feathers" (23). The juxtaposition of Rosa's slovenly room and disheveled personal appearance with her frenzied housecleaning and personal grooming in anticipation of a package containing Magda's shawl signifies the importance of the long-lost child to Rosa's contemporary emotions and accords with psychiatric findings that the attachment to loved ones lost in environments where normal grief and mourning are forbidden remains unresolved.[25] The physically and psychologically oppressive American setting does not replicate Rosa's camp ordeal—it becomes a metaphoric extension of her perpetual grief.

Supporting interpretation of the psychological connection between conflicted present and traumatic past is Ozick's deft imagistic fusion of Holocaust-era sexual assault and contemporary anxiety. As Rosa searches for her missing underpants, she strays onto a fenced private beach and slips into Holocaust association: "To be locked behind barbed wire! No one knew who she was; what had happened to her; where she came from" (49). Like survivors who experience terror when encountering images reminding them of the brutal past, despite the nonviolent postwar context, Rosa is so enraged by the fence that she rebukes the hotel manager, asserting that barbed wire fences are inappropriate in American society. "Only Nazis," she charges, "catch innocent people behind barbed wire" (51). The manager dismisses her as a nuisance, but Rosa's provocative question, "Where were you when we was there?" (51), challenges his ethics and by implication American Holocaust indifference.

Rosa's perceptions of others are influenced by her own history. She views the Miami retirees as being "from the Bronx, from Brooklyn, lost neighborhoods, burned out" and judges that they "left behind a real life" (16). She notes an important distinction between their separation from family and hers, however. They receive letters from children and grandchildren with news of academic and professional triumphs, of marriages, separations, divorces. They are detached, but "they had detached themselves" (29) by their own social planning rather than because of an abrupt and violent externally imposed separation of the type Rosa suffered. That Rosa exists in the present but lives in the past is confirmed in her comment to a man who tries to befriend her. "Without a life," Rosa tells him, "a person lives where they can. If all they got is thoughts, that's where they live" (27–28).

As a mother who was unable to protect her child from Nazi assault, Rosa illustrates Robert Jay Lifton's thesis that survivors are tormented by guilt for their wartime inability to act "in a way they would ordinarily have thought appropriate (save people, resist the victimizers, etc.)."[26] Psychological and psychiatric literature identifies paranoia, suspicion, emotional isolation, and distance, illustrated by unwillingness to forge emotional connections, as symptoms of survivor syndrome. Rosa is a classic exemplar of these symptoms. In addition to the contrast with Stella, Ozick highlights the distinctive traumatic aspects of Rosa's personality by juxtaposing her to Mr. Persky, a pre-Holocaust immigrant whom she meets at a laundromat in Miami. Persky, who left Europe before the conflagration, shares the optimism of prewar Jewish immigrants. He is socially engaged, trusting, at ease with his peers. Conversely, Rosa is withdrawn from Miami Jews, from whom she feels historically and socially alien, judging them to be socialists and idealists whose concern is universalist. Even those who care about survivors distress Rosa, for she believes that they perceive her one-dimensionally, as a refugee, "like a number—counted apart from the ordinary swarm. Blue digits on the arm" (36). Painfully aware of the distinctions separating her from Persky, she responds to his appeal to their common Polish origin by quipping, "My Warsaw isn't your Warsaw" (19). Because he is a pre-Holocaust immigrant, Persky is ineligible for shared witness. His immigrant generation sought escape from nongenocidal Polish antisemitism and a better standard of living in America. His question, "What kind of person are you, you're still afraid?" (19), reveals his ignorance of Holocaust psychic devastation. Even later, when he knows more about Rosa, Persky remains incapable of understanding her suffering. He exclaims, "You ain't in a camp. It's finished. Long ago it's finished" (58). But it is not finished, not for this mother who witnessed her child being hurled against the electrified fence. Her pain endures. This demonstration of profound lack of understanding by the unscathed clarifies Rosa's retreat from ordinary society.

In a remarkably effective association Ozick connects Rosa's ambivalent relationship with Persky to her Holocaust experience. Paranoia and suspicion, commonly associated with survivor syndrome in the psychiatric literature, emerge in Rosa's response to the discovery, on return from her laundromat meeting with Persky, that a pair of her underpants is missing. Ozick adroitly fuses Rosa's obsessive search for the underpants with normally repressed memory of her sexual violation in the camps. Suspicion of Persky triggers memories of her sexual assault. "The shame. Pain in the loins. Burning" (34). Rather than think of the SS men who raped her, she imagines Persky as a "sex maniac, . . . his parts starved" (34). This theme is amplified and connected to the Holocaust in her linked association of her rape and her imagined view of the stained underclothing. That the real and imagined events are united in Rosa's mind is evidenced in her Holocaust image of the underpants "smoldering in an ash heap" (46), in connecting perceived present insult with the past injury. Although Rosa acknowledges being raped by Germans more than once, she staunchly denies Magda's Nazi patrimony, claiming that she was too ill at the time to conceive. In a letter to her beloved child, Rosa invents a pleasing cultivated father of mixed Jewish-Christian blood, the son of her own mother's closest friend, a converted Jew who married a gentile.

Among the devices creative writers use to convey the perpetual Holocaust grief of female characters is their psychological or imaginative restoration of the dead. Like I. B. Singer's Tamara of *Enemies, A Love Story*, who talks to her dead children, and Susan Schaeffer's Anya, who imagines conversations with her murdered parents, Rosa writes to Magda. Copious elegant Polish letters convey pre-Holocaust pleasure and plenty, Holocaust-era deprivation and degradation, and post-Holocaust angst and anger. Unlike Tamara and Anya, however, who see and hear their loved ones as they were in life, Rosa imagines a future for her daughter. Her postwar denial of Magda's death, coupled with her invention of mature and prosperous adult lives for Magda, epitomizes the intensity of the survivor's trauma. This behavior accords with psychiatric theory that contends that when survivors are unable to complete the process of mourning the loss of a child, "various forms of denial, idealization, and . . . 'walling off' become necessary."[27]

A recurrent theme of Ozick's Holocaust fiction is imagined lives. In *The Messiah of Stockholm* a survivor child grown to adulthood without parents takes the name Lars Andemening, the Swedish version of Lazarus. Like one who has risen from the dead, he invents his identity as the son of Bruno Schulz, the Jewish writer-artist shot by the Nazis. A literary critic who worships Schulz, Lars tries to recover the Polish Jew's lost manuscript, just as Rosa tries to preserve Magda's life. And just as Lars withdraws from people unconnected with his preservation project, Rosa withdraws from reality while pursuing Magda's future. Her letters address Magda as "snow queen," "yellow blossom," "cup of sun," and "soul's blessing," vibrant language negating her child's tortured death. Three reveries reveal the mother's invention of the life that should have been. Rosa visualizes Magda as a lovely young girl of sixteen at the threshold of adulthood; at thirty-one, a physician married to a physician living in a large house in a New York suburb; or a professor of Greek philosophy at a prestigious university. Believing Stella's insistence on Magda's death is aberrant, Rosa placates her niece by "pretending" that Magda is dead.

Demonstrating the Holocaust's cataclysmic impact on the survivor's life, Ozick introduces the prewar halcyon days. Letters and interior monologue serve the expository function of introducing Rosa's parents and the cultured life the three enjoyed, allowing readers to comprehend the fundamental change in Rosa's life and to measure her losses. Proustian spontaneous recollection, triggered by Persky's persistent interrogation, revives Rosa's memories. She retreats to an internal field of vision: "All at once the landscape behind her eyes fell out of control" (20), and memories of acculturated Polish life flood her consciousness, as do memories of a laboratory where she excelled in science studies, praise she received from a teacher for her "literary style," and dreams of a career in chemistry. This unbidden recollection leads to willed memory, for she prefers "to live inside her eyes" (21), to relive the good life of reading Tuwim—"such delicacy, such loftiness, such *Polishness*" (20)—and to remember her mother's poetry and father's learning. In this sequence Ozick endows her protagonist with fond memories of a peaceful life: acculturated loving parents, a house filled with ink drawings and replicas of Greek vases and "laden with a thousand books. Polish, German, French; her father's Latin books; the shelf of shy literary periodicals her mother's poetry now and then wandered through. . . . Cultivation, old civilization, beauty, history!" (21). Jealously guarding these memories of the prewar literary life, Rosa brusquely dismisses Persky's efforts to engage her in conversation, volunteering only that she is of an educated family. Guilty of intellectual hubris and social pretension, Rosa dismisses Persky, as her parents dismissed lower-class Jews in Poland. She rejects Persky's invitation to "unload," quipping, "Whatever I would say, you would be deaf" (27). Paradoxically, the woman who destroyed her shop because no one would listen to her Holocaust testimony now rebuffs a willing auditor, intimating that even this sympathetic Jewish immigrant is unworthy of her cultural reminiscence and unequal to her Holocaust recollection.

Contemporary Warsaw Ghetto chroniclers wrote in anticipation of an audience that would share their outrage once informed.[28] Holocaust survivors harbor no such illusions. Survivors who lived through the ordeal of the concentration and death camp universe only to be met with indifference or hostility after liberation are more skeptical of audience response to their witness. *The Drowned and the Saved* reveals Primo Levi's dismayed realization that readers, whose empathy and outrage ghetto writers expected, instead "judge with facile hindsight, or . . . perhaps feel cruelly repelled" by survivor accounts. Levi recognizes that "the experience that we survivors of the Nazi *Lagers* carry within us are extraneous to the new Western generation and become ever more extraneous as the years pass."[29] Rosa shares these views, for she, like Levi and Charlotte Delbo, who bemoans "the indifference of posterity," knows that justice was not served when the world discovered the magnitude of the Nazi crimes. Rosa could agree with Delbo's desire to survive Auschwitz to bear witness, "to be the voice that gives the final reckoning. . . . And there I am. . . . My voice is lost. Who hears it? Who knows how to hear it?"[30] Not only did the triumphant nations do little to aid the Jewish victims; they compounded the crime by failing to inscribe their history. Possessing knowledge more heinous than that which the ghetto writers could imagine, Rosa is unable to share their faith in the civilized world or believe that her witness matters.

As in her other works treating antisemitism, Ozick explores the relationship of the prejudice in conjunction with the Holocaust in "Rosa" and in a novel published during the same year, *The Cannibal Galaxy*. The novel explores a literate, religious Jew's response to antisemitism, manifested by intensified learning in and loyalty to Judaica. Conversely, Rosa's character is a study of a Jewish illiterate who has allowed the prevalent antisemitism of her society to alienate her from her own cultural heritage. Rosa's aversion to her Jewish identity derives not only from Holocaust degradation but from the influence of parents who are self-hating Jews, products of Polish antisemitism, models of radical assimilation gone awry. Unlike many assimilated Jewish Europeans, who balanced their secular cultural interests with Jewish identity, who read European literature but valued their Jewish heritage, the Lublins were infatuated with Polish culture and estranged from their own cultural grounding. They are so Polish that they embrace their compatriots' antisemitism. Rosa proudly recalls that her father identified himself as a "Pole by right" (40), that "there was not a particle of ghetto left in him, not a grain of rot" (21). Consistent with Ozick's ironic distancing from Rosa is her reference to the Lublins' favorite Polish poet. Tuwim was the son of an assimilated family that instilled a love of Poland in him. Despite Tuwim's ardent nationalism and major contribution to Polish literature, he was attacked on antisemitic grounds. Apparently unbeknown to Rosa, but certainly known to Ozick, the Holocaust caused Tuwim to reconsider his position. Writing from an American venue in 1944, he declared his support for a Jewish homeland in Israel and his allegiance to the Jewish people. In "We the Jews of Poland" he wrote that the "only binding ties [are] those based on . . . the blood of martyrs, spilled by villains."[31]

Postwar adherence to her parents' prejudices against observant Jews and Jewish culture defines Rosa as a morally flawed character in Ozick's universe. A remembrance of ghetto incarceration confirms the parental source of Rosa's postwar prejudice against Persky and evidences Ozick's skepticism about the virtues of total assimilation. In a speech cast in antisemitic rhetoric Rosa asks, "Can you imagine a family like us— . . . confining us with teeming Mockowiczes and Rabinowiczes and Perskys and Finkelsteins, . . . walking up and down, and bowing, and shaking and quaking over old rags of prayer books, . . . we were furious because we had to be billeted with such a class, with these old Jew peasants worn out from their rituals and superstitions, phylacteries on their foreheads sticking up so stupidly, like unicorn horns, every morning" (66–67). Ozick's devastating attack on these assimilationists serves a double purpose. She interprets and condemns the Lublins' disdain for their fellow ghetto victims and suggests that their Holocaust shock is all the greater for their delusion regarding their status as Polish citizens. Furthermore, she delineates them as exemplars of self-hatred wrought by antisemitism. The Lublins have internalized antisemitic discourse and characterize pious Jews as the grotesque distortions of their gentile detractors. Through juxtaposition of the sacred image of the phy-lacteries with horns, Ozick distances Rosa from piety and inscribes her as a metaphoric collaborationist, in league with the enemies of Judaism in her representation of ritually clad Jews as horned demons.

The Lublins' preference for Polish and their denigration of Yiddish distin-guish them from most Polish Jews. Living in Warsaw during the golden age of Yiddish literature, the Lublins' library excludes this national writing while privileging most other European languages and literatures. Rosa's mother's disdain for her own mother's Yiddish "cradle-croonings" is echoed in Rosa's antipathy toward Jewish Warsaw, which she describes as a "bitter ancient alley, dense with . . . signs in jargoned Yiddish" (20), and her postwar cha-grin that Americans mistake her for a parochial eastern Jew of Persky's ilk. In contrast to the psychologically healthy, Judaically committed Holocaust survivors in Ozick's fiction—Sheindel in "The Pagan Rabbi," the rebbe in "Bloodshed," and the refugee in "Levitation"—Rosa is guilty of a "certain contempt" for Jews, whom she regards as "primitive" (52). By highlighting the Lublin family's scorn for Yiddish, Ozick, herself a translator of Yiddish poetry and a polemicist who advocates Jewish cultural particularity, explicitly exposes Jewish self-hatred as a corrosive legacy of antisemitism and implicitly rebukes Jews who diminish their own cultural heritage to win the favor of gentile society.[32] Her affection for Yiddish may also be seen in her elegy for the language and its murdered speakers in "Envy; or, Yiddish in America," a work she intended as "a lamentation, . . . because six million Yiddish tongues were under the earth of Europe, and because here under American liberty and spaciousness my own generation, in its foolishness, stupidity and self-disregard, had, in an act tantamount to autolobotomy, disposed of the literature of its fathers."[33]

Ozick's Yiddish poet of "Envy" grieves for a single Kiev Jew and by extension all Jews who were murdered in the Holocaust. Rosa lacks such historic connection to Jewry and grieves only for her personal loss. The fictional poet's lament for the martyred Jews and their language is Ozick's call for revitalization of Jewry through its literature and language, a language true to Jewish thought, a language of Jewish ideational liberation and self-emancipation.

Intrigued by the exploration of alternate perspectives through similar situations, Ozick has created antithetical survivors and Jewish Americans, characters whose real or imagined encounter with the Holocaust has either distanced them from or strengthened their bonds to Judaism and Jewry. Authentic Jewish self-definition stemming from Holocaust awareness appears initially in *Trust* and reemerges as a transformational catalyst in "Bloodshed," "Levitation," and *A Cannibal Galaxy*. The Holocaust is the crucible responsible for Enoch Vand's metamorphosis from political to religious activism, from pre-Holocaust Communist to post-Holocaust observant Jew, but it has left Rosa's assimilationist cultural loyalties and values intact. Despite Enoch's dismay at God's covenantal betrayal, the solidarity he feels with the Jewish people leads to his study of Judaism's sacred books and adoption of Jewish belief. By novel's end, Enoch approaches the Lurianic Hasidic belief in humanity's restorative task in history—freeing the hidden God by liberating divine sparks. With the guidance of a Holocaust survivor, he learns Hebrew, prays and studies the Torah, Talmud, and Ethics of the Fathers, and is committed to the reinvigoration of the Jewish people and rebuilding Judaism. Bleilip, of "Bloodshed," replicates the pattern under the guidance of a Hasidic rebbe, himself a Holocaust survivor. Ozick's believing or returning Jews gain a measure of Holocaust restoration through their commitment to Judaism and the Jewish people. Rosa, like Lushinsky in "A Mercenary," who experienced Holocaust trauma as a child, is characteristic of the dark side of Jewish assimilation and acculturation in a world hostile to Jewry. Nonetheless, the deracination of Lushinsky was born of Holocaust atrocity, whereas Rosa's estrangement from Jewry and Judaism had its genesis in pre-Nazi antisemitism.

Ozick's most sustained contrast of survivors emerges in the characters of her 1983 publications. Rosa is at one pole, and Hester Lilt and Joseph Brill of *The Cannibal Galaxy* occupy the other. Brill and Lilt are authentic, self-defining Jews whose Holocaust experience, dreadful though it was, not only failed to distance them from Judaism or the Jewish community but strengthened their bonds to Jewish civilization and society. In contrast to Rosa's exclusive Polish education, Ozick endows Brill with a dual education. The son of Russian-Jewish parents who immigrated to France, where they continued to honor their ethnic culture, Brill excelled in his secular studies at the Sorbonne and in traditional Jewish education. In contrast to the Lublin aversion for Jewish neighborhoods and the sounds of Yiddish, Brill's family lives in a Jewish working-class neighborhood of Paris, where Joseph savors the vitality of his immigrant neighbors' Kiev, Minsk, and Lithuanian Yiddish dialects. His strong prewar Jewish identity and the experience of studying Jewish canonical texts before and during his Holocaust concealment account for his emergence from the Shoah as a dedicated Jew. Devoted to promoting the harmony of Jewish and non-Jewish Western culture, Brill redirects his career from astronomy to education. His Judaic background underpins his spiritual sustenance during the bleakest period of modern Jewish history and contributes to his relatively healthy survivorship. Conversely, Rosa's Polish acculturation at the expense of the Judaic fails her, and she withdraws to survivor incapacity.

A stronger foil to Rosa is Hester Lilt, who escaped Nazi Europe in a children's transport. Although Ozick neither dramatizes nor reports Lilt's Holocaust experience, we understand that Lilt suffered the loss of her family. Ozick's interest is clearly this character's healthy survivorship, one that is predicated on devotion to Judaic scholarship and illustrated in lectures delivered in the midrashic narrative mode. In marked contrast to Rosa, who is ignorant of Jewish texts but spiritually and intellectually nourished by Polish texts, Lilt is a knowledgeable transmitter of Jewish values and textual tradition. The novelist associates Lilt with the teaching styles of the fictional moral register Rabbi Pult and the celebrated midrashic teacher Rabbi Akiva. She is impressed by the texts of André Neher and Edmond Fleg, contributors to a post-Holocaust Jewish renaissance through Judaic scholarship and

Zionism. Unlike Rosa, whose disinterest in the Jewish nation was learned from her father and is manifested in her denigrating refusal to allow Stella to emigrate to Israel after liberation, where rescue workers would have sent her "to become God knows what . . . a field worker jabbering Hebrew" (40), Lilt presents a public lecture drawing on a narrative by Rabbi Akiva foretelling the restoration of a Jewish homeland in Jerusalem. Rosa claims to have no preference whether her daughter is Jew or gentile, but Lilt's dedication to Jewish survival is implied by the decision to send her daughter to a Jewish parochial school offering Judaic and secular education. Even the characters' names suggest their antithetical identities. Rosa's patronymic is emblematic not only of her Polish assimilation and acculturation but also of the intended annihilation of Polish Jewry, for the city of Lublin, intended "as a reservation for the concentration of Jews by the Nazis, . . . became one of the centers for mass extermination."[34] Hester, a variation of the Hebrew Esther, is the name of a Jewish heroine responsible for the survival of Persian Jewry when it was threatened with annihilation during the time of Haman. Lilt's authenticity is marked by Jewish self-definition, by her choice to live and work as a Jew. Rosa's Jewish inauthenticity is signified by its external imposition. Reading in the context of the canon, one must conclude that despite sympathy for Rosa's Holocaust trauma, Ozick portrays her as ethically debased by her aversion to her Jewish heritage. One need only compare Rosa with Ozick's more sympathetic portraits of observant survivors to recognize the void in Rosa's survivorship. Most of Ozick's survivor protagonists and mentors embrace Emil Fackenheim's thesis, adhering to Judaism and thereby "deny[ing] Hitler a posthumous victory."[35] By insisting on bearing witness and affirming commitment to Judaism, Enoch Vand and his literary descendants, among them Brill and Lilt, resemble the Jew whom Arthur A. Cohen describes in his theological interpretation of the Holocaust: one who voluntarily assumes the task of attaining meaning and wresting instruction from the historical event.[36]

Convinced that literature should make moral judgments, Ozick links widespread passivity to Jewish suffering during the Holocaust with postwar Holocaust amnesia. Rosa feels betrayed by Poles who ride the tram through the Warsaw Ghetto: "Ordinary citizens going from one section of Warsaw to another, ran straight into the place of our misery. Every day, and several times a day, we had these witnesses" (68). They are acquiescent to the ghettoization and persecution of the Polish Jews "because no one regarded us as Poles anymore" (68). Rosa experiences a similar frustration with Americans, who have no interest in hearing her history. Of contemporary

America, Rosa observes, "Nobody knew anything. This amazed me, that nobody remembered what happened only a little while ago" (66). In a letter to Magda, Rosa rages at the world's desire to forget that which she cannot.

Survivors frequently argue that no satisfactory Holocaust analogy exists, that language is inadequate to convey Holocaust reality; yet they are compelled to tell the story. Among the problems encountered by interviewers of Holocaust survivors is "groping to find proper words to express unimaginable and exhausting memories." They describe with "paralyzing, dumbfounding difficulty: the poverty of language to convey emotion and unreal reality." Analyzing the hindrances to discussion of Holocaust experience, one scholar writes: "At the semantic . . . level lurk deeply hidden or repressed meanings; at the narrative level, the tone and style conceal complex emotions, memories, and associations. In the end, we must be resigned to the human inability to duplicate or assimilate those meanings and memories."[37] Sensitive to these difficulties, Ozick demonstrates Rosa's ambivalence. She wants to bear witness, yet she knows that even those who invite her speech do not have the frame of reference to understand it. She cannot communicate the incommunicable. Poverty of language is at the heart of Rosa's incapacity to express herself. Driven inward, Rosa's authentic voice emerges in her Polish letters to her dead daughter. She can utter only vague references to Persky, yet she writes in concrete terms to the child who was too young to understand the Shoah: "You know they took the worst section, a terrible slum, and they built a wall around it. It was a regular city neighborhood with rotting old tenements. They pushed in half a million people, more than double there used to be in that place" (66). Like many survivors, Rosa believes that only victims can comprehend the enormity of the Holocaust. She shares the tension of the survivors whom Elie Wiesel has in mind in his acknowledgment of "the obsession to tell the tale," even though the obsession is accompanied by an equally strong conviction that their experience is impossible to communicate.[38]

Morally sensitive to the potential of fiction to corrupt or trivialize the Holocaust, Ozick introduces the theme of Holocaust transmission and misappropriation in the novella's encounter between Rosa and Dr. Tree, a bogus scholar who writes Rosa a jargon-strewn letter seeking her cooperation for his project "to observe survivor syndroming within the natural setting" (38). Rosa earlier declined the opportunity to reveal her history to Persky because of his innocence. She now spurns the man who presents himself as an expert in the field but is, in fact, an exploiter of Holocaust tragedy, an academic who misappropriates others' suffering to conform data to his thesis. Ozick lavishes the best of her Juvenalian satire on the mindless scholar, who represents pseudo-intellectual Holocaust revisionists. Tree describes his interest in Rosa's camp experience for use in his study on repressed animation and directs the survivor to his chapter, "Defensive Group Formation: The Way of the Baboons." Offended at being addressed as a lab specimen, Rosa recognizes him as a parasite. Painfully aware that Dr. Tree views her as merely a figure with "blue digits on the arm," she condemns his intent to capitalize on the Holocaust, his arrogant pride and belief that he is writing the definitive work on the topic, "to close the books, so to speak, on this lamentable subject" (37). Tree's letter has revealed him as supremely ill-suited to the challenge of Holocaust transmission. A mark of Rosa's sincerity, authenticity, and sanity is her refusal to be a partner to misappropriation of the Holocaust. Ozick earlier described Rosa as "a madwoman and a scavenger" (13), but she was careful to distinguish between ordinary madness of the type afflicting Mrs. Persky and Rosa's justified rage, the sort of survivor Jean Améry views as a healthy response to the Nazi universe.[39] Rosa hurls Tree's manuscript at the ceiling and flushes his letter down the toilet: appropriate acts of conscience rather than the actions of "a madwoman." That Rosa will not contribute her history to an exploitative recorder is an ethical judgment. This response parallels her objection to Stella's repression of Holocaust memory. Misappropriation and denial each dishonor the victims. Rosa's insistence on authentic and appropriate transmission of Holocaust history constitutes a step toward her recovery and return to the Jewish people.

A believer in t'shuva, the redemptive Judaic tenet that opposes classical Greek fatalism, Ozick celebrates the idea that we can change ourselves, that we can change what appears to be our "fate." Therein lies hope for Rosa. By novella's end, Ozick has moved Rosa toward new beginnings. The first stirrings of restoration are evident as Rosa relates a portion of her Holocaust history to Persky, whom she had earlier misjudged and scorned. In her acceptance of the Yiddish-speaking Persky, Rosa finally distances herself from her parents' antisemitism and self-hatred to acknowledge the identity they denied. Emblematic of her new interest in communication are her order to reconnect her telephone, her call to Stella about returning to New York, and her reception of Persky. These small gestures suggest a turning point. More certain signs that healing is under way are Rosa's qualified interest in the shawl when it finally arrives and her recognition that the living, thriving Magda is a figment of her imagination. When Persky arrived, "Magda was away" (70). Earlier in the novella Rosa would have dismissed Persky rather than delay her imagined encounter with Magda. By narrative's end, although she invites Magda's return, she responds to the immediate presence of the living in a manner justifiably interpreted as "an attempt not to replace 'then' by 'now,' but to separate the two and acknowledge that the twin universes she inhabits are distinct."[40] Moreover, in her voluntary social association with a Jew of the sort she disdained during her Polish assimilationist period, she takes the first step to spiritual redemption. Lawrence Friedman astutely identifies the significance of Rosa's acceptance of Persky as "her solidarity not only with the Jewish dead but with the Jewish living."[41] Emphasis on Magda's expected return juxtaposed with Rosa's reception of Persky suggests that although the Holocaust will remain a crucial influence in her life, trauma will be tempered by voluntary community with fellow Jews, leading her toward more effective Holocaust witness. Furthermore, the progression of the letters—beginning in denial characterized by invention of Magda's Polish father and idealization of the Polish past to evade Holocaust memories and concluding in accurate ghetto witness—marks Rosa's reentry into the Jewish community. Although Rosa does not articulate belief in spiritual "turnings," as does Ozick's survivor-rebbe in "Bloodshed," she shares his commitment to remembering Jewish history, a conviction fundamental to Ozick's redemptive vision.

Ozick returns to *The Shawl* in her play of the same title, which is neither a dramatized adaptation of the original nor a sequel.[42] The stage version of *The Shawl* incorporates matter from the short story and the novella, but Ozick's primary purpose in the drama is to counter a new breed of antisemitism, Holocaust denial. Rather than contrast two versions of survival, as she had in the novella, Ozick now juxtaposes the integrity of the Holocaust eyewitnesses with pernicious Holocaust denial. Set in 1979, the year the revisionist, pseudo-academic Institute for Historical Research held its first meeting, Ozick's play opens with the stage in total darkness, "electricity coursing through dangerous wires and the piercing sound of MAGDA'S CRY. Ma . . . ma!" (1). This work dramatizes a Holocaust denier's attempted seduction of Stella and his manipulation of Rosa into signing a document indicating that what happened to Magda was misrepresented, a document intended to bolster revisionist characterization of the Holocaust as a Zionist fabrication. In creating the Holocaust denier, Garner Globalis, Ozick encounters the aesthetic dilemma with which George Steiner wrestled in *The Portage to San Cristobal of A. H.*, namely, how to give the villain his dramatic due without promulgating his cause. Cognizant that the theatrical tradition in which villains deliver powerful speeches is fraught with danger when the subject is the Holocaust, Steiner and Ozick forge ahead nevertheless. Each attributes seductive lines to the Nazis, yet Steiner demonstrates the fraudulent essence of Hitler's speech, and Ozick reveals the denier's cardinal dishonesty and malevolence. Like Milton's Satan, Globalis captivates his victims with charm, in the guise of personas they crave: for Stella, a lover, and for Rosa, an attentive confidant. Progressing beyond the portrait of the pseudoscholar of the novella, who brought the insensitivity and arrogance of a self-aggrandizing academic to a subject demanding humility, in the play Ozick addresses the sinister realm of intentional deceit of Holocaust deniers and revisionists, a dangerous movement making headway among the historically illiterate, who are easily hoodwinked by engaging frauds.

Among changes Ozick instituted for the dramatic form is a shift and elaboration in Rosa's Shoah testimony. Instead of confining her witness to letters written to Magda, Rosa speaks directly to Globalis, Persky, and others, offering more detail about ghetto and camp experiences than she had in the novella. In place of the elegant Polish letters, Rosa speaks haltingly (ellipses are printed in the text) in unembellished, fractured English to recount her ghetto losses: "Over there . . . my father they took away. My brother they took away. My mother was already finished, she couldn't swallow, she couldn't breathe. Her body they took away in a . . . wheelbarrow" (44). Similarly, Ozick replaces the innuendo of the novella with brief but graphic accounts of Rosa's camp brothel experience: "Me they put where . . . they don't let us wear nothing . . . underneath" (44). Rosa now speaks openly of women suffering in long roll calls, ill-clad women standing for hours in the cold, women who are hungry, sick, smelling the stench from the crematoria, their eyes burning from the smoke.

Of special interest to readers of the earlier text are the similarities, departures, and extensions in the characterization of the two Shoah survivors. Rosa's stage incarnation retains the basic character traits established in the novella, with the exception of her newfound tendency to engage in Holocaust discourse. Stella's dramatic manner conforms to Rosa's delineation of her in the novella: a woman who suppresses Holocaust memory to devote her energies to recovery and renewal. In the play's opening scene Rosa rebukes Stella for obliterating their past. When she comprehends that Globalis exploited her to get to Rosa, Stella bitterly concedes that, like Rosa, she is "a piece of human . . . refuse!" Turning on the Holocaust denier, she asks and answers her own question: "Do you think I put my life together any better than Rosa? It may look like it, but it isn't true. . . . Rosa thinks I forgot, I haven't forgotten anything! . . . they starved us . . . we . . . were nothing! . . . I was dying of hunger, I was a child in hell" (59–60). Beneath the facade of normalcy painful recollection lingers. In the end Stella comes to Rosa's support, horrified that Globalis has deceived and manipulated the tormented victim into a false denial. Stella confronts and denounces Globalis directly, mocking his devious inventions: "Bread, the ovens were for baking bread! *(Overwrought)* And the electric fences were only playgrounds for children! Monkey bars, jungle gyms!" (67). Finally, the woman who accused Rosa of making a relic or fetish of the shawl in the novella demands that Rosa show it to the denier: "Tell him what was in it! Get the shawl and show him!" (67). Stuffing a corner of a towel into her mouth in "a gesture reminiscent of the-shawl-that-is-milk" (69), Rosa is too weak to respond with anything other than bewilderment to the fraud Globalis has perpetrated by convincing her that she was signing a paper acknowledging Magda's death when in fact she was signing a statement testifying to her delusionary status and renouncing her Holocaust testimony. It is Stella who takes on the revisionist, identifying him as a Nazi "from the kingdom of lies! . . . exploiter . . . persecutor . . . rapist! . . . you say it never happened, and you rejoice that it did. You want to undo it and you want to do it! You want to take human beings and turn them into nothing! . . . You want to turn the crimes against us into nothing! You want it to happen again" (69).

The play ends in a reconciliation scene between Rosa and Stella: Stella acknowledges her long-term dependence on Rosa, her jealousy of Magda, her sorrow that Globalis has deprived Rosa of Magda. For her part, Rosa confesses that she invented Magda's postwar presence to hurt Stella, to compensate for her rancor that Stella lived and Magda died. The play's closing scenes confirm the disturbing reality that has pervaded the mood of the drama. Although the Holocaust denier has been debunked by Stella and the older generation of Jewish hotel guests have recognized him for what he is, the young gentile receptionist is deceived by his charm and his gifts and agrees to disseminate his pamphlets at her school. The play's conclusion suggests a warmer and more mutually supportive future for Rosa and Stella than does the novella. The play ends with the reconciliation of the survivors, the return of Magda's spirit, Stella's emphatic iteration of the continued presence of Holocaust memory, and her bonding with Rosa in the perpetuation of memory: "I don't think it will ever come to an end. It will never go away, never. Where we were. What happened. What they did to us" (74). Both women retreat to an Edenic garden vision, the idealized Poland of their youth enlarged by the golden-haired Magda in their midst. As the curtain comes down, the women are cradled in each other's arms,

Stella singing a Polish lullaby to Rosa, while the "humming sound of an electric sizzle" and "MAGDA'S CRY. Ma . . . ma!" (75) wash over the audience. The perpetrators remain, the victims remain, the bystanders remain, and the voice covering all is the palpable cry of the most innocent victim, representing generations of Jewish children denied life. By opening and closing the play with Magda's anguished cry, Ozick suggests that the victim's voice will not be silenced; it will remain a haunting presence drowning out the distortions and lies of Holocaust revisionists.

Analyzing the Jewish writers whose work will endure, Ozick argues for those who are attentive to Jewish history and values. She asserts that "the tales we care for lastingly are the ones that touch on the redemptive."[43] Her fictions exhibit these qualities, and they will have a place in literary history as the products of a first-rate imagination and intellect imbued with historic and moral values. The moral injunction to remember is central to Jewish thinking and to Ozick's characters. Enoch Vand argues that history "isn't simply what has happened. It's a judgment on what has happened!"[44] Puttermesser insists that one "must own a past."[45] Edelshtein rebukes those who "court amnesia of history."[46] And Rosa Lublin scorns Holocaust disinterest, misappropriation, and denial. Ozick mourns the loss of "not only the intellect of a people in its prime, . . . but the treasure of a people in its potential . . . lost scholars of Torah . . . loss of thousands upon thousands of achieved thinkers and physicians, nourishing scientists and artists. The loss of those who would have grown into healers, discoverers, poets."[47] Writing about the most celebrated voice of Holocaust remembrance, Elie Wiesel, Ozick urged Jewish writers to "retrieve the Holocaust freight car by freight car, town by town, road by road, document by document. The task is to save it from becoming literature."[48] Ozick's cautionary plea refers to mere literature, to literature that is self-enamored, self-absorbed with its own aesthetic genius. The Holocaust has been a recurrent subject of Ozick's writing, occasionally presented in exquisite lyrical prose. Although her writing is beautiful, dazzling, resplendent, it is a memorial in the finest sense, in the tradition of the great poetic elegiasts who employ beautiful language as an act of commemoration. Ozick's exquisite language does not divert our attention from the Holocaust tragedy to its own artifice. Rather, it binds us to the tragedy, a constant reminder of the Jewish artists who were killed and those never born and the loss to civilization of their brilliance.

Cynthia Ozick is achieving the values she prescribed for Jewish-American literature in her influential essay "Toward a New Yiddish," in fiction that is "centrally Jewish in its concerns" and "liturgical in nature."[49] Her writing pays homage to precursor texts, is enamored of Jewish history, and presents the Holocaust as an orienting event of the twentieth century: "We and all the generations to follow, are, and will continue to be into eternity, witness generations to Jewish loss."[50] Her philosophy of Holocaust witness may be discerned from her long record of witnessing and from her response to a survivor who challenged her representation in *The Shawl*. "Every Jew," she wrote, "should feel as if he himself came out of Egypt. . . . The Exodus took place 4,000 years ago, and yet the *Haggadah* enjoins me to incorporate it into my own mind and flesh, to so act as if it happened directly and intensely to me, not as mere witness but as participant. Well, if I am enjoined to belong to an event that occurred 4,000 years ago, how much more strongly am I obliged to belong to an event that occurred only 40 years ago."[51]

MARGE PIERCY

Writing about the Holocaust and World War II is something Marge Piercy has long understood she would undertake, for those events "changed the lives of everybody [she] knew."[1] She was deeply affected during her childhood by Holocaust coverage in the Jewish press, her maternal family's realization "that Jews were being rounded up, put in camps, and that many were being killed," and her grandmother's "great cry of grief [for] the death of an entire family, a village, a society. . . . What she contemplated as she mourned," Piercy explains, "was the death of a people. She feared there soon would be no more Jews."[2] Piercy also discerns a connection between her mother's wartime observation of the world's indifference to the slaughter of European Jewry and her own moral commitment to "remember always."[3] Although geographic distance from the European catastrophe ensured physical safety, like many American Jews, Piercy has pondered how she might have behaved and what her fate might have been had she been there: whether she would have resisted, whether she would have been spared for slave labor, subjected to medical experiment, or sent to the gas chamber.[4] Her marriage to a French Jew, whose family experienced the war both in France and as refugees in Switzerland, reinforced her connection to the Holocaust. This familial alliance created an opportunity to talk intimately with people possessing direct knowledge of the French Resistance and ready to respond openly to a family member.[5] Those dialogues, and her difficulty securing research funding, proved instrumental in Piercy's decision to focus the Holocaust portion of her book on the French-Jewish experience rather than pursue her initial plan to treat eastern Europe. The resulting novel opens the American Holocaust canon to exploration of a Western nation's Nazi collaboration in the genocide of European Jewry.[6]

In marked contrast to the other works in this study, which focus entirely on the Shoah and its legacy, Piercy treats the Holocaust in the context of the world at war. *Gone to Soldiers* extends the scope of the war novel from the training camp and battle zone perspectives employed by male writers such as Norman Mailer, Irwin Shaw, and William Styron to encompass partisan sabotage, torture chamber, concentration camp, research center, and homefront.[7] A principal virtue of this approach is a politically conscious view of wartime race and gender issues, for she sees "wars fought not between armies but between populations . . . [and she is] aware that in armies there are relatively few men in the front lines in comparison to the vast number of individuals who get involved behind the lines."[8] Populating the novel is a large array of civilians, in the contexts of internment and concentration camps, resistance and intelligence units, and professional or rescue missions at some distance from the war scene.

Although *Gone to Soldiers* was imaginatively conceived, Piercy insists that nothing happens "that had not happened somewhere in the time and place of the work's setting."[9] This supplementing of the fictional with documentary evidence reflects Piercy's conviction that imagined literature on the Shoah is insufficient; it must have external support. Yet, eschewing the approach taken by John Hershey, who made the "recovery" of historical records a central part of the narrative technique in order to simulate history in *The Wall*, Piercy instead integrates documentary evidence organically in the fictional schema of her text. Furthermore, through juxtaposition of varied narrative modes, including refugee interview, diary, journalistic report, dramatic conflict, and dream fantasy, she dissolves boundaries between discourses. The result is an epic novel of monumental scope and vision, one that reflects Piercy's reading of more than three hundred testimonies by survivors, accounts by American soldiers, and histories, a data base "seven times as long as the [seven-hundred-page] manuscript."[10]

Encompassing the European and Pacific theaters of war as well as the American homefront, *Gone to Soldiers* is composed "as a cantata, as a choral work in which there would be many voices."[11] The novel consists of multiple viewpoints "moving regularly from one to the other. . . . Each [character has a specific] social world and history, milieu, problems, . . . family, loved ones." "Each time I change chapters," Piercy says, "I wrench myself from one world to another and . . . do the same for the reader."[12] Related from the viewpoint of a single character at a time, each sequence of the character-titled chapters may be read as an independent novel. In her third draft Piercy wrote each character's tale separately to ensure consistency of the individual's language and tone, and in the fourth draft she reintegrated the segments, intertwining the ten characters' stories.[13] Much of the novel's structural mastery appears in the overlapping yet distinctive perspectives of people who experience the war in the United States, England, France, Germany, and the Far East; from the land, sea, and air; from the trenches, the forests, and the factories; from Milice and Gestapo torture chambers; from Auschwitz and Buchenwald.

The decision to use a cantata structural scheme may have been influenced by the sheer volume of testimonies Piercy read, including historian Emmanuel Ringelblum's famed wartime chronicle, *Oneg Shabbes*, a work composed of multiple voices and drawing on the diverse experiences of east European Jewry. Ringelblum's compilation includes materials gathered by amateur field workers in an effort to record multiple perspectives—young and old, religious and secular, political and apolitical. So, too, Piercy populates her novel with characters from various national, social, and political backgrounds who experience the war and the Holocaust differently.

In accord with other feminist authors who diffuse a singular narrative voice to introduce a structure that foregrounds more than one character, thereby bypassing single, dominant, authoritative points of view, Piercy successfully privileges collective protagonists, multiple points of view, multiple stories. *Gone to Soldiers* may also be read as a "dialogic" novel. Although Piercy has not fashioned an irreconcilable quarrel between opposed voices, like those Bakhtin discovered in Dostoevsky, she negates the idea of a "unity of existence" and a "unity of consciousness" associated with the "monologic" novel. Her cantata of voices offers a fuller sense of the complications of existence, experience, thought, and feelings. In one instance, the July 1942 roundup of French Jews, Piercy presents the same event from four disparate vantage points, to effect a comprehensive rendition of the event but also to attest to varieties of Holocaust experience based on one's political circumstances. Even the protagonist's utterances reveal two contending voices clearly shaped by Shoah events that influence her political and spiritual metamorphosis. *Gone to Soldiers* is, thus, the heterogeneous, polyphonous interaction of voices described by Mikhail Bakhtin as the criterion of the novel as a self-contestatory and self-renewing genre.

Structural unity is achieved by linking the stories of two generations of a multibranched single family and the stories of nonfamily professional associates who are directly engaged in war-related work and the Holocaust. Prewar history of the extended family is quickly sketched through the matriarchal lines of four sisters dispersed in Paris, Shanghai, and Detroit, evidencing the Jewish migration and settlement patterns of the late nineteenth and early twentieth centuries. The Holocaust is chronicled through their families' wartime experience with emphasis on three daughters of the Lévy-Monot family, characters who carry the burden of the next generation from European assimilation and genocide to restoration of the Jewish people in the United States and a national homeland in Israel.

The text's political and sociological authenticity is embedded in the suffering Vichy France imposed on its Jewish population and the composition of the family structure. Lévy-Monot is a native-born French Jew; his wife is a Polish-born Jewish naturalized French citizen; and their three daughters are native-born French citizens. Jacqueline, the eldest, initially feels essentially French in her cultural loyalties and wants no connection to Judaism, whereas the twins, Naomi and Rivka, share Judaic identities reflecting their parents' religious beliefs and political convictions. Symbolic naming provides interpretive direction. Naomi, like her biblical namesake, is loving and a wanderer; Rivka, named for a biblical matriarch, "is the one who should have carried life into the future, but is denied that possibility historically"; and Jacqueline's Hebrew name, "Yakova," "the one who does battle," corresponds to the protagonist's philosophical and dramatic role.[14]

The fully developed female characters arising from Piercy's feminist sensibility are active questers, never restricted to the roles routinely assigned women in war fiction written by men. The characters are pilots, journalists, or resistance fighters; they are passionate activists, forging new directions for women in public life. The strongest, most fully realized characters in the Holocaust chapters of *Gone to Soldiers* are its women: Jacqueline transforms herself from arrogant adolescent Franco-Jewish assimilationist to chastened adult resistance fighter who reclaims her Judaic cultural heritage and adopts a Zionist political philosophy; Daniela, an Orthodox Jew and Zionist, counsels Jacqueline and is her resistance partner; Naomi, a child refugee, is separated from her family and sent to safe haven in the United States; Ruthie Siegal, an American cousin of the young Holocaust victims, is sensitized to American antisemitism and racism through the prism of Nazism; and among the professionals, Louise Kahan, an American journalist, battles press and government bureaucracy to publish documentary evidence of Germany's crime; and Abra, a social scientist, is drawn into research for the OSS.

The chronology and implications of the German war against the Jews of Europe are presented primarily through the investigative agency of two American women and the victimization of the European women. Although Piercy dramatizes most events in the novel, she conveys the early stages of the Nazi rise to power in Germany through Abra's interviews with refugees and the Aryanization of France primarily through Jacqueline's diary accounts. The concentrationary period is presented both dramatically, through Jacqueline's incarceration, and impressionistically, from the distanced imagination of Jacqueline's younger sister, Naomi, who is plagued by survivor guilt, as well as through liberation-era investigative journalism by Louise. Jacqueline's diary and Naomi's speculations and nightmares link public events and private responses, thereby affording Piercy diverse opportunities to develop characters who engage readers and to chart the chronology of the German occupation of France.

Effectively enlarging the Holocaust panorama beyond the circumscribed war-era knowledge of the victims, the Abra chapters convey early periods of German anti-Jewish discrimination and Nazi dominion unknown to the protagonist. Abra chronicles the German misreading of the Nazis as a temporary aberration, the growth and empowerment of Hitler's paramilitary terror squads, support for the Nazis by German industrial barons, inefficacy of the Reichsvertertung as a united front against the Nazis, and collapse of the opposition's delusions that the major world powers would contain Hitler. Her interview scenes with German-Jewish refugees capture the essence of betrayal they felt and function as prologue to the novel's French Holocaust drama. The treachery French Jews will experience under a collaborationist government is anticipated and paralleled in a German refugee's report of confiscation of Jewish property, institution of discriminatory legislation, and arrest and incarceration of Jewish citizens. The refugee's indications of her family's "very German" assimilationist position, their alienation from *Ostjuden* (Jews who emigrated from Poland) and from Zionists, whom they believed to be misguided, foreshadow attitudes that are dramatized in the French sequence. Jacqueline's prewar journal entries, revealing her rejection of any idea that casts doubt on the integrity of her French citizenship, parallels the delusion of native-born Jews that they were secure in French society. Despite living in a Jewish working-class neighborhood, in a household where Yiddish is spoken, and with a father who is active in a Zionist organization, Jacqueline has little patience for Jewish affiliation. "The universal, not the accidental particular" (27), is her ideal. Her notion of the universal, however, is national. She denounces her father's Zionist philosophy and is vexed by her twin sisters' rejection of their French names, Nadine and Renée, in favor of the Hebrew Naomi and Rivka, which Jacqueline classifies as parochial "ghetto" names.

Although the diary form is, in part, homage to the victim and survivor memoirs Piercy read in the course of her research, it serves admirably both as Holocaust chronicle and as venue for the profoundly transformed character to be heard in her own voice. Jacqueline diagrams the Nazification of France: the North is under German military occupation, and in the South, which is ruled by the collaborationist Vichy regime, attendant French antisemitism is manifested in fervent xenophobia and willing enforcement of German anti-Jewish policies, with tragic consequences for native-born and immigrant French Jews.[15] The initial journal entries reveal a young woman apparently oblivious to the political reality of a two-week-old war, writing in adolescent pique about her family's loyalty to Judaism. Not until the third entry, on 21 February 1940, noting her father's mobilization in the French army, does Jacqueline mention the war. Nonetheless, the focus of her meditation is on estrangement from her father, stemming from her disapproval of his dedication to a Jewish national identity. Piercy's development of Jacqueline's assimilationism carries the sociological weight of observations more recently offered by Alain Finkielkraut, the son of Holocaust survivors and a perceptive commentator on French Jewish life. He describes a class of French Jews whose purpose was to "dejewify themselves," to become mimics of the French; in doing so, they "forged a new kind of [Jew], the *Israelite*: reserved, distinguished, conscientious, and smitten with love for France."[16] For this group of assimilationists, the visible Jews, especially east European immigrants, "who persisted in acting as if a Jewish nation might still exist,"[17] who acted Jewish in public and spoke French with a foreign accent, were an embarrassment. Judeophobia was not uncommon among the Israelites, who dreaded being identified as Jewish and openly expressed their contempt, as Jacqueline does at this stage, for Jewish difference. Jacqueline's ready acceptance of the revocation of citizenship of relatives who have lived in France since 1935 is founded on disdain for their continued use of Yiddish and Polish and marks the emotional and political distance she will travel before the novel's conclusion to develop a Jewish sensibility. An exemplar of Alain Finkielkraut's Israelite paradigm, Jacqueline is shaped by her French education and the phenomenon Hannah Arendt characterizes as the self-hating Jew, who lives "in a society on the whole hostile to Jews . . . [where] it is possible to assimilate only by assimilating anti-Semitism also."[18]

Jacqueline maintains her assimilationist naiveté as late as September 1940, when she is certain she is not the subject of French antisemitic wall posters prominently displayed in Paris as part of a propaganda campaign to foster xenophobia among Parisians.[19] She is as French as anyone else, "as thoroughly imbued with French culture as any of my teachers, so it is not me that this vileness is aimed at and I will simply not accept it" (31). Her innocence is shattered when French-born Jews encounter discrimination similar to that which the naturalized and foreign Jews have experienced and are ordered to register with the local police and have *JUIF* stamped on their identity cards.[20] Police registration and her best friend's defection by October 1940 lead Jacqueline to the realization—albeit externally imposed—that her place is in the Jewish community.

Diary entries between August and December 1941 illustrate Piercy's intention to endow her characters with experiences rooted in history. Although she conflates the deprivations and decrees to which Jews in the occupied zone were subject, the authenticity of this section is reinforced by attention to detail, such as attributing Mme Lévy-Monot's continuing employment to her work in the fur industry, one of the few occupations in which Jewish workers were retained to serve the German war effort. Reflective of family hardships and coping strategies are the efforts in Paris of mother and daughters to secure food and fuel while the father, an escaped prisoner of war, purchases a dead man's *Ausweis* (pass) to travel to Marseilles in order to send one child to America. The family receives news of immigrant relatives who have been interned at Drancy.[21] The entire XIe arrondissement, where the largest number of Jewish immigrants lived, is closed; Jewish businesses are expropriated; curfews, hostage taking, arrests, and executions become commonplace. Piercy economically etches the December 1941 arrest of a thousand French Jews, "including all the lawyers who practice at the Paris bar, . . . doctors, writers, and intellectuals" (83).[22] Their incarceration demonstrates that the early differentiation between French and immigrant Jews was transitory, that the Jewish community misread the initial action "as part of the German authorities' attempts to eradicate resistance and not as evidence that the Jews were an expendable commodity, without regard for their nationalities."[23]

The concluding Jacqueline chapter dealing with the early occupation encompasses abominations ranging from the decree compelling the Jews of France to wear the yellow star embossed with the black-lettered word *JUIF* to the roundup and imprisonment of indexed Parisian Jews. Woven between the extended passages on Jacqueline's responses to specific edicts are brief notations on the diminishment of the Jewish presence in society. Every sphere of public life is touched: the Sarah Bernhardt Theater is renamed, as is every Parisian street named for a Jew; writers are withdrawn from publication lists; Jewish students are barred from the Sorbonne, as are Jewish patrons from restaurants, libraries, museums. Even where rights remain, they are sharply curtailed: prohibitions exist against using transportation save the last car of the Metro and shopping beyond one evening hour in restricted establishments.

Readers of the Jacqueline chapters have a double perspective: that of the protagonist, whose knowledge is limited by wartime circumstances, and that of their own privileged post-Holocaust consciousness. Jacqueline's sensibility and perspective are sharply curbed by French and Nazi deceptions practiced on victims. For example, although the diarist notes police registration of the Jews, she is unaware of the implications of the index. Post-Holocaust readers attentive to French collaborationist history understand that the purpose of the registration was to facilitate expropriation of Jewish property and deportation. Names, addresses, nationalities, professions, and property holdings of the indexed Jews were categorized and filed with the Gestapo. Foreign-born Jews were destined to be the victims of the first massive arrests and deportations from Paris. On 16 July, later designated Black Thursday, almost half the Parisian Jews on the index were arrested and interned in Vel d'Hiv as a prelude for transport to Drancy, the embarkation point for deportation to Auschwitz.[24]

Juxtaposed with Jacqueline's fleeting journal references to most anti-Jewish decrees and edicts are multiple delineations of the July 1942 roundup. Jacqueline's entry on the roundup, one of four perspectives, is truncated by her distance from the events. Her diary presentation is void of factual reportage, of the sort historians tender to detail the mechanics of the action and the composition of the 9,000-man French force. Nor does she fuse the mythic and factual, as Cynthia Ozick does in *The Cannibal Galaxy*, characterizing the force as "creatures like centaurs . . . flinging their rods, sticks, rocks, poles. . . . Fangs, hoofs, strange hairiness. . . . Noble French youth. Gendarmes, patrolmen, baby-faced students from the police school, hundreds of cross-strapped blue shirts and armbands."[25] Whereas Ozick's approach functions as the single dramatic representation of the roundup and evocation of the ensuing genocide, Jacqueline's journal recounts her personal grief for her mother and sister. Because she was not an eyewitness, Jacqueline conveys only meager information garnered from the press and from hearsay regarding the thoroughness of the sweep, including the press assessment that the event was "a wonderful idea" (145).[26] Having believed the Vichy deception that only alien Jews, rather than French Jews, would be deported, Jacqueline is stunned by the arrest of French-born Jews and naturalized citizens of many years' standing, the detention of women and children, the aged and the dying.

For postwar readers, the mass arrest of Jews seems a logical development, but until July 1942 it appeared to contemporaries of Jacqueline's background that the harsh measures affecting their economic and social circumstances would be the most critical deprivations French Jews would encounter. Her surprise and outrage that her French-born sister and her long-naturalized mother have been arrested along with recent immigrants illustrates the success of the French antisemites in fostering division within the Jewish community, a phenomenon lasting from the late nineteenth century through the Vichy years. The chapter closes with Jacqueline's desperate isolation and her painful ambivalence regarding French police complicity.

Piercy represents the feelings of the captives at second hand, through Naomi's speculations about her twin's expulsion from the family home. The betrayal by the concierge is the treachery of the French government writ small. In contrast to her older sister's perspective, Naomi's imagined sequence is fashioned through the interior psychology of twin association and captures the physical essence of prisoners suffering sweltering July confinement and discomfort in the Vel d'Hiv glass-roofed stadium.[27] Beyond the physical oppression of parched throats and blistered tongues, insufficient toilets, overcrowding, heat, and stench, Piercy addresses the political ramifications in her attention to the altered demeanor of the French guards: polite during the roundup while under the scrutiny of ordinary French citizens but abusive once their victims had been isolated in the detention site.

Much later in the novel, in Daniela's story, Piercy extends her incremental development of the roundup to incorporate a Jewish political perspective in an allusion to organized Jewish resistance. Unlike Jacqueline, who escaped by chance, Daniela Rubin's family "had word via the network just before it happened" (146) and fled to Nice, where they live under a relatively easy Italian occupation unfettered by Nazi/Vichy racial measures.[28] Although Piercy does not identify "the network" she is alluding to, one of the earliest active resistance efforts of French Jews was the combined work of the Union Generale des Israelites de France (UGIF) and the Communists, who warned their constituents of a projected police measure and saved thousands of lives.[29] In this manner Piercy shifts her focus from individual trauma to the collective response. Among the virtues of this incremental representation of the July roundup are the moving parallels of individual and collective experience, psychological and political nuances.

A transition chapter, entitled "Roads of Paper," continues the focus on the occupation and moves on to Piercy's major themes of resistance and female bonding as a survival strategy, the former rarely treated in American Holocaust literature, and the latter a topic central to women's Holocaust writing. Spanning the period from 11 November, when France was reunited under German rule, to 18 December 1942, the chapter depicts Jacqueline's clandestine existence in a working-class district whose Jewish quarter had been a primary target for the July dragnet and is therefore considered "judenrein." The work of the Resistance during this early period is inscribed in Piercy's references to Jews living under assumed Aryan identities and the philanthropic work of the UGIF, which enabled families of the camp internees to send food. Under false documents bearing the surname Porell, Jacqueline works with a Resistance unit through whose intelligence she learns of impending Drancy deportations. It is not long before she beholds the deportees marched to the trains, among them her barely recognizable sister, "so lean and stooped she looked like an old lady at first" (219), and her mother, also "bone thin" (219).

The Drancy children's deportations are among the most poignant scenes of the novel. Piercy addresses these deportations twice: briefly through rumor and later in extended description. Through her Resistance network Jacqueline learns that German quotas are being met with "a mass deportation of very young children, many of whom had already lost their parents" (217). Confirming and augmenting the intelligence report is an emotionally wrought impressionistic account of a children's deportation filtered through Naomi's reverie, which functions both to record the operation and to imagine her own fate had she remained in France. Rivka, her twin, whose experiences often appear as italicized passages at the end or beginning of Naomi's chapters, observes children *"being called by name, . . . they were too little to have learned their last names or their formal first names. . . . Finally the officials just numbered them. They had to have a thousand children. Little ones were running all about and some officials began to beat them. . . . The children would just lie down and weep. They did not march in neat lines the way the guards wanted them to, into the buses to take them to the train station where the cars were waiting. French policemen were lined up along the way to make sure they did not escape. Children would run up to the guards and beg them to take them to the bathroom so they would not wet themselves, ask them to tie their shoes. . . . The little ones were being shipped east. The French officials had decided the Jewish children must go"* (239). These details are not fictional invention. They represent Piercy's selection and arrangement of data derived from documents such as those appearing in Claude Lévy and Paul Tillard's monumental *Betrayal at the Vel d'Hiv*.[30]

The Jacqueline and Naomi deportation passages are shaped by contemporary and post-Shoah sensibilities. Jacqueline's excerpt is intentionally limited and misfocused, although not entirely misdirected in its accusation against the Germans. It was wholly appropriate for a contemporary French diarist to attribute all the blame for the children's deportations to the Germans, but Vichy documents, revealed after the war, testify to French responsibility for the deportation of the very young.[31] The murder of orphans of stateless Jews deported to Auschwitz, including more than 4,000 taken in the July roundup, stems from Pierre Laval's Eichmann-approved proposal to deport children under age sixteen. Essential to the refugee's imagined scene is her twin's eyewitness to the deportation, itemizing the particulars of young children being beaten and marched to transports. This witness counters the prevailing postwar French desire, held by Gaullists and Communists alike, to suppress the crimes of Vichy. Free of the motivation of politicians and French citizenry to reunite and resurrect the honor of the tragically divided nation, resulting in revisionist memory that maximizes French heroism and minimizes or erases French crimes, Piercy rejects such invention and evasion of Holocaust history.

Paralleling her honest treatment of French collaborationist initiatives is Piercy's correction of the myth that the Jews went passively to slaughter. Paying homage to men and women who fought fascism in the cafés of Paris, the countryside hideouts, the Montaigne Noire and the Pyrenees, and the torture chambers of the Milice and Gestapo, Piercy modeled her resistants on French Jews engaged in armed revolt against the Nazis as members of exclusive Jewish Resistance units or of French Resistance units in which they made up "15 to 20 percent of the active membership . . . although they constituted less than one percent of the French population."[32] The fictional treatment of the Jewish Resistance is derived from extensive historic research and knowledge Piercy gained from her husband's family and their friends. She recalls having heard "stories of Jews . . . who had published clandestine papers carrying news of Allied victories and encouragement to resist, those who had forged papers to enable Jews or escaped prisoners of war to blend into the population or move through the country in hopes of escaping, those who had led children or adults over the heavily patrolled borders into Spain or into Switzerland, those who had committed sabotage or operated illegal radios, those who had helped free prisoners, those who had taken part in armed actions or bombings, those who had taken to the mountains as Maquis, the French guerrilla fighters."[33] Piercy attributes such activity to both major and minor characters. Among Lévy-Monot's multiple roles is that of maquisard leader. Jacqueline and her friend, Daniela Rubin, are couriers and saboteurs. They are joined by a chorus of secondary characters including a Jewish-American woman who helps downed Allied pilots and fugitive Jews escape and an Israeli who joins the French Jewish partisans.

Reflecting historic circumstances, the novel's dominant resistance figures, drawn from the ranks of the Jewish Scout Movement, Zionist organizations, and the Jewish immigrant communities, are shown disrupting German goals and assisting Allied preparation for the cross-Channel invasion. The multifaceted Jewish Resistance is marked by the author's astute political recognition of differences among the factions within the Jewish community, distinctions based on irreconcilable conceptions of Jewish identity.[34] Lévy-Monot's allegiance is to a labor-Zionist organization calling Jews to arms against the Vichy government and to "Armand-Jules," the Jewish army, which acted both independently and in accord with the general French Resistance movement. Descriptions of the maquisard are representative of the novelist's substantive use of Amy Latour's *Jewish Resistance in France, 1940–1944* and its delineation of a maquisard unit as "essentially a military organization, [which] differed from other groups in the general Resistance movement by its Jewish and Zionist ideology."[35] In the Vichy zone Lévy-Monot works with the Eclaireurs Israelites de France (EIF), the Jewish Boy Scouts, and distributes a Jewish Resistance newspaper alerting readers to the dangers of the occupation and urging armed resistance.[36] In the early days of the Resistance, while her father serves in the south, Jacqueline remains in Paris with Daniela, creating Aryan identities for Jewish fugitives by usurping the verifiable names of naturalized non-Jews to produce birth certificates, baptismal records, work permits, and certificates for repatriated prisoners.[37] Jacqueline also serves in networks finding safe housing for children who can pass as gentiles and guiding the inconcealable across the Pyrenees for eventual emigration to Palestine.

In keeping with her focus on authentic portrayal based on research evidencing "how very active women were in the Resistance," Piercy highlights women's resistance roles.[38] Because they were thought to be less vulnerable than men to suspicion of being resistance fighters and because it was easier for women than for men to conceal their Jewish identity, women were particularly numerous as couriers.[39] A minor character, the Jewish-American wife of an aristocratic French collaborator, is modeled on women who worked in and administered the M19 networks that were instrumental in the rescue of thousands of British and American airmen.[40] In addition, Piercy's women experience combat, participate in freeing their colleagues from Milice security and concentration camps, and undergo arrest and torture by the Gestapo.

Much of the novel's focus on the Resistance demonstrates its successes and achievements despite its meager resources, yet Piercy shuns romantic depiction of its exploits and a sentimental view of its self-governance. The heroism she describes is neither a fictional invention nor an exaggeration. Her portrait of the resistance fighters does not exclude unsuccessful missions or aggrandize accomplishments, and it takes note of the burned, bruised, and broken bodies of resistants who have been tortured by the Gestapo and of the beatings and repeated rapes Jacqueline suffers at the hands of Milice thugs. As a feminist, Piercy criticizes sexism among the resistance leadership and in the ranks, exemplified by a commander's objection to Jacqueline's presence at a munitions drop on the very site she scouted and male rejection of prized jobs once women have performed them. Jacqueline foils male resistants who consign women to subordinate, nurturing roles by refusing to nurse an injured partisan unless she is given lessons on the Sten gun.

Even Jacqueline's heroic escape from the Milice prison closely follows details of the Gestapo escape of Marie-Madeleine Fourcade, a Resistance heroine who headed the Alliance network of more than three thousand operatives. Of her prison escape, Fourcade writes:

> One gap seemed big enough to take my head provided I was prepared to push hard. . . . I pushed with all my strength. My head went through. [She retreats as a convoy passes.] . . . Pushing my head through again was even more painful than the first time, but the pain and the fear of failure made me perspire profusely, which helped my skin to slip against the iron. After my neck, I got one shoulder through, then my right leg. Squeezing my hips through was sheer agony. The pain was appalling but I knew that once the head is through the rest of the body will go, while the pain I felt would be nothing compared with what would be in store for me with the Gestapo.[41]

The fictional account varies only in minutiae:

> Pressing my head cautiously against each gap in the bars, I found that the bar nearest the right hand had the largest gap between bar and wall. . . . I began trying to work my head through as soon as the sentry had passed. . . . I forced my head through. It felt as if I had skinned myself and broken my jaw but there I was hanging over the street with my head through the bars. . . . I continued forcing myself through, wishing I were skinnier than I am. . . . My own sweat helped lubricate me. I was sweating heavily, partly from exertion. . . . I thought my arms would rip from their sockets, but the hardest part was my hips. Finally, I lunged and then fell. (500–01)

Fourcade is also the source of Piercy's animal code names for resistance fighters, such as "*Lapin* [Rabbit]" for Jacqueline's father and "Mongoose" for an American major working with the Resistance. Whether Piercy read Fourcade's book is uncertain, but an excerpt from it appears in a book the novelist acknowledges reading, Vera Laska's *Women in the Resistance and in the Holocaust*.

Jacqueline's final journal entry coincides with a bombing raid that takes the life of her father and many others. The chapter concludes with the military journal of a surviving combatant who details the unit's losses, including Jacqueline. Not until her arrival at Auschwitz do readers discover that she is still alive. Readers thereby experience a sudden fissure that parallels the shattering experiences of the victims, who underwent disorienting moves without foreknowledge of their destination. Relinquishing the first-person voice of the diary form, Piercy honors the improbability of maintaining a journal in Auschwitz and validates Jacqueline's transformation from active resistant to disempowered, nameless concentration camp inmate whose history is now presented in the omniscient narrative voice.

Whereas most survivor-writers emphasize the ghetto and concentration-ary settings, Piercy, like native-born American writers, carefully circum-scribes her fictional treatment of the concentration camps. Nonetheless, in two chapters and portions of several others devoted to the camps, she intro-duces a full range of camp themes and skillfully incorporates characteristics of the physical and psychological struggles of prisoners while addressing the moral and social implications of the Holocaust. Her early intention was "to deal with the camps only through the experiences of the twins," and she planned to have Naomi's imagined perception of Rivka and Chava fabricating rocket parts in the hollowed-out mountain of Dora/Nordhausen as the sole concentration camp segment. Fortunately, dealing with the camps "only through this second-level reality" gave way to Piercy's recognition that the novel required direct confrontation with Auschwitz. When, after a year's evasion, Piercy engaged this material, she produced more than twenty drafts and concluded that she had "never written anything more difficult."[42]

The concentration camp universe is initially broached through Naomi's thoughts and imaginings. Playing on the close psychological and emotional bond of twins, Piercy often assimilates Rivka's Holocaust trials and tribula-tions into Naomi's chapters. The guilty survivor twin "*dreaded night when she slipped into Rivka's body*" (515), completely identifying with her sister's pain. Consistent with the initial plan, these segments are generally presented in a mimetic mode. One startling departure appears in the form of an imagined scene of Rivka working as "*a slave in the cavern of the troll king*" in an underground munitions factory whose cave walls "wept" (515). This venture into the realm of the fantastic suggests both the monstrous quality of the camp experience and the difficulty the uninitiated have understanding a world that has no analogue in past human experience.

In contrast to the troll king/slave vision, Naomi's reveries are otherwise composed of realistic scenes of her mother and sister as they endure long roll calls, beatings, intense hunger, and exhaustive labor under falling black smoke and black ash lying "on them like the shadow of death" (311). Her response to their deportation to the east is etched in diction and imagery iterating and linking the passage of imagined vision to existential reality yet distinguishing the imagined from the real, for "deported meant that her bad dreams were true. . . . The place she saw did not come from her subconscious, . . . but was a place that existed there in the east, where the black smoke rose as if from a volcano and hung greasy and potent in the air" (379).

Readers gain an impressionistic overview of camp adversity from Naomi's reveries, but it is through the dramatic presentation of Jacqueline's and Daniela's experience that the daily ignominy of being under the Nazi boot is realized. Forgoing the extended dramatic representation of platform selection and initial camp processing characteristic of Holocaust fiction, Piercy offers a curt single sentence: "In herds of women lashed and beaten, she was stripped, tattooed, shaved of her head and body hair" (570). Despite its brevity, this declarative statement forcefully conveys the depersonalization, debasement, and humiliation of the prisoner. And because of its brevity, the reader, anticipating elaboration, is stunned. Like the dazed victims of Elie Wiesel's and Charlotte Delbo's Auschwitz books, Jacqueline flounders for a time as a compliant automaton, but she soon recognizes the induction system as a ritual passage into the absurd Nazi universe, a rite designed to turn human beings into beasts. A mark of her transformation from active resistant to submissive inmate is her attitude toward bearing witness. Initially, she tries to remember every concentration camp beating and every murder. She soon learns that indignation consumes the energy she needs for survival. All her efforts must be directed toward sustaining herself and Daniela.

Only after the women have been interned for several weeks does Piercy employ the third-person narrative and archetypal Holocaust imagery to render Auschwitz-Birkenau during 1944, when Hungarian Jews by the hundreds of thousands were being gassed: "Every day and every night the sky was red with flames, while heavy ash filtered down on them. . . . Every night large piles of bodies were burned in enormous pyres all around the camp, because the crematoria were overloaded. Ash fell from the sky like oily black snow. The stench of burned flesh hung in the air with the stench of decay. Sometimes half an inch of ash lay on everything" (574).[43]

A short distance from crematoria smoke and falling ash the living are subject to the flagrant camp indignities of poor sanitation, inadequate nutrition, rampant illness, and arbitrary and frequent beatings. Reinforcing the hunger and the squalor designed to degrade the prisoners, a condition sharply heightened by the presence of well-fed SS men and women in immaculate uniforms, is the humiliation of slave labor and the debasement of labor without purpose—inmates carry huge stones from one end of camp to another or run double-time while bearing heavy sacks of cement. For labor designed to support the German war effort, the SS leased prisoners to industrial firms such as I. G. Farben, Hermann Goring Werke, and Krupp's Weichsel Union Metallwerke, which manufactured armaments. Like their historical models, the fictional SS and the Krupp guards drive the slave labor force mercilessly. Military and industrial slave masters alike abuse the women verbally and physically, compelling them to run from place to place while dispensing random blows and exacting hard labor on starvation rations—a system invented to exhaust, to punish, to kill. Sexual humiliation is another feature of the work environment. The women are ordered to strip and parade before SS men and Krupp entrepreneurs, who add sexual mockery to economic exploitation. Unable to escape physically, Jacqueline withdraws mentally and emotionally, imagining "that her body was hidden inside an imitation body. The men could only see the imitation rubber body, but she was the bones hidden inside that they could not see or touch" (574). This response is identified in the psychiatric literature as "psychological removal . . . insulating oneself from the outside stress, developing ways of not feeling so that 'I'm not here,' and 'This is not happening to me.'" Joel Dimsdale explains that "the 'feeling I' no longer has to bear it and instead is replaced by a 'photographic dispassionate I.'"[44]

Since birth and "motherhood made women a target population in the camps," a theme that recurs in countless testimonies written by women, it is not surprising to find inmate response to pregnancy, abortion, and infanticide in the work of a feminist of Piercy's reputation.[45] These subjects enter the novel through secondary characters who collaborate in hiding a pregnancy and birth from camp guards. The pregnancy, we learn, escaped Mengele's detection during the arrival selection, thereby sparing the prisoner immediate gassing or admission to the medical experimentation block, where "he liked to cut open pregnant women, or experiment with the effects of starvation on the fetus or the new born child" (575). Piercy underscores the danger to the women in attendance at the delivery: "If they were caught, they would all be sent to the gas chamber" (576). The scene reflects frequent testimony on the conspiratorial camp deliveries and pays tribute to the heroism of endangered women who provided medical assistance and psychological succor to an inmate who was violating Nazi decree.

It is instructive to compare Piercy's birth scene, written from the perspective of the mother and her accomplices, with another by a survivor who served as a medical attendant. In her capacity as infirmary worker, the survivor objectively describes the instructions given a pregnant woman and her own role in a clandestine delivery. Only after reporting the stark details does she permit herself a subjective comment, a three-word sentence:

> Mancy told her to lie on the ground under the board bed. She herself hid there too. 'Remember,' she said to her quietly, 'you are forbidden to utter a sound. Everything has to take place in complete silence. Nobody should know that you are giving birth. She told me to bring her a bucket of cold water. . . . The birth started. The woman bit her lips in pain until she drew blood. But she did not utter even one sound. She held my hands so tightly that afterwards I had black and blue marks. Finally, the baby was born. Mancy put her hand over his mouth so he would not cry, and then she put his head in the bucket of cold water. She was drowning him like a blind kitten. *I felt faint.* 'The baby was born dead,' Mancy said. Later, she wrapped the dead baby in an old shirt, and the woman who was guarding the entrance took the baby and left to put it on a pile of corpses. The mother was saved. [Italics added.][46]

Among the common characteristics in the writing of the survivor and the novelist are narration by an eyewitness, the mother's need to bear the birth pains silently, and the birth attendant's disposing of the infant to save the mother's life. Whereas the survivor focuses attention entirely on the victims, implying censure of the perpetrators, Piercy explicitly condemns the architects of the tragedy in an ardent moral and political indictment, citing Dr. Mengele's sadistic experimentation on pregnant women and fetuses.

Piercy's birth scene bears much in common both structurally and thematically with innumerable oral and written testimonies and is probably a compendium of several sources. Her more characteristic adaptation of an identifiable source that cites other gender-related humiliations may be observed in a passage faithful to Vera Laska. Laska writes of the arrival at

Auschwitz of Slovakian women who were "issued evening gowns and thus attired . . . helped build the camp."[47] Piercy's protagonist observes evening gown–clad women building the camp in winter. Laska states: "The last gassing took place on October 28, 1944, when most of the 2,000 Jews from the Terezin ghetto went up the chimney, with the additional cruel twist of irony, certainly known to the torturers, that being the Czechoslovak national holiday equal to the American Fourth of July."[48] One of Piercy's secondary characters reports the ghetto liquidation and the transfer of its inhabitants to Auschwitz, using the details Laska cites but shifting the ironic observation to the French calendar of the speaker: "But nobody got to meet them, because on October 28, which was the Czech equivalent of 14 juillet, they were gassed. . . . The execution was arranged to celebrate Czech independence day" (578). Again, the historian's prose is less acerbic, noting "the cruel irony" of the execution date, whereas the novelist adds moral indignation, denoting the inverse Nazi celebration of Czech independence. Maintaining her historico-fictional approach, Piercy concludes the concentration camp sequence with the resistance theme in a passage based on a historic Sonderkommando revolt at Auschwitz, in which female munitions workers smuggled powder to male crematoria workers who manufactured bombs, and the women's removal to Belsen.

Piercy's fidelity to historic fact is matched by her fidelity to women's Holocaust experience and commentary. Central to her representation of women's bonding in pairs or larger surrogate family groups is her recognition that "women tended to try to replicate their lost families, even in concentration camps; . . . women tried to forge relationships, and . . . their survival depended on it."[49] The importance the feminist writer attaches to female bonding is evident in the multiple fictive unions she creates, echoing those of women's memoirs and historians' analyses.[50] The primary fictional association, as in the documentaries, is the sisterly attachment of Jacqueline and Daniela. The supportive relationship established by the two young women dates from their student days and is substantively reinforced by their long period of comradeship in the Resistance and finally in their shared struggle to survive at Auschwitz-Birkenau. Jacqueline's first Auschwitz thought is solidarity with Daniela, determination that she will always keep Daniela in sight, that she will endure whatever her friend endures. When Daniela suffers a brutal beating, it is Jacqueline who blocks her fall, arranges for the column of five to help her reach the barracks, and tends her welts and open wounds. And it is Daniela's Judaic and Zionist mentorship that sustains Jacqueline in survival.

The maternal bond is equally significant in women's Holocaust writing. Supportive maternal relationships are evidenced between Rivka and her mother, Jacqueline and her Aunt Esther, and Auschwitz old-timers and newcomers. In Piercy's universe there is no antagonistic mother-daughter camp union to parallel the secondary father-son relationship in Elie Wiesel's *Night* and the primary relationship in Richard Elman's *28th Day of Elul*, works that trace sons' resentment of burdensome fathers who are ill, march too slowly, or are insufficiently aggressive in securing food. In *Night* a son battles with his father over a piece of bread, and another deserts his father in a death march for fear that he will be killed as a straggler if he keeps pace with the older man; Elman's protagonist deserts his father in their mutual hiding place at the approach of a Nazi search party, for he knows the father will impede his own escape. Piercy is closest to Wiesel in the attention she gives the troubled conscience of the protagonist, who fallaciously blames herself for not doing enough to save her mother when, in fact, she has done everything possible. The devotion of mothers and daughters to each other's survival is exemplified in the relationship of Chava and Rivka Lévy-Monot. Piercy captures the enduring love and support of the pair in the generosity of one starving victim toward the other: "*Maman . . . splitting her piece of daily bread and giving half to Rivka, because she said Rivka's need was more, for she was still growing, although she was not, she could not*" (433); in watching "*the other's few things, the can in which the watery soup was ladled, the scrap of rope, the leg wrappings, the clogs that could not be replaced: any of these stolen could mean death*" (433); in sustaining each other spiritually as well as physically: "*Sometimes Maman sang her Yiddish songs, . . . as they picked the lice from each other, the lice that gave them ulcers and brought typhus that killed*" (434); and in struggling to survive long enough to be of service to the other.

Bonding that took the form of old-timers, or "old numbers," advising newcomers, also a recurrent referent in women's Holocaust writing, is represented in the Auschwitz encounter of Jacqueline with her Aunt Esther.[51] The older woman's privileged indoor accounting job explains her long-term survival and her ability to find and assist Jacqueline, although niece and aunt are so transformed that neither recognizes the other. Like many old-timers who shared their survival strategies and "organized" food or clothing for newcomers, Esther parlays the privilege of an office job to trade with warehouse workers and brings her niece a precious gift, a pair of boots that can be crucial to the wearer's survival.[52] Esther also offers sage advice, warning the newcomer to avoid the hospital, where Dr. Mengele uses human subjects for medical experiments, and counseling her to look lively and masquerade as a factory worker so that she will be considered work-worthy, hence fit to live. She arms Jacqueline with the will to survive by suggesting that she think of her mother and sister as among the living. Her parting message is one of support and resistance, urging a dependable union between Jacqueline and Daniela, one in which they watch out for each other and protect each other's property, and imploring her to "remember, if you die, they win" (573).

A cooperative association, marked by mutual assistance, characterizes the camp relationship of all Piercy's women. They help each other stand through the long roll calls, pick lice from one another, nurse one another through typhus, and support one another through hunger by sharing their memories of food. A scene of recipe sharing echoes the remarks of Gertrude Schneider, a survivor and author of *Journey into Terror*, who observed that the main topic of women's conversation was food, "the most beautiful recipes that anybody could think of"; of Susan Cernyak-Spatz, who testified that "most of our talk when I first arrived in camp was about food: recipes, meals you had eaten, those you hoped to enjoy when you got out"; and of Vera Laska, who writes of the women she lived with in Auschwitz sitting on their bunks in the evenings listening for hours "to stories true and made-up, to lovely poetry and songs of many lands and mainly to tales about food."[53] Similarly, the fictional "women who knew the most recipes and could best describe them were in great demand" (575).

Beyond much-needed physical support, the women nurture one another intellectually, culturally, and spiritually. Jacqueline teaches English and Daniela teaches Hebrew to barrack mates, for whom the lessons offer respite from the hunger, terror, and pain and are a means for feeling human again. At least for the moment, they are not the quivering sacks of bones German oppression has created but women of sound intellect and aesthetic and religious sensibility. Spiritual fortitude is evident in their performance of the Sabbath candle-lighting service, burning "candles of rags or scraps stolen under pain of death" (575). The Passover the women celebrate after transfer to Bergen-Belsen, a seder without food, "slaves telling the story of slaves who had risen up, who had escaped" (607), is derived from the many accounts Piercy had read of Jews observing the holidays in the camps.[54] Furthermore, Piercy's women sustain one another's spirits by developing Zionist postwar plans, insisting they will be a family and go to *Eretz Yisroel*, the land where "no one will ever again call us dirty Jews. No one will make laws against us, ever again" (577).

Jacqueline shares her strategy for retaining her dignity, buoying others' spirits as well as her own. She separates her self-image from the figure she has become, insisting on her humanity. She refuses to see herself in the

Nazi-designed dehumanized mold of bald, stinking, filthy inmate, and it is her rejection of this debased role that is crucial to her endurance. She retains her survival will by establishing goals of witness and judgment that are consistent with her pre-incarceration courage and defiance. Through their generous support of each other and their contributions to the survival of their people, she and Daniela emerge as dignified, proud, admirable champions of decency and honor in the midst of unprecedented evil. Thus, Piercy joins Karmel and Schaeffer in the importance she assigns the efficacy of female bonding as a survival strategy in a universe designed to dehumanize and demoralize victims as prelude to their murder.

For a more comprehensive Auschwitz perspective advancing beyond the knowledge to which victims were privy, the novelist incorporates the vantage point and objective voice of the investigative reporter. A foreign correspondent, Louise Kahan, has access to evidence denied the captive. During a postwar journalists' briefing in a salt mine serving as a warehouse for German war plunder, Louise learns of the extensive, carefully invento-ried Nazi cache of various currencies, art treasures, Jewish ritual artifacts, and assorted personal possessions of victim populations. While the other reporters remain professionally objective and detached, the Jewish woman, "as one of those intended to be robbed of her life . . . had no choice but to contemplate what passed understanding . . . how and where this loot had been gathered. . . . All those women whose rings had been taken from their hands, dead. All the children whose toys had been carefully preserved while the children were burned" (629). The vehicle of the journalists' information session serves Piercy as she moves from documentation of the vast scope of Nazi pillage to the voice of the individual to present the larger perspective and articulate her moral outrage.

A political writer, Piercy is more interested in the sociopolitical ramifica-tions of survivorship than in the individual's psychic stress, the major theme in *Anya* and *The Shawl*, as well as in I. B. Singer's *Enemies, A Love Story* and Saul Bellow's *Mr. Sammler's Planet*. Jacqueline's changing discourse signifies her political transformation. As a young Francophile, her discourse was that of a French citizen confident of her place in the body politic; as a hounded Jew of Nazi-occupied Europe, she alternates between caustic lapses into Nazi-Deutsche and resistant defiance; and as an Auschwitz survivor, her voice is again double-edged: she is at once the Holocaust-burnished victim and the triumphant Zionist, a self-defined Jew. Schaeffer's Anya and Ozick's Rosa speak in short bursts of dialogue, reverberating their pain. Piercy's Jacqueline delivers political speeches rejecting the Hannah Arendt banalityof-evil thesis and passionately denouncing racism and sexism as generators of violence, "brutality given a license . . . a uniform, a credo" (571).

Although most of the novelists whose texts are explored in this book treat antisemitism, Piercy more so than the others exposes its diverse social and political manifestations. Her fiction corroborates the view of historians who attribute the success of Germany's war against European Jewry to the continent's enduring Christian antisemitic sympathies, evidenced in centuries of edicts, expulsions, pogroms, and mass murders. Piercy's is one of several noted American literary voices emphasizing the intimate relationship between traditional Christian antisemitism (a hatred that holds Jews responsible for the crucifixion of Christ and therefore rationalizes and justifies the persecution of Jews throughout history) and Nazi racist antisemitism, the product of social Darwinism, obsessed with the binary oppositions of superior/inferior, Aryan/Jew. Like most Jewish-American novelists who treat antisemitism and the Holocaust, Piercy quickly disposes of biologically based Nazi racial ideology. Instead, she directs the reader's attention to the traditional economic, political, social, religious, and militant forms of antisemitism practiced in Christian nations as a critically supportive agency of Nazi efforts to annihilate world Jewry. Whether manifested in the violent pogroms of Russia or the social and economic structures of the West, antisemitism is revealed for the pathology that it is as a leitmotif in chapters devoted to nine of the novel's major and minor characters.

Jacqueline's intellectual journey from alienated Jew to self-defining Jew begins with her encounter of French antisemitism and her recognition of French collaborationist sympathy for German anti-Jewish measures. Representative of the novelist's superb integration of historic and invented matter is her reference to an art show at the Palais Berlitz, exhibited by L'Institute Français des Questions Juives, an organization formed to publicize Nazi anti-Jewish propaganda in the name of French citizenry.[55] The signature billboard of the elaborate campaign designed to bolster support for anti-Jewish legislation is "an enormous four-story-high poster of an old man with a beard and a long nose . . . digging claws into a globe, where France was drawn in" (79). The caricature's "signs of Jewishness" establish a binary opposition between being Jewish and being French. Assuming that Jacqueline is a French Catholic, a bystander, whose language is simultaneously tinged with Nazi racism and emblematic of long-standing French Catholic antisemitic discourse, urges the young woman to attend the show to learn how to keep herself pure for the "New France." Jacqueline rebukes herself for failing to contest the antisemite's bigotry and thereby begins her transformation.

Her criticism shifts from antipathy for her father's Zionist sympathies to contempt for French antisemites, who made her feel "like a cockroach they were trying to crush under their well-shod feet" (79). The word *cockroach* evokes both Jacqueline's newly discovered vulnerability and Nazi-Deutsche rhetoric identifying Jews as vermin deserving extermination. Piercy links banal antisemitism and the Shoah by juxtaposing the propagandistic art exhibit scene with a report of the destruction of six Parisian synagogues. The antisemitism of the French press is revealed in its insistence that the desecration was "a spontaneous act of the French people who want . . . the so-called foreign element, thrust out" (80). Piercy's introduction at this juncture of Nazi racist discourse conveys the affinity of German Nazis and French collaborationists, "who are rejecting us as they reject a disease or a poison" (80), and expresses Jacqueline's contempt for press support of the July roundup of Jews, which was described as "France . . . being cleansed and purified" (80).

The novel carries the Francophone from these discoveries to alienation and rejection of postwar French residency. Jacqueline delivers a bill of accusation against French officials who cooperated with the Nazis by passing antisemitic legislation, supplying records, and assisting in rounding up and deporting Jews. Estrangement from her compatriots is the result of Jacqueline's Holocaust-wrought understanding that Jews are hated not "because we did something or said something. They make us stand for an evil they invent and then they want to kill it in us'" (255). Jacqueline now counts herself among the Jewish "we," and the gentile French have become "they," the "others." Remaining in France after liberation is untenable, for she would "stare into faces and . . . wonder, what did you do? Whose side were you on?" (697).

To underscore the pervasiveness of Christian Holocaust culpability, Piercy links the novel's European and American antisemitic scenes. Manifold forms of American "widespread and almost pervasive" antisemitism that Piercy experienced in Detroit during the Depression and World War II, such as housing covenants that kept Jews out of neighborhoods, "hate tracts that the worker-preachers distributed, the rant of Father Coughlin pouring from [the] radio," are explored in the novel's chapters devoted to Ruthie Siegal and her circle of family and friends.[56] A peaceful Easter tableau of worshipers leaving church triggers Ruthie's recollection of her grandmother's story of Easter-season anti-Jewish violence, "how there would be pogroms some years. Other years the goyim would simply come and beat and kill one or two, for sport" (88). Old World hatred of Jews based on church teachings depicting them as Christ-killers is reincarnated in the New World, drama-tized in several American characters' references to the radio ministries of Reverend J. Frank Norris, who ranted against "the international godless Jewish conspiracy" (275), and "Father Coughlin, who spewed out his diarrhea of the mouth against Jews from all the radios in the Catholic neighborhoods around . . . Detroit" (109). The American churchmen iterate the religious base in their charges of Jewish "godlessness" and invoke *The Protocols of the Elders of Zion*, an infamous forgery purporting a Jewish world conspiracy. The memory of church slander that emerges in the context of a Jewish merchant marine's engagement with a Nazi U-boat indicates the historic and literary connection between religious and race-based antisemitism. Ruthie's reference to "Gerald K. Smith's *Cross and Sword* . . . with their Jewish conspiracy headlines and some of the local klan offshoots . . . down-with-the-Jews leaflets" (309) similarly links the history of the media arm of the church with that of the Ku Klux Klan in propagating and inflaming antisemitic passions. Ruthie's contemplation of whether "what made Nazis out of Germans wasn't something she felt and saw around her here" (276) explicitly correlates Christian antisemitism with Nazism. Through these references Piercy literally and metaphorically links Christian and Nazi antisemitism, each embracing violence, the earlier religious variant preparing the world for the extraordinary success of the later genocidal racial variant.

The novel scrutinizes the pervasive American political antisemitism that flourished during the thirties and forties in Congress, the State Department, the press, industry, and the military. Piercy explores the prevalence of antisemitism in the military through two characters, incidentally via a reference by Ruthie's brother, Duvey, during his wartime merchant marine service and through extended passages devoted to Ruthie's fiancé, a Jewish marine. The only other Jew aboard Duvey's ship believes he must conceal his Jewish identity, unless speaking with another Jew, because when "you said you were a Jew, they wanted to start in on you. They thought all Jews were patsies and you had to be twice as tough" (107). Murray, the object of persistent harassment of the sort experienced by Jewish service personnel in Irwin Shaw's *Young Lions* and Norman Mailer's *Naked and the Dead*, routinely suffers the antisemitic hooliganism and insults of his platoon, who are encouraged by the example of their sergeant. Their invective ranges from mockery to classic Nazi propaganda indicting all Jews for warmongering and cowardice. Paralleling the German mold, this verbal abuse soon gives way to a murder threat when the sergeant warns, "Jew-boy. When we land the landing force, you're going to die here" (633).

The social and economic spheres of civilian life manifest similar hostility toward Jews. Paralleling the survival of European Jews under false identities, Louise Kahan must adopt a Christian name and appearance to be published. Ruthie Siegal, a college student, is grateful to work in a typing pool, "a lucky job for a Jew to find" (157) in an era when Jews are routinely denied office jobs. Oscar Kahan is one of two professors in the social sciences at Columbia, "which made Columbia more liberal than most schools of its caliber" (230) in an American university system that maintained exclusionary admission quotas for highly qualified Jewish students and enjoyed a near perfect *Judenrein* professoriate.

The filtering of antisemitism from the institutional level to the private social sphere is illustrated in Abra's story, specifically in the response of her family to her relationship with Oscar Kahan. They disapprove of her working with a Jew and are later appalled by her romantic involvement with another, cautioning her about the social ostracism she will encounter. Her jilted WASP lover admonishes the New England maiden for studying under "Kraut Jews" (34), and her brother rebukes her for "following some Jew professor to wartime London" (463). Abra's eventual marriage to another Jew leads to her disinheritance. Her patrician brother's warning "that doors will be closed to you that formerly swung wide" (684) conveys the sentiments of genteel antisemites.

More ominous than the social antisemitism enunciated by Abra's family is the flagrant support for the Nazi state by the German-American community of Yorkville: "Swastikas openly displayed, . . . Nazi films playing the movie theaters, . . . the German-American Bund passing out anti-Semitic tracts" (14). The potential for the seemingly harmless brand of Nazism exhibited in the American German Bund to become lethal if associated with power is conveyed in the juxtaposed scene of Abra's interview of a German-Jewish refugee who explains the German system and Jewish self-delusion within the German sphere: "You see, we were so used to being denounced, and business as usual. Every other German was an anti-Semite accustomed to rant about the Jewish problem and the Jewish influence and the Zionist conspiracy. But they would expect you to understand, they didn't mean you personally. It was the others, the bad Jews. You grow used to thinking that they don't really mean it when they make the little jokes about Jews. You just let it pass over and wait for them to act human again. We were almost comfortably accustomed to all those little and big insults, just so we prospered and lived our individual lives" (93). No matter what course Jews took, antisemites found fault with the Jews in their midst. Thoroughly assimilated Jews were a danger to the state because they blended with the host population, making their machinations difficult to detect. Zionists, on the other hand, were guilty of dual loyalties. Too German or insufficiently German, capitalist or communist, it made no matter. Where the antisemite reigned, the Jew as enemy was all that mattered. This salient juxtaposition clearly implies Piercy's political message that sanctioned or even tolerated religious, social, or political antisemitism is but prologue for anti-Jewish violence.

Piercy joins critics such as David Wyman, author of *The Abandonment of the Jews: America and the Holocaust, 1941–1945*, in condemning Western acquiescence to the annihilation of European Jewry, damning not only perpetrator nations but bystander nations for complicity with the Nazi genocide.[57] Paris knew, London knew, and Washington knew what the Final Solution meant, and through the voluntary collaboration of France and the passive neglect or active hindrance of the United States and Britain, Hitler's goals were facilitated. Piercy's ire and political invective are boldly directed not only at British and American failure to intervene but more justifiably and forcefully at their obstructionist policies thwarting Jewish resistance and immigration. The U.S. State Department and British Foreign Office had no interest in rescuing large numbers of Jews, fearing the Axis release of thousands of Jews into Allied countries. The fact that America and Britain ignored authenticated reports of the systematic annihilation of European Jewry as early as 1942 and failed to respond to pleas to bomb the rail lines leading to the extermination camps confirms their antipathy to saving Jews. Piercy details the U.S. government's sins of omission and commission, ranging from President Roosevelt's failure to speak out on the destruction and assign priority to the rescue, to State Department and congressional policies of repressing Holocaust news, to congressional curtailment of Jewish immigration to the United States.[58] Through the dialogue of American Jews whose rescue efforts are systematically blocked, Piercy dramatizes rejection of the Wagner-Rogers Bill, which would have allowed the entry to America of 10,000 threatened Jewish children during 1939–40. The enthusiastic admission of thousands of non-Jewish British child victims of the blitz, juxtaposed with "the tiny legal trickle [of Jews] which the State Department as a policy attempted to stop at the source in Europe" (386), affirm the anti-Jewish bias. Of the blatant British and American disregard for opportunities to save Hungarian Jewry in 1944, when the mass murder of the Jews was common knowledge, she writes: "The State Department remained as hostile as ever toward intervening on behalf of Jews, and no government expressed interest in the negotiations to save that population. The British would not budge on refusing passage to Palestine. No country wanted more Jews, so they would go up the chimneys for lack of caring" (446). Rather than employ sweeping statements of moral indignation at lackluster American and British efforts to halt the genocide, Piercy presents a meticulously detailed history lesson of Allied failures and invites readers to draw their own conclusions.

In apparent league with government suppression of reports of mass killings and of the death camps was silence of the mainstream press. Piercy's criticism of media and government suppression of news of German atrocities is given voice through Louise Kahan's frustration with editors' reluctance to publish such reports and her contempt for the Office of War Information and its "policy of putting out no information on what was known about the [concentration] camps and the fate of the Jews in Europe" (340). The Siegal family's resentment of obfuscation of the genocide by the State Department and the mainstream press parallels Holocaust-era frustrations in Piercy's own family. In "The Dark Thread in the Weave," an essay about the impact of the Holocaust on her life, Piercy debunks the notion that the killing operation of the camps was unknown, because "the Jewish papers were full of stories and occasionally photographs that had been smuggled out. . . . There were occasional small stories in the regular press, . . . that Jews were being killed in large numbers was certainly known."[59]

In the manner of most American novelists treating the Holocaust, Piercy turns her attention to the problematic of postwar survival. Departing, however, from the focus on long-term survival found in the works of Bellow, Ozick, Potok, Singer, Wallant, and Schaeffer, among others, Piercy explores survivorship in wartime, while her subjects are still uncertain of the fate of their loved ones, and in the immediate aftermath of the Shoah. Naomi and Jacqueline feel guilty for their survival while their mother and another sister remain in jeopardy. Jacqueline can occasionally repress her shame by fighting against the Nazis, but Naomi's geographic distance from the catastrophe heightens her anxiety and rage. Her feelings are further complicated by anger and ambivalence toward the parents who saved her life by sending her away. Naomi's vacillation is seen in her resentment and adoration of her father. She is angry at their separation and longs for him to rescue her and return her to an intact family. Like the adults of Claudine Vegh's psychological study, who harbor ambivalent feelings toward parents who sent them into distant safety, Naomi is at once angry with her parents and devoted to them.[60] Similarly, like Lore Segal, who wrote about living as a refugee in other people's houses and never feeling she belonged, long after Naomi has settled into living with American relatives, she feigns interest in matters of no concern to her and conceals her thoughts, "because she was in someone else's country and someone else's house" (378).[61] Naomi's feeling that she has been "cast out by her family" (121), that "she no longer really belonged to anybody" (236), may also be grounded in feelings Piercy attributes to her first husband, who she says felt rejected when he was placed with a Swiss family that "insisted he go to church and observe Christianity" while his parents were interned in a Swiss camp.[62]

Beneath her superficial adjustment to a life of school and friends, Naomi endures Holocaust anxieties in silence, for she recognizes that language is insufficient to convey her knowledge to innocent American children. She is cognizant of how different she is from her American peers, who have never witnessed bombs falling, cities burning, or crematorium chimneys spewing smoke and ash, children for whom war is something in the movies or a comic strip. Survivor reluctance to speak of the Holocaust with nonwitnesses, a recurrent pattern in psychiatric and creative literatures, is evident in Naomi's character. Though she and Ruthie are devoted to each other, Naomi hides her Holocaust fears and anger from Ruthie and others in her supportive American family. The burden of her experience and the knowledge of mass murders she acquires from the Yiddish press is borne in isolation. Unlike Anya Savikin and Rosa Lublin, survivors of ghettos and labor and concentration camps who remain silent in the conviction that their experience is ineffable, this sheltered child's silence is primarily predicated on the wish to please her benefactors and the desire to fit in with schoolmates, an attitude common among children who were being protected during the war.[63]

Piercy locates all of Naomi's Holocaust trauma internally, in misconceptions, memories, dreams, and imagined sequences of the July 1942 Paris roundup, confinement in the Vel d'Hiv, Drancy, and Dora/Nordhausen. Typical of the postwar survivor, Naomi associates ordinary events and circumstances with Holocaust experiences. Wakened by the loud noise of a truck backfiring or clanging garbage cans, she cries out in French for her mother and sister. She conceals such incidents and her horrendous nightmares of camp hardships, believing others would see such revelations as confirming her strangeness. During the Detroit race riot she overhears teachers speaking of massing combatants, of people coming with guns, and "she wonder[s] if this [is] an invasion" (305). When a classmate suggests she join the Jewish group and step away from her black friend, Naomi assumes,

"They'll come to take us away. . . . They'll separate us out the way they took Maman and Rivka" (306). She considers whether the Germans or the Japanese are coming and concludes that "if it was the Japanese, maybe they wouldn't pick her out to take away" (307). Shattered glass on the Detroit streets recalls *Kristallnacht*, and the blacks are perceived as "the local Jews, the ones they picked out to beat up when they got excited and started running around in the streets" (307). Detroit of 1943 feels like Paris of 1940. She even interprets social relations through a Holocaust lens, appraising the suitability of a boyfriend by imagining that the Germans are coming and she is going into hiding with him and fantasizing in another instance that she and a lover are spies, partisans underground.

Piercy attests to the complexity and contrariness of survivor guilt by revealing Naomi's alternate embrace and rejection of it. When her nightmares subside, she is contrite for wanting them to abate. During a period of romantic infatuation the nightmares diminish even further, and she is troubled by feeling disconnected from Rivka, unable to sense whether her twin is dead or alive. Despite these episodic detachments from Holocaust associations, the refugee's obsession with the Holocaust is affirmed near war's end. Pregnant, she claims the baby, not as part of her union with her former lover, but as her own, as "Rivka returned, to grow up again and be loved" (693), in an expression somewhat analogous to Rosa Lublin's effort to give her slain daughter life. Naomi's pregnancy, like those sustained by prisoners, may be read metaphorically as well as literally, as "an affirmation of Jewish identity and the continuation of Jewish life."[64] In contrast to her imagined partisan heroics, bearing a Jewish child is tangible resistance to the genocidal objective.

Through Jacqueline's character Piercy explores survivor syndrome during and after the war. Guilty for escaping, for being away when the French police came for Maman and Rivka, for failing to secure their release from Drancy, Jacqueline considers herself "living on borrowed time, time she had stolen," and justifies working for the Resistance and taking risks by rationalizing that she is trying "to make amends" (214). As is the case for Schaeffer's Anya and Ozick's Rosa, the war does not end for Jacqueline when combat ceases and she is liberated. Starvation and typhus have shriveled her to seventy-one pounds, and an old bullet wound may necessitate amputation of her arm. She is disoriented: "Every morning when she woke, she was back in the camp" (641). She is haunted by nightmare-ravaged sleep in which ill-clad women are lined up for the winter *Appell*, the woman beside her clubbed to death. In dream "she smelled the burning flesh, . . . saw the open glazed eyes of [the] dead . . . the smear on the wall that was the brains of a child dashed to death by a grinning guard . . . the blood pouring from the severed breast of a woman with a dog set on her, tearing now at her throat" (641–42). The nightmare landscape is the essential reality; the hospital is "an unplace, among unpeople" (641–42).

The survivor's life is Shoah-obsessed, Shoah-driven. Jacqueline is always hungry; she hoards her hospital food: "She ate whatever she could get. It seemed to her . . . she was never full, that she never would be full" (644). She remains fearful: "She still cringed when she heard German spoken. . . . It was hard to overcome the habit of cowering, of never meeting a gaze. She had been a piece too long, a slave, a number" (644). Freedom is overwhelming. Being outdoors for the first time is suffocating. She speaks in language symptomatic of posttraumatic syndrome, referring to a period "back when I was alive" (643) and describing herself as "twenty-three going on seventy" (679). As Jacqueline recognizes signs of her own physical regeneration—her body's response to food and medicine, the resumption of menstruation and breast development—her thoughts turn to hope that her mother and Rivka have also survived, hope that sparks her determination to recuperate quickly and search for them. News of her mother's death at Dora/Nordhausen and the continued uncertainty about Rivka's survival return her to feelings of overwhelming sorrow and guilt: "It was herself who should not be alive, with those she loved murdered" (645).

Like Bellow, Ozick, and Schaeffer, Piercy employs the failure to pursue prewar ambitions and professions as a sign of continuing Holocaust response. She differs from these writers, however, who use the disruption primarily to signify long-term, Holocaust-induced diminished ambition or capacity. Instead, she shifts the focus from Holocaust paralysis to regeneration and renewal through survivor mission in the form of communal service. Jacqueline no longer aspires to teach French literature or be a great French actress; rather, she will serve the Jewish state and people. Her first postwar job, accepted to facilitate a search for Rivka, is in a displaced-persons office. Shoah-wrought career revision to serve the surviving remnant is seen also in a young Israeli colleague who fought with her in the Jewish Resistance. Trained, "in another life" (678), to be a Talmudic scholar, he now knows more about warfare than religious law. Instead of devoting his life to textual study, he will spend it defending Israel from Arab belligerents who promise a second Holocaust rather than tolerate a Jewish nation in their midst.

Under the chapter title *L'Chaim*, the Hebrew word for life, Piercy announces new beginnings for the surviving Lévy-Monot sisters and, by extension, regeneration for the Jewish people in their sovereign nation. Although the search for Rivka is fruitless, Jacqueline is reunited with Naomi and is dedicated to nation-building. She welcomes Naomi's pregnancy and chooses to make a family with other survivors, ready for a "deeper and more primitive, tribal, familial, sisterly, motherly [love]. . . . She would give her strength, her love, her knowledge, her history, her self. They would cobble a family together out of refuse and rubble; they would scavenge their debris into a life" (683). Jacqueline's metamorphosis is complete. The Holocaust has transformed her from self-denying nominal Jew to self-affirming and communal-affirming Zionist. Repair of the Diaspora Jew and regeneration as an Israeli engaged in building a Jewish nation and homeland is the former assimilationist's response to Shoah tragedy, a response that is self-healing and group-serving.

Piercy does not seek to explain the Holocaust theologically, nor does she put God on trial in the manner of Wiesel and Singer. No female character in Piercy's fictional universe raises her voice, as does the religiously educated male protagonist in Wiesel's world, who rebels against blessing God in traditional Yom Kippur prayer, "*yitgadal viyitkadach shmé raba* . . . May His Name be blessed and magnified." The all-powerful Lord of the Universe has chosen silence in the midst of his people's genocide, and the boy who had been enamored of God rejects Him. Only Naomi briefly questions the wisdom and purpose of a deity who would tolerate the Holocaust and wonders whether there really is a God, "because even though it's a sin to think that . . . life could be better arranged, besides wars and Nazis even" (160). Unlike Wiesel and Singer, for whose characters theological turmoil and protest become major Holocaust responses, Piercy's characters, like those of the other writers studied here, remain theologically mute. Writing in her own voice, however, in "The Dark Thread in the Weave," Piercy reveals the impact of the Holocaust on her religious thinking, claiming that she "cannot imagine a world that contains both the Holocaust and a personal omnipotent G-d. . . . [She] cannot imagine that any petition of [hers], rising would have any impact on something that would not be moved by the anguish of several million pious and fervid Jews or the cries of babies thrown living into the fire."[65] Yet she does not put Judaism on trial.

In accord with the views of Emil Fackenheim in *God's Presence in History* and of Eliezar Berkovitz in *Faith after the Holocaust*, that Jews must deny Hitler a posthumous victory by rededicating themselves to Judaism and the Jewish people, Piercy, a Reconstructionist Jew, returns her characters to Judaism.[66] In this regard her work is more closely aligned with that of Wiesel, Singer, and Ozick than other novels in this book, which steer clear of religious themes. Some characters in *Gone to Soldiers* are estranged from Judaism and the Jewish people before the Holocaust, but they, like some apostates in the fiction of Singer, return to religious, cultural, or political Jewish affiliation in response to the Holocaust. Oscar, Louise, and Jacqueline assert their Jewish identity by performing religious rites and using liturgical Hebrew, and Jacqueline will presumably give up her beloved French for Hebrew as the language of daily discourse when she takes up residence in Israel—behaviors they would earlier have avoided. Sustaining Judaism and the Jewish people and creating a safe nation in the land of their forefathers are viable Holocaust responses for these characters, who interpret the Shoah as an orienting event in history, as does Marge Piercy: "Knowledge of the Holocaust is knowledge of the darkest secret, the worst obscenity about being human. It is a sore that cannot heal, a pit that swallows light. Yet survivors triumphed by surviving, and Jews exist. . . . It gives even more . . . importance to reshaping and revitalizing Judaism than it might otherwise have had, or had not for generations that did not grow up into the sense of it as one of the boundaries of human existence."[67]

The impact of the Shoah is represented not only in dramatic character reversals but also in the novel's choral voices, which echo and amplify the protagonist's voice. Parallel development of Oscar, Louise, and Jacqueline reinforces the theme of connection to Jewish collective experience. The Holocaust accounts for Oscar's manner of mourning his sister, who died a horrible death at Ravensbrück. He slashes the lapel of his army jacket in accord with the biblical injunction to rend clothing as a symbol of a broken heart, and he recites the mourner's Kaddish and the *Aleinu*, simultaneously mourning his sister and all the Holocaust dead. For the professorial oss researcher, deeply involved in chronicling the human costs of the catastrophe, the Holocaust "was a wound in the fabric of existence" (631). It is this cosmic interpretation that leads him to express his grief in accord with Jewish custom. Complementing Oscar's cosmic Holocaust interpretation is the new understanding Louise posits of the Holocaust as an orienting event in history, the measure by which to judge other events. She is driven by her vision of inmates in Bergen-Belsen, who had been "stripped of home, possessions, work, family, friends, community, country, everything they had loved, all connections now smashed, murdered, gone" (661).

The religious and cultural commitment marked by Oscar and Louise are prologue to Piercy's treatment of the concluding stage in Jacqueline's metamorphosis. Her assessment of Oscar's need "to learn to place himself and connect with his own history" fits Jacqueline as well.[68] Nowhere in the fiction are the regenerative postures of return to Judaism and identification with the Jewish people more dramatically enacted than in Jacqueline's cultural and political transformation. As we have seen, the pre-Shoah adolescent was an avowed assimilationist, "rejecting her Jewishness because of the marginalization it implies," impatient with her father's Zionism, dismissive of the family's religious observances.[69] She argued that being Jewish is a part of "the accidental particular . . . a matter of coincidence and has no lasting importance" (27). As the transformative agency of her life, the Shoah teaches Jacqueline that Jewish identity can be externally imposed regardless of the individual's wishes. Genocidal threat and segregation with believing Jews of her own generation serves as a catalyst for developing a self-defined Jewish identity.

Before Auschwitz, Sigmund Freud wrote, "My language . . . is German, my culture, my attainments are German. I considered myself German intellectually, until I noticed the growth of anti-Semitic prejudices in Germany and German Austria. Since that time, I prefer to call myself a Jew."[70] A similar realization eventually dawns on the assimilated French Israelite. Jacqueline's transformation is not a sudden turn but has been amply developed in the course of five treacherous years. The diary format, an apt vehicle for chronicling this transformation, reveals that her amended perspective coincided with Shoah knowledge and with her disapproval of another resolute assimilationist's position. The young woman who had once considered being born into a Jewish family as a "contingent peripheral part of [her] being, not part of [her] essence," later acknowledges that Jewish identity "defines" her (252). Instrumental in Jacqueline's transformation are her Holocaust experiences, new respect for her father's Zionism, and the influence of Daniela, whom she admires for feeling "thoroughly and proudly Jewish." She and Daniela share their thoughts about Judaism and Zionism and hold "long involuted discussions about how Judaism could be more responsive to women" (252).[71] If Jacqueline is to affirm and claim Judaism for herself as Daniela has, if she is to be herself, "entire, authentic, . . . [she] must find a way of being Jewish that is . . . an affirmation in this identity, as Papa and Daniela have" (252–53). Having had Jewish identity "thrust" on her, she now defines herself first as a politically committed Jew and secondarily as a religiously defined Jew. She participates in religious observance, lighting makeshift candles, reciting Sabbath prayers, and celebrating Passover with barrack mates. In marked contrast to prewar arguments with her father about Jewish solidarity, they speak amicably in the worst of times about Lévy-Monot's dream of the people's regeneration through adherence to Judaism and establishment of a Jewish homeland rather than living as marginalized citizens on a continent where one-third of world Jewry has been willfully transformed into ash. Lévy-Monot expresses himself in Hebraic liturgical discourse, alluding to the exodus from Egypt, drawing an analogy between Jewish biblical and contemporary history, evoking the ancient transformation of the Jewish people from slaves in an alien land to a sovereign nation in Zion. His quotation of the concluding line of the Passover seder service, "Next year in Jerusalem," conveys the contemporary longing of a Diaspora Jew for return to Jerusalem. Just as the ancient Jewish bondage in Egypt was followed by autonomy in the promised land, so too contemporary Jews are determined to pass from slavery and slaughter in German-occupied Europe to freedom and sovereignty in Zion. In a speech that is to be echoed by the Auschwitz survivor, Lévy-Monot bemoans France's betrayal of its Jews, citing the Vichy government's voluntary passage of antisemitic legislation depriving French Jews first of their civil rights and then of their lives. Zionist sentiments similar to Lévy-Monot's are enunciated by Daniela, who longs to join her fiancé in Palestine, where Jews will be safe and valued citizens.

Jacqueline's gradual religious and political metamorphosis is also conveyed through her response to Jewish texts and religious observance. For example, she defines her commitment to Daniela and Daniela's principles by quoting the Book of Ruth: "Whither thou goest I will go. . . . Thy people shall be my people and thy gods my gods" (604). Against the backdrop of Chanukah, a Jewish celebration of release from religious despotism, Jacqueline broods that there are no Jews left in her Paris apartment to light the holiday candles and memorialize the dead as "all the candles of lives blown out" (401), an image evoking both Chanukah liberation and Shoah memorial. Similarly, in a wartime letter to Naomi, Jacqueline comforts her sister, asserting that in her American exile she is the sole member of the family who is "free to be a Jew and . . . should be proud" (380). Jacqueline's postliberation engagement with Judaism is signified in her language during the Jewish New Year season. She identifies the holiday by its Hebrew name, *Rosh Hashanah*, and extends a heartfelt traditional Hebrew greeting to her fellow Auschwitz survivor, praying that they both will be inscribed for a good year. In a marked departure from her prewar view of Jewish ritual as primitive, the Holocaust survivor performs the ancient custom of *tashlich*, throwing bread crumbs into the river, symbolically casting out sin.

Jacqueline's political connection with the Jewish people, signified by her commitment to build a Jewish state, is a direct outgrowth of the Holocaust.

Drancy was transmogrified as a way station to Auschwitz; Frenchmen turned France into Vichy; French ideals of liberty, equality, and fraternity were replaced by tyranny, bigotry, and fratricide. In her last chapter Jacqueline echoes her father's rejection of French repatriation: "She belonged to no one but the friends who had survived and who were going, as Jews, to make a place where Jews could never be stateless" (683). No longer content to be a Diaspora Jew, the Israelite in a France that views the Jew as Other; no longer grateful for a host nation's tolerance, she has a new perception of Jewry's place in the world. That resistance fighters such as Daniela, Jacqueline, Lev, and Lévy-Monot wish to go to Palestine and, if need be, fight for their nation is congruent with Piercy's impression of Israelis as Jews who refused to be victims, Jews who could fight, Jews who could be powerful.[72] By novel's end, Jacqueline is serving as an official spokesperson on behalf of Jewish immigration to Palestine, and she claims Naomi, and the child Naomi is carrying, for the Jewish nation.

Piercy never suggests that the creation of a Jewish state is an acceptable outcome of the Holocaust or that the meaning of the Shoah is found in Israel's formation. Rather, she testifies to the need for a safe haven for a people subjected to centuries of persecution and to continuing discrimination and murder in the postwar era. Questioned about the relation of her characters' cultural and political transformations to those of prewar French assimilationists such as Edmond Fleg and André Neher, whose Holocaust experiences generated their ardent Zionism and advocacy of Jewish civilization, Piercy acknowledged that she was "aware of the impact the war had on many Jews who thought of themselves as being French, until they discovered they were not French, they were French Jews."[73]

There is broad agreement among literary critics that the distinction of the Piercy canon springs from the union of the personal and the political. Characteristic is Susan Mernit's observation that Piercy "sees human beings as interconnected in a social network, having both duties and responsibilities to one another; and it is this conviction, more than anything, that makes her fiction political."[74] *Gone to Soldiers* is consistent with and extends Piercy's narrative pattern of relating the personal to the political, compellingly addressing racism and sexism in the private and public spheres. Personal history, in Piercy's fictional universe, is powerfully shaped by political, social, and religious beliefs and responsibilities. In this era of Holocaust deniers and other antisemites laboring to minimize Jewish Holocaust losses, Marge Piercy believes Jews must keep Holocaust memory alive. She has contributed to that mission with distinction in *Gone to Soldiers*, grounding her fiction in verifiable details of Holocaust history, producing a work that is both political and deeply moral.

About her own commemoration and lamentation for the resistance fighters who became the models for her characters, Piercy writes, "I have eaten your history and made it myth."[75] Just as memory becomes prayer for the poet of "Black Mountain," so too, for the war-ravaged Jacqueline on the verge of beginning a new life in Palestine, "memory had become a religious function . . . and she studied how to keep it intact and powerful" (683). Memory is clearly a form of prayer for Piercy, too. Her Holocaust writing embodies a profound sense of obligation to the living and the dead, based on the understanding that art makes vivid the history that might otherwise be obscured.

NORMA ROSEN

Cynthia Ozick and Norma Rosen have shared a decades-long personal and literary friendship that has included contemplation of and writing about the Holocaust, albeit in distinct literary styles. Each writer has invented American characters who wrestle with the social and personal implications of the Holocaust, depicted the Holocaust plight of women and children, fashioned a postwar confrontation of Jew and German, and introduced the problematic of Holocaust transmission as a literary theme. Rosen is convinced that the Holocaust is "the central occurrence of the twentieth century . . . the central human occurrence."[1] She therefore embraces as her recurrent theme a topic that Ozick introduces intermittently, that is, "what might happen to people [who were 'not there'] who truly took into consciousness the fact of the Holocaust . . . the meaning to human life and aspiration of the knowledge that human beings—in great numbers—could do what had been done."[2]

Rosen's 1974 essay "The Holocaust and the American-Jewish Novelist" addresses the feasibility and propriety of writing about the Holocaust and queries, "How could the virtues of fiction—indirection, irony, ambivalence—be used to make art out of this unspeakable occurrence?"[3] Thirteen years and several Holocaust works later she argues that the paradox for novelists working in this sphere lies "in the tension between writing and not writing about it. If the writer treats the subject, the risk is that it may be falsified, trivialized. Even a 'successful' treatment of the subject risks an aestheticizing or a false ordering of it, since whatever is expressed in art conveys the impression that it, too, is subject to the laws of composition. Yet not to write means omitting the central event of the twentieth century."[4]

Like Susan Fromberg Schaeffer, Marge Piercy, and Cynthia Ozick, Norma Rosen is an exemplar of Elie Wiesel's authentic Jews, who consider themselves "inside the whirlwind of the Holocaust, even those born afterwards,

even those who heard its echoes in distant lands."[5] A diligent reader of
Emmanuel Ringelblum's diary of the Warsaw Ghetto and *The Black Book of
Polish Jewry* and an avid observer of the testimony of eyewitnesses during the
televised Eichmann trial, Rosen has inscribed the Shoah on her mind. She
describes herself as a "witness-through-the-imagination," a "documenter of
the responses of those who 'had heard the terrible news,'" a role she considers
appropriate for the American novelist.[6]

Paralleling themes engaged by other writers considered here, but departing radically in her representation, Rosen privileges female characters and
addresses the plight of mothers in the camp universe. Instead of directly
presenting women in ghetto and camp, she propels readers to contemplation of the Holocaust through the mediating lens of engaged American
women. Removed in time and space from the Holocaust landscape but
powerfully affected by its enduring resonance, Rosen's women are Jews
and gentiles, wives of survivors or empathetic citizens, who respond to the
horrific ordeal Jews experienced. She writes of a pregnant gentile's reaction
to camp birthing, an American innocent so troubled by revelations of human
capacity for evil that she vows to remain childless, another who wants to
effect reconciliation between a Holocaust survivor and postwar Germans,
and a Jewish American torn between the desire to spare her child his father's
traumatic childhood story and to develop Shoah remembrance. Although
not subjected to direct experience of the camps, Rosen's women remember
those who were there and consecrate the memory of murdered European
Jewry.

Norma Rosen's *Touching Evil* bears witness to Holocaust crime through
the sympathetic response of gentile American women to the plight of
Holocaust victims. Her narrative is removed in space and time from the
historic concentration camp universe: its time is 1961, during the Jerusalem
Eichmann trial, and its setting the United States. As the foreword to the
1990 paperback reissue of the novel explains, "*Touching Evil* is about the
Holocaust, but there are no living Jews in it, only the shadows of dead
ones." Jews appear only as imagined Holocaust victims and as televised
court witnesses, evoking ghostly specters of the victims. Because Rosen
perceives the Holocaust as a human rather than a Jewish problem, she
has developed non-Jewish characters who experience Jewish history vicari-
ously, as "witnesses-through-the-imagination."[7] Although many Holocaust
scholars would disagree, Rosen believes "the malaise, the malediction of
[Holocaust] knowledge has entered the psyche of Jew and non-Jew alike."[8]
She would probably find greater endorsement for her view that non-Jews

ought to be moved, the genesis of her decision to replace her original Jewish protagonist with two gentile mediators.[9] Refuting critics who have disparaged her approach as universalizing the Holocaust, weakening Jewish Holocaust specificity, Rosen counters, "If a novel says . . . that the Holocaust experience is so intense that it radiates out to affect non-Jews who then experience it through the imagination, then that is not universalizing, not a generalizing, a spreading and thinning-out of the Jewish trauma, it is the opposite: a bringing of the non-Jew into Jewish experience. It is not universalizing; it is Judaizing."[10] Rosen's atypical gentiles could not be more obsessed with the Holocaust were they Jewish.

The first of the novel's two epigraphs from Carl Gustav Jung's *Memories, Dreams, Reflections* argues, "Touching evil brings with it the grave peril of succumbing to it. We must, therefore no longer succumb to anything at all, not even to good." The American women are touched by the radical evil of Nazism but reject Jung's hypothesis. Instead, they are more attuned to Isaac Rosenfeld's stance, arguing "that because we have to live with the knowledge of evil greater than evil, we also have to find a good greater than good. . . . 'Terror beyond evil and joy beyond good: that is all there is to work with. . . . May the knowledge of joy come, . . . and the knowledge of terror never leave!'"[11] To that end, the American protagonists seek joy and fulfillment in their personal lives yet allow their Holocaust knowledge to transform them. The friendship of Jean Lamb and Hattie Mews springs from their daily meetings to view the Eichmann trial, sessions described as "holy ritual." Moments of Holocaust consciousness impinge on one another, varying in intensity from fleeting to all-consuming, and penetrate the emotions and intellects of each woman. Rosen conveys the need for Shoah commemoration in succeeding eras by creating coprotagonists from two generations. Hattie's response reveals the dismay of initial encounter with Holocaust evil, whereas Jean is a "reflector . . . distanced from her own revelation."[12] Past and present collide and merge as the novel alternates between diary recollections of 1944, the year Jean Lamb learned of the Shoah through newspaper photographs of concentration camps, and 1961's Eichmann trial, the vehicle for Hattie's initial discovery and Jean's confirmation of the centrality of the Holocaust in her life.[13]

Grounding the sources of the women's Holocaust knowledge in the trial and photography and in a later introduction of a newspaper account, Rosen clearly distinguishes between the documentary and the fictive worlds of her novel. Refraining from re-creating the Holocaust universe, she separates what actually happened from the fictive tale that depicts the impact of the

Holocaust on her imagined characters. The survivors' excruciating court-room appearances, "their faces designed into masks, . . . their voices, in translation, disembodied" (52), create the aura of testimony without actually duplicating it. Rosen relies on readers' knowledge of the legal proceedings and the Holocaust to suggest the content of the trial, and she reminds us that our perspective limits and influences our understanding. The characters, and by implication the readers, are unavoidably removed, distanced: "Something about the way we both move—or don't move—while we are watching. Hattie and I are an experimental, silent film reacting to a film on TV. . . . We fall endlessly, soundlessly from our chairs. We roll on the floor, we clutch our wombs. Soundless, endless groans" (52). Separating "fact" from "fiction," Rosen intensifies our understanding of documentary and of narrative and clarifies the difference between knowing the Shoah through experience and through empathetic imagination.

The Eichmann trial reaffirms Jean's acceptance of the Holocaust as her own catastrophe. Fifteen years after the initial shock she hopes the receding immediacy will free her from Shoah reimmersion. Despite temporal distance from the event, and contrary to her expectations, she is reclaimed by history. For Jean, watching the trial with Hattie evolves into a second Holocaust cataclysm. Her mind and heart are violated once more. Almost two decades after the initial trauma Jean describes herself as "up to my ears again in corpses" (25). The horrors reappear, not instantaneously in a unified photo-graphic composition but piecemeal in daily doses of devastation: "Machine guns punching bullet holes, . . . clubs beating against bone" (209), visions of the starving and screaming, the bodies forever falling, piercing the psyches of heretofore immune Americans.

The Holocaust's continuing effect on future generations is conveyed through Hattie's absorption in the trial. The pregnant woman is both physi-cal foil and emotional double to the intentionally childless Jean. Astonished by the trial revelations, Hattie concurs with Jean's judgment that the Nazis defiled life itself, and she too expresses reservations about propagating the species. The fictive reference to the trial allows Rosen to represent the younger generation's initial Holocaust exposure in juxtaposition to its continuing impact on the previous generation. Setting the fiction during the sixties trial rather than in the wartime era is Rosen's proclamation that the Shoah ought not be conveniently put to rest; it continues to have an im-pact on thinking, sensitive people. In provocative contrast to Hollywood's *Judgment at Nuremberg*, which muted the "Jewishness" of the Holocaust by privileging the Nazi judiciary's crimes against the German people and drawing parallels between Nazi and American racism, Rosen adroitly uses the Eichmann trial to direct attention to the systematic annihilation of European Jewry.

That the Shoah alarms so few people profoundly distresses Jean, who had expected it to evoke horror comparable to that expressed in Picasso's *Guernica*. Modeled on Rosen's experience as a Mount Holyoke undergraduate, the passive response of Jean's fellow students to the news of the concentration camps is reflective of global indifference to the destruction of European Jewry. As the war in Europe ended and the death camps were discovered, "like monsters' lairs, full of stinking bones" (74), the college president spoke of "troubled times," and campus life proceeded as usual: "The girls still brushed their Stroock tweed skirts and cold-water washed their cashmeres" (74). These young women were self-satisfied with their war efforts: knitting for Russian War Relief, dancing with soldiers at the local USO, reading to psychiatric patients in the Veterans' Hospital, and harvesting apples on nearby farms whose workers were at war. Skeletal corpses of Jews did not merit their concern. Conversely, Jean Lamb understood at first sight of the photograph of "the piled-up stick bodies at the bottom of a lime pit" that "a catastrophe has changed the world. The old forms have no more meaning" (74).

Holocaust insensitivity is sustained in the post-Holocaust era. Representative of the larger world's apathy are the attitudes of the men closely associated with Jean and Hattie. Hattie's husband is a photographer aesthetically distanced from flesh and blood, devoted instead to creating pleasing patterns, to the arrangement of horizontals and verticals. Hattie's brother-in-law responds contemptuously to her talk about the trial and the impact it has made on her: " 'Don't you understand,' he asks, 'that all this happened to other people?' " (84). Jean's absent lover, Loftus, who brought the two women together to enable Hattie to get through the trial, is, as his name suggests, above these concerns. Loftus, like most people who had "lived through this whole business the first time news of it came around" (28), does not understand the Holocaust any better in 1961 than he did in 1945. His concern is not for the victims, not for the significance of the Shoah for the human condition, but for the sensibilities of his American lover, who just might lose her joie de vivre if she succumbs to "the horrors of the monster's cave" (28). He warns Hattie and Jean that the lesson of Pandora's box is not a warning against curiosity: "It's a warning not to hope the garbage of the world won't dump itself on your heads" (26). His advice to Jean is to persuade Hattie to stop watching the trial: "What's the good of watching—a child like that" (28). Evidence that "the child" has matured is her rejoinder that the killers are still free: "Their possibilities are always with us. . . . They are saying to us, 'This, *this* is what people are capable of.' I curse them for showing it. Curse them for being it. How do they expect us to go on?" (84).

For those who are sensitive to Holocaust reality, the luxury of pre-Holocaust normality can never be regained. Isaac Rosenfeld, one of America's leading intellectuals of the World War II era, spoke for his generation and for future generations when he argued in 1949 that terror had become the model reality of our time. If one attains Holocaust knowledge, Rosenfeld concluded, life cannot go on as before: "It is impossible to live, to think, to create, without bearing witness against the terror."[14] That Norma Rosen shares Rosenfeld's view is evident from her second epigraph, drawn from his *Age of Enormity*, and her representation of the fictive women's obsession with Holocaust thought and imagery. An early title for the novel, *Heart's Witness*, reflects the importance Rosen assigns the compassionate witnessing role. Sharing Rosenfeld's view that Holocaust evil is beyond any kind of evil we know, and despairing of the American creed of "business as usual," Rosen casts Jean Lamb's post-Holocaust life in a radically altered mode.[15] "Nothing of her life would, after she learned of the existence of the death camps, be as before." Jean Lamb "was to be someone so profoundly affected by the news that she would vow never to live the life that had been lived by people till now."[16] For a considerable time, the mere mention of the words "concentration camps" was, Jean recalls, an occasion when "my body and soul emptied out. I was ready to faint, to fall down. I marveled at anyone who remained standing" (77). At war's end, as others sought to return to prewar pursuits, Jean elected sacrifice. That Jean's Holocaust epiphany occurred while making love and that her response is refusal to bear children illustrate her feminist rebuttal to Holocaust history. Jean Lamb inherits the loss of Jewish mothers and the unborn millions who were never conceived, who never came to term. Marriage and motherhood are luxuries she no longer allows herself. Through a willed political act she makes the catastrophe her own. In choosing deprivation for herself, she allies herself with her European sisters and testifies to humanity's loss of Jewish progeny.

Jean's romantic involvement is also Holocaust-directed. She accepts a lover primarily because he had been a camp liberator. She acknowledges, "He wooed me . . . with that, though he didn't know it." For Jean, "there were only two kinds of people . . . those who knew and those who didn't know. And it had nothing to do with reading newspapers" (77). Just as her relationship with her lover is based on shared Holocaust interest, so her friendship with Hattie is Shoah-predicated. Hattie's response to the television coverage of the trial echoes Jean's earlier reaction to military and newspaper photographs of the camps. The fictive pregnant woman, like the author who watched the trial during her own pregnancy, absorbs the Holocaust experience, takes it thoroughly into her consciousness, senses it in her body. "Hattie drinks in the words . . . sucks up the images. . . . Her shoulders watch, her knees watch. Her fetus thrusts forward to watch" (68).[17]

The scene in which Jean first learns of the genocide is among the most skillfully structured and imagined in an American context. Juxtaposed to the 1961 report of trial witness testimony about the killings, "on a beautiful clear October morning" (69), is Jean's recollection of another "October Morn at college," where she is in the psychology lab with her professor, mentor, lover, who moves their conversation from the "dear little mice in their electrified cages" to "the reality of now," which he has recently discovered from an army psychologist friend who has shared news of the photographs he has seen. The professor lectures the student: "All this is happening now. . . . Happening! In 1944! Has been going on for years and still is, in the midst of war. . . . Experimental cell blocks, drains in the tiled floor, all that. It hardly matters that these are Germans. . . . What matters is that men have done it. . . . Teachers, students, lovers of science. They have replaced the mice in the maze with men" (72).

The response of Rosen's women to visual and imagined Holocaust representation is analogous to the response of another American woman, Susan Sontag. Writing of her own exposure to the Holocaust through the medium of photographic journalism, Sontag explains: "It was photographs of Bergen-Belsen and Dachau which I came across by chance . . . in 1945. Nothing I have seen in photography — or in real life — ever cut me as sharply, deeply, instantaneously. Indeed, it seems plausible for me to divide my life into two parts. . . . When I looked at those photographs, something broke. Some limit had been reached, and not only that of horror; I felt irrevocably grieved, wounded, but a part of my feeling started to tighten; something went dead; something is still crying."[18]

Although *Touching Evil* shares its documentary approach with other Holocaust fiction, it is distinctive in its deliberation on American reaction and feminine perspective. The two gentile American women become witnesses for those Jewish women who did not live to testify to the devastation. They empathize powerfully and repeatedly with the women of the camps, Jean with the woman who "was shot but did not die, and who dug her way from under a mountain of corpses that spouted blood" (221) and Hattie with a far-gone pregnant woman on a forced march and with another giving birth in lice-infested straw. Hattie directly addresses the intense association she feels with the victims: "Can you see how it happened to another woman? I can feel it in my body how it did" (86). As Jean stumbles over a broken pavement and makes her way through the crumbling of the urban landscape, her thoughts return to "the bloody woman, the digger through the rubble of last night's corpses" (50). The resurrected digger becomes a recurrent presence in Jean's imagination, a shadowy companion overwhelming her spirit, clawing her way into the American consciousness as she had clawed her way through the corpses. Failure to watch the trial and listen to the survivor testimony on behalf of the "gaunt ascetics of the camps" and those "who had passed beyond hunger and terror" (221) is interpreted by Hattie as an act of supreme betrayal. The Americans' association with the Europeans is complete. Hattie has developed the "ability to slip inside the lives of other people" (220). Jean is finally overwhelmed and needs distance from the trial, from "that special group whose agonies we had somehow . . . held in the circle of our arms" (221).

For the Hatties and Jeans of the world, suffering will not heal with time; the dead will not depart from their thoughts but burrow ever deeper. The Holocaust becomes their categorical imperative, the touchstone by which they measure all else in their lives, their central interest and motivating force. And since their perspective is also within the context of female experience, it is entirely appropriate and realistic that Rosen employs feminist imagery and rhetoric. Echoing the voices of Ilona Karmel's women, the rhetoric of Rosen's novel renders not only the Nazi brutalization of the Jewish people but the regenerative Jewish will to survive, to rise from the ashes in stubborn pursuit of life.

Rosen's propensity for combining Holocaust images with those of pro-creation and sexuality elicited negative criticism. To suggest, as Nora Sayre does, that Rosen is making a feminist assertion that hospitals, or labor rooms in particular, are like concentration camps is to ignore their role as objective correlative, as Hattie's postwar referent for the despised helplessness and vulnerability of the camp inmate.[19] Hattie's compassion for a powerless woman subjected to the cruel indifference of an overworked inner-city hospital intern is significant, for it provides another connection with the Jewish woman, completely powerless and humiliated, giving birth in a prison barrack beneath the gaze of a booted soldier of the master race. The American patient's "unsightly genitals, bleeding, gaping, oozing," in the presence of and at the mercy of the medical personnel of a New York

City hospital in their starched white uniforms, are Hattie's postwar link with the testimony of the woman "who squeezed her baby out into a world of concrete, straw, and lice" (252). Hattie's acceptance of the Shoah legacy is the source of her elemental cry: "Cursed be the booted feet. Cursed be the legs that stood on them. . . . Curse the Hun heart that shit on this grace!" (252–53). Jean's rape is a physical referent by which she may imagine the arbitrary violence perpetrated against European Jewry, the utterly senseless brutality one people imposed on another. Although Rosen deliberately removes her novel from the setting and time of the Holocaust, the event is intended to be a felt experience, not an abstraction. The lives of nonparticipants are to be touched, intimately, penetratingly, violently, and with lasting effect, by the insidious evil of the Holocaust. The feminine rhetoric that can, at first reading, seem peripheral to the Holocaust subject is skillfully and powerfully linked to it.

Edward Alexander charges *Touching Evil* with presenting "a womb's eye view" of the Holocaust and being "diverted by the temptations of analogy, of heavy symbolism, and feminist topicality."[20] Although the impact of the novel is diminished by peripheral digressions, feminist rhetoric and analogies are not the offenders. Far from being distracting, feminist rhetoric provides the authentic voice through which Rosen's women understand and claim the Holocaust. It is through this language and imagery that Jean and Hattie relate humanely, elementally, and personally to the women of the camps. Rosen's diction of sexuality and biology is intrinsic to expression of the will of her characters to remember the women of the Shoah and to recall the Nazi ideology of linking one's destiny to one's biology. Similarly, the diction of childbearing serves Rosen's thesis that the Holocaust legacy must pass from generation to generation. In an age of aborted dreams, an age of Nazi perversion, evocation of life and death processes in terms of children denied and children delivered is apt. Rather than criticize Rosen for her use of feminist rhetoric, one should acclaim her for recognizing the validity of this language to describe the brutality Jewish women suffered in the camps and to forge a connection between the living and the dead.

The procreation/birth control dichotomy Rosen employs in the novel is sustained by effective juxtaposition of the creative and destructive impulses of art. Devastated by televised testimony detailing the murder of mothers and children, Hattie and Jean meet at the Museum of Modern Art so that Hattie may gaze on statues of serene mothers surrounded by healthy, exuberant children, a vision of holiness to counter the destructive visions engendered by the trial. As she contemplates the marble mother, a testament to creative human genius, Hattie reads a newspaper account she has brought with her of the destructive evil Germany unleashed against Jewish parents and their children. The passage resembles a description of the deportation of French children from Drancy to Auschwitz that is found in the historical record.[21] Like Piercy, Rosen writes movingly of the physical and psychological plight of the most vulnerable of the innocent victims of Nazism: "The children were covered with sores. They had diarrhea. They screamed and wept all night in the empty rooms where they had been put. There was nothing in the rooms but filthy mats full of vermin. . . . Terror had overcome them. The halls were a madhouse. When the orders were given to take the children to Auschwitz, it was as if they sensed what was in store. Then the police would go up and the children, screaming with terror, would be carried kicking and struggling to the courtyard" (224). This scene highlights once again the important distinction between the "factual" and the "fictional" that Rosen introduced in her trial-watching scenes, separating an actual account of Holocaust atrocity from the impact on the imagined characters. Jean senses an outraged scream filling the silent sculpture hall and imagines the great goddesses "on broken toes, with hands severed at the wrists" (223), suddenly struck blind, petrified by the testimony of human degradation. The children clinging to the mutilated marble figures now evoke Holocaust mothers and children. Rosen's integration of documentary evidence and artistic evocation emphatically melds the destructive and creative impulses that typify the twentieth century and anticipates images of sculptural Holocaust memorials that have appeared decades after the novel's publication.

In "The Holocaust and the American-Jewish Novelist" Rosen explains that "the question the book was asking [is]—What kind of daily lives can people live after they have touched an evil so absolute that it overpowers all the old ideas of evil and good?"[22] The Holocaust has so permeated the lives of Jean and Hattie that it is indeed their Kantian category of reference. Holocaust imagery and associations inform their thinking, their speech, and a chorus of voices that surround them, voices that at once appropriate and misappropriate Holocaust terms. As Rosen notes in her important essay "The Second Life of Holocaust Imagery," "For a mind engraved with the Holocaust, gas is always that gas. Shower means their shower. Ovens are those ovens. A train is a freight car crammed with suffocating children."[23] Her characters exemplify this sort of association that comes unbidden into the mind deeply affected by the Holocaust. Contemporary events, people, and conditions evoke Holocaust classifications and definitions. A neighbor describes a personal betrayal as "telling the police where Anne Frank is hiding"; a person of ignoble behavior is described as "a gold tooth salvager" or "an informer" (60). A skeletal Chinese laundryman with a cadaverous face is compared to "the near-corpses of last evening's televised trial" (43) and perceived by Hattie as a camp inmate whose will to live had been destroyed. For Jean, whose new consciousness was initiated by the 1945 photograph of American soldiers evacuating "stick bodies, two and three to the armful" (78), from the concentration camps, the Eichmann trial confirms the ever-present specter of evil. Unlike Sylvia Plath and others, who misappropriate Holocaust tropes to aggrandize phenomena of lesser historical or psychological import, Rosen's women reflect on the contemporary situation as a means of entry or return to the Holocaust context. Their utterances are acts of commemoration, in Cynthia Ozick's apt description, "for the universalizing sanctification of memory."[24]

Repudiation of God or, at the very least, anger for divine inaction in the face of absolute evil is the characteristic response of orthodox Jewish male voices in the works of Elie Wiesel and I. B. Singer, and the occasional woman in Singer's fiction. Unlike most female protagonists in women's Holocaust writing, Rosen's characters agonize over God's responsibility for the six million. Like Wiesel's adolescent survivor, Eliezer, whose faith was temporarily extinguished in the same flames that consumed his family, Jean Lamb judges and denounces divine failure. Jean's assertion of God's Holocaust complicity is reminiscent of Eliezer's anguished misgiving about blessing the name of God, who "has had thousands of children burned in His pits . . . kept six crematories working night and day . . . created Auschwitz, Birkenau, Buna, and so many factories of death."[25] Her prayer-parody is a vitriolic denunciation of the merciless God of Auschwitz: "God of the medical-experiment cell block . . . God of the common lime-pit grave . . . God of chopped fingers . . . of blinded eyes, God of electrodes attached at one end of a jeep battery and at the other to the genitals of political prisoners" (233). The language of prayer is Shoah-stained, grotesquely evocative of Gestapo torture and Nazi murders. Rosen's use of this construction evokes the traditional Jewish response of countercommentary that parodies or inverts sacred texts to suggest the subversion of God's principles in the historic context. Jean's prayer disrupts the traditional liturgical text as Nazism disrupted the lives of its victims. The harsh tone of the fictional prayer is mitigated in the author's voice eighteen years later. But sadness and ambivalence about the God of mercy remain in "Justice for Jonah, or, a Bible Bartleby." In this meditation on the biblical text the petitioner asserts:

"Show me a text that speaks of God's unbounded mercy, and images of the Holocaust appear before my eyes. . . . Theology doesn't help. . . . Perhaps my generation will have to die out in the desert before God can appear again on an untarnished mercy seat."[26] Hattie's transformation to nonbeliever is charted in her reflections—first, of personal relief: "There but for the grace of God go I"; then an expression of doubt: "What when there is no grace of God?"; and, finally, denial: "There but for the grace of God and there is no grace of God, we see that there is none—so I go sideslipping into the life of that woman who gave birth in the typhus-infested straw" (131). And when Hattie asks whether God sees us, the older initiate responds, "It seems irrelevant. . . . Isn't it enough that we see each other? Witnessing and being witnessed without end?" (238).

The subject of Holocaust transmission attains both thematic and structural significance in *Touching Evil*. Transmission of the awesome tale leads to Rosen's narrative design of manuscript within manuscript within manuscript for subjective responses, as opposed to her incorporation of newspaper accounts and reference to trial testimony to convey historical evidence. The narrative is structurally unified by a series of Jean's letters and Hattie's diary entries, which reveal the connection between receiving the news and making it one's own. The distance between listening and telling is traversed as Jean's revelatory memory is sparked by trial testimony. Acting as both Jean's foil and her double, Hattie embraces the responsibility for transmitting Holocaust history to the next generation through her diary, a form that evokes victim and survivor diaries and testimonies and simultaneously suggests how personal the Holocaust has become for this "witness through the imagination." Among Rosen's objectives for *Touching Evil* "was to try to find a way to break through the conventional distancing of the novel and get at something intense enough, into-the-marrow enough, which is how reading about the Holocaust strikes us down."[27] The women's writings concurrently demonstrate their absorption of Holocaust pain and testify to the continuing impact of the Nazi crime against humanity, a crime destined to haunt each succeeding generation.

Unlike André Schwarz-Bart and I. B. Singer, who deal with the Holocaust as part of Jewish history, citing calamities through the ages, Rosen separates the Shoah from the larger Jewish historical context and reveals it as the paramount crime of the modern era. That iniquity of such magnitude demands perpetual remembrance appears in Rosen's delineation of multigenerational witness. One woman attains Holocaust knowledge in 1944, another in 1961, another is a newborn who will inherit her mother's diary, and the public will have her novel and play. The need to continue to bear witness is manifested in testimonial voices at the Eichmann trial two decades after the atrocities and in Hattie's writing. The pattern of transmission is established for another generation: as history has been passed from Jean to Hattie, so it will be from Hattie to her daughter. Each woman bears witness directly, Jean in her diary-letters and Hattie in multiple manuscripts for a play, a memoir, a novel. Hattie's writing, incorporated in the novel as long italicized interludes in Jean's letters, becomes the life force of Jean's childless existence. These gentile coprotagonists join a gallery of fictional Jewish Holocaust scribes who attest to the importance of Holocaust memory: Arthur Cohen's Nathan, who brings the dedication of a Torahic scribe to his narration; Saul Bellow's Arthur Sammler, who abandons his literary and philosophic scholarship to cover the Six Day War for a news journal because he believes a second Holocaust threatens; I. B. Singer's writer-protagonists, creative writers and journalists, who record the lives of the murdered Jews, chronicle shtetl memories to commemorate the victims, or act as facilitators through whom survivors may tell their stories; and Cynthia Ozick's Enoch Vand, who records Holocaust statistics for the OSS.

Touching Evil encourages readers to consider the larger philosophical implication of the Holocaust, that the Shoah has transformed our perceptions of humanity. One cannot simply curse the Nazis and forget them: "Their possibilities are always with us" (84). Since the Nazis "passed for human beings," Rosen asks, "what does that say about human beings?" (84). To our shame, "a poison went into the atmosphere. Just as when an atomic bomb explodes. Each generation in turn will be sickened, poisoned with disgust for the human race" (84).

Rosen's short stories generally turn from "witness through the imagination" of non-Jews to the Holocaust concerns and impressions of Jewish Americans and Holocaust survivors. She continues to maintain distance, never setting the fiction directly in the Holocaust arena, yet her Holocaust-haunted characters grow ever more complex as they live with knowledge of the Shoah. Her achievement in short fiction lies not in the re-creation or representation of the Shoah universe but in the delineation of the consequences of the Holocaust for the lives of people who were not there yet are concerned on a humanitarian level or intimately associated with survivors and the children of survivors. Rosen and her empathetic women are among those whom Arthur Cohen describes as "the generation that bears the scar without the wound, sustaining memory without direct experience."[28] In an essay about her cultural background Norma Rosen explains that she was "born of an immaculate Jewish conception . . . [of] parents, who were Jews by birth, refrained from intercourse with the Jewish religion and proudly passed [her] . . . untainted . . . into the world." Her assimilated parents provided her with "no religion, no philosophy, no language, no literature, no custom."[29] News of the Holocaust and marriage to a Holocaust survivor provided Rosen intimate, if indirect, association with Jewish history, which profoundly influenced her intellectual and artistic life. The intellectual journey she describes in *Accidents of Influence: Writing as a Woman and a Jew in America* includes her self-directed ongoing Jewish education and its influence on her writing. Several of her short stories incorporate a husband-survivor and an American wife, who exhibits various degrees of sensitivity to and understanding of her husband's Holocaust background and its influence on his postwar decisions. In other writing Rosen's survivors and Jewish Americans confront Germans with Holocaust history. In these works themes emerge regarding the impact of the Holocaust on the second generation and problems inherent in Holocaust transmission.

Congruent themes of protest against God's Holocaust silence and the validity of religious practice in the post-Holocaust era take a more prominent place in Rosen's short fiction and recent essays. Authorial protest against God's silence in the face of the Shoah finds expression in an essay on the biblical Jonah. In this text Rosen invents a fantastic narrative illuminating the biblical text, a midrash of Jonah inside the great fish receiving images of future "scenes from inquisitions and expulsions and ghettos and pogroms and, at last, death camps and crematoria" (93). Divine forgiveness and rescue of the pagan sinners of Nineveh, compared with failure to intervene on behalf of the millions of innocents who perished in the Holocaust, remains an unresolved enigma for the faithful Jonah.

At the heart of "What Must I Say to You?" is the issue of religious validity in the post-Holocaust age.[30] The husband and wife of this narrative are dramatized in conflict about placing a mezuzah, a small case enclosing a roll of parchment transcribed with two biblical passages concerning the love of God and divine precepts, on their front doorframe, as prescribed by Judaic law. The husband, a survivor and Jewishly educated, whose family has been annihilated in the Holocaust, insists on traditional observance. The American-born Jewish wife, uneducated in Judaica, rejects the mezuzah, arguing, as Jean Lamb does, that pre-Holocaust and post-Holocaust lifestyles cannot be similar. Acknowledging that the words inscribed on the parchment might move her, if she were to permit it, she insists, "I will not allow them to" (64). To support her contention, the wife, who shares Jean Lamb's interest in the Eichmann trial, quotes the passage about deported children struggling with their Nazi captors that Hattie had read in the museum scene of *Touching Evil*. She is astonished that despite this abomination, her husband rejects neither God nor Judaism. In her mind, as in Lamb's, the Holocaust invalidates religious faith and observance. Disregarding the wife's argument for rejection of faith and religious observance as an expression of Holocaust protest, the husband attributes the decline of American Jewish religious observance to assimilationist goals rather than Holocaust reaction. To his quotation of the social and economic upward mobility of practicing European Jews, the wife cynically retorts, "I'm sure that helped them a lot!" This is as close as she dares venture to "speaking the unspeakable" (65). Instead, she silently imagines an encounter with a German whom she confronts in the name of the murdered children. Although Rosen does not explore the survivor's Holocaust thoughts either through interior monologue or in dialogue, she shows him defiantly continuing the religious traditions of the murdered, stubbornly and proudly preparing to guide the next generation Judaically and thereby sustaining the people targeted for annihilation. The wife relents, not because she has altered her objections but to appease the man she loves. She cannot resist a verbal jab, however. Her parodic reference to the affixed mezuzah, "when mezuzahs last in doorway bloomed" (68), evokes Walt Whitman's magnificent elegy for Abraham Lincoln and reminds us simultaneously of the unceremonial burial of the murdered millions and the need to remember and commemorate their lives—as they were lived and lost.

"The Cheek of the Trout," an autobiographical story, returns to the theme of Holocaust confrontation, this time with a real encounter.[31] The narrative is set in postwar Vienna, the city of the survivor's birth and early childhood, where he and his American wife meet Austrians and Germans. Rosen writes that it is "a fiction based on truth (though with altered characters and point of view), an almost-memoir about the way something happened: a trip to Vienna with my husband, who was born there."[32] With or without these fictional changes, the story asks the one question worth asking: How, after the Holocaust, can we live now? Vienna, filled with beautiful architecture, music, and monstrous Holocaust history, is the perfect backdrop to the contrapuntal perceptions of the returned survivor and his American wife. The story's opening line establishes the polarities of the characters. The husband tells his wife, "Enjoy the city for me" (398). Clearly, his enjoyment of the city is clouded by his memories of lost family and his own removal in a children's transport. Despite his wife's empathy, the survivor knows, "She could never understand. She almost agreed" (398). The rich details of the narrative dramatize the nuances of understanding and misunderstanding. When the couple walks into the older districts, the husband identifies the sites, always with a Holocaust footnote. The sight of his uncle's former shop, still prospering, inspires speculation about which neighbor benefited from the confiscation of Jewish property. Husband and wife stand silently before the doorway of his family home, follow his path to school, and sit on the park bench where the family enjoyed their Sunday outings. When emotion overtakes the survivor, he walks away. The tension brought on by this trip invades the couple's relationship and the individual's self-perception: "From the beginning they knew the trip would be too painful. From the beginning it was too full of silences between them" (400). The wife responds by alternating between striving to make her husband understand that she has absorbed his pain and realizing that she has only limited Holocaust knowledge. Indignation at her husband's apparent resentment toward nonsurvivors' appropriation of Holocaust memory engenders her challenge: "I'm not a tourist! How could I know you and not think of what went on here? I would think of it even if I didn't know you!" (404).

Departing from her convention of allowing American women to approach the Holocaust as "witnesses through the imagination," Rosen reverses the pattern for this protagonist, who imagines escape from Holocaust reality, albeit briefly. She envisions alternate, younger identities for herself and her husband in which her husband's father is the survivor. As she feels guilty for this temporary alleviating gesture, another voice invades her thoughts, one representative of the misguided proponents of Holocaust amnesia and silence, those who want to obliterate Holocaust memory. It chides her to yield to the glories of Vienna and liberate herself from the constraints of the survivor, "who can't allow people to give themselves to the present now where they're completely safe and well" (401). This is but a fleeting presence, one quickly and suitably consigned to oblivion.

Imagination surrenders to a more plausible reality. The couple visits a graveyard, where the husband delusively envisions his father's ashes are interred. Comforting as such a pretense may be, Rosen denies the possibility through the wife's skeptical correction: "Would the bureaucrats of Buchenwald, where his father died of typhus, have ordered the ashes of individuals to be carefully scooped and labeled and sent home because it was still in the early years of killings, or had they shoveled and dumped the bushel-loads and picked names to call them?" (401–02). The city's history is revealed in its cemetery. Juxtaposed to elaborate gothic-lettered stones identifying the pre-Holocaust dead as city administrators and professionals are modest stones testifying to the Holocaust slaughter of Vienna's betrayed Jews: "Vergast Belsec, Gestorben in Theresienstadt. . . . Verschleppt nach Auschwitz. Umgekommmen in Dachau. Ermordet in Belsen" (Gassed at Belsec, died in Theresienstadt. . . . Deported to Auschwitz. Succumbed in Dachau. Murdered in Belsen) (402).

Reality also traps the couple at a village with mountain trails at one end and thermal pools at the other. As they gaze upward at the healthy Austrian mountain climbers, they resist joining them because "they were all about the right age" (406) to have served the Hitler cause. Instead, they join the invalids and less hearty tourists who have come for the baths, among them Jews from various countries: a Rumanian couple that comments on Polish antisemitism, "those who would not 'set foot in Germany,' and those who made a point of it" (407). These Jews are still struggling with the impact of the Holocaust, trying to temper their feelings toward nations that abandoned them and those that persecuted them. As the American couple prepares to dine with a German couple young enough to be free of Holocaust taint, the American wife imagines Heinrich's father counseling him: "If you meet any Jews, don't hang your head. It's true your grandfather joined the Nazi party for business reasons, and I became an S.S. officer when I was young, but whatever we did, you're another generation, you had nothing to do with it, and you don't owe an apology" (408–09). Although one sees logic in the elder's advice to his son that the younger generation is free of the sins of the fathers, the remaining discourse reveals his sustained, post-Holocaust Nazi inclinations: "If you meet a Jew, you can be friendly, offer a glass of wine, if you can stand to be with them, but on no account are you required to apologize" (409). In the American Jew's mind the Nazi is not rehabilitated, an echo of the conclusion reached by Cynthia Ozick's protagonist in "The Suitcase." The actual "confrontation" amounts to little. The Americans acknowledge their difficulty with Germans and Austrians of an age to have been involved in Hitler's war. Heinrich and Elsa agree that it is a "natural" and "understandable" reaction. Although this story lacks the acrimony between Jew and German evident in "The Suitcase," which features the evasions of a German who was an adult during the Hitler period, Rosen's muted encounter of Shoah and post-Shoah generations raises similar questions. Her characters remain polite: Rosen's protagonist experiences fury but contains it internally.

The civilized outrage of the American wife's reverie is confirmed in symbolic pattern, however. As the evening and the story conclude, the couples dine on trout, evoking, as Rosen explains in the accompanying essay, Schubert's *Die Forelle* (The Trout). This allusion to classical music signifies the ease with which Nazis moved between art and atrocity. In the essay Rosen reminds readers that "concentration camp commandants were often men of 'culture' who would finish the day's hideous work and then repair to an evening of beautiful German music. In Auschwitz the S.S. commandant kept a quartet of gifted prisoners playing German music day and night as Jews stumbled to the gas chambers" (396). Her allusion to *Die Forelle* is also reminiscent of Fania Fenelon's memoir, *Playing for Time*, focusing on the women's orchestra in Auschwitz whose function was to perform for their oppressors.

The novelist's progression from confrontations imagined by her characters to an actual clash of Jew and German is most directly represented in "The Inner Light and the Fire."[33] Here Rosen dramatizes the encounter through the agency of an innocent American woman determined to reconcile a victim and a perpetrator's heir. The American decides that her Jewish tailor, a survivor, must meet her newfound German friends, a visiting academic and his wife, in order that he "forever after take them into account when he thinks of Germans" (5). What the Germans are to take from this meeting is left unarticulated.

Unlike other survivors of Rosen's fiction, who are reticent to speak of their wartime experience, Mr. Shneider is forthcoming, and the American woman thinks she wants him to share his wisdom, his legacy of "Man in extremis" (5). Yet when he reveals his story, she reacts as though she were being assaulted. Each statement by the survivor is punctuated with the word "Thump!" suggestive of its impact on the auditor: " 'The S.S. put me to work in a storehouse!' Thump! 'First they send trucks to take out everything from Jewish stores. And if something is missing from the inventory, they shoot the storekeeper!' Thump! 'In the ghetto they are starving. They are dropping down.' Thump!" (6). As the survivor enumerates degrees of persecution, the American auditor absorbs each reference as an affront to her innocence. Although she wants the Traugotts to hear the survivor's testimony, she is protective of the cultured Germans, naively transferring the diction of assault to the victim of Nazi brutality and consigning vulnerability to the descendants of criminals: "Brave Gretel, so thin and full of inner light, so vulnerable, has bravely delivered the sword into Mr. Shneider's hands, and must now be brave enough to let it cleave" (6). In response to Gretel's naive observation regarding the presence of kosher butcher shops in Boston and their absence in Germany, Shneider informs her that the lack of such shops corresponds to the absence of Jews. In contrast to Gretel, who claims to be unaware of her country's Holocaust crimes, Walter confesses that his family knew what was happening and recalls walking with his father in the fields where he saw a hundred ghostlike women herded to work. Lest we think Walter is apologizing for the gravity of Germany's criminal past, Rosen suggests the limitations to full witness common to many of his countrymen with his quick and ardent disclaimer of continued German antisemitism, "with just a trace of residual national pride that pokes, hard as a rock, through the soft snowblanket of general atonement, [he adds,] 'this is all so much changed now'" (7).

The American woman and the German couple are eager to put the past behind them and bask in self-delusive optimism regarding the present, but Shneider cuts to the essence of their deceptions and offers his testimony to help convict Nazi criminals who have thus far eluded justice. His witness is expanded from unofficial purveyor of the news to all who would listen, in the manner of the "ancient mariner," to official court witness against a camp commandant whose sadistic behavior he witnessed during a deportation session, a man who transferred his prisoners to another concentration camp when he realized there was insufficient time to shoot them all before the Russians arrived to liberate the camp.

The repatriated Germans send their American friend a newspaper article and their own exuberant commentary hailing the building of a new synagogue in Germany, which "gives the appearance of 'a folded paper construction.' Yet it is the epitome . . . 'of the age of concrete and steel'" (8). The contemporary architectural analogy suggests the duplicity that pervaded the Nazi administration of the Final Solution, when entry signs to concentration camps announced freedom through labor and poison gas dispensers looked like ordinary shower heads. Mr. Shneider ignores the architectural commentary and raises the issue the German newspaper fails to report, that is, "the synagogue that formerly stood on this spot was destroyed by fire" (8) set by the Nazis. Why express glee at the building of German synagogues now that there are no Jews to worship in these buildings? The erection of the synagogue in a Jewless Germany evokes the Nazi plan for a postwar museum of an extinct race.

Neither architecture nor the judicial system redresses Germany's criminal past and contemporary support of Nazis at home and abroad. As to the outcome of the trial in which Shneider testified, he speculates that as the camp commandant is now seventy-nine years old, he will be considered too old to be punished for his crime: "So you see, if you don't allow other people to live to be seventy-nine, and if you escape long enough, then your defense can be you yourself are now seventy-nine!" (8). Through Shneider's voice Rosen expresses her moral outrage at the failure to bring the criminals to justice and for the second injustice society and the courts perpetrated against the victims who testify.

The final section of the story returns the reader to the American's consciousness. She listens to Shneider's report of his Holocaust-era witness at Gestapo headquarters, where he was working as a tailor caring for SS uniforms. Here he observed the sadism common to the supermen of the Reich as a group of SS men nailed a living man into a wooden box and threw the box down two flights of stairs. The American, for whom " 'Never Forget!' was an idle slogan" (9), failed to provide an epiphany for Shneider and the German couple, but she experiences her own epiphany. Defeating her conscious suppression of Shneider's testimony, the unconscious controls her sleep and disturbs her dreams with "a figure, horribly pierced, . . . its clothes drip blood" (9). A few days later her husband discovers that a large painted wooden box presented by the German couple as a farewell gift and heretofore treasured has been relegated to the basement. Her dream of "Mr. Shneider's man [standing] up in the Traugotts' box! Pale, dishevelled, his face and body torn" (9), has finally clarified Holocaust reality for her, and the crying voice she continues to hear affirms that Holocaust memory cannot, and ought not, be put to rest. Thus, in an ironic reversal, the American who thought the Holocaust victim needed to be unburdened of Holocaust memory is herself transformed by the encounter. That she has the Traugott box removed suggests that she will progress from unconscious to conscious acceptance of the enormities of Holocaust history, joining Rosen's female sympathizers whose Holocaust knowledge engenders a significant change in their lives.

In the symbolic and multilayered short story "Fences," whose title alludes to concentration camp fences as well as the psychological barriers survivors erect and dismantle between themselves and nonwitnesses, Rosen returns to the theme of religious response to the Shoah.[34] Here she develops the delicate psychological balance of survivors in dialogue and dramatic presentation more thoroughly than before and introduces the theme of Holocaust impact on the second generation. A family member's discovery of a package containing her dead father's prayer shawl is the catalyst for debate regarding transmittal of Holocaust memory and assumption of Judaic religious identity for post-Holocaust generations.

The narrative's survivor chorus of the rescued consists of two primary voices and a minor one. The dominant voices are those of two male survivors, one who was rescued from the conflagration and the other who witnessed it directly. The protagonist, Edward, left his mother and elder sister behind when he escaped Vienna in a children's transport bound for England, after his father's murder in an early concentration camp. His antagonist is the family lodger, Frederick, who was an adult during the war and suffered the loss of his wife and child. The muted voice is that of Edward's older sister, Bryna, who remained in Austria with their mother. Representative of survivors "coddling the flesh because the heart won't heal" (81), Bryna is more psychologically fragile than Edward and Frederick and is reluctant to view her father's prayer shawl, fearing its deterioration.

The lodger is the exemplar of clinical psychiatric writings on survivor syndrome and is closest among Rosen's characters to Cynthia Ozick's troubled survivor, Rosa Lublin of *The Shawl*. Frederick, too, remains unmarried, lives in a rented room in another survivor's apartment, and maintains silence about his lost family. He shares Rosa Lublin's bitterness over international abandonment of the Jews, her contempt for people whose interest in survivors is inauthentic, and her conviction that "no one can enter the Holocaust" (80). His complex and ambivalent reaction to those who demonstrate postwar interest in the Shoah appears in his contradictory observations of "limits of human capacities! Breaking points! Possibilities for nobility or degradation or heroism! How fascinated they are by us now. Not while it was happening, no. But now, later, they want to know everything!" (80).

Perhaps because Frederick no longer has a child to protect, as Edward does, he permits his rage to emerge unbridled while commenting on the indifference to the slaughter of European Jewry. Frederick articulates a dilemma at the center of Rosen's Holocaust writing: "Between the reality-witnesses and the imaginers there can be no accord. The imaginers . . . wish in subtle ways to extract meanings that the survivors themselves avoid" (80). As choral commentator and author of "a social history of the western world in the Twenties and Thirties" (76), Frederick attests to the difficulties of Holocaust transmission explicitly and evokes a quintessential Holocaust image to articulate the story's theme: "All around there are electrified fences. As the grandparents could not get out, so no one else can ever get in" (77).

Although Rosen does not explain the family's Holocaust silence, it may be attributed to the parents' effort to shield their ten-year-old son and to Edward's attempt to cope with contemporary life. Initially, Edward fears that the sight of the prayer shawl will lead to painful questions from Daniel. Yet it is at his son's urging that Edward's memories take voice. In response to the child's question about when his grandfather stopped wearing the prayer shawl—a query euphemistically phrased in diction that evades Holocaust reality—the father responds forthrightly, abandoning a protective veneer: "When did my father die, do you mean, Daniel? He was taken to a concentration camp when I was your age. After six months he died" (79). In contrast to this direct approach, Edward later hesitates to answer Daniel's question about his grandmother's history. He seeks not to spare his son but to award his mother an extra moment of life, if only metaphorically, as he revels in the memory of her nurturing role before disclosing that she was transported "to the East, and shot . . . in a field of snow" (81).

Edward transmits more than Holocaust history to his son. Like the survivor-father of "What Must I Say To You?" he transmits the Judaic heritage in the act of sharing the prayer shawl, the tallit, with Daniel.[35] Enacting the ritual associated with donning the tallit—kissing the embroidered calligraphic neckpiece, emblematic of embracing the commandments—he covers his head and upper body in the column of black and white stripes and recalls for his son how he had shared a similar religious experience with his father. In Edward's gesture of draping the prayer shawl over his amenable son, Rosen symbolically intimates and then explicitly declares the survival of Jewry and Judaism in the post-Holocaust era. This gesture is confirmed in her explanation of the prayer shawl's survival through its many migrations in wartime and in peace, thereby signifying that Judaism and the Jewish people will survive, given the devotion of adherents who cherish and transmit the legacy to future generations prepared to embrace it.

Paralleling Frederick's role is that of Daniel's American mother, who wavers between engagement and withdrawal. Sensitive to her husband's psychic trauma yet protective of her young son's innocence, she observes the conferral scene with trepidation, mentally urging her son to resist vicarious association with his father's Viennese tribulations. Aware of the perils of "imaginary shifting into other people's places" (77), Rebecca fears that the impressionable boy will be permanently scarred by Holocaust knowledge. Paradoxically, anxiety for the son leads to the mother's epiphany, "with the clarity of sudden electrification" (82). The visual stimulus of the prayer shawl's broad black stripes against the white of the bedspread leads the parents to polar perspectives. For Edward, the black stripes suggest Torahic calligraphy. For Rebecca, Judaically unschooled, like the wife in "What Must I Say to You?" the black stripes evoke concentration camp uniforms. She sees the tallit on her ten-year-old son's shoulders as metaphor for his assumption of the mantle of oppression, whereas for Edward the son is accepting a sacred inheritance. Before Rebecca can remove the prayer shawl, she collides with Frederick, whose reaction to the conferral prompts an action that thwarts Rebecca's renunciation. Formerly secretive about his family, Frederick now shares a photograph that Rebecca presumes to be either his son or the young Frederick himself. This gesture heralds the beginning of his healing, a sign that he welcomes communication. Rebecca's response is to refrain from intruding on Holocaust transmittal by father to son, just as she accepts their commitment to a Jewish future. The implication here, as in much of Rosen's later work, which has become increasingly Jewish, is that collective Jewish memory must include the Holocaust, but that the Shoah no longer obviates faith in God and Judaic observance. The American wife finally realizes what her survivor-husband has long known, that Holocaust restoration lies in the individual's voluntary acceptance of Jewish identity and of building Jewish community.

Writing of her own knowledge of the Holocaust, Rosen notes: "There is no beginning and no end to thinking about the Holocaust. We spend our lives reading witness books, looking at films of testimony, and we know nothing. Behind every degradation, every terror published or recounted, horrors we cannot know lie buried with those who could not survive."[36] Her response to this history places her among artists who will help future generations understand one of the saddest and most bestial episodes in human history, when a people that considered itself the master race instituted a program of genocidal intent against Jews by employing humanity's technological genius. Furthermore, she has achieved this feat in a manner that noted critic Irving Howe attributes to "the canniest writers," those who "know or sense that their subject cannot be met full face. It must be taken on a tangent, with extreme wariness, through strategies of indirection and circuitous narratives that leave untouched but always invoke or evoke it as a hovering shadow."[37]

Rosen's careful meditation about the Holocaust, her exploration of the radical change visited on humanity by the Shoah, has earned her critical acclaim. Representative is Sidra DeKoven Ezrahi's conclusion that in *Touching Evil* Rosen achieves "a partial balance between the narrative of commonplace events in the lives of a few people in New York in 1961 and the subterranean forces of Holocaust evil and suffering which constantly threatens those events."[38] Alan Berger concludes that Rosen, far from universalizing the Holocaust, "wishes the Jewish experience to be read as a cipher of the human condition, . . . [making clear that] survival has moral implications and thus is much more than . . . Darwinian survival." Berger asserts that "authentically encountering the Holocaust means taking its pain and moral challenge into one's soul and body."[39] Norma Rosen has.

A generation after the Holocaust we have a body of imaginative literature that has sought to understand a force hitherto beyond the imagination. Norma Rosen has participated in that endeavor in a significant way, not by re-creating the Holocaust universe but by demonstrating that the subject is and should be of concern to thinking people, convincingly illustrating that "the central question was—and is still—how to write as a Jew after the Holocaust."[40] Rosen's contribution to Holocaust literature has been the rendering of Holocaust-metamorphosed lives, lives transformed by a malevolence so absolute that it overpowers earlier conceptions of good and evil. In the process, the daughter of Jewishly estranged parents has become a Jewish writer, honoring a central moral injunction to remember collective Jewish history.

CONCLUSION

Of the significance of memory, Primo Levi writes: "It has been observed by psychologists that survivors of traumatic events are divided into two well-defined groups: those who repress their past *en bloc*, and those whose memory of the offense persists, as though carved in stone, prevailing over all previous or subsequent experiences. Now, not by choice but by nature, I belong to the second group. Of my two years of life outside the law I have not forgotten a single thing. Without any deliberate effort, memory continues to restore to me events, faces, words, sensations, as if at that time my mind had gone through a period of exalted receptivity, during which not a detail was lost."[1]

Collective memory is realized through reading histories and testimonies. It is also achieved through subjecting the documentary to the artistic imagination. Historians have performed the valuable work of gathering and analyzing the raw data of the Holocaust. Creative artists' search for truth, especially when dealing with the Shoah and its essential mystery, reaches beyond reporting the data surrounding the event. The facts of the Shoah constitute the given of the novel, which then proceeds from the factual to a deeper truth. Alvin Rosenfeld describes it as "an attempt to express a new order of consciousness, a recognizable shift in being."[2] The Holocaust novel is not just an account of what happened. Its concern is with bearing witness, with engaging memory as something more than recollection, thereby making the past a significant part of the present and the future. Like history and testimony, fiction of the Shoah struggles to wrest meaning from the event. The fiction examined in this book self-consciously ponders history, reflects on the tragedy and its implications, rescues memory from oblivion, and petitions future generations to accept the legacy of the Shoah and remember in perpetuity. The novelists inscribe the Holocaust images on our consciousness and thereby sustain memory.

Theodor Adorno's cautionary injunction against aesthetic exploitation of the Holocaust is honored by these writers. They use their art not primarily or essentially to provide aesthetic pleasure but to shape personal and collective memory in ways that ensure its enduring relevance. The European-born bear witness to horrors they endured, and the American-born join them in solidarity as "the generation that bears the scar without the wound, sustaining memory without direct experience."[3] Together survivor and American-born writers unite with the larger Jewish community in mourning. Whether they reconstitute the past from direct knowledge and memory as eyewitnesses or through documentary research and artistic imagination, these writers create memorable literature. They open and broaden the American literary canon and the Holocaust canon by giving full voice and visibility to Holocaust history, by creating fiction that allows readers to read referentially and aesthetically, with the sense that "this is true" and that "this is constructed." The voices of these writers are both literary and historiographical. They demonstrate that representation of history through the lens of male hegemony is incomplete. They affirm that the story of the Shoah is also a Jewish woman's story, that the past has a gendered dimension. They honor the memories of the men, women, and children who died in and lived through the Shoah. Recounting the lives and deaths of European Jewry and interpreting the survivors' stories denies the Nazis and their collaborators a posthumous victory and honors the biblical mandate to remember.

NOTES

Introduction

1. Paula Hyman, "Gender and Jewish History," *Tikkun* 3, no.1 (Jan.–Feb. 1988): 35.

2. Claudia Koonz, *Mothers in the Fatherland* (New York: St. Martin's Press, 1987), 5–6.

3. Eichmann's comments were reported by Rudolf Hoess in his autobiography *Commandant of Auschwitz*, trans. Constantine Fitzgibbon (Cleveland: World Publishing, 1960), 242; qtd. by Alan Berger in *Crisis and Covenant: The Holocaust in American Jewish Fiction* (Albany: State University of New York Press, 1985), 12.

4. Mary Lowenthal Felstiner, *To Paint Her Life: Charlotte Salomon in the Nazi Era* (New York: Harper Collins, 1994), 207; qtd. by Myrna Goldenberg in "'From a World Beyond': Women in the Holocaust," *Feminist Studies* 22 (fall 1996): 669.

5. Among important contributions to women's Holocaust history are Sybil Milton's "Women and the Holocaust: The Case of German and German-Jewish Women," *When Biology Became Destiny: Women in Weimar and Nazi Germany*, ed. Renate Bridenthal, Anita Grossman, and Marion Kaplan (New York: Monthly Review Press, 1984), 297–333; Marion Kaplan's "Jewish Women in Nazi Germany: Daily Life, Daily Struggles, 1933–1939," *Feminist Studies* 16 (fall 1990): 579–606; Konnilyn Feig's fine chapter, "Women and the Third Riech, Part 1: Ravensbrück—For Women Only," in *Hitler's Death Camps: The Sanity of Madness* (New York: Holmes & Meier, 1979), 133–56; and Germaine Tillion's *Ravensbrück* (Garden City: Doubleday, 1975). The works by Milton, Feig, and Tillion are central to understanding women's camp experience. Margaret L. Rossiter, *Women in the Resistance* (New York: Praeger, 1986), and *Women in the Resistance and in the Holocaust*, ed. Vera Laska (Westport CT: Greenwood Press, 1983), contribute valuable studies of women serving in resistance movements. An important source of women's Holocaust experience and response is the proceedings of the first conference on women and the Holocaust at Stern College in 1983, attended by more than 400 scholars and survivors, *Proceedings of the*

Conference, "Women Surviving: The Holocaust," ed. Esther Katz and Joan Ringelheim (New York: Institute for Research and History, 1983).

6. Marlene Heinemann's *Gender and Destiny: Women Writers and the Holocaust* (New York: Greenwood Press, 1986) is a pioneering study of women's Holocaust memoirs that isolates gender-based Holocaust experience and the manner in which women write about the Holocaust encounter. Corroborative essays on women's memoirs include Sara Horowitz's "Memory and Testimony of Women Survivors of Nazi Genocide," *Women of the Word: Jewish Women and Jewish Writing*, ed. Judith Baskin (Detroit: Wayne State University Press, 1994), and several works by Myrna Goldenberg: "Different Horrors, Same Hell: Women Remembering the Holocaust," *Thinking the Unthinkable: Meanings of the Holocaust*, ed. Roger S. Gottlieb (New York: Paulist Press, 1990), 150–66; "Lessons Learned from Gentle Heroism: Women's Holocaust Narrative," *Annals of the American Academy of Political and Social Science* (Nov. 1996): 78–93; "From a World Beyond: Women and the Holocaust," *Feminist Studies* 22 (fall 1996): 667–87; and "Testimony, Narrative, and Nightmare: Experience of Jewish Women in the Holocaust," *Active Voices*, ed. Mauri Sacks (Urbana: University of Illinois Press, 1995), 94–108.

7. Sociologist Ruth Linden offers an account of interviewing Holocaust survivors and interpreting their stories in *Making Stories, Making Selves: Feminist Reflections on the Holocaust* (Columbus: Ohio State University Press, 1993). Carol Rittner and John Roth have edited an anthology of women's Holocaust writing, *Different Voices: Women and the Holocaust* (New York: Paragon House, 1993), that is entirely devoted to excerpts from well-known survivor testimonies, diaries, and feminist scholarship on women's Holocaust experience.

8. Groundbreaking essays by Joan Ringelheim, a central voice in women's Holocaust studies, include "The Unethical and the Unspeakable: Women and the Holocaust," *Simon Wiesenthal Center Annual* 1 (1984): 69–87; "Thoughts about Women and the Holocaust," *Thinking the Unthinkable*, ed. Gottlieb, 141–49; "Women and the Holocaust: A Reconsideration of Research," *Signs* 10, no.4 (1985): 741–61, rpt. in an abridged and revised version as "Women and the Holocaust: A Reconsideration of Research," *Jewish Women in Historical Perspective*, ed. Judith R. Baskin (Detroit: Wayne State University Press, 1991), 243–64, and with a postscript adding new historic evidence in *Different Voices*, ed. Rittner and Roth, 373–418, prelude to a forthcoming book by Ringelheim, *Double Jeopardy: Women and the Holocaust*.

9. Ringelheim, "Thoughts about Women and the Holocaust," 147.

10. Ringelheim, "Women and the Holocaust," *Signs*, 743.

11. Ringelheim, "Women and the Holocaust," *Signs*, 747, 743.

12. Ringelheim, "Women and the Holocaust," *Different Voices*.

13. In Appelfeld's *Badenheim 1939* a woman senses something terrible about to

befall the guests at the spa. "Kitty" and *Tzili* each revolve around a woman's experience. Kitty, in hiding in a convent, resorts to voluntary muteness in her struggle to submerge her Jewish identity and negate her feminine sexuality. Tzili's story of survival has much in common with women's recording of female Holocaust experience, particularly in its focus on her persecution as a sex object and her strategy of adopting a gentile identity for survival. Similarly, I. B. Singer's female characters approach the abyss in *Shosha* and are of primary concern in his studies of the impact of the Shoah on survivors' psychological and religious identities in "The Cafeteria," "Hanka," "The Mentor," and *Enemies, A Love Story*.

14. Horowitz, "Memory and Testimony of Women Survivors," 263–64.

15. For analyses of women's Holocaust narratives in books by single authors, see Edward Alexander, *The Resonance of Dust: Essays on Holocaust Literature and Jewish Fate* (Columbus: Ohio State University Press, 1979); Alan Berger, *Crisis and Covenant: The Holocaust in American Jewish Fiction* (Albany: State University of New York Press, 1985); Lawrence Langer, *The Holocaust and the Literary Imagination* (New Haven: Yale University Press, 1975); S. Lillian Kremer, *Witness through the Imagination: Jewish American Holocaust Literature* (Detroit: Wayne State University Press, 1989), 218–78; Lawrence Langer, *The Age of Atrocity: Death in Modern Literature* (Boston: Beacon Press, 1978); Lawrence Langer, *Versions of Survival: The Holocaust and the Human Spirit* (Albany: State University of New York Press, 1982); Lawrence Langer, *Holocaust Testimonies: The Ruins of Memory* (New Haven: Yale University Press, 1991); Lawrence Langer, *Admitting the Holocaust* (New York: Oxford University Press, 1994); and Alvin H. Rosenfeld, *A Double Dying: Reflections on Holocaust Literature* (Bloomington: Indiana University Press, 1980).

16. Examination of women's Holocaust literary expression is the subject of Dorothy Bilik's *Immigrant-Survivors: Post-Holocaust Consciousness in Recent Jewish American Fiction* (Middletown CT: Wesleyan University Press, 1981), and Ellen S. Fine's "Women and the Holocaust: Strategies for Survival," *Reflections of the Holocaust in Art and Literature*, ed. Randolph L. Braham (Boulder: Csengeri Institute for Holocaust Studies; New York: Graduate School and University Center of the City University of New York, 1990). Sidra DeKoven Ezrahi writes penetrating analyses of several women writers in *By Words Alone: The Holocaust in Literature* (Chicago: University of Chicago Press, 1980). Worthy analyses appear in Sara Horowitz's essay "Ilona Karmel," *Jewish American Women Writers: A Bio-Bibliographical and Critical Sourcebook*, ed. Ann R. Shapiro (Westport CT: Greenwood Press, 1994), 146–57, and "The 'Pin with Which to Stick Yourself': The Holocaust in Jewish American Women's Writing," *Daughters of Valor: Contemporary Jewish American Women Writers*, ed. Jay L. Halio and Ben Siegel (Newark: University of Delaware Press, 1997), 141–59. I write about women's Holocaust literature in "Holocaust-Wrought Women:

Portraits by Four American Writers," *Studies in American Jewish Literature* 11 (fall 1992): 150–61; *"An Estate of Memory*: Women in the Holocaust," *Holocaust Studies Annual*, ed. Sanford Pinsker and Jack Fischel (New York: Garland Publishing, 1992), 99–110; "Holocaust Writing," *The Oxford Companion to Women's Writing in the United States*, ed. Cathy N. Davidson and Linda Wagner-Martin (New York: Oxford University Press, 1994), 395–97; "The Holocaust and the Witnessing Imagination," *Violence, Silence, and Anger: Women's Writing as Transgression*, ed. Deirdre Lashgari (Charlottesville: University Press of Virginia, 1995), 231–46; "Norma Rosen: An American Literary Response to the Holocaust," *Daughters of Valor*, ed. Halio and Siegel, 160–74.

17. *Different Voices* includes memoirs and critical essays, and *Women in the Holocaust* (New York: Remember, 1993) is a collection of women's testimonies, compiled and translated by Jehoshua Eibeshitz and Anna Eilenberg-Eibeshitz. Among works focused on Holocaust writing that include women's works are *Truth and Lamentation: Stories and Poems on the Holocaust*, ed. Milton Teichman and Sharon Leder (Urbana: University of Illinois Press, 1994); *Art from the Ashes: A Holocaust Anthology*, ed. Lawrence Langer (New York: Oxford University Press, 1995); *The Literature of Destruction: Jewish Responses to Catastrophe* (New York: Jewish Publication Society, 1988), ed. David G. Roskies; and *Blood to Remember: American Poets on the Holocaust*, ed. Charles Fishman (Lubbock: Texas Tech University Press, 1991). Other anthologies, whose subject is not the Holocaust but which include women's Holocaust writing, are *Against Forgetting: Twentieth-Century Poetry of Witness*, ed. Carolyn Forché (New York: W. W. Norton, 1993); *Follow My Footprints: Changing Images of Women in American Jewish Fiction*, ed. Sylvia Barack Fishman (Hanover NH: University Press of New England, 1992); *The Woman Who Lost Her Names: Selected Writings by American Jewish Women*, ed. Julia Wolf Mazow (San Francisco: Harper & Row, 1980); *America and I: Short Stories by American Jewish Women Writers*, ed. Joyce Antler (Boston: Beacon Press, 1990); *Nice Jewish Girls: A Lesbian Anthology*, ed. Evelyn Torton Beck (Boston: Beacon Press, 1992); *Writing Our Way Home: Contemporary Stories by American Jewish Writers*, ed. Ted Solotaroff and Nessa Rapoport (New York: Schocken Books, 1992); and *The Global Anthology of Jewish Women Writers*, ed. Robert and Roberta Kalechofsky (Marblehead MA: Micah Publications, 1990).

18. Women were subjected to many medical experiments. Historian Konnilyn Feig points out that "in terms of maiming operations—cutting up, cutting into—it is quite clear that [Nazi] subjects were far more often women than men. . . . Since [the Nazis] believed women were inferior to men, they were even less restrained in effecting the physical destruction of a woman's body prior to its death" (Feig, 171–72).

19. Norma Rosen coined the phrase "witness through the imagination" in her essay

"The Holocaust and the American-Jewish Novelist," *Midstream* 20 (Oct. 1974), rpt. in Rosen, *Accidents of Influence: Writing as a Woman and a Jew in America* (Albany: State University of New York Press, 1992), 3–17.

20. Demetz remarked on her appreciation of Karmel's book in response to my question about the Holocaust texts that influenced her. Hana Demetz, interview with S. Lillian Kremer, 20 May 1988.

21. Elaine Showalter, "Women and the Literary Curriculum," *College English* 32 (May 1971): 858–59.

22. Ilona Karmel, *An Estate of Memory* (Boston: Houghton Mifflin, 1969), 321. Subsequent citations from this text appear in parentheses.

23. Myrna Goldenberg's analysis of women's memoirs and testimonies, in "Different Horrors, Same Hell," identifies repetition of themes and incidents, especially the frequent acknowledgment of their vulnerability as sexual beings, as distinguishing female from male writing.

24. See Ringelheim, "Women and the Holocaust," *Signs*.

25. Charlotte Delbo, *None of Us Will Return*, trans. John Githens (Boston: Beacon Press, 1968), 122.

26. Bruno Bettelheim argued that the SS was successful in its efforts to infantilize prisoners in its control of the use of latrines. The SS humiliated prisoners by reducing them to pre–toilet training status, forcing them to soil themselves and to request permission to relieve themselves. With loss of their habitual standards of cleanliness, some prisoners regressed to the instinctual behavior of early childhood. "Individual and Mass Behavior in Extreme Situations," *Journal of Abnormal Psychology* (1943): 417–52.

27. For an analysis of the different treatment of pregnancy and motherhood by scholars and women writing Holocaust testimony, see Horowitz, "Memory and Testimony of Women Survivors," 258–82.

28. Heinemann, 17.

29. Representative of the shift from wholly positive to flawed mother figures are Schaeffer's Anya, characterized as overprotecting her daughter, and Rebecca Goldstein's mother in "The Legacy of Raizel Kaddish," who manipulates the life of her daughter by trying to make her a compassionate saint in contrition for her self-perceived moral lapse while in a concentration camp.

30. Elie Wiesel, *Night*, trans. Stella Rodway (New York: Hill & Wang, 1958), 42.

31. Tadeusz Borowski, *This Way for the Gas, Ladies and Gentlemen*, trans. Barbara Vedder (Middlesex: Penguin Books, 1967), 45–46.

32. See ghetto historians Chaim A. Kaplan, *Scroll of Agony: The Warsaw Diary of Chaim A. Kaplan*, ed. Abraham I. Katsh (New York: Collier, 1973), 327–28, and Emmanuel Ringelblum, *Notes from the Warsaw Ghetto: The Journal of Emmanuel*

Ringelblum, ed. Jacob Sloan (New York: Schocken Books, 1974), 172. In 1942 Kaplan wrote that ragged six- or seven-year-olds were immediately recognizable by the humps on their backs filled with potatoes and onions. Likewise, Ringelblum recorded efforts of emaciated three- or four-year olds crawling through rainwater conduits and culverts to bring merchandise into the ghetto from the Aryan side of Warsaw. For fictional delineation of child smugglers, see Arnost Lustig, *Diamonds of the Night*, trans. Jeanne Nemcova (Evanston: Northwestern University Press, 1978), and Leslie Epstein, *King of the Jews* (New York: New American Library, 1979).

33. Ellen Fine, "Women and the Holocaust," 82.

34. Ringelheim, "Women and the Holocaust," *Signs*, 745–46.

35. See Konnilyn Feig on the Nazi-supervised births in Birkenau and the prescribed manner of drowning the newborns in small barrels (184).

36. Sara Nomberg-Przytyk, "Esther's First Born," *Auschwitz: True Tales from a Grotesque Land*, trans. Roslyn Hirsh, ed. Eli Pfefferkorn and David Hirsh (Chapel Hill: University of North Carolina Press, 1985), 69, rpt. in *Truth and Lamentation*, ed. Teichman and Leder, 87.

37. Susan Cernyak-Spatz, qtd. by Goldenberg in "Different Horrors, Same Hell," 159.

38. Livia Bitton Jackson, *Elli: Coming of Age in the Holocaust* (New York: Times Books, 1980), 94.

39. Feig, 161.

40. Leonard Tushnet, *The Uses of Adversity: Studies of Starvation in the Warsaw Ghetto* (London: T. Yoseloff, 1966), qtd. by Milton, 311–12.

41. This position is frequently advanced by Lawrence Langer not only in his repudiation of Martin Gilbert's recognition of ghetto and death camp resistance in the closing paragraph of *The Holocaust: The Jewish Tragedy* (London: Collins, 1986) but in dissent from other scholars who address resistance and heroism at conferences, in his analysis of video testimonies from the Yale Holocaust Archives in oral presentations, and in *Holocaust Testimonies*, 162–63.

42. Olga Lengyel, *Five Chimneys*, trans. Clifford Coch and Paul B. Weiss (Chicago: Ziff-Davis, 1947), 95.

43. Terrence Des Pres, *The Survivor: An Anatomy of Life in the Death Camps* (Oxford: Oxford University Press, 1976), 136, 138.

44. Judith Tydor Baumel concludes from her study of Plaszow women's mutual assistance that the behavior was both gender- and religiously motivated, citing women who invoked Torahic and Talmudic teaching to the effect that Jews were responsible for one another and that "[s]he who saves one life, it is as if [s]he saves an entire world." Judith Tydor Baumel, "Social Interaction among Jewish Women

in Crisis during the Holocaust: A Case Study," *Gender and History* 7 (April 1995): 65. Cited by Goldenberg, "From a World Beyond," 670.

45. Ringelheim, "Woman and the Holocaust," *Signs*, 749.

46. Primo Levi, *Survival in Auschwitz*, trans. Stuart Woolf (New York: Macmillan, 1960), 88.

47. Langer, *Admitting the Holocaust*, 105.

48. Tillion, *Ravensbrück*, 230.

49. Milton, 313.

50. Milton, 313–14.

51. Goldenberg, "Testimony, Narrative, and Nightmare," 101.

52. Ilona Karmel, interview with S. Lillian Kremer, 24 May 1988.

53. Ezrahi, 67.

54. Agnes Roza, *Diary from Camp Nuremberg, 1944* (Budapest: Magioto, 1978), 44, qtd. by Michael Unger in "The Prisoner's First Encounter with Auschwitz," *The Nazi Holocaust: Historical Articles on the Destruction of European Jews*, ed. Michael R. Marrus (London: Meckler, 1989), 1164.

55. Viktor Frankl, *From Death Camp to Existentialism: A Psychiatrist's Path to New Therapy*, trans. Ilse Lasch (Boston: Beacon Press, 1959), 38.

56. *Survivors, Victims, and Perpetrators: Essays on the Nazi Holocaust*, ed. Joel E. Dimsdale (Washington DC: Hemisphere Publishing, 1980), 168.

57. Fine, "Women and the Holocaust."

58. Writing of her work for the resistance inside Birkenau, Olga Lengyel explains the value of her position as an infirmary nurse for disseminating news among the inmates. Men who were assigned to special labor details in the women's section came to the infirmary, where Lengyel spread the war news and served as a "post office," accepting and delivering letters and parcels from one resistance member to another. This work became Lengyel's "new reason for living." Lengyel, 67–68.

59. Milton, 316.

60. Although Ettinger refused to detail the specifics of her missions or identify her group during our 23 May 1988 interview, she confirmed her association with a resistance unit.

61. Elie Wiesel, qtd. by Alan Berger in "Holocaust Survivors and Children in *Anya* and *Mr. Sammler's Planet*," *Modern Language Studies* 16 (winter 1986): 81.

62. Charlotte Delbo, *Auschwitz and After*, trans. Rosette C. Lamont (New Haven: Yale University Press, 1995), 230.

63. Among male Americans who treat survivor syndrome are Edward Lewis Wallant, Saul Bellow, Bernard Malamud, I. B. Singer, and Chaim Potok. See chapters on these writers in Kremer, *Witness through the Imagination*.

64. Patricia Brenner, Ethel Roskies, and Richard S. Lazarus, "Stress and Coping under Extreme Conditions," *Survivors, Victims, and Perpetrators*, ed. Dimsdale, 242.

65. E. C. Trautman, "Fear and Panic in the Nazi Concentration Camps," *International Journal of Social Psychiatry* 10 (1964), qtd. by Leo Eitinger in "The Concentration Camp Syndrome and Its Late Sequelae," *Survivors, Victims, and Perpetrators*, ed. Dimsdale, 146.

66. Sidney M. Bolkosky, "Interviewing Victims Who Survived: Listening for the Silences that Strike," *Annals of Scholarship* 4 (winter 1987): 34.

67. Charlotte Delbo, *La mémoire et les jours* (Paris: Berg International, 1985), 14. Lawrence Langer discusses Delbo's theories at length and uses them extensively in his study of survivor memory, *Holocaust Testimonies*.

68. On post-Holocaust study and observance of Judaism in Ozick's fiction, see Kremer, *Witness through the Imagination*, 218–78.

69. James Young, *Writing and Rewriting the Holocaust: Narrative and the Consequences of Interpretation* (Bloomington: Indiana University Press, 1988), 63.

70. Alvin Rosenfeld, "Jean Améry as Witness," *Holocaust Remembrance: The Shapes of Memory*, ed. Geoffrey H. Hartman (Oxford: Blackwell, 1994), 60.

71. Etty Hillesum, *An Interrupted Life: The Diaries of Etty Hillesum*, trans. Arnold J. Pomerans (New York: Pantheon, 1984), 146.

72. Arthur A. Cohen, *The Tremendum: A Theological Interpretation of the Holocaust* (New York: Crossroad, 1981) 23.

73. Berel Lang, *Act and Idea in the Nazi Genocide* (Chicago: University of Chicago Press, 1990), xiii.

74. George Steiner, "A Kind of Survivor," *Language and Silence: Essays on Language, Literature, and the Inhuman* (New York: Atheneum, 1977), 143–44.

75. Qtd. by Irving Abrahamson, ed., in *Against Silence: The Voice and Vision of Elie Wiesel* (New York: Holocaust Library, 1985), 1:44.

76. Lang, 125–35.

77. Theodor Adorno, *Aesthetics and Politics*, trans. and ed. Ronald Taylor (London: New Left Books, 1977), 188; T. W. Adorno, *Aesthetic Theory*, trans. Christian Lenhardt (London: Routledge & Kegan Paul, 1970), 352–54, 443–44; T. W. Adorno, *Prisms*, 245–71, qtd. by Sidra DeKoven Ezrahi in "'The Grave in the Air': Unbound Metaphors in Post-Holocaust Poetry," *Probing the Limits of Representation: Nazism and the "Final Solution"*, ed. Saul Friedlander (Cambridge: Harvard University Press, 1992), 260.

78. Emil Fackenheim, who was incarcerated at Sachsenhausen, asserts that it was not until years later, when he read a study of that camp, that he felt he truly understood his own experience and what had occurred there. Qtd. by Rosenfeld in *Double Dying*, 17–18.

79. Among the biblical injunctions to remember and bear witness are Leviticus 5:1; Deuteronomy 25:17–19, 32:7; and Exodus 13:3.

80. Langer, *Holocaust Testimonies*.

81. Maurice Blanchot, *The Writing of the Disaster*, trans. Ann Smock (Lincoln: University of Nebraska Press, 1986).

82. Rosenfeld, *Double Dying*, 180.

83. Friedlander, ed., *Probing the Limits of Representation*.

84. Lang, xi.

85. Hartman, "Introduction: Darkness Visible," *Holocaust Remembrance*, ed. Hartman, 10.

Ilona Karmel

1. Ilona Karmel, interview with S. Lillian Kremer, 24 May 1988. Subsequent citations to this interview appear as Karmel interview.

2. A collection of the sisters' Polish poems was published as *Spiew za Drutami* (Song behind the wire), and several were later translated into Yiddish. Like her sister, Henia Karmel-Wolfe has published two Holocaust novels. *The Baders of Jacob Street* situates political and apolitical, religious and nonreligious, parochial and assimilationist Jews, professionals and laborers as members of a viable neighborhood, representative of the world of Polish Jewry before the genocide. Karmel-Wolfe's subject is the prelude to the catastrophe, the onset of the Aryan aggression, culminating with the establishment of the Cracow Ghetto. *Marek and Lisa* is a love story involving the Holocaust tribulations, separation, and eventual reunion of lovers. Karmel interview.

3. Archibald MacLeish, with whom Karmel studied writing at Harvard, brought *Stephania* to Houghton Mifflin (Karmel interview). Martin Rice cites the poet's praise of the book as "one of the most dramatic incidents in the cultural record of our time," in *Saturday Review* 36 (9 May 1953): 21. J. H. Raleigh compared the novel to *Magic Mountain* in the *New Republic* 128 (4 May 1953): 19, and it is described by Frances Gaither as "a testament to the human spirit indestructible" in the *New York Times Book Review* (29 March 1953): 4.

4. Ilona Karmel, *Stephania* (Boston: Houghton Mifflin, 1953), 314. Subsequent references to this edition appear parenthetically in the text.

5. Levi, 123.

6. Unsigned review, *Times Literary Supplement* (2 April 1954): 213.

7. Ilona Karmel, *An Estate of Memory* (Boston: Houghton Mifflin, 1969). References to this edition appear parenthetically in the text.

8. Rice, 21.

9. Karmel and her sister each delineate maternal resourcefulness based on their mother's example. Their father was dead by the time they entered the ghetto, and

they depended solely on their mother. Ilona Karmel credits her mother with saving her life. When she was hospitalized with typhus, at a time when the ill were already being shot, her mother "stole [her] out through the back door." Another time, her mother saved both daughters by hiding them under a mattress during a selection, an incident Karmel incorporates in her fiction. So competent was her mother that she even nursed and adopted a young woman who was not a relation, welcoming her into their bunk and caring for her during a typhus epidemic. Karmel interview and Horowitz, "Ilona Karmel," 147.

10. Henia Karmel-Wolfe also develops the passing theme in *The Baders of Jacob Street*, but with an ironic reversal: the Jewish woman is overcome with remorse and fear after having to taunt Jewish slave laborers and voluntarily returns to the ghetto to share the fate of her parents. Ilona Karmel's treatment of the fabrication of Christian identity has commonalities with that of another Plaszow survivor who writes of her family's experiences while traveling as Polish Catholics with false identity papers. See Berta Ferderber-Salz, *And the Sun Kept Shining . . .* (New York: Holocaust Publications, 1980), 26–27.

11. Malvina Graf, *The Krakow Ghetto and the Plaszow Camp Remembered* (Tallahassee: Florida State University Press, 1989), 86–91.

12. Skarzysko (also known as Skarzysko-Kamienna) was established in August 1942 and functioned until August 1944. The camp consisted of three factory camps for the HASAG concern, designated Werke A, B, and C. The workers of A and B units produced ammunition, and those in Werke C produced underwater mines filled with picric acid. The prisoners of C died of poisoning within three months of their assignment. Living conditions were horrendous. Prisoners received seven ounces of bread a day and a pint of watery soup twice a day. They slept on bunks with two or three tiers of wooden shelves. Epidemics of dysentery and typhus were common. In late 1943 and early 1944 mass executions were carried out in Werke C. In July 1944, mass killings were again conducted in preparation for liquidating the camp. Several hundred prisoners were also killed during an escape attempt during the liquidation. The total number of Jews brought there is estimated at 25,000 to 30,000 and the number who died at 18,000 to 23,000. Survivors were sent to Buchenwald. Felicja Karay, "Skarzysko-Kamienna," *Encyclopedia of the Holocaust*, ed. Israel Gutman (New York: Macmillan, 1990), 4:1360–61.

13. For an eyewitness account of frequent arrests, beatings, and executions at Plaszow, see Jacob Stendig, "Execution at Plashow [*sic*]," trans. Moshe Spiegel, *Anthology of Holocaust Literature*, ed. Jacob Glatstein et al. (New York: Atheneum, 1982), 32–37, 250–52.

14. A woman prisoner who worked with noxious chemicals confirms Karmel's description of the toll taken on prisoners. She writes: "The work which would appear

to be easy, injured our health severely. The sulphur dust made us yellow — our hands, clothing, and even our faces were yellowed, and so we were called 'the yellows.'" Iren Darvas, "Women in a Nazi Munitions Factory," *Yad Vashem Bulletin* 7, no.21 (1967): 31–32.

15. Des Pres, 134–35.

16. Lengyel, 40.

17. Karmel modeled her treatment of women caring for the sick on the evidence surrounding her, including her mother's "adoption" of a young typhus patient whom she nursed as she did her own children. Karmel interview.

18. Aurelia's pregnancy is modeled on that of a woman Karmel met in Leipzig who bandaged herself to conceal pregnancy. Karmel recalls that this woman would fall asleep at work and that the others would push her to wake her. The portion of Aurelia's story that relates to smuggling the child from the camp has its source in an incident that occurred in the Cracow camp which involved smuggling a drug-silenced child out in a sack. Karmel interview.

19. Ruth Angress, "Afterword," *An Estate of Memory*, 446.

20. Levi, 160.

21. Ezrahi, *By Words Alone*, 83.

22. Karmel interview.

23. Zdena Berger, *Tell Me Another Morning* (New York: Harper & Brothers, 1959), 135, 149.

24. Frankl, 38.

25. Ezrahi, *By Words Alone*, 82–83.

26. Sara R. Horowitz, "Memory and Testimony of Women Survivors," 269.

27. Ezrahi, *By Words Alone*, 87.

28. Horowitz, "Memory and Testimony of Women Survivors," 269.

29. See Lengyel.

30. The model of Barbara's character is a woman named Tamara whom the author admired, a woman whose looks and arrest on Aryan papers are incorporated in the text. Karmel interview.

31. Karmel interview.

32. Ilona Karmel, letter to S. Lillian Kremer, 10 January 1998.

33. Karmel interview.

34. Confirming Karmel's presentation of Goeth's criminality are memoirs of other survivors. Henry Orenstein notes Goeth's greed with reference to selling safe block elder positions and using his subordinates to accumulate wealth obtained by searches of new prisoner arrivals. Eventually, the Gestapo discovered Goeth's private hoard of prisoner property and arrested him. Orenstein, Graf, and Ferderber-Salz offer lengthy documentation of Goeth's sadism, including his penchant for using prisoners

as sharpshooting targets, and note that under Goeth's command "frequent selections were conducted in the camp hospital and those too sick or weak to work were . . . shot." See Henry Orenstein, *I Shall Live: Surviving against All Odds, 1939–1945* (New York: Beaufort, 1987), 197–98, 206, 179; Graf, 92–93; and Ferderber-Salz, 80, 179.

35. Karmel interview.

36. This man chose the older and weak-looking women for transport to Skarzysko, among them Karmel and her sister, because he knew the remaining Plaszow inmates would be sent to Auschwitz, where the elderly and the weak would have little chance for survival. Karmel interview.

37. Karmel interview.

38. The genesis of the Aurelia-Alinka fictional relationship is located in two distinct biographical sources. The mother-daughter association reflects the experience of a girl Karmel knew in Skarzysko who joined forces with an older woman. The story of their initial meeting during the Radom Ghetto liquidation is based on the history of two women Karmel met in the Cracow Ghetto hospital who told her of their "meeting in the grave." Karmel interview.

39. Karmel letter to Kremer.

40. Karmel interview.

41. Ezrahi, *By Words Alone*, 78.

42. Levi, 86, 45.

43. Karmel interview.

Elżbieta Ettinger

1. Elżbieta Ettinger, interview with S. Lillian Kremer, 23 May 1988. Subsequent references to this interview appear as Ettinger interview.

2. The life and death of the Warsaw Ghetto is described in meticulous detail in a journal kept by a trained historian, Emmanuel Ringelblum, and in the archives of the *Oneg Shabbes* (Sabbath celebrants), a secret society created by Ringelblum to preserve the record of the destruction of Polish Jewry. Ringelblum's diary and notes, which he had hidden, were found in the ruins of the ghetto. The scope of the entries is wide-ranging, covering all of life in the ghetto and much that was happening in the rest of Poland.

3. Elżbieta Ettinger, letter to S. Lillian Kremer, 29 August 1988.

4. Ettinger interview.

5. Ettinger interview.

6. Ettinger interview.

7. Ettinger interview.

8. Elżbieta Ettinger, *Kindergarten* (Boston: Houghton Mifflin, 1970), 2. Subsequent references to this edition appear parenthetically in the text.

9. Rachel Auerbach, "*Yizkor*, 1943," *Literature of Destruction*, ed. Roskies, 460.

10. Helen Lewine, who became a member of the underground resistance at age thirteen, addresses bearing witness in a manner similar to Elli. She reports that a few days before the ghetto liquidation her father told her, "Remember, if you survive, tell your children and your children's children what those beasts did to us." Lewine contends that through all the hardships she endured she always heard her father's voice telling her, "Tell your children, your children's children," and that made her survive. Another survivor, Vladka Meed, argued before a group of survivors, "I am convinced that we survived, because we are witnesses and we have to tell the story; otherwise there is no meaning to our survival." *Proceedings of the Conference, "Women Surviving: The Holocaust,"* ed. Katz and Ringelheim, 69–70.

11. Ettinger attributes the decision to use an authentic diary in its present form to the advice of her editor, who thought it would be a shame not to make use of the diary in her possession. The editor believed the diary should stay intact rather than be incorporated into the narration. Once that decision was taken, the chronological order was abandoned. Ettinger interview.

12. Marek Wilczynski, "Trusting the Words: Paradoxes of Ida Fink," *Modern Language Studies* 24 (fall 1994): 25–28.

13. Ettinger interview.

14. Lawrence Langer made this distinction between chronological and durational memory in a presentation of survivor testimony to a National Endowment for the Humanities seminar at Brandeis University, 22 July 1996.

15. All Jews in state, community, and public enterprises were dismissed. Aryan firms were prohibited from employing Jewish workers, and Jews were forbidden to use libraries, theaters, movies, railroads, and streetcars. Jewish property outside the ghetto boundaries was confiscated. Although a ghetto for Warsaw was proposed as early as November 1939, administrative conflicts within the German hierarchy delayed its implementation. In the summer of 1940, before the ghetto was officially established, the Germans built 11 miles of eight-foot-high walls separating the section where Jews were concentrated from the rest of the city. All Jews living outside the walled area were directed to move in, and all Poles had to depart. On October 3—Rosh Hashanah—the Nazis proclaimed the establishment of the ghetto, and by mid-October almost 400,000 people were concentrated within 100 city blocks. Until 15 November 1940 it was still possible for Jews to leave the ghetto and work outside. Then, without warning, on 15 November the ghetto was sealed and the Jews trapped behind its walls. Nora Levin, *The Holocaust: The Destruction of European Jewry, 1933–1945* (New York: Schocken Books, 1973), 207–08.

16. By the early months of 1942 food allocation allowed by the Germans consisted of 194 calories per Jew per day. Outside the ghetto the Poles of Warsaw were allowed

634 calories and the Germans 2,310 calories. The Nazis ensured death by starvation of thousands of Jews who were without illegal means of getting supplementary food. Martin Gilbert, *Final Journey: The Fate of the Jews in Nazi Europe* (London: George Allen & Unwin, 1979), 101.

17. Vladka Meed, a heroine of the Warsaw Ghetto, described the purpose of clandestine cultural and political activities: "To remain a human being in the ghetto one had to live in constant defiance, to act illegally. We had illegal synagogues, illegal classes, illegal meetings and illegal publications. We were trying to live through the war, the hard times, in the ways which were known to us before the war." Qtd. by Yitzhak Rabi in "Living on Both Sides of the Ghetto Wall," *Forward*, 24 November 1995: 8.

18. Zygmunt Bauman, *Modernity and the Holocaust* (Ithaca: Cornell University Press, 1989), 130.

19. Ettinger, the author of *Hannah Arendt/Martin Heidegger* (New Haven: Yale University Press, 1995), is no doubt familiar with Arendt's withering attack on the Jewish Councils in her book *Eichmann in Jerusalem*.

20. Chaim A. Kaplan, *The Scroll of Agony*, excerpted in *Literature of Destruction*, ed. Roskies, 437–38.

21. Ettinger interview.

22. All Nazi-occupied countries had some Christian rescuers who operated either independently or as members of religious or underground resistance organizations that saved a small number of Jewish children. See Nechama Tec, "A Historical Perspective: Tracing the History of the Hidden Child Experience," *The Hidden Children: The Secret Survivors of the Holocaust*, ed. Jane Marks (New York: Fawcett Columbine, 1993).

23. The danger and trauma of the fugitives' encounters with blatant antisemitism is thoroughly documented and examined by survivors and social scientists. For cases of Jewish children on the Aryan side who heard antisemitic outbursts by Polish guardians unaware of the children's Jewish origins, see Emmanuel Ringelblum, "Children of the Warsaw Ghetto," *Jewish-Polish Relations during the Second World War*, excerpt trans. S. L. Shneiderman, *Congress Bi-Weekly* 30.7 (April 1963): 16.

24. Tec, 287.

25. Holocaust historians have made a convincing case that the one area of agreement between many Poles and Germans was the need for the elimination of the Jews and that the major Polish resistance group was explicitly antisemitic. Many Poles did not regard Jews as Poles and identified them with communism, further exacerbating anti-Jewish feelings. See George M. Kren, "The Holocaust as History," *Echoes from the Holocaust: Philosophical Reflections on a Dark Time*, ed. Alan Rosenberg and Gerald E. Meyers (Philadelphia: Temple University Press, 1988), 19.

26. Tec, 277.

27. Levin, 217.

28. Ettinger interview.

29. Emmanuel Ringelblum, qtd. by Marie Syrkin in "The Literature of the Holocaust," *Midstream* (May 1966): 14.

30. Meed, 194.

31. Tec writes: "When taking a step into the Christian world the destinies of the Jewish children were influenced by their appearance and the extent to which it conformed to the stereotypical 'Jewish look.' How well we could blend socially into the environment also made a difference" (285–86).

32. By the time Elli completes her education, she shares the views of Ida Fink's seventeen-year-old, who is reluctant to admit her Jewish identity even to an American liberator. She explains: "You don't know what it means to say, 'I am Jewish.' For three years I heard those words day and night but never, not even when I was alone, did I dare to say them aloud. . . . Do you know what it means to live in fear, lying, never speaking your own language, or thinking with your own brain, or looking with your own eyes?" Ida Fink, "Night of Surrender," *A Scrap of Time and Other Stories*, trans. Madeline Levine and Francine Prose (New York: Pantheon, 1987), 99–100.

33. Ida Fink, *The Journey*, trans. Joanna Weschler and Francine Prose (New York: Farrar, Straus, Giroux, 1992), 78.

34. Fink takes up a similar theme in her tale of two sisters whose "seemingly quiet days were in fact full of anxiety and insecurity . . . walking on shaky ground, mined with guesses and speculations . . . [the sisters] dissected every fragment of every sentence; every look; every smile" (*The Journey*, 87).

35. Vladka Meed, *On Both Sides of the Wall: Memoirs from the Warsaw Ghetto*, trans. Steven Meed (New York: Holocaust Library, 1979).

36. Tec, 287.

37. Saul Friedlander, *When Memory Comes*, trans. Helen R. Lane (New York: Farrar, Straus, Giroux, 1979), 110, qtd. by Susan Rubin Suleiman in *Risking Who One Is: Encounters with Contemporary Art and Literature* (Cambridge: Harvard University Press, 1994), 210.

38. Like her character, Ettinger worked in a German office and saw documents addressing the Final Solution. Ettinger interview.

39. Ettinger interview.

40. Maturity and good luck were at the heart of Susan Suleiman's survival at the same age as the fictional Emmi. Having successfully escaped a Nazi dragnet of her Budapest neighborhood with her parents, Suleiman was placed with Christian farmers and then retrieved by her parents when they were able to secure work under false papers. The Harvard professor recalls: "My name was Mary. My mother whispered to me every morning not to forget it, never to say my real name, no matter who asked. I told her not to worry, I wouldn't tell. I felt grown-up and

superior, carrying a secret like that." Living in the same house were people who were suspicious of the family. When one asked what her mother's maiden name was (it was Stern, a Jewish name), she was unable to reply—not because she did not know but because she did not know what "maiden name" meant. So complete was the child's indoctrination that at war's end a year later, when the family first returned to their home, she knew, "I was no longer Mary, but for a moment I could not remember my name." Suleiman, 220, 224.

41. Fink, "Night of Surrender," 94–95.

42. Elżbieta Ettinger, *Quicksand* (London: Pandora, 1989). References to this edition appear parenthetically in the text.

43. Iwona Irwin-Zarecka, *Neutralizing Memory: The Jew in Contemporary Poland* (New Brunswick: Transaction, 1989), 54–55.

44. Qtd. by Eva Fogelman in "The Psychology behind Being a Hidden Child," *Hidden Children*, ed. Marks, 299.

45. Fogelman, 301.

46. Ettinger experienced Soviet-style antisemitism at her job and reports that she was harassed to leave her position in foreign trade beginning in 1960. She explains that Jews were suspected of having contacts with Western countries. Ettinger interview.

Hana Demetz

1. Hana Demetz, interview with S. Lillian Kremer, 20 May 1988. Subsequent references to this interview appear as Demetz interview.

2. Demetz interview.

3. On Freundlich, see Patrizia Guida-Laforgia, *Invisible Women Writers in Exile in the U.S.A.* (New York: Peter Lang, 1995). Demetz revealed her own political purpose during the course of our interview.

4. Demetz interview.

5. Demetz interview.

6. Hana Demetz, *The House on Prague Street*, trans. Hana Demetz (New York: St. Martin's Press, 1980), 2. Subsequent references to this edition appear parenthetically in the text.

7. In 1930 there were 117,551 persons of the Jewish faith in Bohemia, Moravia, and Silesia and 136,737 in Slovakia, approximately 1.7 percent of the general population of 14,729,536. In Bohemia, Moravia, and Silesia 33 percent of the Jewish population declared Jewish nationality, 36.7 percent declared Czech nationality, and 30.3 percent declared German nationality. See "The Jews of Czechoslovakia," *The Jewish Communities of Nazi-Occupied Europe*, Research Institute on Peace and Post-War Problems, American Jewish Committee (New York: Howard Fertig, 1982), 1.

8. Bauman, 58–59; emphasis in original.

9. See Richard Elman's *The Reckoning* (New York: Charles Scribner's Sons, 1969), Edward Lewis Wallant's *The Pawnbroker* (New York: Harcourt Brace Jovanovich, 1961), and Ladislaw Grossman's *The Shop on Main Street* (Prague: Hlada Fronta, 1966).

10. Fink, *Scrap of Time*, 13.

11. Before the occupation Czechs and Jews lived harmoniously in Bohemia and Moravia. During the early period of the protectorate Czechs continued their private friendliness to the Jews and patronized Jewish cafés in demonstration of their hostility to the Germans. See "Jews of Czechoslovakia," 17–18.

12. In the protectorate a special German agency, Hadega (Handelsgesellschaft), was established for the registration of Jewish property. Nazi legislation permitted the *Reichprotektor* or his agency "trustees" to liquidate or supervise Jewish businesses in the Reich. In 1940 the *Reichprotektor*'s decree "for the elimination of the Jews from the Protectorate economy" made it "legal" for Jewish property to be "transferred" to non-Jews. "Jews of Czechoslovakia," 9.

13. Jiri Weil, *Life with a Star*, trans. Ruzena Kovarikova and Roslyn Schloss (New York: Farrar, Straus, Giroux, 1989), 50.

14. On these discriminatory laws, see "Jews of Czechoslovakia," 1–28.

15. Demetz interview.

16. Demetz claims that her mother's family did not identify as Jews but considered themselves Czech. As fully assimilated "modern" Jews, their self-identities were national rather than religious or culturally Jewish. Demetz interview.

17. Demetz did similar work in an ammunition factory. Demetz interview.

18. This episode is one of the rare instances in which Demetz departs from autobiography for fictional invention. Unlike Richter, the novelist's father was not killed by a Czech mob. He was deported to eastern Germany as an alien in 1946 and escaped to West Germany via Berlin in 1951. He died of a heart attack in 1958. Fortunoff Video Archive for Holocaust Testimonies, Yale University, tape T-177, testimony of Hana D.

19. Hana Demetz, *The Journey from Prague Street* (New York: St. Martin's Press, 1990). References to this edition appear parenthetically in the text.

20. Demetz interview.

Susan Fromberg Schaeffer

1. Qtd. by Irving Halperin from *Letters*, no. XV, in "Etty Hillesum: A Story of Spiritual Growth," *Reflections of the Holocaust in Art and Literature*, ed. Randolph L. Braham (New York: Columbia University Press, 1990), 10–11.

2. Heinemann, 120.

3. Susan Fromberg Schaeffer, interview with S. Lillian Kremer, 18 May 1988. Subsequent references to this interview appear as Schaeffer interview.

4. Susan Fromberg Schaeffer, *Anya* (New York: Macmillan, 1974), 9. Subsequent references to this edition appear parenthetically.

5. Schaeffer confirmed her reliance on actual rather than invented atrocities in response to a student's question about the historic precedent for the novel's account of the disfiguring of the faces of Jewish female students by their male classmates. Schaeffer conversation with the author's Holocaust literature class, Kansas State University, 4 April 1995.

6. Susan Fromberg Schaeffer, Edward Lewis Wallant Award acceptance speech, 27 April 1975.

7. Schaeffer interview.

8. Schaeffer, Wallant Award acceptance speech.

9. Schaeffer interview.

10. Under the auspices of the Ribbentrop-Molotov agreement of 23 August 1939, which contained a secret appendix relating to Lithuania and Vilna, it was established that the northern frontier of Lithuania would constitute the boundary between the German and Soviet zones of influence. In accord with that provision Germany and the USSR recognized the interests Lithuania had in the Vilna region. A week after signing the pact the Germans invaded Poland, and on 17 September 1939 the Red Army entered Vilna. By 25 September the USSR had transferred Vilna to Lithuania. In September 1939 the eastern part of Poland was annexed to the Soviet Union, and the Jewish population of this area, in addition to Polish-Jewish refugees who fled Nazi-occupied territories, came under Soviet and then Lithuanian rule.

11. Shootings continued without respite at Ponar during the summer of 1941. Martin Gilbert cites the diary entry for 27 July 1941 of a Polish journalist from Ponar, W. Sakowicz: "Shooting is carried on nearly every day. . . . People say that about 5000 persons have been killed in the course of this month. . . . About two hundred to three hundred people are being driven up here nearly every day. And nobody ever returns." He also notes that on 31 August 1941, a few days before the Vilna Ghetto was established, the predominantly Jewish section of Vilna was surrounded by an *Einsatzkommando* unit, together with several hundred armed Lithuanians, who took people indiscriminately from their houses and beat them and then delivered them by trucks to the pits at Ponar, where 2,019 Jewish women, 864 men, and 817 children were murdered. Even after the two ghettos were established, the *Einsatzkommando* slaughter of thousands continued every Sunday in September, and on the Day of Atonement 3,000 were taken from the ghetto to be shot at Ponar. Martin Gilbert,

The Holocaust: A History of the Jews of Europe during the Second World War (New York: Holt, Rinehart & Winston, 1985), 177–78, 192–93, 194, 206.

12. In Vilna, as in other cities, two ghettos were created—one with a working population, the other for Jews whose annihilation was imminent. The ghetto of unskilled workers was liquidated within a month. The second, comprising 12,000 skilled workers and their families, survived for two years.

13. Yitzhak Arad, *Ghetto in Flames: The Struggle and Destruction of the Jews in Vilna in the Holocaust* (Jerusalem: Yad Vashem, 1980); Leonard Tushnet, *The Pavement of Hell* (New York: St. Martin's Press, 1972).

14. See Arad for a thorough description of ghetto conditions, including insufficient sewers, water supplies, toilets, and showers and an abundance of bugs and lice, burst pipes, clogged drains, and garbage piles. This unhygienic state, coupled with shortages of food, clothing, and firewood, created ideal conditions for disease. Arad, 315.

15. Anatol Fried, chairman of the Vilna Judenrat, appointed Jacob Gens commander of the ghetto police in September 1941. In July 1942 the Germans dismissed the Jewish Council and appointed Gens head of ghetto administration. Gens promoted the idea of "work for life," recognizing that the survival of the Jews depended on their productivity until Germany was defeated.

16. Tushnet, 157.

17. Jacob Gens was informed by a sympathetic German that he was on an execution list and given the opportunity to escape. He refused, fearful that thousands of Jews would pay with their lives. Tushnet, 196.

18. The Polish ghettos received food supplies from official and unofficial sources. Official supplies were distributed on the basis of ration cards issued by the German authorities, rations far short of those allocated to the non-Jewish population in the occupied areas. In the second half of 1941 the daily food ration allotted to Jews in the *Generalgouvernement* consisted of 184 calories, approximately 7.5 percent of normal requirements, whereas Poles were given 26 percent and Germans received a full ration. This starvation policy was noted by Hans Frank in a speech on 24 August 1942 when he claimed, "In passing, may I say that we are sentencing 1.2 million Jews to death by hunger." Zbigniew Landau, "Ghettos, Nutrition in," *Encyclopedia of the Holocaust*, ed. Israel Gutman (New York: Macmillan, 1990), 2:583.

19. Tushnet, 165.

20. The fictional account is probably modeled on the historic murder of duped Vilna volunteers who were told they would be taken to work at Kaunas, a ghetto reputed to have better food and housing. Instead, they were taken to Ponary, the prewar picnic area outside Vilna, where the entire transport was shot. See Tushnet, 182–83.

21. Fink, *Scrap of Time*, 42–46.

22. On the psychological impact of the Holocaust on children and their play, see George Eisen, *Children and Play in the Holocaust: Games among the Shadows* (Amherst: University of Massachusetts Press, 1988).

23. Qtd. by Levin, 249.

24. Tadeusz Borowski, "This Way for the Gas, Ladies and Gentlemen," *This Way for the Gas*, 43.

25. Arad, 431–32.

26. Horowitz, "Memory and Testimony of Women Survivors," 278–79.

27. Cynthia Haft, *The Theme of Nazi Concentration Camps in French Literature* (Paris: Mouton, 1973), 33.

28. Feig, *Hitler's Death Camps*, 170.

29. See Gertrude Schneider, *The Journey into Terror: The Story of the Riga Ghetto* (New York: ARK House, 1979), 126. For a similar description of the Kaiserwald induction ritual, see Hannelore Temel, "A Sad Time to Be Young," *Muted Voices: Jewish Survivors of Latvia Remember*, ed. Gertrude Schneider (New York: Philosophical Library, 1987).

30. Levi, *Survival in Auschwitz*, 22.

31. Zdena Berger, *Tell Me Another Morning* (New York: Harper & Brothers, 1959), 90.

32. Tushnet, 146.

33. Had Schaeffer conducted research beyond limited survivor interviews, she could have presented a fuller account of the heroic resistance of the United Partisan Organization, which carried out sabotage from the surrounding forests, smuggled weapons into the ghetto, printed and distributed illegal newspapers, disseminated news to other ghettos, assisted Russian prisoners of war, and mined trainloads of German troops. For dramatic treatment of the role of partisans in the Vilna Ghetto, see Irena Klepfisz's play, *Bread and Candy: Songs of the Holocaust*, published in *Bridges* (fall 1991), 14–41.

34. Schaeffer interview.

35. Victor Frankl, *Man's Search for Meaning: An Introduction to Logo Therapy*, rev. ed. of *Death-Camp to Existentialism*, trans. Ilse Lasch (Boston: Beacon Press, 1962), 66, 65. I quoted Victor Frankl and asked Schaeffer whether she agreed with his theory. She responded affirmatively.

36. Susan Rubin Suleiman, "Maternal Splitting: 'Good' and 'Bad' Mothers and Reality," *Risking Who One Is: Encounters with Contemporary Art and Literature* (Cambridge: Harvard University Press, 1994), 38–54.

37. See Suleiman's discussion of this psychoanalytic projection in her essay "Writing and Motherhood," *Risking Who One Is*.

38. Ferderber-Salz, *And the Sun Kept Shining* . . . , 31.

39. Yehuda Bauer provides an example of the continuing rabid antisemitism of the local population in the postwar era: "In the village of Eisiskes in the Vilna area five of the few Jews who had survived were murdered. In some of the pockets of their clothes the following Polish inscription: 'This will be the fate of all surviving Jews.'" Hundreds of Jewish Holocaust survivors were murdered throughout Poland. Representative were 42 killed in the town of Kielce who were accused of blood libel, harking back to the Middle Ages, when trumped-up charges of killing Christian children for ritual purposes were common. The pogrom that followed, in which government forces participated and the local bishop refused to intervene, provoked a mass exodus of remaining survivors to the American and British zones of Germany. Yehuda Bauer, *A History of the Holocaust* (New York: Franklin Watts, 1982), 340, 341.

40. Qtd. by Alan Berger, without attribution to the specific Wiesel source, in "Holocaust Survivors and Children," 81.

41. Berger, 82.

42. Anya's struggle with memory may be compared with that of an Auschwitz survivor who reports a similar change in her behavior, from suppressing memory in youth to fostering it later in life. Like Anya, this survivor speaks of lying awake at night haunted by the Holocaust, guilty that she survived when the rest of her family perished, remembering her family, and trying to emulate their holiday customs. Fortunoff Video Archive for Holocaust Testimonies, Yale University, tape T-71, testimony of Eva L.

43. Schaeffer interview.

44. Emil L. Fackenheim, *God's Presence in History: Jewish Affirmations and Philosophical Reflections* (New York: New York University Press, 1970).

45. Berger, 120.

46. Alexander, *Resonance of Dust*, 133.

47. Berger, 112.

Cynthia Ozick

1. Cynthia Ozick, "Roundtable Discussion," Writing and the Holocaust Conference (State University of New York at Albany, 5–7 April 1987), pub. in *Writing and the Holocaust*, ed. Berel Lang (New York: Holmes & Meier, 1988), 284.

2. Francine Prose, "Idolatry in Miami," *New York Times Book Review*, 10 September 1989: 23; Cynthia Ozick, interview with S. Lillian Kremer, 28 December 1986. Subsequent references to this interview appear as Ozick interview.

3. Cynthia Ozick, interview with Tom Teicholz, *Paris Review* 102 (spring 1987): 185.

4. Ozick, "Roundtable Discussion," 284.

5. Ozick, "Roundtable Discussion," 282–83.

6. For a full analysis of Ozick's Holocaust works, aside from *The Shawl*, see S. Lillian Kremer, "The Dybbuk of All the Lost Dead: Cynthia Ozick's Holocaust Fiction," *Witness through the Imagination*, 218–78.

7. Prose, 39.

8. Cynthia Ozick, *The Shawl* (New York: Alfred A. Knopf, 1989), 5, 6, 7, 9. Subsequent references to "The Shawl" and "Rosa" from this edition appear in the text in parentheses.

9. Delbo, *None of Us Will Return*, 124.

10. Cynthia Ozick, "The Pagan Rabbi," *The Pagan Rabbi and Other Stories* (New York: Alfred A. Knopf, 1971), 7.

11. Amy Gottfried, "Fragmented Art and the Liturgical Community of the Dead in Cynthia Ozick's *The Shawl*," *Studies in American Jewish Literature* 13 (1994): 42.

12. Gottfried, 43.

13. Berger, *Crisis and Covenant*, 53. According to Berger, "Ozick's shawl/*tallit* is a talisman which protects both Rosa and Magda when they either wear or hold it" (53). In addition to physical protection, Berger interprets the shawl as a metaphor for spiritual survival and affirmation of Judaism, since it is associated with cinnamon and almond fragrance evocative of the ritual spice box of the Sabbath-end havdalah ceremony. For a Christological interpretation of the shawl, see Victor Strandberg, *Greek Mind/Jewish Soul: The Conflicted Art of Cynthia Ozick* (Madison: University of Wisconsin Press, 1994), 143.

14. Ozick interview.

15. Ozick, "Roundtable Discussion," 279.

16. Ozick wrote: "*Anya* makes experience—no, gives it, as if uninvented, or as if, turning around in your own room, you see for the first time, what has happened, who you are, and what is there, and why. Susan Fromberg Schaeffer is one of those consummately natural writers who seem not to make novels but life itself." Book endorsement.

17. Ozick interview.

18. Joseph Lowin, *Cynthia Ozick* (Boston: Twayne, 1988), 121.

19. Fania Fenelon, *Playing for Time*, qtd. by Feig in *Hitler's Death Camps*, 186.

20. Lawrence Langer, "Myth and Truth in Cynthia Ozick's 'The Shawl' and 'Rosa,'" *Admitting the Holocaust*, 141.

21. Elie Wiesel, *Night Dawn Day*, trans. Anne Borchardt (New York: Aronson, 1985), 303.

22. Dan Bar-On, "Transgenerational After-Effects of the Holocaust in Israel: Three Generations," *Breaking Crystal: Writing and Memory after Auschwitz*, ed. Efraim Sicher (Urbana-Champaign: University of Illinois Press, 1997), 104.

23. Nelly Sachs, "The Chorus of the Rescued," *O the Chimneys!* (New York: Farrar, Straus, Giroux, 1967).

24. Martin S. Bergmann and Milton E. Jucovy, eds., *Generations of the Holocaust* (New York: Basic Books, 1982), 8.

25. In an analysis of the effects of survivor syndrome Jack Terry isolates the unresolved loss of a child as among the most traumatic Holocaust experiences. He argues: "The most profound effect of the Holocaust on those who survived invariably revolves around the loss of libidinal objects. In concentration camps, mourning would have been impossible even if it had been permitted. Grief in itself threatens the integrity of the ego, and under circumstances in which the intensity of the affect is too great or the ego has been so weakened—both of which were the case in the Holocaust—mourning cannot take place. Thus, the attachment to the lost object remains unresolved." Jack Terry, "The Damaging Effects of the 'Survivor Syndrome,'" *Psychoanalytic Reflections on the Holocaust: Selected Essays*, ed. Steven A. Luel and Paul Marcus (New York: KTAV, 1984), 145.

26. Robert Jay Lifton, "The Concept of the Survivor," *Survivors, Victims, and Perpetrators*, ed. Dimsdale, qtd. by George Kren in "The Holocaust Survivor and Psychoanalysis," *Healing Their Wounds: Psychotherapy with Holocaust Survivors and Their Families*, ed. Paul Marcus and Alan Rosenberg (New York: Praeger, 1989), 7.

27. Henry Krystal, "Integration and Self-Healing in Psychotraumatic States," *Psychoanalytic Reflections on the Holocaust*, ed. Luel and Marcus, 125.

28. See writers in "Scribes of the Warsaw Ghetto," *Literature of Destruction*, ed. Roskies.

29. Primo Levi, *The Drowned and the Saved* (New York: Summit Books, 1988), 78, 198.

30. Charlotte Delbo, qtd. by Sara Horowitz in "Voices from the Killing Ground," *Holocaust Remembrance: The Shapes of Memory*, ed. Geoffrey H. Hartman (Oxford: Basil Blackwell, 1994), 52.

31. Qtd. by Elaine Kauvar in *Cynthia Ozick's Fiction: Tradition and Invention* (Bloomington: Indiana University Press, 1993), 186. I am indebted to Elaine Kauvar for shedding light on Tuwim's life and poetry and its relationship to Rosa's circumstances.

32. A devotée of Yiddish literature, Cynthia Ozick has endeavored to support a vibrant Yiddish culture by translating Yiddish poetry, including the work of David Einhorn and Jacob Glatstein, and writing about the art and problematics of translation from Yiddish to English in her essay "Prayer Leader," *Prooftexts* 3.1 (Jan. 1983): 1–8, rpt. "A Translator's Monologue," *Metaphor & Memory* (New York: Alfred A. Knopf, 1989), 199–208.

33. Cynthia Ozick, "A Bintel Brief for Jacob Glatstein," *Jewish Heritage* 14 (Sept.

1972): 60, qtd. by Deborah Heiligman Weiner in "Cynthia Ozick, Pagan vs Jew (1966–1976)," *Studies in American Jewish Literature* 3 (1983): 187.

34. Kauvar, 186.

35. See Emil Fackenheim, *God's Presence in History: Jewish Affirmations and Philo-sophical Reflections* (New York: New York University Press, 1970).

36. Cohen, *The Tremendum*, 2.

37. Bolkosky, "Interviewing Victims Who Survived," 34.

38. Harry James Cargas, *In Conversation with Elie Wiesel* (New York: Paulist Press, 1976), 87.

39. See Jean Améry, *At the Mind's Limits: Contemplations by a Survivor on Auschwitz and Its Realities*, trans. Sidney Rosenfeld and Stella P. Rosenfeld (Bloomington: Indiana University Press, 1980).

40. Langer, "Myth and Truth," 144.

41. Lawrence S. Friedman, *Understanding Cynthia Ozick* (Columbia: University of South Carolina Press, 1991), 120.

42. The play appeared originally under the title *Blue Light*, a reference to the blue lights of Warsaw. My observations are to an unpublished manuscript, "The Shawl: A Play in Two Acts."

43. Cynthia Ozick, "Innovation and Redemption: What Literature Means," *Art & Ardor: Essays* (New York: Alfred A. Knopf, 1983), 245.

44. Cynthia Ozick, *Trust* (New York: New American Library, 1966), 229.

45. Cynthia Ozick, "Puttermesser: Her Work History, Her Ancestry, Her After-life," *Levitation: Five Fictions* (New York: Alfred A. Knopf, 1982), 36.

46. Cynthia Ozick, "Envy; or, Yiddish in America," *The Pagan Rabbi and Other Stories* (New York: Alfred A. Knopf, 1971), 74.

47. Cynthia Ozick, "Notes toward Finding the Right Question," *Forging New Identities*, 134, orig. pub. as "A Vindication of the Rights of Jewish Women," *Forum* 35 (spring–summer 1979): 37–60.

48. Cynthia Ozick, "The Uses of Legend: Elie Wiesel as Tsaddik," *Congress Bi-Weekly* (9 June 1969): 19, qtd. by Amy Gottfried, 40.

49. Cynthia Ozick, "Toward a New Yiddish," *Art & Ardor*, 174–75.

50. Ozick, "Finding the Right Question," 134.

51. Letter from Cynthia Ozick to survivor, 20 April 1983, qtd. by Sarah Blacher Cohen in *Cynthia Ozick's Comic Art: From Levity to Liturgy* (Bloomington: Indiana University Press, 1994), 148.

Marge Piercy

1. Marge Piercy, interview with S. Lillian Kremer, 26 May 1988. Subsequent citations to this interview appear as Piercy interview. See also Marge Piercy, "A

Woman Writer Treads on Male Turf," conversation with Alvin Sanoff, *U.S. News and World Report*, 8 May 1987: 74. In a letter to the author Piercy wrote, "World War II was too important to my life, to what happened to women, to Jews, to the United States, to leave only to men to write about it in the limited ways they often have" (26 Sept. 1988).

2. Marge Piercy, "The Dark Thread in the Weave," *Testimony: Contemporary Writers Make the Holocaust Personal*, ed. David Rosenberg (New York: Random House, 1989), 173, 177.

3. Marge Piercy, "My Mother's Body," qtd. by Piercy in "Dark Thread in the Weave," 172.

4. Piercy, "Dark Thread in the Weave," 179.

5. Piercy went to France with her first husband, Michel Schiff, whom she describes as "a French Jew who had what was generally regarded as a good war, i.e., his parents had crossed the border to Switzerland illegally but successfully" (Piercy interview). In her poem "The Ram's Horn Sounding" Piercy commemorates the Holocaust experience of her husband's relatives, who sewed contraband into their coat linings and used forged passports. *Available Light* (New York: Alfred A. Knopf, 1988), 127.

6. Piercy interview.

7. Marge Piercy, *Gone to Soldiers* (New York: Summit Books, 1987). Citations to this edition appear parenthetically in the text.

8. Piercy, "Woman Writer," 74.

9. Marge Piercy, "After Words," *Gone to Soldiers*, 702–03.

10. Piercy, "Woman Writer," 74.

11. Piercy interview.

12. Marge Piercy, interview with Sue Walker and Eugenie Hammer, *Ways of Knowing: Essays on Marge Piercy*, ed. Sue Walker and Eugenie Hammer (Mobile: Negative Capability Press, 1991), 151.

13. Piercy, "Woman Writer," 74.

14. Piercy interview.

15. In 1939 there were approximately 270,000 Jews in France, 200,000 of whom lived in Paris. Of the total, 150,000 were foreign born, of whom more than half were "stateless," refugees from countries that were under German domination or had passed anti-Jewish legislation depriving Jews of nationality.

16. Alain Finkielkraut, *The Imaginary Jew*, trans. Kevin O'Neill (Lincoln: University of Nebraska Press, 1994), 63.

17. Finkielkraut, 63.

18. Hannah Arendt, letter to Kurt Blumenfeld, qtd. by Elaine Marks in *Marrano as Metaphor: The Jewish Presence in French Writing* (New York: Columbia University Press, 1996), 147.

19. Piercy refers to antisemitic posters in a 1940 entry, prior to the institution-

alization of anti-Jewish propaganda displays that began on 11 May 1941 by Theo Dannecker, aide to Adolf Eichmann, specialist in anti-Jewish activities. See Claude Lévy and Paul Tillard, *Betrayal at the Vel d'Hiv*, trans. Inea Bushnaq (New York: Hill & Wang, 1967), 248.

20. French-born Jews whose families had been living in France for generations generally referred to themselves as *Israelites*, believing the term to be less pejorative than *Juif*, the word used to define the foreign or immigrant Jew.

21. Roundups of Jews were already under way by the diarist's August entry. On 14 May 1941, 3,649 naturalized Polish Jews living in France were sent to concentration camps. In August there was another abduction of 3,429 Jews, who were interned in Drancy, Pithiviers, and Beaune-la-Rolande, camps located in the occupied zone. See Levin, 433.

22. On the roundups of specific segments of the Jewish population, see Lévy and Tillard, 256, and Jacques Adler, *The Jews of Paris and the Final Solution: Communal Response and Internal Conflicts, 1940–1944* (New York: Oxford University Press, 1987), 11.

23. Adler, 41.

24. Lévy and Tillard, 242–43, 3.

25. See Kremer, "Dybbuk of All the Lost Dead," 259, for a detailed comparison of Ozick's fictional representation in *The Cannibal Galaxy* (New York: Alfred A. Knopf, 1983), 24, with her source in Michael R. Marrus and Robert O. Paxton's *Vichy France and the Jews* (New York: Basic Books, 1981), 250–51.

26. After the July 1942 raids the collaboration press published Nazi misinformation indicating that all arrestees were black marketeers or otherwise criminal. Lévy and Tillard, 200.

27. The Vel d'Hiv was not prepared for the reception and retention of thousands of prisoners. For the 7,000 prisoners, 4,051 of whom were children, there were 10 lavatories and approximately 20 urinals, half of which were cordoned off because they contained windows facing the street that could have been used for escape. By the end of the morning the lavatories were blocked and the urinals overflowing. For eight days, 7,000 people were locked into this sports stadium without food or water, without sanitary conveniences, in unbreathable air, conditions contrived to humiliate and break the internees. Among them were the critically ill, pregnant women in labor, and people with contagious diseases. Some lost their reason. Of the many attempted suicides, 10 were successful. Lévy and Tillard, 45, 72–73, 68, 49.

28. On the efforts of the UGIF, Yiddish press, and Communists to warn their constituencies of the imminent roundups and deportations, see Lévy and Tillard, 17, 181–83; on the Italian position vis-à-vis the Jews during the joint Nazi/Fascist occupation of the Vichy zone, see Levin, 449–54.

29. Theo Dannecker ordered the Jewish section of the Gestapo to merge all the French Jewish philanthropic organizations in a single organization, which, like the index, was to facilitate the deportations. The UGIF amalgamated all Jewish activities in its role as a philanthropic and social service body, providing assistance to tens of thousands of Jews whose situations became increasingly difficult. Ironically, and inadvertently, the UGIF took part in the organization of the deportation of Jews arrested on 16–17 July, preparing name tags and providing medical care in the Vel d'Hiv. Although the motive of the Jewish members was to help their fellows in terrible times, they were forced to administer German policy, much as the *Judenräte* of eastern Europe did, but short of preparing deportation lists. Lévy and Tillard, 247–48.

30. See the eyewitness account offered by a social worker assigned to the children. Lévy and Tillard, 158–59.

31. For detailed descriptions of the Drancy children's deportations and copies of the documents exchanged on the matter between German authorities in France and Berlin, see Lévy and Tillard, 94–96, and Gerhard Schoenberner, *The Yellow Star: The Persecution of the Jews in Europe, 1933–1945*, trans. Susan Sweet (London: Corgi Books, 1969), 107.

32. Leon Poliakov, "Jewish Resistance in France," YIVO: *Annual of Jewish Social Science* 8 (1953): 261.

33. Piercy, "Dark Thread in the Weave," 181.

34. French Judaism defined itself in French national terms. The fundamental rift between the UGIF and Jewish immigrants was based on the UGIF belief, until the beginning of 1943, that native French Jews would be protected by Vichy, whose quarrel was with foreign Jews. The French Jews who resorted to communal help were satisfied with the UGIF role. The foreign Jews, who benefited from the UGIF relief policy, differed in their belief that a militant response to internment was necessary. Ideological differences also existed between the Communist and Jewish national resistants, with the Communists emphasizing the anti-Nazi character of their activities and the Zionists stressing Jewish nationalist ideals.

35. Amy Latour, *The Jewish Resistance in France, 1940–1944*, trans. Irene R. Ilton (New York: Holocaust Library, 1970), 107.

36. According to Leon Poliakov, a member of the French Resistance and postwar research director of the Centre du Documentation Juive Contemporaine, the EIF found homes for refugees and evacuated children from the cities to the provinces. The homes served not only as shelters but as schools for professional and skilled training in various fields with the intention of building a strong cadre of pioneers for Palestine. The EIF had cooperative contacts among the clergy, police, municipal authorities, and professional smugglers. Poliakov, 257–59.

37. On the process of creating false identities and transforming foreign Jews who did not speak proper French and might even have a Yiddish accent, see Latour, 132–33.

38. Piercy interview.

39. According to Jan Karski, a Polish Resistance leader, women were better suited for undercover or conspiratorial work because they were quicker to perceive danger, more optimistic of mission outcome, more cautious and discreet, less inclined to risky bluffing, and could make themselves less conspicuous. He praised the "liaison women," or couriers, who were more exposed than the organizers, planners, or executors because they often carried incriminating materials or anti-Nazi literature for distribution. Laska, introduction, *Women in the Resistance and in the Holocaust*, ed. Laska, 7. See also Rossiter, *Women in the Resistance*.

40. See Airey Neave, "Postman across the Pyrenees," *Women in the Resistance and in the Holocaust*, ed. Laska, 131–36, orig. pub. in Neave, *The Escape Room* (Garden City NY: Doubleday, 1970), 126–38.

41. Marie-Madeleine Fourcade, "The Woman in Charge of Noah's Ark," *Women in the Resistance and in the Holocaust*, ed. Laska, 146–47, orig. pub. in Marie-Madeleine Fourcade, *Noah's Ark: A Memoir of Struggle and Resistance*, trans. George Allen Unwin (New York: E. P. Dutton, 1974). Fourcade was known as "Hedgehog," and because all the members of her network worked under animal code names, they were dubbed "Noah's Ark" by the Gestapo.

42. Piercy, "Dark Thread in the Weave," 183–84; Piercy interview.

43. The largest portion of the six million Jews murdered by the Nazis were killed in Auschwitz. According to various War Crime Investigation Commissions, approximately four million men, women, and children, Jews and non-Jews, perished in Auschwitz alone. Most arrivals to Auschwitz went directly to the gas chambers, which were located, along with the crematoria, in the Birkenau section.

44. Joel E. Dimsdale, "The Coping Behavior of Nazi Concentration Camp Survivors," *Survivors, Victims, and Perpetrators*, 168.

45. On the burdens of motherhood, see Heinemann, *Gender and Destiny*.

46. Nomberg-Przytyk, 70.

47. Vera Laska, "Auschwitz—A Factual Deposition," *Women in the Resistance and in the Holocaust*, ed. Laska, 174.

48. Laska, "Auschwitz," 174.

49. Piercy interview.

50. Representative of testimony given by women survivors attesting to the significance of bonding and their support groups are the remarks of Susan Cernyak-Spatz, a survivor of Theresienstadt, Auschwitz, Birkenau, and Ravensbrück, regarding the aid of others during illness and procurement of supplementary food. Susan

Cernyak-Spatz, panelist quoted in *Proceedings of the Conference, "Women Surviving: The Holocaust,"* ed. Katz and Ringelheim, 146.

51. See Nomberg-Przytyk, 23–27.

52. Susan Cernyak-Spatz, a privileged worker in the Kanada-kommando, notes, "It was understood that the suitcases that had been confiscated from the transports and which contained food were to be for the unit's use. It was a tacit understanding we had with the Nazis that if they let us have the food, we wouldn't report their own theft of clothing and valuables." Susan Cernyak-Spatz, "The 'Normality of Evil': Two Years in Auschwitz-Birkenau," *Jewish Currents* (Jan. 1987): 15.

53. Gertrude Schneider, qtd. in *Proceedings of the Conference, "Women Surviving: The Holocaust,"* ed. Katz and Ringelheim, 153; Cernyak-Spatz, "Normality of Evil," 16; Laska, "Auschwitz," 183.

54. Piercy interview.

55. The mission of the Institute for the Study of Jewish Affairs, which regularly published and distributed hate literature to the public, was "to organize meetings, invite anti-Jewish speakers, and make sure that the walls of Paris were permanently covered with anti-Semitic posters." Lévy and Tillard, 248.

56. Piercy, "Dark Thread in the Weave," 175, 174.

57. David Wyman, *The Abandonment of the Jews: America and the Holocaust, 1941–1945* (New York: Pantheon, 1985).

58. Capitalizing on fears that the Germans had infiltrated the refugee stream with agents, Breckenridge Long, director of the State Department's Special Problems Division, became one of the most adamant foes of rescuing the Jews. The State Department conspired to conceal cable 354, which instructed Leland Harrison to cease forwarding reports of mass murder. Henry Feingold, "The Government Response," *The Holocaust: Ideology, Bureaucracy, and Genocide*, ed. Henry Friedlander and Sybil Milton (New York: Kraus International, 1980), 248–49.

59. Piercy, "Dark Thread in the Weave," 173.

60. See Claudine Vegh, *I Didn't Say Goodbye*, trans. Ros Schwartz (London: Caliban Books, 1979). The survivor-psychologist, who experienced the war as a child separated from her parents, analyzes her own story and presents case studies of seventeen survivors who discuss their wartime feelings about their parents and their postwar family relationships or lack thereof. An appended analysis by Bruno Bettelheim confirms Vegh's views.

61. Lore Segal, *Other People's Houses* (New York: Harcourt, Brace & World, 1964).

62. Piercy, "Dark Thread in the Weave," 180.

63. See Segal for an excellent autobiographical rendition of a child who escaped post-*Anschluss* Austria as part of an experimental children's transport to England and who led an awkward life as a refugee among strangers.

64. Kerstin W. Shands, *The Repair of the World: The Novels of Marge Piercy* (Westport CT: Greenwood Press, 1995), 124.

65. Piercy, "Dark Thread in the Weave," 189.

66. Piercy's last three novels, *Gone to Soldiers, Summer People*, and *He, She, and It*, demonstrate that the Jewish heritage has become an increasingly significant factor in her writing. This contrasts with the understated, even submerged, Jewish identity in much of her earlier fiction.

67. Piercy, "Dark Thread in the Weave," 191.

68. Katherine Usher Henderson, "Marge Piercy," *Inter/View: Talks with America's Writing Women*, ed. Mickey Pearlman and Katherine Usher Henderson (Louisville: University of Kentucky Press, 1990), 69.

69. Sherry Lee Linkon, "'A Way of Being Jewish That Is Mine': Gender and Ethnicity in the Novels of Marge Piercy," *Studies in American Jewish Literature* 13 (1994): 98.

70. Sigmund Freud, qtd. by Sander Gilman in *Freud, Race, and Gender* (Princeton: Princeton University Press, 1993), 16.

71. Given Piercy's strong feminist positions, it would be easy to misinterpret this passage as a feminist critique of Judaism. On the contrary, Piercy parts with many feminists who view Judaism negatively. In a review essay entitled "The Repair of the World" (1984) "Piercy protests the view that Judaism is a particularly oppressive and staunchly patriarchal religion. She writes: 'A great deal of nonsense is talked and written about Judaism by those who are not Jews. The general consensus among many Christians and among many feminists seems to be that Judaism is a quaint relic or else the apotheosis of patriarchy, and that the attachment of Jews to our identity is a form of masochism or a sign of unheightened consciousness'" (Shands, 7).

72. Piercy, "Dark Thread in the Weave," 178.

73. Piercy interview.

74. Susan Mernit, "Suburban Housewife Makes Good," *Women's Review of Books* 1:11 (Aug. 1984): 18.

75. Piercy, "Black Mountain," *Available Light*.

Norma Rosen

1. Norma Rosen, "The Holocaust and the American-Jewish Novelist," *Midstream* 20 (Oct. 1974), rpt. in Rosen, *Accidents of Influence*, 8–9.

2. Rosen, "Holocaust," 12.

3. Rosen, "Holocaust," 9.

4. Norma Rosen, "The Second Life of Holocaust Imagery," *Accidents of Influence*, 49.

5. Qtd. by Abrahamson, ed., in *Against Silence*, 1:44.

6. Rosen, "Holocaust," 10.

7. Rosen, "Second Life," 51.

8. Norma Rosen, "Notes toward a Holocaust Fiction," *Testimony: Contemporary Writers Make the Holocaust Personal*, ed. David Rosenberg (New York: Times Books, Random House, 1989), 394, rpt. in *Accidents of Influence*, 107–23.

9. Rosen writes: "When I began to write . . . *Touching Evil*, the woman . . . who had learned of the existence of the Nazi camps and who thereafter felt that she must not go on with any sort of ordinary 'good' life, was Jewish. But as I went on writing, the idea took hold of me that she ought not [be] Jewish. Because, I thought, this was how gentiles ought to feel. And in my book, at least, they would." Norma Rosen, "Living in Two Cultures," *Response: A Contemporary Jewish Review* 16 (winter 1972–73): 107.

10. Rosen, "Second Life," 51.

11. Norma Rosen, *Touching Evil* (New York: Harcourt, Brace & World, 1969), 57–58. Subsequent references to this edition appear in parentheses in the text.

12. Norma Rosen, interview with S. Lillian Kremer, 19 May 1988. Subsequent references to this interview appear as Rosen interview.

13. Rosen writes: "When I wrote of the devastation in the woman who makes her discovery at the time the camps were opened and photographs were released, I believed it was invention. Later, I read Susan Sontag's *On Photography* and found her description—'a negative epiphany'—of her first sight, at age twelve, of photographs from the camps in 1945." "Holocaust Fiction," 108.

14. Isaac Rosenfeld, "The Meaning of Terror," *An Age of Enormity: Life and Writing in the Forties and Fifties* (New York: World Publishing, 1962), 209.

15. Rosen interview.

16. Rosen, "Holocaust," 11.

17. Rosen was pregnant in 1961, "watching the Eichmann trial, . . . asking the question, 'How can we live now?'" "Holocaust Fiction," 395.

18. Susan Sontag, *On Photography* (New York: Farrar, Straus, Giroux, 1977), 19–20.

19. Nora Sayre, *New York Times Book Review* (14 Sept. 1969), 26.

20. Alexander, *Resonance of Dust*, 132.

21. See Lévy and Tillard, *Betrayal at the Vel d'Hiv*, 157–59.

22. Rosen, "Holocaust," 13.

23. Rosen, "Second Life," 52.

24. Ozick, "Roundtable Discussion," *Writing and the Holocaust*, ed. Lang, 281.

25. Wiesel, *Night*, 73.

26. Norma Rosen, "Justice for Jonah, or, a Bible Bartleby," *Congregation: Contemporary Writers Read the Jewish Bible*, ed. David Rosenberg (New York: Harcourt Brace Jovanovich, 1987), rpt. in Rosen, *Accidents of Influence*, 87.

27. Norma Rosen, letter to the author, 15 Jan. 1998.

28. Cohen, *The Tremendum*, 2.

29. Norma Rosen, "On Living in Two Cultures," *Accidents of Influence*, 128.

30. Norma Rosen, "What Must I Say To You?" *Green* (New York: Harcourt, Brace & World, 1967), rpt. in *Woman Who Lost Her Names*, ed. Mazow. References are to the Mazow edition and appear in parentheses in the text.

31. Norma Rosen, "The Cheek of the Trout," *Testimony*, ed. Rosenberg, 398–411.

32. Rosen's husband left Vienna on a children's transport a few weeks after Kristallnacht. The Jewish Kultesgemeinde managed to save his life, but not those of his parents and extended family. Rosen and her husband traveled to Vienna four decades later "and saw it in inverse relation to its perfection now: the shadow that lies beneath, the past within the present." "Holocaust Fiction," 396.

33. Norma Rosen, "The Inner Light and the Fire," *Forthcoming: Jewish Imaginative Writing* 1 (fall 1983): 4–9.

34. Norma Rosen, "Fences," *Orim: A Jewish Journal at Yale* 1 (spring 1986): 75–83.

35. This story has parallels to Rosen's own family history. She notes that her husband's father's prayer shawl was retrieved in the same way and that the experience was very moving for her. The rest of the story, including the conferral of the tallit, is invented. Rosen interview.

36. Rosen, "Holocaust Fiction," 393.

37. Irving Howe, "Writing and the Holocaust," *Writing and the Holocaust*, ed. Lang, 194.

38. Ezrahi, *By Words Alone*, 209–10.

39. Berger, *Crisis and Covenant*, 172–73, 174.

40. Norma Rosen, "The Literature of Contempt," *Accidents of Influence*, 42.

Conclusion

1. Primo Levi, *Moments of Reprieve*, trans. Ruth Feldman (New York: Summit Books, 1987), 10–11.

2. Rosenfeld, *Double Dying*, 13.

3. Cohen, *The Tremendum*, 2.

INDEX

Page references set in *italic* indicate inclusive treatment of that work.

Adorno, Theodor, 29, 153
Aichinger, Ilse, 4
Akiva, Rabbi, 167
Alexander, Edward, 4, 148, 220
American German Bund, 200
Améry, Jean, 170
Angress, Ruth, 47
anti-Jewish legislation, 70–71, 105–6, 108
antisemitism, 72, 74–77, 98; American practice of, 149, 179, 198–99, 200; assimilated Jews' response to, 165, 181; cast as anti-Zionism, 97, 99; Christian, 53, 103, 140, 197–98; cultural, 141; economic, 141, 200; Ettinger's experience with, 66; European anti-Jewish violence, 149; in European history, 140–41; French practice of, 181–83, 197–98, 263–64 n.55, 267; fugitives' experience with, 252 n.23; German and Russian practices compared, 99, 140–41; Holocaust denial and, 171; Jewish immigration curtailed by U.S. Congress, 201; Jewish response to, 142–48, 164–68, 170–71; Jewish self-hatred stemming from, 165–67; Ozick's experience of, 149; Polish-German agreement on, 252 n.25; Polish practice of, in *Anya,* 122–23, 141–42; —, in *An Estate of Memory,* 54; —, in *Kindergarten,* 74–77, 85; —, in *Quicksand,* 93, 99; —, in *The Shawl,* 164; and Polish refusal to arm Jews, 76, 85; political, 197,

199; in postwar Poland, 142–43, 259 n.39; practiced by Polish partisans, 80; in prewar Poland, 122–23, 141–42; racial, 103; in radio broadcasts by Father Coughlin, 149, 198–99; similarities of religious and racial varieties of, 140–41, 197–99; social, 197, 200; Soviet, 99; and suppression of Holocaust news and information, 202; in U.S. State Department, 199, 201, 267 n.58; as theme in *Anya,* 140–42; as theme in *An Estate of Memory,* 53–55; as theme in *Gone to Soldiers,* 197–202; as theme in *The Shawl,* 164
Anya (Schaeffer), 6, 7, 12–13, 22–25, *119–48,* 154, 243 n.29, 257 n.20, 260 n.20
Appelfeld, Aharon, 4, 240–41 n.13
Arad, Yitzhak, 124
Arendt, Hannah, 1, 181, 198
Aryanization: in *Gone to Soldiers,* 182–83; in *The House on Prague Street,* 103, 105–6, 255 n.12; in *Kindergarten,* 70
Auschwitz, 26, 100, 129, 133, 135–36, 151–52, 221–22, 266 n.43; in *Gone to Soldiers,* 193–96, 210; writing about, 189
Auschwitz-Birkenau, 21, 43, 111; gassing of Hungarian Jews at, 190–91; in *Gone to Soldiers,* 190–91, 193

Bakhtin, Mikhail, 178
Bar-On, Dan, 158
Bauman, Zygmunt, 103
Baumel, Judith, 244 n.44
Bellow, Saul, 145, 196, 224

Drancy, 182–83, 204, 210, 221, 264 n.20;
children's deportations from, 185, 265 n.31
Dubnov, Simon, 27

Eclaireurs Israelites de France (EIF; Boy
Scouts), 187, 265 n.36
Edward Lewis Wallant Award, 148
Eichmann, Adolf, 2, 186; trial of, 213, 214–16,
222, 224, 226
Einsatzgruppen massacre, 124, 256–57 n.11
Elman, Richard, 18, 147
émigré writers, compared to American-born
writers, 23–27
Epstein, Leslie, 14, 125
An Estate of Memory (Karmel), 6, 9, 13, 19,
22, 31–32, *35–65*
Ettinger, Elżbieta, 9, 12–13, 22, 24, 25–26,
66–99, 254 n.46; compared to Amery,
88; compared to Arendt, 74; compared
to Fink, 68, 77–78, 81, 90–91, 253 n.32;
compared to Friedlander, 82–83; compared
to Kaplan, 74; compared to Karmel, 66,
68, 80, 99; compared to Kestenberg,
96; compared to Levin, 77; compared to
Lustig, 77–78; compared to Meed, 78;
compared to Ozick, 73, 94; compared to
Piercy, 68; compared to Schaeffer, 93–94;
compared to Singer, 93–94, 96; compared
to Tec, 76–77, 82–83; compared to Wiesel,
77–78; contributor to *Oneg Shabbes*, 66;
life of, in postwar Poland, 66; service as a
partisan, 66, 245 n.60; as victim of postwar
antisemitism, 66; Works: *Kindergarten*, 6,
9, 12–13, 22, 25, *67–92*, 251 n.11; *Quicksand*,
6, 22, 24, *92–99*
Ezrahi, Sidra DeKoven, 5, 51, 52–53, 62, 234,
241 n.16

Fackenheim, Emil, 147, 168, 206, 246 n.78
Farben, I. G., 191
Feig, Konnilyn, 2, 15, 242 n.18, 244 n.35
feminist historiography, 2–3
"Fences" (Rosen), *231–34*, 270 n.35
Fenelon, Fania, 157
Ferderber-Salz, Berta, 141
Final Solution, 201
Fine, Ellen, 5, 21
Fink, Ida, 4, 58, 103, 126–29, 253 n.32 n.34
Finkielkraut, Alain, 181
Fleg, Edmond, 167, 210

food rationing, 107–8, 113; camp
conversations about, 195; women's
writing about, 194–95
Fourcade, Marie Madeleine, 188–89, 266 n.41
France, 184–85, 210; Aryanization of,
179–81; betrayal of Jews in, 209;
German occupation of, 180; government
distinctions between foreign and native-
born Jewish citizens of, 264 n.20, 265 n.34;
Jewish population of, in 1939, 263 n.15;
postwar, Jews in, 198; pro-Nazi press in,
198, 264 n.26; roundup of Jews in, 183,
264 n.21, 22; status of Jews under Nazi
occupation and Vichy government, 264
n.20, 265 n.34
Frank, Anne, 13, 222; compared to Demetz
character, 112–13; *Diary* of, compared to
Ettinger's fictional diary, 71
Frank, Hans, 257 n.18
Frankl, Victor, 20, 138
Freud, Sigmund, 208
Fried, Anatol, 257 n.15
Friedlander, Saul, 20
Friedman, Lawrence, 171

The Garden of the Finzi-Continis, 116
gender: Holocaust humiliation based on,
192–93; bonding and solidarity, 17–20,
35, 45–47, 47–48, 52, 62, 64, 134, 266
n.50; issues explored in *Anya*, 132–34, 141;
issues explored in *Gone to Soldiers*, 188,
193–96; issues explored in *The House on
Prague Street*, 109; issues explored in *The
Shawl*, 151, 162; maternal vulnerability, 86;
and medical experiments, 242 n.18; and
nursing roles, 46–47; sexual vulnerability
of women during incarceration, 11, 133;
women's bodies and deprivation, 41,
43–44; women's mutual assistance, 45,
244–45 n.44; women's resourcefulness, 16,
41, 247–48 n.9
Gens, Jacob, 257 n.15 n.17; in *Anya*, 124–25
Gestapo, 110, 115; in *Anya*, 125, 126, 138, 139,
141, 144, 146; in *Gone to Soldiers*, 178, 183,
186, 187, 188
ghettoization: German deception practiced
in, 101; and food rationing, 257 n.18
Gilbert, Sir Martin, 16, 256 n.11
Goeth, Amon, 40, 57–58, 65, 249–50 n.34
Goldenberg, Myrna, 2, 19, 240 n.6, 243 n.23